T0388614

Chamber Music in Europe (1850-1918): Composition, Mediation and Reception

SPECVLVM MVSICAE

EDENDUM CURAVIT
ROBERTO ILLIANO

VOLUME LII

PUBLICATIONS OF THE CENTRO STUDI OPERA OMNIA LUIGI BOCCHERINI
PUBBLICAZIONI DEL CENTRO STUDI OPERA OMNIA LUIGI BOCCHERINI
PUBLICATIONS DU CENTRO STUDI OPERA OMNIA LUIGI BOCCHERINI
VERÖFFENTLICHUNGEN DES CENTRO STUDI OPERA OMNIA LUIGI BOCCHERINI
PUBLICACIONES DEL CENTRO STUDI OPERA OMNIA LUIGI BOCCHERINI
LUCCA

CHAMBER MUSIC IN EUROPE (1850-1918)

COMPOSITION, MEDIATION AND RECEPTION

EDITED BY

CATRINA FLINT DE MÉDICIS

AND

FRANÇOIS DE MÉDICIS

BREPOLS

TURNHOUT

MMXXIV

The present volume has been made possibile by the friendly support of the

Palazzetto Bru Zane – Centre de musique romantique française

**PALAZZETTO
BRU ZANE**
CENTRE
DE MUSIQUE
ROMANTIQUE
FRANÇAISE

© BREPOLS 2024

All rights reserved. No part of this publication may be reproduced,
stored in a retrieval system, or transmitted, in any form or by any means,
electronic, mechanical, photocopying, recording, or otherwise, without
the prior permission of the publisher.

D/2024/0095/110

ISBN 978-2-503-61176-1

Printed in Italy

CONTENTS

National Identities and Cultural Transfer

Introduction

THE CONCEPT OF 'CHAMBER MUSIC' has a long history in Western music: since the Middle Ages, it has pervaded through various social classes within various political regimes, from the *bassa musica* or *basse musique* in the Medieval courts or the aristocratic *musique de la chambre du Roi*, to music making within the bourgeois and working classes. Its works have been composed for and directed towards a variety of performers: it might be played directly by its composer or communicated through manuscripts to nearby performers or through publishers or other markets to a wider community, both professional and amateur. 'Chamber music' may be very simply defined, as music for small ensembles, for performance in private and relatively intimate venues. Indeed, it is tempting to tuck this type of music away, into the early nineteenth-century Biedermeier drawing rooms of the emerging middle class or the larger venues available to the aristocracy and the *haute bourgeoisie* who presided over musical salons (alongside political and literary salons). As Tia DeNora has explained, the dismantling of patronage for court orchestras led the aristocrats to redirect their support for musicians towards the salon, where both the nobility and the wealthy bourgeois could vie for prestige[1].

If chamber music is closely linked to the private realm, paradoxically, its repertoire may be defined by its relationship to music in more 'public' genres. Indeed, chamber music was not limited to new repertoires conceived specifically for its private venues. It also included music derived from works given in commercial halls: before the advent of the gramophone or the radio, an orchestral work or symphony might be read at the piano, in a four-hand reduction. Likewise, familiarity with an opera might be gained through arrangements of individual airs, or a piano-vocal score[2]. Thomas Christensen has rightly attributed the surge in piano-vocal scores to at least two of the factors that also underpinned a growth in chamber music repertoire: the development of the fortepiano after 1770, and an increased demand for scores from amateur music makers[3].

In parallel to these types of arrangements of 'public' works for 'private' spaces, the nineteenth-century witnessed a substantial proliferation of various repertoires directed

---

[1].   DeNora 1995.

[2].   On the proliferation and practice of four-hand piano reductions and piano-vocal scores in nineteenth-century private spaces, see Christensen 1999, pp. 255-298 and Christensen 2000, pp. 67-94.

[3].   Christensen 2000, p. 76.

primarily towards intimate performance settings: vocal music such as the German *Lied*, the French *romance* or the more *recherché* French *mélodie*; piano works ranging from more formal piano sonatas to more lyrical and evocative miniature pieces (nocturnes, album leaves, *moments musicaux*, impromptus, and bagatelles, for example), published individually or assembled in sets or cycles. Relatively standardised multi-instrumental repertoires such as the violin sonata, string quartet, and piano quartet were common fare for chamber music performances, while other works were written for more unusual combinations that might wend their way into specific music societies, such as Camille Saint-Saëns (1835-1921) and Vincent d'Indy's (1851-1931) trumpet septets written specifically for *La Trompette*, founded in 1860[4].

During the eighteenth century, as the sheet music market expanded and an upper class endowed with ample time and money for leisurely activities swelled, chamber music developed to satisfy the musical practices of both simple music lovers and practitioners, as well as *amateurs éclairés*, or, the musically 'enlightened'. Soon enough, the line between amateur and professional chamber music became blurred. The most impressive developments might arguably first be observed in the genres of piano music and the string quartet. As is well known, the demands of Beethoven's string quartets reached such technical difficulties that they were simply beyond the reach of most amateur ensembles — not to mention their audiences, challenged as they were by the daring style of these works. This contributed significantly to the rise of professional ensembles dedicated to this genre, such as the Baillot and Schuppanzigh string quartets in Paris and Vienna.

Salons across Europe became launching pads for many a performer's career; another result of changes to the musical market. As a way of amplifying his reputation, Ludwig van Beethoven (1770-1827) wrote piano sonatas to play in salons, as a sort of *faire-valoir* for showcasing his virtuosity. It was no longer repertoire conceived with amateur pianists in mind, for the sale of sheet music, as was W. A. Mozart's (1756-1791) contribution to the genre (and Joseph Haydn's (1732-1809), for all but his last two piano sonatas). And like Beethoven, countless piano virtuosi aimed to impress the high society figures that peopled Europe's elegant salons, with private performances of their music. Fryderyk Chopin's (1810-1849) career is a well-known case in point: following his move to Paris, demand for his performances in the high-class salons of the day surged to the point that the composer was able to forego playing in public. With their faint echo of *bel canto* arias from the public stage, Chopin's character pieces, in his hands, moved irretrievably into closed, private venues for the fortunate few[5].

In the decades that followed the mid-eighteenth-century growth of 'public' or 'subscription' concerts, and in contrast to the glare of the theatre's lights and the gaze of those behind opera glasses in their fashionable dress and elegant coiffures, many chamber music

---

[4]. AUGÉ DE LASSUS 1911.

[5]. On *bel canto* opera and Bellini's influence on Chopin, see Charles Rosen's insightful observations in ROSEN 1998, pp. 325-328 and 344-349.

performances also became a privileged means for a Romantic form of escape to the private and inner realm. Some works seem eminently appropriate for this type of setting: for many music historians, the late Beethoven string quartets spring readily to mind, with their probing inwardness, marked at times by dense counterpoint, harmonic meanderings, and formal discontinuities and liberties that, as we mentioned earlier, made them so inaccessible[6]. But as we dig deeper into our understanding of the genre, we must acknowledge the multiplicity of meaning that chamber music held for nineteenth-century composers, musicians, and audiences, particularly from 1850 onwards.

First and uppermost in mind for many is the association of chamber music with 'serious' or 'high-brow' art, perhaps as a reaction to the substantial growth in mass-produced or mechanically-produced cultural products. Consider only the explosion of the press in the second half of the nineteenth century or the advent of photography, with the challenges they posed to conceptions of art after 1850[7]. As Emmanuel Reibel has shown, music in no way remained immune to this industrial revolution[8]. But this brand of 'serious' chamber music existed alongside 'low-brow' repertoires that included arrangements of Giacomo Meyerbeer's (1791-1864) opera arias, and popular dances like the waltz, the polka and the galop. The venues for chamber music also transformed at this time, with a growth in music societies which often held their events at public recital halls and theatres, although their gatherings were not always open to the public. The concerts of new French music organized by the Société nationale de musique from 1871 onward are a good example of this. In the early years, access to its events were limited to subscribers and their guests. This was soon emulated in other new music societies with the Spanish Sociedad Nacional de Música (1915-1922) or the Società Italiana di Musica Moderna (founded in 1917) and it anticipates in many ways the policy of Schoenberg's Society for Private Musical Performances (or Verein für musikalische Privataufführungen, 1918-1921).

Newer, public performance outlets for chamber music did not preclude private performances (see Perreault and Fenton in this volume), or necessarily dislodge Romantic visions of this repertoire as most 'serious' and 'sublime' (see Katalinić). But they did create the opportunity for the expanded reception and perhaps even the conception of chamber works as emblems of nation or national identity (see Bunzel, Branda, and Sá). Under the pressure of widespread nationalist affirmation and the struggles for political autonomy, the nineteenth century saw the emergence of new national traditions in the Polish, Czech, and Hungarian lands, in Russia, among various nations, alongside the long-established musical traditions of

---

[6]. See KERMAN 1979.

[7]. On reactions to products of mass culture, see HUYSSEN 1986, in particular Chapter 3, for nineteenth-century associations of mass culture with the feminine. On the cultural history of photography see MARIEN 2002, Part 2.

[8]. See REIBEL 2023.

France, and both German and Italian-speaking countries. Far from being confined to the concert halls and salons of their respective nations, these newer, 'nationalist' genres of chamber music often reached a variety of audiences beyond their borders, and at a range of diverse venues. For these societies also had the potential to become sites for cultural transfer, serving their adopted nations as models for new music and gathering grounds for individuals who shared similar socio-political persuasions (see Reißfelder and Thomason).

The involvement of women in the organisation and performance of chamber music also bears study. For young, middle, and upper-class women of the years between 1850 and 1918, chamber music performance became a vehicle for *Bildung*, or growth and education, along with other accomplishments such as reading and drawing. Some of them would develop these interests far beyond the expectations of their patriarchal society, to the dismay (or disdain) of those who scorned women endowed with intellectual aspirations as 'blue stockings'. With the public sphere especially out of reach for most women, those who overcame the difficulties of engaging in professional composition often concentrated their efforts on chamber music repertoire. These works they wrote for salons which they could freely access, and even direct, as well as for the press. For every Augusta Holmès (1847-1903) — with the opera *La montagne noire* (1895) and grandiose symphonic poems to her credit — how many Fanny Mendelssohn-Hensel's (1805-1847), Clara Wieck-Schumann's (1819-1896), Pauline Viardot's (1821-1910), and Mel Bonis's (1858-1937) faithfully penned chamber pieces for private and public consumption? Women who neither composed nor performed nonetheless found ways to play an instrumental part in the dissemination of this repertoire. If the work of the *salonnière* Marguerite de Saint-Marceaux (1850-1930) may be viewed as a form of creation and cultural mediation (see Perreault), the musical events organized by Alice Warder Garrett (1877-1952) might be considered vehicles for diplomacy (see Fenton). Still, the full extent to which women were able to enter fully into either public or private performances of this genre remained and continues to remain questionable (see November).

This is where good, old-fashioned, gendered associations with the 'serious' and by implication, the 'masculine', come into play, alongside what Sylvia Kahan observes in this volume as an «[...] outsized interest in the Beethoven's late string quartets [...]». For in parallel with the growth of chamber works for the public, came the seeds of a musical canon of chamber pieces alongside patterns of emulation amongst composers at a time when it was nearly impossible to ignore the legacy of Beethoven. Beethoven's legacy proved impossible to disregard for countless nineteenth-century composers such as Felix Mendelssohn (1809-1847), Franz Liszt (1811-1886), Richard Wagner (1813-1883), Johannes Brahms (1833-1897), and Gustav Mahler (1860-1911)[9]. In France, the Beethovenian tradition appears to have left a

---

[9]. For the enormous influence of Beethoven on nineteenth-century symphony, and the problem of the very different nature of the borrowings according to each composer, see DAHLHAUS 1980, pp. 152-153.

profound mark on the composer César Franck (1822-1890), though it may well be Beethoven's symphonies and not his quartets that wielded their influence on his String Quartet in D Minor (see Strucken-Paland), or the 'heroic' works from his second period that made themselves felt in the celebrated Quintet (see de Médicis). More generally still, Romantic conceptions of the mature or 'late' Beethoven may inevitably creep into our conceptions of chamber works penned by composers in their final years — it is almost inevitable given longstanding traditions in composer biography that routinely divide the artist's output into early, middle, and late-style works. In this, Edward Said's two notions of late style seem particularly relevant; one offers a distillation of «[...] age and wisdom in some last works that reflect[s] a special maturity, a new spirit of reconciliation and serenity[...]»; and the other «[...] involves nonharmonious, nonserene tension, and above all, a sort of deliberately unproductive productiveness going *against*»[10]. Yet if we look more closely at Antonín Dvořák (1841-1904) or Saint-Saëns's final string quartets, this model founders (see Campo-Bowen and Deruchie).

For Andrew Deruchie, Saint-Saëns's Second String Quartet, written in his later years and linked by the composer to experiences of aging, reveals a musician both «[...] engaged with the present and mindful of the future». For him the work represents «[...] not a rebuke to the innovative spirit but a lesson on how music could evolve within the aesthetic standards the composer believed would prevail in the future [...]». In Deruchie's analysis, this 'late' work does not come to a close with an epiphany as one might expect at the end of life, but rather with a burst of Haydnesque laughter. Similarly, Christopher Campo-Bowen challenges the notion of 'lateness' in the music that Dvořák composed near the end of his life. Peering through the lens of Beethoven's late career, in search of a Dvořák who has retreated from society «into an alienated yet transcendent creative existence» proves futile in the case of this composer, who enjoyed popular and critical success in both Vienna and Prague. In view of this, and considering various musical factors, Campo-Bowen rightly asks: «How would our perceptions of music history change if, instead of valuing alienation and struggle, we were to value joy and ease?».

Described in the writings of Vincent d'Indy as 'Beethovenian', close analysis of César Franck's chamber works reveals a much more detailed view. Christiane Strucken-Paland reminds readers that the French composer referred to Beethoven's process for the finale of the Ninth Symphony in relation to his own writing for the String Quartet of 1889. And while this work bears the imprint of the German composer's symphonic style, in contrast to Beethoven, «Franck's finale no longer functions as the apotheosis of a teleological development». Instead, it establishes a static experience of time. Through his analysis of the Quintet, François de Médicis also establishes Franck's indebtedness to Beethoven's musical narrative arcs of *per aspera ad astra* and the race to the abyss. These are featured prominently in the German composer's works from his second period and left their mark on the music of some of his followers (e.g.,

---

[10].   SAID 2006, cited in WHEELDON 2009, p. 1.

Liszt and Brahms). Thus for de Médicis and contrarily to d'Indy, it was probably not the 'late' style of Beethoven that cast its shadow over Franck, but rather the 'Heroic' works, including the Piano Sonata, Op. 57 (*Appassionata*).

In the realm of chamber music performance, Nancy November argues that the works of Beethoven and other composers within the Austro-German canon served a social purpose to provide specifically men with activities that appeared free of political associations. But this same body of works seems to have been denied to women musicians, who turned to other repertoires, and moreover adopted a performance style of self-effacement in order to allow the composer to speak directly. Isabelle Perreault also points to the toning down or restriction of female bodies within the phenomenon of 'serious' listening. Silent, near reverent, and in the well-lighted interior of the home, this practice constituted a veritable 'Wagnerian' experience in Marguerite (Meg) de Saint-Marceaux's salon, «without the exuberance displayed by certain society audiences» she so disdained. In addition to hosting these near spiritual gatherings, Meg de Saint-Marceaux's salon functioned as an important platform or forum for performers and composers alike to network and try out new works.

Performances in private salons such as Saint-Marceaux's were regularly referred to in the Parisian press, alongside those given in public. From Sylvia Kahan, we learn that while aristocratic or bourgeois dailies such as *Le Figaro* and *Le Gaulois* published only superficial accounts of these concerts and recitals during the Third Republic, serious attention was paid to these events in the pages of *Le Temps*. Still, in the thrall of Beethoven mania during this time, French music often received little attention compared to works from the Austro-German canon. Pointing to the near complete absence of commentary on some forty performances of Debussy's string quartet, Kahan cautions readers of a significant disconnect between public and private programming, and commentary from the press.

For the American and at times Italian press commenting on the 'private' performances of the Musical Art Quartet, criticism was more consistently directed at the performers than it was at the music itself. Kathryn Fenton explores the work and reception of this ensemble, specifically for events supported by Alice Warder Garrett that were intended as a means of American musical diplomacy. For Fenton, the tenor of the press reception that followed the quartet's performances was manipulated to some degree by the American Embassy in Italy. The quartet even garnered praise from Benito Mussolini himself, who viewed the ensemble's concerts as an effort to foster friendship between the two nations. Emphasis on the performers also characterized the reception of Dvořák's 1892 'Farewell Tour', featuring the *Dumky* Piano Trio Op. 90, as we learn from Eva Branda, who also underscores a critical perception of the composer's chamber works as 'intimate', since, in the words of Josef Boleška «[...] every idea comes from his *inner-being* (*nitro*)». More importantly, for Branda, Czech chamber music works were not considered markers of Czech national identity in the same way as opera and symphony. Thus, for Branda, «[...] the marking out of chamber music as

[Dvořák's] 'niche' insulated him from criticism, helping to secure, in this area at least, his wider success among the Czechs».

At the same time, for Anja Bunzel, the case of a chamber music concert series given in Prague, known as *Free Musical Entertainments*, is very much connected to Czech nationalism:

> [...] within the wider context of Czech musical culture the most important outcomes of these *Entertainments* were not primarily the promotion of individual composers such as Dvořák, or, indeed, the popularisation of new Czech works. Rather, these events offered a platform to explore openly whether and how panslavism might have a place in music and also how it might lead to a more effective formation of national identity in Czech musical culture.

Like the English concerts of French music that David Reißfelder addresses in this volume, the *Free Musical Entertainments* might be interpreted as a means of countering German influence on Czech culture. These events also provided an opportunity for audiences to experience newer, unpublished works — a sort of testing ground for composers, much like Meg Saint-Marceaux's salon, but conducted in public. Although these concerts began as purely vocal events, which might be considered more reflective of the nation — as Eva Branda points out — they evolved fairly quickly into mainly instrumental concerts. Sometimes 'Czechness' was asserted not by the composers, but by the performers. Moreover, the whole issue of 'seriousness' that marked the salon of Saint-Marceaux and the concerts of French music in England, as well as the need for self-effacement patent in the performances of all-female string quartets (see November) appears largely absent from the *Free Musical Entertainments*.

Vjera Katalinić's chapter on concerts organized by the Committee for the Promotion of Chamber Music in Zagreb tells a much different story. There the consolidation of chamber music events appears to have coincided with a decreased need to establish national identity, though Katalinić concedes that (as Bunzel and Branda also find), issues of nation were more greatly bound up in opera and vocal music. At the turn of the nineteenth and into the twentieth century, Zagreb witnessed a growth in interest for 'sublime' chamber music that superseded performances of works that might be considered 'low brow' (i.e., operettas and acrobatic performances). While local performers took part in these events, the Committee also invited a significant number of outside musicians to perform in concerts. To some extent, this also reflects the international nature of many chamber music events given in Lisbon, considered in Hélder Sá's chapter. In terms of music, the range of repertoire for solo violinists and violin duos in Lisbon was fairly broad in terms of nationality and historical era, belying any sort of 'ethnic-linguistic' nationalist privileging of home-grown talent. As was the case in France and England, the repertoire for string quartet and trio concerts often relied heavily on works by Beethoven.

This kind of musical migration, from one nation to another, is often referred to as 'cultural transfer', and the period under study — from 1850 to 1918 — proved an ideal time for this. Music had circulated previously in the form of publications; Haydn, for instance, published with every major publisher in Europe. Virtuosi also toured extensively, though often to deliver concertos. But as railways expanded and economic pressure eased during the *Belle Époque*, chamber music could travel more easily with its performers, who were also, sometimes, its composers. England in particular benefitted from an influx of French music in the years leading up to the First World War. David Reißfelder's chapter examines the role that works from across the Channel played in helping to define musical modernity, particularly new British music. He underscores the significance of the Franck Quartet and Quintet (works discussed by Strucken-Paland and de Médicis in this volume):

> While in 1901 it was still doubtful whether Franck would ever equal Schumann and Brahms in rank, a decade later, the significance of his works — the more austere Quintet and Quartet included — was beyond question […]. Franck's chamber music, by the beginning of the First World War, was regularly performed by British musicians. Twenty years after his death, he was unreservedly perceived as 'modern' and appeared in concert series focused on contemporary (and often British) repertoire […].

And London critics were reading their d'Indy, dressing up Franck as a new, but French Beethoven. Indeed, French chamber music provided the English with an alternative model through which to explore new musical styles that stood apart from German models. These new elements, drawn from French music, might be considered derivative, but they might also represent freedom from the kinds of German music that had dominated many chamber music societies. Geoff Thomason's work on the Ancoats Brotherhood concerts provides a case in point. Initially a society founded for working class people, the Brotherhood eventually transformed into a middle-class chamber music society, with concerts solidly rooted in the Austro-German canon for some time. The most notable of these were events featuring the Brodsky String Quartet, an ensemble that often travelled back and forth between England and Europe. But the First World War proved a catalyst for change that was already beginning to rear its head, notably through the repertoire chosen by women musicians — modern French and British works — which increasingly overtook the Austro-German canon in the years leading up to and beyond 1914.

While they may well be smaller works for smaller spaces, chamber music in the later years of Romanticism and the early years of Modernism occupied an important place in Western music making. This repertoire provided hefty cultural capital for private salons, allowing the women who oversaw these intimate spaces to exert much wider influence outside the walls of their homes. It could become a means of expressing or exploring nationhood, or just as easily, it could provide a more neutral, but still personal ground for bringing audiences together. Beethovenian tropes and models may hover to far too great a degree in the background of any consideration of this genre. But confronting these tropes and models allows those in the present to live, to some extent, the experiences of those who, during a relatively recent time, composed, performed, and listened to that most intimate and personal genre of music.

François de Médicis & Catrina Flint de Médicis
Montréal, December 2023

Bibliography

AUGÉ DE LASSUS 1911
AUGÉ DE LASSUS, Lucien. *La Trompette: Un demi-siècle de musique de chambre*, Paris, C. Delagrave, 1911.

CHRISTENSEN 1999
CHRISTENSEN, Thomas. 'Four-Hand Piano Transcription and Geographies of Nineteenth-Century Musical Reception', in: *Journal of the American Musicological Society*, LII/2 (1999), pp. 255-298.

CHRISTENSEN 2000
ID. 'Public Music in Private Spaces: Piano-Vocal Scores and the Domestication of Opera', in: *Music and the Cultures of Print*, edited by Kate van Orden, New York, Garland Publishing, 2000, pp. 67-93.

DAHLHAUS 1980
DAHLHAUS, Carl. *Neues Handbuch der Musikwissenschaft. 6: Die Musik des 19. Jahrhunderts*, Wiesbaden, Akademische Verlagsgesellschaft Athenaion, 1980.

DENORA 1995
DENORA, Tia. *Beethoven and the Construction of Genius: Musical Politics in Vienna, 1792-1803*, Berkeley (CA), University of California Press, 1995.

HUYSSEN 1986
HUYSSEN, Andreas. *After the Great Divide: Modernism, Mass Culture, Postmodernism*, Bloomington-Indianapolis, Indiana University Press, 1986.

KERMAN 1979
KERMAN, Joseph. *The Beethoven Quartets*, New York, W. W. Norton & Company, 1979.

MARIEN 2002
MARIEN, Mary Warner. *Photography: A Cultural History*, New York, Harry N. Abrams, 2002.

REIBEL 2023
REIBEL, Emmanuel. *Du Métronome au gramophone. Musique et révolution industrielle*, Paris, Fayard, 2023.

ROSEN 1998
ROSEN, Charles. *The Romantic Generation*, Cambridge (MA), Harvard University Press, 1998.

SAID 2006
SAID, Edward, W. *On Late Style: Music and Literature Against the Grain*, New York, Pantheon Books, 2006.

WHEELDON 2009
WHEELDON, Marianne. *Debussy's Late Style*, Bloomington, Indiana University Press, 2009.

WITHIN, AROUND AND BEYOND THE 'BEETHOVENIAN'

Antonín Dvořák's String Quartets Opp. 105 and 106 and the Question of Late Style

Christopher Campo-Bowen
(Virginia Tech)

WE MIGHT SURMISE that, upon his return to Bohemia in the late spring of 1895, Antonín Dvořák was quite tired. He had spent much of the last three years either in the United States or traveling from there back to his native land, and in the months after his return he eventually decided that his American adventures were over. For most of the year Dvořák did little in the way of composing, confining himself to revising and creating reductions of his own works. Prior to leaving New York City, he had begun work on a quartet in A-flat major, sketching a portion of the first movement. It was not until November that he began composing again in earnest, but when he did, it was with renewed gusto. Between 11 November 1895 and 9 December, he wrote the String Quartet in G major, Op. 106, and by 30 December he had returned to and completed the String Quartet in A-flat major, Op. 105. From there, Dvořák's creative impulse would carry him first into the realm of programme music, with five tone poems appearing in the next two years, and then into opera, where he would produce *Čert a Káča* (1899), *Rusalka* (1900), and *Armida* (1903).

The last two string quartets composed by Antonín Dvořák have long occupied a curious place in accounts of the composer's life and works. Given their genre and their chronological position within the composer's life, the quartets in G and A-flat have been frequently apostrophised as the last pieces of 'absolute music' that Dvořák ever wrote. Both contemporary observers, like the Viennese critic Robert Hirschfeld, and later writers, such as the composer's first biographer Otakar Šourek, saw the Opp. 105 and 106 quartets as a last stage of normalcy before Dvořák departed for the uncharacteristic wilds of tone poems and opera. Twentieth-century biographers' dislike for the tone poems — *Vodník* (The Water Goblin), *Zlatý kolovrat* (The Golden Spinning Wheel), *Polednice* (The Noon Witch), and *Holoubek* (The Wild Dove), all composed in 1896 — was not helped by the often-gruesome content of the works' source texts: Czech folk ballads written by the poet and folklorist Karel Jaromír Erben, based on tales he collected. Indeed, in much of the twentieth-century biographical literature on Dvořák, his four Erben tone poems and the *Píseň bohatýrská* (Heroic Song, 1897) were viewed with indifference or a sort of genteel distaste, as though authors were mildly annoyed that the composer of the Symphony No. 7 in D minor, the, 'American' String Quartet, and the Cello Concerto would stoop to something as gauche as programme music[1]. The following quote is emblematic: «What one is inclined to regret is that during the next couple of years or so he should have devoted so much of his time to attempts to express his devotion to his homeland in "programme music", a branch of composition in which now and again Smetana had shown supremacy but for which Dvořák's great talents, many-sided though they were, were less well-fitted»[2]. Engagement with the last three operas required a quite different rhetorical apparatus than the 'absolute' works like the symphonies or string quartets, and so they tend to occupy their own self-contained realm within Dvořák's reception[3]. In short, one is greeted by a profusion of compositional genres in the last ten years of his life, before he died in 1904 at the age of 62 — a period that, by the examples of other composers, might be termed his 'late period'. Yet the idea of lateness very rarely, if ever, intrudes upon discussions of Dvořák's life and works[4].

In this chapter, I revaluate the historical position of the last two quartets in Dvořák's life with an eye toward a vexed question in music history: that of 'late style'. To some extent this is a problem of the dog that did not bark: the absence of lateness in Dvořák's reception is indicative of a larger issue than simply his music and life not fitting into established models of how the impending end of life affects creative work. I should be clear that I am not trying to recuperate Dvořák into a model of lateness, or to argue that he should be included among the 'great' composers who are seen as possessing late styles. Rather, I suggest that the example of Dvořák's last works exposes the contingency and exclusionary nature of the label 'late', and his willingness to shift genres, audiences, and aesthetic principles in the last years of his life places him outside conventional biographical and musical models. Following from Gordon McMullan and Sam Smiles, I too contend that «there is arguably an ethical obligation to find a more appropriate, a less (or even an un-) mythologised means of validating the productions of old age or of proximity to death»[5]. Dvořák's last string quartets present an opportunity to rethink how we construct composer-career narratives, and how we unwittingly perpetuate exclusionary models that privilege certain identities, certain world views, and certain kinds of music.

---

[1]. See, for example, HUGHES 1967; BUTTERWORTH 1980; and SCHÖNZELER 1984.

[2]. HUGHES 1967, p. 186.

[3]. More on the character and reception of Dvořák's operas can be found in SMACZNY 1997.

[4]. While it is difficult to prove a negative example, suffice it to say that Dvořák's entry in the *Grove Dictionary of Music and Musicians*, the paradigmatic Anglophone reference work, only uses the word 'late' in the sense of late style once, and that only in passing, in a discussion of the last three operas. See DÖGE 2001.

[5]. See MCMULLAN – SMILES 2016, p. 12.

LATE STYLES IN MUSIC

The *locus classicus* of late style in music is, of course, Ludwig van Beethoven. In a famous essay entitled 'Spätstil Beethovens' Theodor Adorno characterises the composer's late style as full of contradictions, as alienated from its social and artistic surroundings, and as difficult, irascible, and unyielding[6]. In most biographical accounts, the composer's impending death seems to cast a shadow backward into his own life, and it is the awareness of the futility of striving in the face of mortality that causes the subjective to come through at the expense of the teleological force of earlier works. Adorno resisted this psychological interpretation of the works as outgrowths of Beethoven's increasing subjectivity, as though the late works, the string quartets in particular, mirrored his increasing suffering at the close of life by breaking through Classical form with the force of 'personality'. He instead preferred to interpret subjectivity in Beethoven's late works as deriving from their embrace of convention alongside their wilful disregard for the drive toward an organic unity, paradoxically rendering their expressionlessness expressive of the ultimately intractable inability to bridge the gap between subject (the composer and/or the musical theme) and object (the musical work and/or its formal framework)[7]. Because of the apparent disunion and irreconcilability of Beethoven's late works, Adorno says, «in the history of art, late works are the catastrophes»[8]. Alongside this collapse of social connectedness and artistic form is a collapse of temporal sequentiality: as Edward Said says of Adorno's conception of late style, «lateness is being at the end, fully conscious, full of memory, and also very (even preternaturally) aware of the present»[9].

The quality of lateness, it should be said, may be based not only on the facts of biography, but may also inhere as a historical category, grounded in a dialectical model of musical progress and characterized by a sense of anachronicity — a category in which Dvořák also fails to fit, by virtue of the same differences that obviate his correspondence to the biographical model of lateness[10]. Related to the idea of anachronism, both Adorno and Said ascribe to lateness a characteristic stylistic and artistic inconsistency, a tendency to bounce back and forth between genres, musical styles, and aesthetic priorities. Though Dvořák did move between three different genres — string quartet, symphonic poem, and opera — in his last years, he did so in blocks, so that he produced only works in that genre for a given time. Not only does this indicate a certain

---

[6]. See ADORNO 2002, pp. 564-568.

[7]. Richard Leppert also notes that the genre of the string quartet itself also highlights another aporia, that between the «utopian social balance» of the individual with the collective embodied in the string quartet, on the one hand, and authoritarian dominance of the composer. See discussion in *ibidem*, pp. 516-525.

[8]. *Ibidem*, p. 567.

[9]. See SAID 2006, p. 14.

[10]. The distinction between biographical and historical models of lateness is discussed in WOOD 2006, pp. xii-xiii.

level of consistency, but subsequent historiography has tended to view the progression from symphonic poem to opera as a teleological narrative. Dvořák's first biographer, Otakar Šourek, alongside all those who drew from him, positioned the Erben symphonic poems as preparatory exercises for the return to opera, a narrative diametrically opposed to the idea of inconsistent flitting between genres and styles[11].

Part of the problem with the concept of late style is that, in music, it is almost inevitably reliant on the Beethovenian model of the artist-hero composer, who struggles, overcomes, and, in inescapably failing to overcome mortality's inexorable pull, retreats from society into an alienated yet transcendent creative existence. Composers like Franz Schubert have supported other narratives of late style, but he too suffers from the inevitable comparison with his elder contemporary. Schubert was only 31 at the time of his death, but his last works are as equally invested with an aura of lateness as those of Beethoven, even if the sense of lateness is somewhat different. According to the musicologist Lorraine Byrne Bodley, Schubert's «[late] music is an indication of the composer's "self-guiding artistic destiny"; it elaborates an alternative argument to the prevailing Beethovenian aesthetic and to the forces of illness and death, which at once dehumanize and liberate the human spirit [...]. What grips us is [Schubert's] transcendence of struggle, a continual striving toward synthesis and the creative energy that endured and redoubled in the face of crisis and death»[12]. In this view, while Schubert's late style may be more affirming than that of Beethoven, it nevertheless replicates the model of the hero-genius who overcomes (or, in Joseph Straus's model, accommodates) in order to deliver musical transcendence to the listener — just as Beethoven 'overcame' his deafness, so Schubert overcame his terminal illness, if only temporarily[13].

This model is, to say the least, limiting. At its most basic level, it is reliant on a music-historiographical model of style analysis that privileges an evolutionary progression from an early, 'immature', less complex style to one that is late, 'mature', and ever more profoundly complex[14]. Furthermore, the overcoming genius model presupposes the idea that the artist must suffer in order to achieve musical excellence, while also relying on a valuation of music based on an early Romantic concept of transcendent metaphysical meaning. The idea that music was

---

11. An example of this can be found in ŠOUREK 1933, pp. 42-44.

12. BODLEY 2016, p. 10.

13. Straus argues, in distinction from other critics of Schubert's late music, that Schubert does not overcome the musical or biographical problems of his last years but rather accommodates their presence. Nevertheless, both models position illness (and its association with mortality) as something to be dealt with, a narrative problem in need of resolution. For more on the resonances of the heroic composer model with theorisations of disability, especially with regard to ableism and the cultural tendency to reward narratives of overcoming, see STRAUS 2011, pp. 45-71.

14. See, for example, BODLEY 2016, p. 1. For a broader discussion of the legacy of evolutionary categories in musical style history, see MUNDY 2014.

capable of disclosing unique metaphysical truths went unchallenged at least through the first stirrings of European musical modernism in Richard Strauss's late nineteenth-century tone poems, and it remains partially if not wholly latent throughout Adorno's twentieth-century writings on the *Wahrheitsgehalt* of Beethoven and Arnold Schoenberg's music. At this point it also goes without saying that the musical transcendence of late style is and was heavily reliant on a specifically German philosophical and aesthetic tradition, one that has a tendency to erase difference and particularity through appeals to the universalising category of the 'genius'.

Antonín Dvořák, for all his creative excellence, compositional fecundity, and profound musical imagination, had trouble fitting the model of the nineteenth-century genius. His irrevocable ethnic and cultural difference as a Czech composer meant that his creative talent was presupposed to be naïve and natural, as opposed to the cerebral and studied creative genius of figures like Beethoven and Johannes Brahms[15]. The works that brought him closest to that category were precisely those that trafficked most heavily in the aesthetic discourses of the German-speaking world, for example the String Quartet No. 10 or the Symphony No. 7, so lauded by the Viennese critical establishment led by Eduard Hanslick and other partisans of 'absolute' music — a style that Michael Beckerman, in one of his many felicitous phrases, has termed the 'High Habsburg' style[16]. It was in the circles that valued such music, which privileged the idea of immanent musical meaning, emphasised a compositional practice focusing on the organic development of motives, and disdained the idea of programme music in favour of absolute music, that Dvořák made his name, and from which his music spread across Europe and thence elsewhere.

DVOŘÁK'S LAST QUARTETS

It is thus no surprise that, in a musicological literature heavily reliant on German music history and historiography, Dvořák's last two string quartets would be privileged as his final, valedictory statement in the realm of absolute music. Most commentators agreed that the last two quartets represented a departure from the simpler style that had characterized the composer's American period, and that they could be read as a return to the musical language that characterized his pre-American maturity. Dvořák's efforts in the realm of the string quartet were well-known in the musical milieus of both Vienna and Prague, and the genre itself was seen as a bastion of German musical conservatism through the end of the nineteenth century, prizing as it did the works of Haydn, Mozart, Beethoven, and Brahms[17].

---

[15]. For an extended discussion of Dvořák's reception history and its relationship to Austro-German ideas of musical value and creativity, see BOTSTEIN 1997.

[16]. See BECKERMAN 2003, pp. 10-13.

[17]. See DAVERIO 2004, pp. 348-349.

Ex. 1: String Quartet in G Major, Op. 106, Movement No. 2, Climax.

Dvořák's last two quartets are deeply indebted to Classical models, with both featuring the standard four-movement plan: a sonata-form first movement, a slow movement, a scherzo, and a sonata or rondo form fourth movement, though the first and fourth movements of both display tendencies toward expansion and modification of their normative formal types. Neither displays much in the way of musical material that might be described as alienated, catastrophic, or even necessarily difficult (though the pieces are certainly technically challenging). Indeed, on the contrary, Dvořák seems to go out of his way to provide thematic unity, evocative contrast, and lyricism. Two examples should suffice to illustrate this point: the second movement of the Quartet in G (see Ex. 1) and the final movement of the Quartet in A-flat (see Ex. 2).

Šourek considered the slow movement of the Quartet in G the culminating part of the work and «one of the loveliest and most profound slow movements in Dvořák's creation»[18].

---

[18]. ŠOUREK 1978, p. 114. See also ŠOUREK 1930, pp. 234-255.

Ex. 2: String Quartet in A-flat Major, Op. 105, Movement No. 4, Opening.

The Prague music critic Karel Knittl, after the premiere of the work on 8 October 1896, called the movement the pinnacle of the quartet as a whole; later that same year, down in Vienna, Robert Hirschfeld also singled out the movement as exceptional, writing that the quartet as a whole often went beyond the sonic borders of the string quartet into the realm of the orchestral[19]. The movement is cast in a theme and variations structure, and a single theme is developed over the alternation of minor and major modalities. After a series of contrasting variations, the music eventually comes to a broad climax, emphasising the main theme in rhythmic unison and an outpouring of pathos.

The deeply felt lyricism of this movement provides moments of alternating emotional intensity and repose, as well as a broader contrast to the sunny and energetic first movement. Indeed, both the Quartet in G and the Quartet in A-flat seem to be suffused with feelings of joy and thanksgiving. Such qualities were interpreted as having been occasioned by Dvořák's

---

[19].   See Knittl 1896 and Hirschfeld 1896.

Ex. 3a: First appearance of the second theme in the String Quartet in A-flat Major, Op. 105, Finale, bb. 81-92.

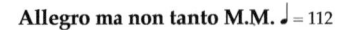

return to his beloved Bohemia and his deliverance from the difficulties of living and working in the United States[20]. This is not necessarily to privilege a biographical motivation for these works — whatever the reason for their musical exuberance, and whatever the formal oddities of their respective first movements, I would argue the quartets do little to suggest incoherence or fissured textures.

While the second movement of the Quartet in G delivers emotional tension and catharsis in the familiar guise of variation technique, the final movement of the Quartet in A-flat provides surprises from the outset. It begins with an E-natural, alien to its home key and made all the more strange by the final sonority, F major, that ended the third movement. The cello's introductory motive ends on F-sharp, another foreign pitch and bass note for an extremely unstable harmony

---

[20]. See, for example, ŠOUREK 1978, p. 105.

Ex. 3b: Second appearance of the second theme in the String Quartet in A-flat Major, Op. 105, Finale, bb. 333-344.

consisting of two superimposed tritones, E-natural/B-flat and F-sharp/C-natural. Out of this harmonic no-man's land Dvořák conjures a quick switch into A-flat major and the movement proper begins, recalling Franz Joseph Haydn in his more playful moments.

Formally, the fourth movement of the Quartet in A-flat is a combination of sonata and rondo form, featuring three complementary themes connected by motivic derivations of the first theme. Indeed, the entire movement is suffused by the anacrusis gesture that opens the movement of three sixteenth-notes leading into a longer downbeat, which provides an overall sense of motivic unity.

The exception to the interconnectedness of the final movement is the lyrical second theme, which stands apart in all of its appearances. However, each time it is emphasised in such a way as to mark a gradually building narrative throughout the movement. The calmness of its first appearance contrasts sharply with the busyness of the musical texture throughout

Ex. 3c: Third appearance of the second theme in the String Quartet in A-flat Major, Op. 105, Finale, bb. 509-521.

the first part of the movement, and the second appearance intensifies the theme's lyricism by specifying it be played *sul G*, adding a warmth of sonority unique within the movement. Finally, the second theme appears in the coda, carried by the viola and cello in rhythmic augmentation while the two violins weave a two-octave, A-flat pedal above it.

This final appearance has a triumphant quality to it, bringing the quartet to a joyful close. All told, in their lyricism, emotional variety, motivic coherence, and just plain joyfulness, the last two quartets stand in direct opposition to the primary affective markers of late style as it is typically discussed in music.

Beyond 'Late Style'

Apart from the musical qualities of his last two string quartets, there are several other reasons why, to my mind, Dvořák evades the category of late style. One such reason, mentioned above, was his willingness to change musical genres suddenly and wholly when it came to composition. After the last two quartets, Dvořák turned to orchestral programme music, writing five tone poems in less than two years. The last five tone poems represent Dvořák's most sustained engagement with the genre of programme music. As I mentioned earlier, four of the tone poems were based on the poetry of Karel Jaromír Erben, a writer and collector of folksongs and folktales. The works — *Vodník* (The Water Goblin), *Polednice* (The Noon Witch), *Zlatý kolovrat* (The Golden Spinning Wheel), and *Holoubek* (The Wild Dove) — follow their textual inspirations quite closely, to the point that Dvořák wrote the poetry into the score above the corresponding musical passages, almost as if setting text. His final tone poem, *Píseň bohatýrská* (Heroic Song), featured a more abstract programme, and as such was almost immediately claimed by anxious partisans of absolute music as a return to form[21].

These programmatic pieces formed the background against which the last two quartets were initially measured and received, as the quartets were not heard publicly until late December 1896 — after the premieres of *Vodník* and *Polednice*. Hirschfeld, having lauded Dvořák's string quartet writing as quasi-orchestral, characterized the appearance of the tone poems in the following manner: «In general Dvořák seems to undergo a development that, precisely by virtue of the ease with which he composes, is far more erratic than we can see in, say, Brahms»[22]. Such a statement reinforces the idea that there is both a proper way, in terms of both aesthetics and genre, for composers to develop their musical output, as well as the notion that Brahms (and, by extension, the composers whose lineage he represented) stood for this proper path. It also perhaps subtly reiterates the idea of Dvořák as the naive creative talent, from whom music could not but flow, as opposed to the cerebral, carefully worked-out compositions of Brahms, Beethoven, Bach, *et al.* It is precisely Dvořák's compositional ease that prevents his assimilation into the discourses of late style — rather than being based in a creative impasse or the inability to properly communicate the profound interiority of lateness, Dvořák's inconsistency was borne of the fact that he simply could not help himself.

Nevertheless, at the same time that Hirschfeld reinforced a narrative that seemed to relegate Dvořák to a lesser tier, he reaffirmed Dvořák's new path. The composer had, in Hirschfeld's estimation, come to the end of what was possible with instrumental music, and had

---

[21]. See Campo-Bowen 2016.

[22]. Hirschfeld 1896, p. 16: «Im Allgemeinen scheint Dvorak eine Entwicklung durchzumachen, die eben vermöge der Leichtigkeit seines Schaffens weit mit mehr sprunghaft ist, als wir etwa bei Brahms gewahren können».

apparently been so overpowered by the desire to express himself poetically that he had turned to programme music. While to the critic this development seemed erratic, it simultaneously underscored Dvořák's facility with all manner of different musical genres in the most positive of ways — Hirschfeld ended his feuilleton with the encomium: «Since he can do everything, everything is possible for him»[23]. At the risk of reinforcing the primacy of biographical readings in understanding lateness, such a sentiment also militates against any ascriptions of late style: a composer for whom everything is possible, and who finds favour with critics and audiences in both worldly, imperial Vienna and his native Prague, hardly seems alienated from his creative and social surroundings.

All of Dvořák's last five tone poems were in some sense essays in musical storytelling, which (according to Šourek) Dvořák seems to have used as preparation for his last three operas: *Čert a Káča* (The Devil and Kate, 1899), *Rusalka* (1900), and *Armida* (1903). Dvořák likewise wrote these in relatively quick succession. What is notable here is the completeness with which Dvořák devoted himself to a single genre at a time — aside from revisions to older works and a few sketches, Dvořák's compositional attention was wholly focused on only three genres, each in a self-contained period, in the final eight years of his life after his return from the United States. Other notable musical examples of late style, for example Beethoven, Schubert, Brahms, and even Ravel, tended to switch between genres more rapidly. In this context, Hirschfeld's comment about Dvořák's 'erratic' development might be understood more as a comment on his movement between the supposedly circumscribed, opposed aesthetic realms of absolute and programme music. Moreover, with the exception of Ravel, none of those four composers turned to opera in their last works[24].

This somewhat compartmentalized way of reading Dvořák's last works inherently violates the historical model of developmental stylistic evolution, largely institutionalized by Guido Adler (with help from Charles Hubert Parry) and which formed the core of musicological inquiry for much of the twentieth century[25]. The adaptability of a composer's works to this model was what positioned them within not only a hierarchy of musical value, with but also of ethnic difference[26]. Even if the more explicitly essentialist implications of the model were disavowed later in the twentieth century, style criticism and analysis still retained many of its characteristic features[27]. Dvořák's generic oddity, alongside his incompatibility with the

---

[23]. HIRSCHFELD 1896, p. 17: «Da er Alles kann, ist ihm Alles möglich».

[24]. KELLEY 2016, p. 158.

[25]. See MUNDY 2014, pp. 738-742.

[26]. For a discussion of late, nineteenth-century hierarchies of musical value and their relationship to ethnicity, race, and the music of Czech composers, see CAMPO-BOWEN 2019.

[27]. *Ibidem*, pp. 754-756.

biographical model of the mainstays of the Austro-German symphonic tradition — heroic overcoming is absent from most accounts of his life and works, except perhaps in contemporary writing that would have had him overcome his innate Czechness to approach Austro-German symphonic greatness — helps him evade the category of late style[28].

In sum, there are at least three ways in which Dvořák departs from the model of 'late style'. His last string quartets defy the musical expectations for the category of late style, and instead appear to continue from Dvořák's previous efforts in the genre. His last works in general moved away from the vaunted category of absolute music and appeared in an atypical fashion. Finally, and most importantly, Dvořák did not fit, or fit only with difficulty, into the inherited model of the heroic overcomer, the hero-genius who withdrew from the world into creative alienation. Indeed, Dvořák himself lauded the importance of opera as a public genre in the last year of his life, indicating his devotion to and desire for connection with his audience. Additionally, as Beckerman trenchantly quipped, Dvořák was only «invited to the Great Composers' party» — for whom late work was a marker of exceptional genius — «on the condition that he arrive in national dress»[29].

This is where we come to the invitation that Dvořák's last works, including the string quartets, grant us — that we dispense with the idea of late style and its associated categories of 'genius' and the 'canon' in Western music, which themselves index pervasive hierarchies of race and ethnicity, among other such social categories. In this context, late style is a marker of musical worth. Acknowledging the presence of these rhetorical and aesthetic constructs in our efforts to understand composers like Dvořák, if not attempting to discard it altogether, has the benefit of allowing us to seek new ideas of musical value and new models for our interpretation of composers. This is not to say that Dvořák and his last quartets should replace Beethoven or Schubert and their late quartets in the canon, but rather that the musical values that have led, and that lead us to privilege the latter works should be questioned. How would our perceptions of music history change if, instead of valuing alienation and struggle, we were to value joy and ease? What if, instead of a canon of masterworks, we were to seek out those works that speak to the musical and artistic needs of the moment, that enable us to envision aesthetic worlds that do not privilege suffering and proximity to death as the keys to musical profundity? Dvořák's last string quartets might not be those works themselves, but they open up the interpretive space to question late style, release its assumptions and associated concepts, and attempt to imagine something new.

---

[28]. For an accounting of such contemporary criticism, see Brodbeck 2014, pp. 143-184.

[29]. Beckerman 2003, pp. 223-224.

BIBLIOGRAPHY

ADORNO 2002
ADORNO, Theodor Wiesengrund. 'Late Style in Beethoven', in: *Essays on Music*, edited by Richard Leppert, translated by Susan H. Gillespie, Berkeley (CA), University of California Press, 2002, pp. 564-568.

BECKERMAN 2003
BECKERMAN, Michael. *New Worlds of Dvořák: Searching in American for the Composer's Inner Life*, New York, W. W. Norton & Co., 2003.

BODLEY 2016
BODLEY, Lorraine Byrne. 'Introduction: Schubert's Late Style', in: *Schubert's Late Music: History, Theory, Style*, edited by Lorraine Byrne Bodley and Julian Horton, Cambridge-New York, Cambridge University Press, 2016, pp. 1-16.

BOTSTEIN 1997
BOTSTEIN, Leon. 'Reversing the Critical Tradition: Innovation, Modernity, and Ideology in the Work and Career of Antonín Dvořák', in: *Dvořák and His World*, edited by Michael Beckerman, Princeton, Princeton University Press, 1997, pp. 11-55.

BRODBECK 2014
BRODBECK, David. *Defining «Deutschtum»: Political Ideology, German Identity, and Music-Critical Discourse in Liberal Vienna*, Oxford-New York, Oxford University Press, 2014.

BUTTERWORTH 1980
BUTTERWORTH, Neil. *Dvořák: His Life and Times*, Kent, Midas Books, 1980.

CAMPO-BOWEN 2016
CAMPO-BOWEN, Christopher. 'Bohemian Rhapsodist: Antonín Dvořák's *Píseň bohatýrská* and the Historiography of Czech Music', in: *19th-Century Music*, XL/2 (2016), pp. 159-181.

CAMPO-BOWEN 2019
ID. '«A Promising, Political Sound»: Epistemologies of Empire and Bedřich Smetana's *The Bartered Bride* at the 1892 Vienna International Exhibition of Music and Theater', in: *The Musical Quarterly*, CII/1 (2019), pp. 31-81.

DAVERIO 2004
DAVERIO, John. '*Fin de Siècle* Chamber Music and the Critique of Modernism', in: *Nineteenth-Century Chamber Music*, edited by Stephen E. Hefling, Abingdon-New York, Routledge, 2004, pp. 348-382.

DÖGE 2001
DÖGE, Klaus. 'Dvořák, Antonín', in: *Grove Music Online*, 20 January 2001, <https://www.oxfordmusiconline.com/grovemusic/>, accessed December 2023.

Hirschfeld 1896
Hirschfeld, Robert. 'Feuilleton. Musik. Neue Werke', in: *Wiener Abendpost*, 31 December 1896, pp. 15-17.

Hughes 1967
Hughes, Gerase. *Dvořák: His Life & Music*, New York, Dodd, Mead & Co., 1967.

Kelly 2016
Kelly, Barbara. 'Ravel's Timeliness and His Many Late Styles', in: *Late Style and Its Discontents: Essays in Art, Literature, and Music*, edited by Gordon McMullan and Sam Smiles, Oxford-New York, Oxford University Press, 2016, pp. 158-173.

Knittl 1896
Knittl, Karel. 'První provedení kvarteta z G od Antonína Dvořáka', in: *Dalibor*, xviii/42-43 (17 October 1896), pp. 329-331.

McMullan – Smiles 2016
McMullan, Gordon – Smiles, Sam. 'Introduction', in: *Late Style and its Discontents: Essays in Art, Literature, and Music, op. cit.*, pp. 1-12.

Mundy 2014
Mundy, Rachel. 'Evolutionary Categories and Musical Style from Adler to America', in: *Journal of the American Musicological Society* lxvii/3 (2014), pp. 735-768.

Said 2006
Said, Edward. *On Late Style: Music and Literature against the Grain*, New York, Pantheon Book, 2006.

Schönzeler 1984
Schönzeler, Hans-Hubert. *Dvořák*, New York, Marion Boyer, 1984.

Smaczny 1997
Smaczny, Jan. 'Dvořák: The Operas', in: *Dvořák and His World, op. cit.*, pp. 104-133.

Šourek 1930
Šourek, Otakar. *Život a dílo Antonína Dvořáka Část třetí 1891-1896*, Prague, Hudební matice Umělecké besedy, 1930.

Šourek 1933
Id. *Život a dílo Antonína Dvořáka Část čtvrtá 1897-1904*, Prague, Hudební matice Umělecké besedy, 1933.

Šourek 1978
Id. *The Chamber Music of Antonín Dvořák*, translated by Roberta Finlayson Samsour, Westport, Greenwood Press, 1978.

STRAUS 2011
STRAUS, Joseph. *Extraordinary Measures: Disability in Music*, Oxford-New York, Oxford University Press, 2011.

WOOD 2006
WOOD, Michael. 'Introduction', in: *On Late Style: Music and Literature against the Grain, op. cit.*, pp. xi-xix.

Saint-Saëns's Second String Quartet and the Art of Composing 'Oldly'

Andrew Deruchie
(University of Manitoba)

Andrew Deruchie
(University of Manitoba)

How might Camille Saint-Saëns (1835-1921) have been remembered had he died around the time of his near contemporary Johannes Brahms (1833-1897)? According to received music-historical narratives, Saint-Saëns's works of the 1870s through the 1890s brought his career to its apogee and made him the leader of a new wave of high-minded French composers. After the turn of the century such narratives have Saint-Saëns, who on the face of things persisted in his established aesthetic vein, falter creatively. He fades into irrelevance behind Debussy, Richard Strauss, and Stravinsky, and even becomes a vindictive opponent of these new protagonists.

What accounts for this fall from hero to bit player or even villain? Basic assumptions of twentieth-century historiography have clearly not served the musician well. Its familiar fetishisation of 'progress' and veneration of the avant-garde make the Saint-Saëns of the twentieth century ripe for casting as a 'conservative' foil to the modernists. His loud and ongoing espousal of an ostensibly obsolete art from this perspective appears a failure — to change with the times, or at least to step aside quietly.

Calls to re-assess the composer have recently emerged, and the current intellectual climate, suspicious of canonising narratives, may yet foster a more sympathetic view[1]. The reception of the musician's later career, however, has also been shaped by another set of ideas, distinct from — if easily assimilated to — the tenets of modernist historiography. Saint-Saëns's career began as a child prodigy, and it continued until his death at the age of 86, when he was very old. Perhaps he had been old for some time: in 1911, men aged 75 years or more accounted for just two percent of France's population[2]. Naturally, perceptions of old age arise from the cultural

---

[1]. See, for example, Botstein 2012.
[2]. Bourdelais 1993, pp. 406-407.

standards of communities and are complicated by aging individuals' varying appearances, physical and cognitive abilities, outlooks, and so on. Useful generalisations nonetheless remain possible. According to the historian of old age Pat Thane, «over many centuries and places there was remarkable continuity in how old age was defined in both popular and official discourse. In ancient Greece and Rome, throughout medieval and early modern Europe, in nineteenth-century North America and Australasia, old age was believed to begin somewhere between ages 60 and 70, as it still is»[3]. Saint-Saëns, then, may have been 'old' — or have been of an age where observers, then and now, could perceive him this way — for the final 20 years or more of his career. In this light, the received narratives put the composer on his downward slide into creative impotence and irrelevance when he began to be old.

Recent scholarship suggests this is no accident. The emerging interdisciplinary field of age studies conceives of old age as less a biological fact or medical condition than a cultural construct resembling gender, race, and (dis)ability; some writers postulate old age as a similarly minoritised and stigmatised identity[4]. As such, old age is known through the formal and informal stories told about it, and it imposes expectations or 'cultural scripts' upon old people. Some stories seem positive: elders may be revered for their experience and wisdom. But the prevailing views of old age emphasise degeneration, diminishing autonomy and productivity, intransigent persistence in old ways, and regression into a second childhood marked by dependence, sexual innocence, weakness, and so on. Cultural historians, including in the sphere of music Joseph Straus, have demonstrated that the reception of aging artists, writers, and musicians tends to mirror such stories and scripts remarkably[5]. An artist's final works or 'late style' may seem a transcendent culmination of a lifetime's experience — or they may appear as embarrassing evidence of diminishing abilities[6]. As we shall soon see, central themes in the reception of Saint-Saëns's post-1900 career instantiate some of the most stigmatic ideas surrounding aging.

Stigmas and scripts, of course, can — and should — be deconstructed and resisted. Like their counterparts in disability studies, scholars of old age have emphasised that the experiences and outlooks of aging people may differ radically from the stories told about old age, and the elderly may rightly find the expectations imposed upon them oppressive. Accordingly, recent critics including Straus, Linda and Michael Hutcheon, and Joy Calico have revisited the ostensibly problematic late-life œuvres of old composers such as Richard Strauss, Igor Stravinsky, Benjamin Britten, Arnold Schoenberg, and Milton Babbitt, developing sensitive and sympathetic accounts rooted in these musicians' lived experiences of old age. Works typically

---

[3]. THANE 2005, p. 17.

[4]. See, for example, GULLETTE 2004 and GULLETTE 2017.

[5]. STRAUS 2022A-E.

[6]. See BARONE 1995.

viewed as evidence of waning creative powers or senility become examples of composing 'oldly': responses to disability and other challenges of aging, products of late-life material circumstances, or manifestations of certain outlooks on aging and creativity[7].

To re-frame the question posed at the outset, how might Saint-Saëns be remembered absent the stories and scripts? How might the figure of the aging Saint-Saëns appear in light of his own outlook? How might Saint-Saëns's late-life music exemplify an art of composing oldly? This chapter sketches some answers. Its first section interrogates broad themes of Saint-Saëns reception, demonstrating how these intersect with important received ideas about old age. It then re-examines some of the musician's writings, arguing these exemplify an outlook theorists call «generativity», whereby elderly individuals, remaining productive and dynamic, assume a didactic posture beneficial to themselves and to younger generations. The final sections offer a critical account of the Second String Quartet, written in 1918 when Saint-Saëns was 82 years old. The composer had long associated this genre with maturity and mastery; having abandoned youthful attempts in the 1850s, he did not issue his first quartet until 1899, explaining, «[...] you can only write a quartet at age twenty, when you've got the rashness and ignorance of youth, or at sixty, when you possess consummate experience and your art no longer lacks anything»[8]. Saint-Saëns's correspondence, moreover, indicates that experiences of aging factored in this work's conception. A brief letter to his long-time friend Charles Lecocq reported, «I have just finished the second movement of the quartet [...]. The first movement portrays youth, the second, the regret of having lost it. Consequently, it is perhaps the saddest movement I know»[9]. This work, we shall see, aestheticises key ideas laid out in the musician's late-life writings. The art of composing 'oldly' it exemplifies evinces both Saint-Saëns's ongoing engagement with current musical culture and lessons he believed would benefit the future of music. It also allegorically takes aim at the cultural scripts surrounding old age that were already constraining the composer's reception. The finale refuses to end according to formal convention — another kind of cultural script — instead carrying on energetically and adventurously long after it should have concluded.

---

7. STRAUS 2022a-e, HUTCHEON – HUTCHEON 2015, and CALICO 2015.

8. Quoted in LALO 1900. On the composer's abandoned early quartets, see GUILLOUX 2017, pp. xlvii-xlviii. Some of the composer's correspondence suggests he viewed the Second Quartet as the belated realisation of these youthful attempts. On 9 August 1918, he wrote to Philippe Bellenot: «Now, this quartet was planned when I was eighteen! But I wouldn't have been able to write it at the time». The work even enfolds a material connection to Saint-Saëns's teenage years. Fabien Guilloux has identified a draft of the work's opening fanfare (but none of its other elements) in a sketch apparently dating from the 1850s. See *ibidem*, pp. xlviii and lxi; the sketch is reproduced on p. ci; the letter to Belenot is quoted on p. lxi.

9. Saint-Saëns to Charles Lecocq, 29 July 1918, quoted in HARKINS 1971.

OLD FOOL, AGED AVENGER

In his superb five-episode audio podcast *Musicking While Old*, Joseph Straus helpfully synthesises recent insights from the field of age studies to delineate a number of interconnected ideas that collectively define old age as a cultural construct. Most are negative, condemnatory, and stigmatising: old age brings decline, dependency, diminished productivity, and a return to the incapacities of childhood; old people cling to old ways and attempt to block progress. Such ideas, Straus shows, define the roles of old opera characters and govern the reception of old composers and performers.

Most of these ideas factor to some extent in Saint-Saëns reception, but two loom especially largely. The first is the commonplace belief that old age brings decline:

> Decline is the master narrative of old age. It's a time when everything gets worse. The story of decline shapes negative assessments of the late work of composers; its faults are now attributed to their declining creativity, a seemingly inevitable consequence of aging. [...] In the decline story, old composers often become old fools: their skills deteriorate, their creativity and originality wane, the quality of their music degenerates. They may try to do what the young people are doing, or the things they themselves did when they were young, and the result is embarrassing. We pity their loss of competence[10][.]

This «master narrative of old age» is also the master narrative of Saint-Saëns's career from around the age of sixty-five. In a 1923 biography, his erstwhile acquaintance Georges Servières parsed his œuvre into a conventional three phases, but on the bases of achievement and recognition instead of the usual criterion of style. The first period, «the years of youth», extends from 1852 to around 1870. The second, running into the 1890s, has the composer's talent ripen, reaping public success in the theatre and concert hall. Servières characterised the musician's «final 20 or 25 years» euphemistically, as a period of «official honours and tributes paid more to the composer's past than to the present»[11]. At issue was not Saint-Saëns's productivity as such. Beyond his seventieth birthday, he continued touring widely and frequently as a pianist and conductor, and his output as a composer kept pace: some 40 percent of his opus numbers date from after 1895. Nor did Saint-Saëns's technique suffer. In the critic's judgment, the final works match the expertise of their counterparts from the 1880s. According to Servières, the aging Saint-Saëns stagnated creatively: the final period includes «some interesting works, but these do not show any true evolution, either aesthetic

---

[10]. STRAUS 2022c.
[11]. SERVIÈRES 1923, pp. 83-84. Quote on p. 84.

or technical»[12]. The old Saint-Saëns worked prolifically and competently, but his creative powers failed, leaving him, Servières implies, unequal to the challenges posed by the radical early twentieth-century environment.

Such an organic trajectory of growth, bloom, and decline of creativity characterises most subsequent accounts of Saint-Saëns's career, with the turning point usually located around 1900. The final chapter of a recent biography by Jean-Luc Caron and Gérard Denizeau bears the title 'Une inspiraion déclinante'. In these twentieth-century years, «the creative vein that had brought [...] such high artistic achievements rapidly becomes exhausted. [...] The Fifth Piano Concerto [1896] stands as his last great masterwork». The subsequent music lacks «what might be called the renewal of inspiration»[13]. Jacques Bonnaure cautions that unlike some other old composers, Saint-Saëns, «not a prodigious old man», did not redeem his career with a brilliant final burst of creativity: «His output contains no equivalent to Verdi's *Falstaff* or Strauss's *Four Last Songs*»[14].

The structures of many Saint-Saëns biographies imply creative decline. The narrative almost always accelerates conspicuously upon reaching 1895 or 1900, as though the story were by this point exhausted, the many works to come notwithstanding. Servières devotes a scant six pages of his 78-page biography to the composer's final 20 years, Philippe Majorelle allots just six of his biographical narrative's 105 pages to the same period, and Jean Gallois skims through the post-1900 years in a meagre 39 of 360 pages[15]. Recent English-language life-and-works volumes by Brian Rees and Stephen Studd offer more proportionate coverage, but the flavour of both narratives changes: chronicles of the 1870s and 80s highlighting achievements as a composer give way to accounts of the twentieth-century years lingering on honorary doctorates, audiences with royals, and jubilee concerts[16]. Tributes paid more to the past than to the present take over the story.

Late in his life, Saint-Saëns experienced some events usually reserved for the dead. In February 1921, Jean Chantavoine presented lectures on the still-living composer's theatre works at the Concerts historiques Pasdeloup, a series, true to its name, otherwise spotlighting deceased musicians[17]. In 1907, Saint-Saëns had attended the dedication of a statue in his honour in Dieppe. (Satire proved irresistible: *Comœdia* ran an article titled 'Les Deux Saint-Saëns à Dieppe' with the caption «Saint-Saëns yesterday inaugurated the statue of the illustrious composer Saint-Saëns»[18].) Such events bespeak perceptions of the musician's great age, and they

---

12. *Ibidem*, p. 84.
13. Caron – Denizeau 2014. Quote on p. 139.
14. Bonnaure 2010, p. 151.
15. Servières 1923, Majorelle 2009, and Gallois 2004.
16. Rees 2008 and Studd 1999.
17. These lectures were later published as Chantavoine 1921.
18. Thorel 1907.

testify to his eminence in French musical culture. Some commentators take them as emblematic of the composer's faltering powers and even his creative death. For Studd, Saint-Saëns's forces of invention had by 1907 become so depleted as to reduce «this grand old man of French music» to a «museum piece». The creativity of Studd's aging Saint-Saëns undergoes a kind of transubstantiation, symbolised by the statue, from flesh and blood to bronze and stone[19].

Perceptions of Saint-Saëns's decline additionally stem from some of his many press articles. To cite one important example, in 1914 he plunged into a debate over the place of German music in wartime France with a series of polemics appearing in *L'Écho de Paris* under the title 'Germanophilie', later gathered into an eponymous pamphlet[20]. A lifelong admirer of the great eighteenth- and early nineteenth-century Germanic traditions, and an early advocate of Wagner, Saint-Saëns in the 1880s grew sceptical of the latter composer's mounting influence and began denouncing French Wagnerism in print. Now, in light of the invasion, enemy atrocities, and the sacrifices of French soldiers, he campaigned for a boycott of German music written since the nationalistic nineteenth century, especially Wagner's 'holy German art'. And the author admonished his compatriots to reflect on what he considered the outsized place of German aesthetics in French musical culture. These writings drew some support but aroused much hostility. Saint-Saëns's side suffered a decisive defeat, and he was widely ridiculed as an old fool, embarrassingly out of touch with the times. Albert Gavy-Bélédin, director of the science-and-culture monthly *Le Gerbe*, expressed this view most succinctly: «The *boches* are monsters; they are hateful to us. M. Camille Saint-Saëns is an old man. He arouses pity»[21]. Recalling the fray a decade on, the Belgian musicologist and composer Ernest Closson remembered *Germanophilie* as the «senile opposition» of an «egotistical old man»[22]. Even Chantavoine, who knew and admired Saint-Saëns, felt embarrassed by the screed of an old fool: «some reservations must be expressed about certain articles written during the War of 1914-1918 [...]. Age showed itself here as irritability rather than serenity, and his pen lashed out»[23].

Some commentators suspected the author of disingenuous motifs. Jean Marnold took *Germanophilie* for a self-serving attempt to preserve power in a musical world that was leaving Saint-Saëns behind[24]. This view adumbrates another important story about aging identified by Straus:

> Old people try to impede progress. They cling to the old ways and prevent
> young people from exploring what is new and better. In literature and opera, old

---

[19]. STUDD 1999, pp. 249-250.
[20]. SAINT-SAËNS 1916.
[21]. GAVY-BÉLÉDIN 1919.
[22]. CLOSSON 1924.
[23]. CHANTAVOINE 1947.
[24]. MARNOLD 1917.

> characters commonly either attempt to block the progress of the young hero or block the union of the young lovers. They may cling to power [...]. In both cases, the narrative requires them to yield. They may step aside gracefully and permit a happy comic resolution [...] or they may fight to hold onto power [...] and be forcefully, even violently pushed aside [...]. Composers persisting in writing the same sort of music they have previously written are often understood to defy contemporary trends and the progressive historical evolution of musical style[25].

In their attempts to impede progress, old people (and composers) may act as 'aged avengers', angry, vindictive, and raging over their loss of power, as Marnold casts the Saint-Saëns of *Germanophilie*.

Like the decline narrative, the progress-impeding, aged-avenger story has become a truism of Saint-Saëns reception. Even the most sympathetic biographers portray the elderly musician as dogmatically clinging to anachronistic stylistic and aesthetic values, relentlessly crusading against modernism, and indeed repudiating virtually all new developments. As Caron and Denizeau summarise, «at the time the young Debussy's audacities were beginning to reverberate in the musical world, Saint-Saëns wilfully pursued a militant classicism, historically backward, even reactionary, and above all contrary to the commitments of his conquering youth»[26]. According to James Harding, the composer's «attitude towards the new music of his day was hostile». Strauss's operas «filled him with horror [...] [and] reminded him of the tortures in Dante's *Inferno*»; *Le sacre du printemps* left him «frozen in disbelief»[27]. Like Harding, most writers cannot help portraying the old composer's outlook as pitiful, their unease manifest in the denigrating humour in which they typically wrap his irresistibly quotable comments on the modern music he rejected («one can like *Salome* — children like cod liver oil»).

The old Saint-Saëns sometimes appears downright malevolent. According to the critic Pierre Lalo, the composer in his final decades was «beset by a strange hatred of the musicians of the following generation». Recalling Marnold's assessment of *Germanophilie*, Lalo attributed this development to the insecurities of an aging composer threatened by new currents[28]. On the basis of a sarcastic 1915 letter to Gabriel Fauré, some writers claim Saint-Saëns conspired to block the terminally ill Debussy's election to the Institut[29]. A frequently recounted anecdote has the composer delaying a vacation expressly to denounce the premiere of Debussy's only opera. Some biographers mockingly transliterate the musician's lisp («I've thayed in Parith to thpeak ill of Pelleath et Melithande», as rendered by Harding), as though to make slapstick

---

25. STRAUS 2022c.
26. CARON – DENIZEAU 2014, p. 141.
27. HARDING 1965, pp. 214-15.
28. LALO 1947, p. 96.
29. See STUDD 1999, p. 271 and HARDING 1965, p. 215.

of the comment[30]. Here again, Saint-Saëns is portrayed as a comically pitiful opponent of new music. The aged avenger shades into the old fool.

GENERATIVITY

One way recent cultural historians have resisted the decline narrative, the aged-avenger story, and other pernicious tropes has involved looking to artists' lived experiences of old age and to the purposes motivating their late-life creativity. In the case of Saint-Saëns, the concept of generativity, whereby the elderly view themselves as teachers of the young, assuming the didactic tasks of conserving, passing on, and leading, seems helpful. The developmental psychologist Erik Erikson first theorised generativity in the 1950s as a mid-life «concern for establishing and guiding the next generation»[31], though he came to see its relevance to old age: generativity could stave off what he called stagnation, a lack of interest or initiative, resulting in a sense of giving up[32]. For subsequent psychologists, and more recently gerontologists, generativity has become a disposition especially associated with, and beneficial to, elderly people. Such researchers emphasise that teaching future generations yields benefits to the self: generative acts may satisfy «an inner desire grounded both in a drive for leaving a lasting legacy that survives the self and an impulse to be needed by others and be useful», and they may fulfil «a cultural demand, representing social expectations to play mentoring, supporting and leading roles in the family, community or the institutions of the wider society»[33]. More broadly, generativity assumes an outlook on old age as a time of continuing growth, learning, and exploration. In all of these ways, generativity stands diametrically opposed to the stories and cultural scripts long associated with aging — and reflexively associated with Saint-Saëns. The elderly remain dynamic (not static) and engaged (not isolated or insular); they grow and develop (rather than decline), they look to the future (rather than ensconce themselves in the past), and they remain fundamentally productive.

A generative outlook appears manifest in some of Saint-Saëns's writings, including the polemics often considered evidence of his decline or his desire to block progress. The musician tended to frame such texts as a kind of public service, identifying current and potential future consequences of aesthetic developments he considered detrimental to French musical culture and society more broadly. In the introduction to *Harmonie et mélodie* (1885), the author

---

[30]. *Ibidem*, p. 215.

[31]. ERIKSON 1963, p. 103.

[32]. *Ibidem*.

[33]. MCADAMS 2001. For a helpful survey of current views on generativity, see VILLAR – SERRAT – PRATT 2023.

worried, not unreasonably, about the fate of native aesthetic values such as clarity, order, and charm amid a seemingly unabating tide of French Wagnerism. He presented his case partly as a civic matter: if French refinement became engulfed by Teutonic grandiloquence, concert- and theatregoers could suffer a diminished sense of their own French identities[34].

Thirty years later, he proposed the 'Germanophilie' articles similarly. His angry, confrontational, and patronising tone ruffled many feathers, but Saint-Saëns put forth nuanced and coherent arguments meant to benefit France. The German military attack behoved Frenchmen to acknowledge the insidious creep of an ongoing aesthetic invasion that had, he claimed, suppressed the national values for which he had feared in the introduction to *Harmonie et mélodie*. For all its virtues, German music was not superior to French; even Wagner, the idol of Saint-Saëns's ostensible Germanophiles and a composer he continued to admire, did not lack flaws, a point he made with an adroit and hilarious litany of continuity problems in the plot of *Parsifal*. Reclaiming France's stages and concert halls for French music and musicians — whence his call to boycott German music — would benefit the nation's solidarity, and reclaiming French aesthetics for French art would help secure its future.

Saint-Saëns most explicitly adopted a generative posture in 'L'Évolution musicale', a text penned at the age of 70 addressing the future of music[35]. The article opens:

> As one advances in age, one seems to ascend to a high tower, from which increasingly vast horizons can be seen. Little by little, one becomes less interested in immediate concerns and more interested in observing the entirety of all facts, like the links of an immense chain — elements of a gradual, inevitable evolution. Whereas contemporary art still interests us, the whole of art interests us more, and we discover that in the history of art, as in that of humanity, similar causes have similar effects[36].

The wisdom of old age, he believed, afforded him a privileged view of art's historical development. This perspective enabled him to foresee a future in which the radical directions of the present day would appear as aberrations and yield to a core of normative aesthetic values ratified by centuries of the art form's evolution:

---

34. SAINT-SAËNS 1885.

35. SAINT-SAËNS 1906.

36. Translated in SAINT-SAËNS 2012: «En avançant en âge, il semble qu'on s'élève lentement sur une haute tour d'où l'on embrasse des horizons de plus en plus vastes; on se désintéresse peu à peu des choses immédiates pour observer l'ensemble des faits, qui nous apparaissent comme les chaînons d'une chaîne immense, comme les facteurs d'une évolution graduelle et inévitable. Si l'art actuel nous intéresse toujours, l'ensemble de l'art nous intéresse davantage et nous découvrons que dans son histoire, comme dans celle de l'humanité, les mêmes causes ramènent les mêmes effets».

> [At present,] we are returning [...] to stone filigree, to keystones crushing vaults instead of strengthening them, to the imbalance of leaning towers. If the lessons of the past do not lie, a reaction is near. What will it be? No one can say, but one can hope that a powerful genius will condense the chaos into a vast synthesis where the voice — that living divine instrument — will resume the place it is owed, where line, pattern, and color will join together in perfect equilibrium, where tonalities, instead of dancing a mad, pointless round, will give one another mutual support [...]. Thus, a magnificent future is doubtless reserved for music, the modern art par excellence, the phoenix that never dies[37].

Saint-Saëns doubtless produced such articles with an eye to establishing his legacy and ensuring continuity between his accomplishments and music to come. He clearly envisioned a future rooted in classical values — here coded as line, pattern, equilibrium, order, and expressive restraint — that had always underpinned his music. Between the lines of texts such as *Germanophilie* and 'L'Évolution musicale', it seems easy to see an «impulse to be needed by others and be useful»[38]. One, of course, might justifiably quibble with these texts' assumptions, arguments, and politics. There is, however, little reason to doubt the sincerity of Saint-Saëns's desire to lead others in directions he considered beneficial and necessary. In this light, seeming truisms about the musician appear somewhat differently. Saint-Saëns aimed not to block progress but to guide it; he did not single-mindedly cling to the past but looked to the future. His denunciations of some modern music perhaps stemmed not from malicious defensiveness but from a sense of pastoral duty. In such writings, in sum, we can just as easily see an elderly Saint-Saëns confidently engaged with the present and eager to deploy his experience and insights to the benefit of the future as we can an aged avenger or an old fool. It is perhaps worth recalling that some of the old musician's prognostications, about music and society alike, proved prescient. Reflecting on the horrifying results of technological progress in the Great War, he feared a future conflict would involve «some means of destruction by which entire cities disappear, as though in a dream»[39]. And as some commentators have observed, a radical reining-in of pre-war musical modernism's excesses was indeed near at hand: Stravinsky began his Octet mere months after Saint-Saëns died[40].

---

[37]. *Ibidem*: «Nous revenons [...] aux dentelles de pierre, aux clefs écrasant les voûtes au lieu de les consolider, au déséquilibrement des tours penchées. Si les leçons du passé ne sont pas mensongères, la réaction est proche. Que sera-t-il? Nul ne pourrait le dire, mais il est permis d'espérer qu'un génie puissant condensera le chaos en un une vaste synthèse où la voix — l'instrument vivant, l'instrument divin —reprendra la place qui lui est due, où la ligne, le modelé et la couleur s'uniront dans un parfait équilibre, où les tonalités, au lieu de danser une ronde folle et sans but, se prêteront un mutuel appui [...] et un magnifique avenir est sans doute ainsi réservé à la musique, l'art moderne par excellence, le phénix qui ne saurait périr». Pasler's translation is given here in its original, American standard English.

[38]. See footnote 33.

[39]. Quoted in REES 2008, p. 431.

[40]. ADAMS – PASLER 2012.

Ongoing Exploration

The example of the Second String Quartet — a work, as noted earlier, the composer linked to experiences of aging — demonstrates that we may likewise see in Saint-Saëns's maligned late oeuvre a composer engaged with the present and mindful of the future. This quartet's reception parallels the prevailing views of Saint-Saëns's later career. During his final few years, it attracted little attention, far less than the First Quartet of 1899, which received early performances by leading ensembles and even elicited press coverage, relatively rare for contemporary French chamber music[41]. French performers passed over the new work. The premiere apparently took place on 1 August 1919 — documentary biographers have yet to trace the quartet's performance history — at the Kurhaus, a seaside resort hotel and concert hall in Scheveningen, a district of The Hague[42]. That October, it featured at the Berkshire Festival of Chamber Music in overseas Massachusetts; the same ensemble gave a performance in New York the following month. The quartet does not appear to have made its French recital-hall debut until 1933, though Parisians could have heard it via radio broadcast as early as 1930[43]. The French musical press likewise ignored the new work. After the Berkshire performance, Richard Aldrich, music critic for the *New York Times*, dismissed it as the product of an aged avenger, an assessment that has typified its reception ever since: «This quartet might be considered as a rebuke by the aged French composer to the innovative spirit of some of his younger fellow-countrymen with which he is notoriously out of sympathy»[44]. Following the reprise in New York, he similarly characterised it as the «protest and reproof» of «an octogenarian who has held fast to the principles and methods that have guided his life's work»[45].

The generative outlook manifest in 'L'Évolution musicale' and other texts presents an alternative optic, through which this work appears very differently. The quartet offers not a rebuke to the innovative spirit but a lesson on how music could evolve within the aesthetic standards the composer believed would prevail in the future: principles of form descended from the eighteenth century, a system of pitch organisation committed to projecting a single tonic within a chromatically embellished major-minor system, and an ensemble of classicising values prioritising delight over the profound, play over the expression of subjectivity, and

---

[41]. On the First Quartet's reception, see Deruchie 2020.

[42]. See *De avondpost* 1919. My thanks to Stephanie Frakes for locating and translating this document. The composer's correspondence reveals that a private hearing had taken place at the home of his publisher Jacques Durand in May of 1919; see Guilloux 2017.

[43]. For the earliest evidence I have located of a public performance in France, see *Ménestrel* 1933. Programme guides printed in French newspapers reveal at least a dozen broadcasts between 1930 and 1939 on Le Poste parisien, Radio Tour Eiffel, and Radio Paris.

[44]. Aldrich 1919a.

[45]. Aldrich 1919b.

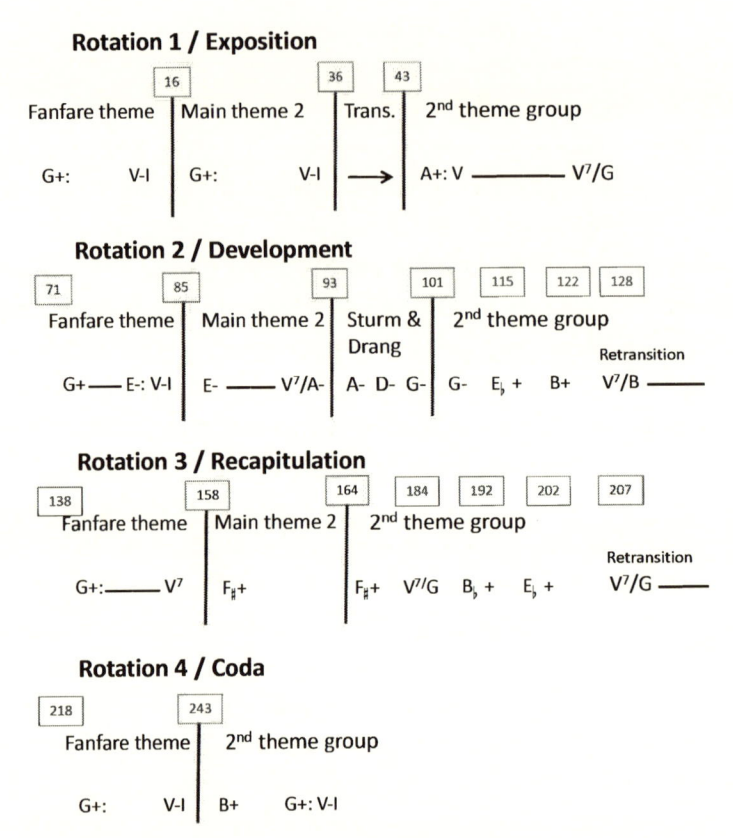

FIG. 1: Saint-Saëns, Second String Quartet, Movement 1, form.

beauty over the sublime. Rather than preserving Saint-Saëns's past ways, the quartet evinces his ongoing exploration of possibilities and his willingness to learn — even from the modernists he denounced.

Two of many possible examples, the large-scale form of the first movement and the quartet's tonal syntax, may serve to illustrate. Most commentators view the opening movement as a straightforward sonata-allegro of eighteenth-century cast, but the form is deceptively complex. The movement unfolds in four rotations, each beginning with the fanfare theme heard at the outset and cycling through an ensemble of thematic elements in a similar order (see FIG. 1). These in some ways correspond to the major divisions of the expected sonata form, as this design was cultivated by Vincent d'Indy, Guy Ropartz, Paul Dukas, Maurice Ravel, Fauré, and Saint-Saëns himself. The exposition-like first rotation features a pair of main themes (the fanfare theme and another at b. 16/Rehearsal 1), each reaching an authentic cadence in the G-major tonic[46]. A brief transition (from b. 36/Reh. 3 – 4) leads to a loosely knit second group

[46]. Because the widely available 1919 Durand edition lacks bar numbers, score locations are also indicated by rehearsal marks (abbreviated 'Reh.'). Where relevant, the number bars before or after the mark is indicated

(b. 44/Reh. 3 + 4) introducing some new thematic elements and hovering on the dominant of A major. The second rotation (from b. 71/Reh. 6 – 2) at first suggests a repeat of the exposition. Miniscule chromatic alterations, however, deflect the fanfare theme's cadence to E minor (b. 85/Reh. 7 + 4). From here, the rotation takes on standard attributes of a development section, including tonal instability, the *Sturm-und-Drang* topic, fragmentation and recombination of themes, and a concluding retransition featuring a pedal (albeit on the dominant of the 'wrong' key, B major). If the second rotation registers as development, the third (b. 138/Reh. 11) seems like a recapitulation: the fanfare theme returns in the home key (a delightful, surprise resolution of the preceding dominant), with most other thematic elements following. The final rotation (b. 218/Reh. 16 + 3), shorter than its predecessors, suggests a coda.

Much, however, does not square with contemporary French sonata-form convention. In the second rotation, tonal instability is confined to brief passages, and the *Sturm-und-Drang* segment lasts just 6 bars. On the whole, the rotation does not convey the degree of activity and motion typical of contemporary French development sections, including the composer's own. In the 'recapitulation', no elements of the second group return in the tonic. The section, moreover, explores as much tonal territory as its predecessor and is equally given to developing and recombining themes; it concludes with an even more emphatic retransition (from b. 205/ Reh. 16 – 8), this time emphasising the 'correct' dominant. In sum, this rotation seems as development-like as the development itself.

Still more incongruous with generic convention, all four rotations begin with a complete statement of the fanfare theme — in the home key. This attribute not only distinguishes the movement from the many other 'rotational' sonata forms of the eighteenth through early twentieth centuries. It also radically undercuts the narrative, 'there-and-back' tonal trajectory that had defined sonata form since its inception (and had underwritten its seventeenth-century binary-form precursors). Saint-Saëns re-shapes the teleological arc traditional to first-movement form into a spiral-like, iterative design that repeatedly returns to its origins. The movement's large-scale plan therefore might profitably be described as a hybrid of sonata and variation forms. Like variations, the rotations depart from the same point and strike out on diverging paths, each moving through different tonal territory and developing melodic-motivic materials in its own way, all while retaining certain generic characteristics of sonata form.

In this movement, the octogenarian Saint-Saëns not only found a new path through a standard form, something he had been doing his whole career. He also realised a deeper re-imagining of the design, finding new possibility in its generic traditions. *Pace* Servières and Aldrich, the movement hardly evinces a decline of creativity or a lack of new initiative. With it, Saint-Saëns perhaps saw himself leading younger colleagues by demonstrating potential

---

respectively by '–' or '+'; 'Reh. 3 – 3' indicates 3 bars before rehearsal mark 3; 'Reh. 3 + 4' indicates 4 bars after rehearsal mark 3.

for renewal in the formal language he believed would carry music into a future beyond early twentieth-century modernism.

Saint-Saëns approaches tonal syntax similarly. Harmonic progressions move around the circle of fifths remarkably frequently for a work dating from 1918 by a composer who in the past had often availed himself of chromatic third relationships and occasionally octatonic cycles. Harmonies Arcangelo Corelli could have written underpin the first movement's first main theme, which after the opening fanfare expresses I-V-ii-vi, reversing these chords ten bars later at its cadence. Fifth relationships play out at other structural levels. A fifteen-bar segment of the opening movement's 'development' rotation moves from E minor through the keys of A minor and D minor to settle on G minor (b. 85/Reh. 7 + 4 to b. 99/ Reh. 9 – 8). Progressions by fifth sometimes seem downright ostentatious, as at b. 25/Reh. 22 + 8 to Reh. 23 of the second movement, where a sequential transition proceeds an extravagant seven notches around the circle of fifths, from the dominant of F to G-flat. The finale features even more flamboyant circle-of-fifths motion, including one stretch of twenty-two consecutive chords (b. 247/Reh. 50 + 8 to b. 292/Reh. 53 + 5).

Into a syntax rooted firmly in the seventeenth and eighteenth centuries, Saint-Saëns integrates pitch devices favoured by the modernists. The slow movement offers many examples. Saint-Saëns makes extensive use of the Phrygian mode, especially in the recurring main theme (from b. 6 in Ex. 1). As melodic degrees, the flat second and seventh occur frequently. These also factor in the harmony, notably at cadences, such as at bb. 9-10, where B-flat and D-flat make for a modally inflected 'dominant'. Examples elsewhere include the half cadences on the minor dominant at bb. 82 and 83/Reh. 30 + 3 and 30 + 4. Enriching the non-diatonic flavour are the frequent E-naturals, which give the effect of a 'fluctuating' folk mode, a resource sometimes employed by d'Indy (and well known in the music of Bartók). Saint-Saëns treats such modal inflections motivically by working them into the deeper structure of the movement. The Phrygian D-flats in Ex. 1 get composed out as the key of the second theme (from b. 17/Reh. 22); when the theme returns in F-sharp minor (b. 34/Reh. 24, not shown in Ex. 1), the same inflection foreshadows the G-major starting point of the ensuing transition (b. 41/Reh. 25). Beyond the slow movement, such procedures take the music through an extraordinary amount of tonal space, to which Saint-Saëns draws attention with frequent changes of key signature. Over the four movements, every chromatic pitch class other than A-flat/G-sharp serves as a tonic designated with a key signature.

Saint-Saëns occasionally deploys the whole-tone scale, a device closely associated with Debussy. Normally confined to the bass, this collection invariably prolongs a diatonic scale step. In bb. 15-16 (see again Ex. 1), the bass ascends a tenth through the whole-tone scale from A-flat to C-natural to expand the dominant of D-flat. In bars 29-31/Reh. 23 + 1 to Reh. 23 + 3, a whole-tone descent in the bass from F to B-double-flat converts G-flat major (the arrival point of the seven-notch circle-of-fifths journey) into G-flat minor, immediately re-spelled as F-sharp minor, for the above-mentioned reprise of the main theme.

Ex. 1: Saint-Saëns, Second String Quartet, Movement 2, bb. 1-17.

Most strikingly, in this movement Saint-Saëns takes up a procedure employed extensively in the atonal music of Schoenberg (though also in some works by Hugo Wolf and other German modernists of the '1860s generation'): chromatic saturation, wherein all twelve pitch classes circulate in a given passage, with the completion of the chromatic aggregate typically marking a point of formal articulation. As Ex. 1 reveals, the opening four-bar phrase employs all twelve chromatic pitches, with first violin's B-flat on the downbeat of b. 4 completing the aggregate and closing the phrase. Lest attentive listeners (or analysts) suspect a mere accident here, Saint-Saëns immediately repeats the procedure: the two-bar phrase spanning bb. 4-5 likewise introduces all twelve pitch classes, the aggregate this time completed with the introduction of F-sharp on the final eighth note of b. 5.

As with the first movement's form, Saint-Saëns's treatment of tonal syntax hardly evinces intransigence or creative stagnation. Indeed, the composer's adoption of pitch methods favoured by modernists — including Schoenberg — reveals a willingness to learn from younger generations. He perhaps meant to offer a wise old man's lesson in return: by integrating modal harmonies, the whole-tone scale, and chromatic saturation into a syntax governed by the circle of fifths, he demonstrated that the «magnificent future» he foresaw could reconcile radical innovations with the *sine qua non* of «tonalities giving one another mutual support».

The *Vieillard* Laughs

A committed classicist, Saint-Saëns remained sceptical of appeals to music to express individual experience or autobiography (though this did not diminish his admiration of Berlioz). Nonetheless, it seems easy to hear in the quartet the 'programme' he sketched in the letter to Lecocq cited earlier («the first movement portrays youth, the second, the regret of having lost it. Consequently, it is perhaps the saddest movement I know»). Much about the opening allegro accords with the scenario: bubbling rhythmic energy, mainly sunny skies, and perhaps a naïveté suggested by eighteenth-century mannerisms such as the galant-style opening fanfare. The spiral like form perhaps suggests youthful notions of a boundless future. The slow movement, by contrast, takes an inward turn to psychological torment. Saint-Saëns derived the pitch techniques just surveyed from the modernist languages of epochal lateness, decadence, and nostalgia, here pressed into service to evoke suffering over lost youth. The movement's form, moreover, involves an accelerating series of rotations through the beleaguered main theme and a tragically vulnerable pastoral subject, culminating in a sequence (from bb. 59-68/ Reh. 27 – 2 to 28) of rapid and brutal collisions between these disparate elements. The fractures and discontinuities of Beethoven's late quartets here seem intensified by lessons drawn from Stravinsky's Russian ballets. The passage probably stands as the most fragmented music Saint-Saëns ever composed.

Ex. 2: Saint-Saëns, Second String Quartet, Movements 3 and 4, bb. 29-63.

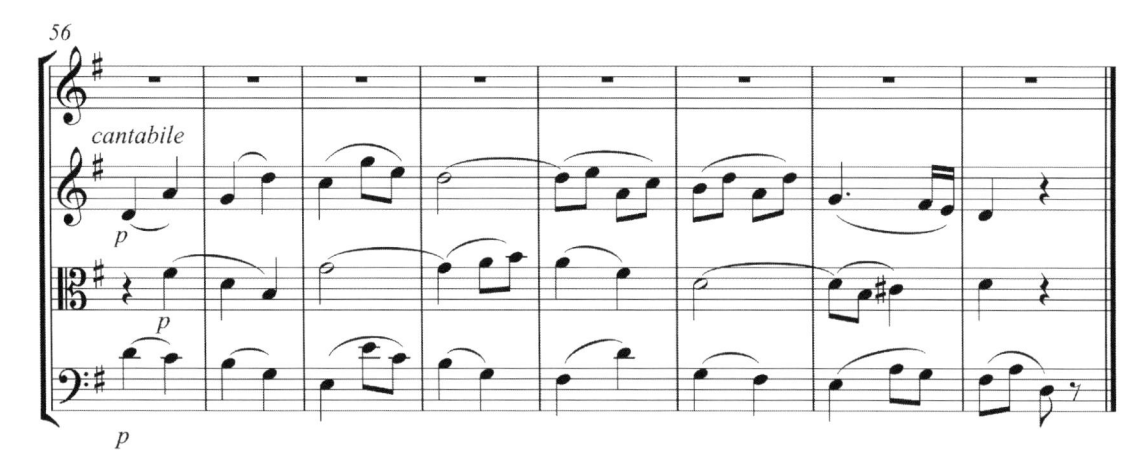

When he wrote to Charles Lecocq, Saint-Saëns had completed just the first two movements. What follows youth and suffering from its loss? The remaining movements, a brief interlude and a rollicking finale, run together. The interlude continues from the agonised dénouement of the adagio. Marrying the profound, introspective character of the first movement of Beethoven's Op. 131 or the Cavatina of Op. 130 with chromatic counterpoint recalling the Prelude to Act 3 of *Parsifal*, the interlude seems to meditate, contemplating the anguished turmoil of the slow movement at some remove. This movement does not so much conclude as dissolve into a pregnant pause (Ex. 2). The first notes of the finale puncture the silence, not with an epiphany in the tradition of the long nineteenth century (a transcendent victory after the struggle) but with Haydnesque playfulness: the first violin plucks the open strings, as though tuning up; a sustained chord checks the intonation. After the viola and cello do the same, the first violin laughs at the joke (b. 54/Reh. 35 – 2). The quartet then launches into the first of two main themes, an innocent folk song, as far removed from all the gravitas as one could imagine, of a type Saint-Saëns had long employed in his instrumental finales.

These bars invite interpretation in light of both the letter to Lecocq and the composer's generative outlook. Faced with the inevitable challenges of aging, Saint-Saëns's music carries on just as it always had, and as the musician perhaps saw himself carrying on as a tireless performer, public intellectual, and perennially productive composer. The passage also offers another lesson to posterity consistent with the sagely insights he claimed in 'l'Évolution musicale'. Lightness here dispels the ponderous, delight displaces the expression of subjectivity, charm and innocence succeed lateness and decadence: the classicising principles in which Saint-Saëns foresaw the aesthetic cornerstones of the art form's future emerge from an aporia of overripe expression. The first violin perhaps laughs not just at the joke, but also at the self-seriousness of the second and third movements, as though existential (or *fin-de-siècle*) crises were simply not the stuff of music.

The remainder of the movement brings more delight and playful humour. From the folksong, the finale promises to unfurl a compact and straightforward ABACA rondo form (FIG. 2). A second G-major main theme, based on the laughing motif, follows the folksong; next come an episode, a reprise of the laughing theme, and a longer second episode. This last is a punishingly relentless perpetual-motion fugato, evoking the first movement of Beethoven's Op. 130 quartet. Just when the onrush of constant figuration and endless *Fortspinnung* threaten to engulf listeners, the joke from the outset repeats: the violin, viola, and cello again pluck their open strings and check the intonation, dissolving the sublime mood with delightful humour. The violin again laughs; the quartet again launches into the innocent and charming folksong, initiating a full, tonic-key recapitulation of the main themes.

Rondo

	m.84	116	129	186	214	270	296	317	344
A		B	A	C	A (RECAPITULATION) Coda				
Folk Song	Laughing Theme	Episode	Laughing theme	Episode: Fugato	Folk Song Laughing Theme	Fugato theme		Embedded Recap.	Embedded Coda
G+			G+		G+ D♭, A♭, E♭, C-	D-	E-	G+	B♭, A♭, B E G+
Allegretto				Animato	Tempo 1	Allegro	Tempo 1		

FIG. 2: Saint-Saëns, Second String Quartet, Movement 4, form.

In the end, the old composer himself has a laugh — and offers a final lesson, of a different kind. A recapitulation, of course, conventionally brings closure to the form and betokens the coda and the end. The finale, however, refuses to end according to this 'cultural script': an entirely new formal section ensues, replete with fresh thematic development and more harmonic adventure. This ostensible, Beethovenian coda begins with more classicising humour, which becomes all the more delightful in light of Saint-Saëns's programme and his outlook on his old age. At first, the music stagnates, sitting awkwardly on G major for a full 8 bars, as though uncertain of what to do next (Ex. 3). A ham-fisted harmonic progression (from b. 222/Reh. 48 + 4) leads from C major through D major and G major to a dominant-seventh on A, replete with glaring parallel fifths and octaves between all chords. These parallels do not, like their counterparts at the outset of coda to the *Eroica* Symphony's first movement, groan with a force of will impelling the music to continue, but register like the purposefully vulgar writing with which Haydn sometimes evokes clumsy peasants, such as in the heavy-footed trio of Symphony No. 88's minuet. The music comically stumbles forward — as though surprised to find itself still going at this apparently terminal stage of the form.

The new section into which it lurches turns out to be the finale's longest by far, at 204 bars accounting for more than half of the movement. If this is a coda, it assumes extravagant proportions, even by Beethoven's standards. It is also the most formally complex and tonally adventurous of the form's sections. From the bumbling progression, it explores D-flat major

Ex. 3: Saint-Saëns, Second String Quartet, Movement 4, bb. 214-227.

(b. 226/Reh. 49 – 1), A-flat major (b. 238/Reh. 50 – 1), E-flat major (b. 246/Reh. 50 + 7), C minor (b. 250/Reh. 51 – 4), D minor (b. 270/Reh. 52), and E minor (b. 297/Reh. 54) before finally settling back on the tonic. On this journey, it passes through three tempos, picks up loose threads (including a reprise of the fugato's theme and texture), and, after all the new development, embarks on another recapitulation (from b. 317/Reh. 55 + 4). The section even features its own nested coda (from b. 344/Reh. 57 + 4), which itself evinces a closure-defying tonal restlessness, rapidly cycling through B-flat major, A-flat major, B major, and E major before a composed accelerando finally consumes the movement in a burst of virtuosity.

The finale, in sum, thwarts listeners' expectations by energetically carrying on long after it seems destined to conclude and remaining adventurous through its final bars. Coming at the end of a work thematising aging in the shadow of lost youth, this upending of the form's expected course may stand as an allegory for how the composer saw his late-life career in the face of the prevailing cultural stories of decline, diminishing inspiration, and so on. In this defiant coda to a movement replete with humour, the old composer makes the point with an irreverent laugh at the judgments, soon to be canonical, passed on his old-age career by the likes of Aldrich, Gavy-Bélédin, and Servières: after the apparent end, which was really only the middle, there remains a lot of music, including some exciting, delightful, and adventurous stuff. In the tradition of classical comedy, the laugh enfolds a final lesson to posterity, one that all who write about this — or any other — old fool or aged avenger ought to heed.

BIBLIOGRAPHY

ADAMS – PASLER 2012

ADAMS, Byron – PASLER, Jann. 'Saint-Saëns and the Future of Music', in: *Camille Saint-Saëns and His World*, edited by Jann Pasler, Princeton, Princeton University Press, 2012, pp. 312-318.

Aldrich 1919a
Aldrich, Richard. 'Prize Sonata at Music Festival', in: *New York Times*, 28 September 1919.

Aldrich 1919b
Id. 'Music', in: *New York Times*, 19 November 1919.

Barone 1995
Barone, Anthony. 'Wagner's «Parsifal» and the Theory of Late Style', in: *Cambridge Opera Journal*, vii/1 (1995), pp. 37-54.

Bonnaure 2010
Bonnaure, Jaccques. *Saint-Saëns*, Arles, Actes Sud, 2010.

Botstein 2012
Botstein, Leon. 'Beyond the Conceits of the Avant-Garde: Saint-Saëns, Romain Rolland, and the Musical Culture of the Nineteenth Century', in: *Camille Saint-Saëns and His World, op. cit.*, pp. 370-401.

Bourdelais 1993
Bourdelais, Patrice. *Le nouvel âge de la vieillesse: histoire du vieillissement de la population*, Paris, O. Jacob, 1993.

Calico 2015
Calico, Joy. 'Old-Age Style: The Case of Arnold Schoenberg (1874-1951)', in: *New German Critique*, no. 125 (2015), pp. 65-80.

Caron – Denizeau 2014
Caron, Jean-Luc – Denizeau, Gérard. *Camille Saint-Saëns*, Paris, Bleu nuit, 2014.

Chantavoine 1921
Chantavoine, Jean. *L'Œuvre dramatique de Camille Saint-Saëns*, Paris, Heugel, 1921.

Chantavoine 1947
Id. *Camille Saint-Saëns*, Paris, Richard-Masse, 1947.

Closson 1924
Closson, Ernest. 'Faut-il, ne faut-il pas rejouer Wagner?', in: *La Revue belge*, 1 October 1924.

De avondpost 1919
'Scheveningen', in: *De avondpost*, 1 August 1919.

Deruchie 2020
Deruchie, Andrew. 'Saint-Saëns's First String Quartet, Cyclic Form and the Aesthetics of Charm', in: *Nineteenth-Century Music Review*, xvii/1 (2020), pp. 69-95.

ERIKSON 1963
ERIKSON, Erik. *Childhood and Society*, New York, Norton, 1963.

GALLOIS 2004
GALLOIS, Jean. *Charles-Camille Saint-Saëns*, Sprimont, Mardaga, 2004.

GAVY-BÉLÉDIN 1919
GAVY-BÉLÉDIN, Albert. 'D'une revue', in: *Le Gerbe*, 1 July 1919.

GUILLOUX 2017
GUILLOUX, Fabien. 'Preface', in: *Camille Saint-Saëns, Œuvres instrumentals completes. Série III: Musique de chambre. 1: Quatuors et quintette à cordes*, edited by Fabien Guilloux, Kassel, Bärenreiter, 2017.

GULLETTE 2004
GULLETTE, Margaret Morganroth. *Aged by Culture*, Chicago, University of Chicago Press, 2004.

GULLETTE 2017
EAD. *Ending Ageism, or How Not to Shoot Old People*, New Brunswick (NJ), Rutgers University Press, 2017.

HARDING 1965
HARDING, James. *Saint-Saëns and His Circle*, London, Chapman & Hall, 1965.

HARKINS 1971
HARKINS, Elizabeth. *The Chamber Music of Camille Saint-Saëns*, unpublished Ph.D. Diss., New York (NY), New York University, 1976.

HUTCHEON – HUTCHEON 2015
HUTCHEON, Linda – HUTCHEON, Michael. *Four Last Songs: Aging and Creativity in Verdi, Strauss, Messiaen, and Britten*, Chicago, University of Chicago Press, 2015.

LALO 1900
LALO, Pierre. 'La Musique', in: *Le Temps*, 18 January 1900.

LALO 1947
ID. *De Rameau à Ravel*, Paris, Albin Michel, 1947.

MAJORELLE 2009
MAJORELLE, Philippe. *Saint-Saëns: le Beethoven français*, Paris, Séguier, 2009.

MARNOLD 1917
MARNOLD, JEAN. 'Germanophilie', in: *Le cas Wagner: la musique pendant la guerre*, Paris, Bossard, 1917.

McAdams 2001
McAdams, Dan. 'Generativity in Midlife', in: *Handbook of Midlife Development*, edited by Margie Lachman, New York, Wiley, 2001, pp. 395-443.

Ménéstrel 1933
'Quatuor Pierre Reitlinger, José Figueroa, Jarecki, et Lemaire', in: *Le Ménéstrel*, 7 April 1933.

Rees 2008
Rees, Brian. *Camille Saint-Saëns*, London, Faber & Faber, 2008.

Saint-Saëns 1885
Saint-Saëns, Camille. 'Introduction', in: *Harmonie et mélodie*, Paris, Calmann Lévy, 1885, pp. i-xxxi.

Saint-Saëns 1906
Id. 'L'Évolution musicale', in: *Le Ménéstrel*, 24 June 1906.

Saint-Saëns 1916
Id. *Germanophilie*, Paris, Dorbon, 1916.

Saint-Saëns 2012
Id. 'Musical Evolution', translated by Jann Pasler, in: *Camille Saint-Saëns and His World*, *op. cit.*, pp. 318-322.

Servières 1923
Servières, Georges. *Saint-Saëns*, Paris, Félix Alcan, 1923.

Straus 2022a
Straus, Joseph (Host). *Musicking While Old: Old Age as Culture (1/5)*, [Audio Podcast], SMT Pod, 2022, <https://smt-pod.org/episodes/season01/#e1.2>, accessed December 2023.

Straus 2022b
Id. *Musicking While Old: Old Age + Opera (2/5)*, [Audio Podcast], SMT Pod, 2022, <https://smt-pod.org/episodes/season01/#e1.4>, accessed December 2023.

Straus 2022c
Id. *Musicking While Old: Old Composers (3/5)*, [Audio Podcast], SMT Pod, 2022, <https://smt-pod.org/episodes/season01/#e1.8>, accessed December 2023.

Straus 2022d
Id. *Musicking While Old: Old Performers (4/5)*, [Audio Podcast], SMT Pod, 2022, <https://smt-pod.org/episodes/season01/#e1.13>, accessed December 2023.

Straus 2022e
Id. *Musicking While Old, Old Listeners (5/5)*, [Audio Podcast], SMT Pod, 2022, <https://smt-pod.org/episodes/season01/#e1.16>, accessed December 2023.

STUDD 1999
STUDD, STEPHEN. *Saint-Saëns: A Critical Biography*, London, Cygnus Arts, 1999.

THANE 2005
THANE, Pat. *A History of Old Age*, Los Angeles, the J. Paul Getty Museum, 2005.

THOREL 1907
THOREL, René. 'Les deux Saint-Saëns à Dieppe', in: *Comœdia*, 28 October 1907.

VILLAR – SERRAT – PRATT 2023
VILLAR, Feliciano – SERRAT, Rodrigo – PRATT, Michael. 'Older Age as a Time to Contribute: A Scoping Review of Generativity in Later Life', in: *Ageing and Society*, XLIII/8 (2023), pp. 1860-1861.

César Franck: The String Quartet at the Nexus of Tradition and Innovation

Christiane Strucken-Paland
(César Franck Association, Hürth)

Origin

THE STRING QUARTET in D minor is one of César Franck's last great compositions. Composed in 1889, the piece may be understood as a 'late work' par excellence, in which traditional and innovative elements enter into particularly tense play with each other. On one hand, the piece features an almost experimental overall arrangement, which in its «manneristic mastery of form»[1] and «stunning harmonic design»[2] represents, as it were, the sum of Franck's compositional achievements. At the same time, it remains unmistakably linked to the genre traditions of absolute music, shaped above all by Ludwig van Beethoven. César Franck evidently held the string quartet genre in great awe, for it was very late in life that he ventured to compose his only contribution to the genre. In the spring of 1889, he wrote down the first sketches for the Quartet[3]; in the fall of 1889, he began to work them out, completing the composition in January 1890. According to Vincent d'Indy, during this time Franck repeatedly studied the quartets of Beethoven, Franz Schubert, and Johannes Brahms at the piano[4].

Throughout France as well, the string quartet was considered a supremely intimate genre, requiring maturity and respect, and the impact of the Viennese classical quartets, especially Beethoven's, was very strong. Even after the founding of the Société nationale de musique

[1]. See RATHERT 1990, p. 327, «manieristische Formbeherrschung».

[2]. See HINRICHSEN 2004, p. 89, «atemberaubende, harmonische Konstruktivität».

[3]. See D'INDY, p. 165.

[4]. According to *ibidem*, Franck was thinking of a Quartet as early as 1888: «Ce fut au cours de sa cinquante-sixième année que César Franck osa penser à la composition d'un quatuor pour archets; et encore, en cette année 1888 où nous remarquions avec surprise, étalées sur son piano, les partitions des quatuors de Beethoven, de Schubert et même de Brahms, ne fit-il qu'y penser sans rien écrire, et ce n'est que du printemps de 1889 que datent les premières esquisses». There are no Brahms or Schubert quartets in what remains of Franck's music library. But there is the Collection of Ludwig van Beethoven's Quartets arranged for piano 4 hands by Henri Roubier.

(1871) with its expressed goal of promoting French music, Beethoven's works continued to dominate programmes. Franck, in his late creative period, took his bearings from the genres and instrumental combinations for which Beethoven had set new standards, retaining the framework of the traditional sonata form. He then developed it further in a highly innovative manner through his formal concept of the cyclical interconnection of movements, hollowing out the form from within, as it were. This left a mark on his composition of, most significantly, the D-minor Symphony, and, in the area of chamber music, on the Violin Sonata and especially the String Quartet[5]. In what follows, I provide a detailed examination of Franck's post-Beethovenian cyclical process, with special attention to the formal design of the String Quartet's outer movements[6].

SYMPHONIC FEATURES

Even in his chamber music, Franck primarily looked to Beethoven's symphonies as a guideline. How did this come about? In nineteenth-century music, the larger the dimensions of a given composition, the more a composer felt the problem of unity in the work to be crucial. Especially in the field of symphonic composition, where monumentality and grandeur become thematic in a special way, a flexible shaping of the idea of unity seemed necessary. Hence quite a few nineteenth-century composers endeavoured to structure works, especially those with a symphonic character, using cyclic linking techniques. Given this tendency, it may be postulated that cyclic principles should basically be understood as primarily *symphonic* procedures. The tendency to link movements cyclically even in chamber music, for example in Franck's String Quartet, closely correlates with the transformation of the nineteenth-century concept of the symphony: from a genre to a stylistic concept rooted not so much in the instrumentation as in the work's musical texture. Thus, Franck's String Quartet also exhibits *symphonic* characteristics, which require corresponding cyclical unification efforts. In the sense proposed by Siegfried Oechsle, the concept of the symphony should be understood here as a paradigm, as a model of aesthetically autonomous music, to which no actual single work corresponds, and which is signified by the collective singular 'the' symphony.

The primacy of the symphony as the supreme genre of instrumental music developed because, in the Romantic sensibility, it ranked as the highest of all the arts; it was autonomous, and therefore, the 'purest' of the arts. In contrast to chamber music, the instrumental parts in the symphonic orchestral apparatus tend to be evened out in a grand ensemble. In the 1830s, Beethoven's influence spread throughout Germany, and thanks to performances of all of his symphonies by the conductor François Antoine Habeneck, they even reached Paris, a city then

---

[5]. KRAUS 2004, p. 32.
[6]. See STRUCKEN-PALAND 2010.

dominated by opera[7]. As a result, composers evinced an increasing tendency toward symphonic writing. Beethoven's symphonies in particular became the epitome of the genre and also determined the normative foundations of composition[8], especially with respect to the aesthetic idea of symphonic monumentality and grandeur inherent in the genre. The symphonic style transformed from a generic to a stylistic term that denoted not simply the instrumentation but also the very construction of the music. The tendency toward symphonic writing, to which composers felt committed in their confrontation with Beethoven, went well beyond chamber music genres such as the string quartet and the piano sonata. Franck's works display symphonic characteristics even in his chamber music and organ music, which subsequently could also be explained by his focus on the 'symphonic' in his appreciation of Beethoven. Indeed, even after the Franco-Prussian War of 1870/1871, the composers of the *jeune école française* that Franck initiated continued to refer to Beethoven as their ideal and model. One musical event that would have had a lasting influence on Franck's symphonic-orchestral compositional style was certainly the sensational performances of Beethoven's piano trios given by Franz Liszt in 1837, which resulted in the genre of the trio, then increasingly popular, becoming the «symphonie des salons»[9].

In all its exceptional monumentality and grandeur, the symphony was intended for the general public, for audiences taking part in a rapidly expanding bourgeois musical life. In a concurrent development, chamber music was becoming increasingly integrated into public concert life and now also addressed a broad audience; the incorporation of symphonic features within the genre was intended to render this chamber music comprehensible to listeners. In Franck's String Quartet, the idea of 'large form', monumentality, and grandeur are particularly noticeable in the finale with its huge dimensions: with its 881 bars, it has symphonic proportions. Compared to each of the preceding movements, it is so substantial that the Quartet might rightly be called a 'finale quartet', that is, a work in which the finale is a self-sufficient quartet in its own right[10].

In addition to these *quantitative* symphonic features, the symphonic style always includes the *qualitative* impetus to create formal connection, organic cohesion, and unity of the work as a whole, above all via thematic motifs and harmonic elements, rather than resorting to extra-musical literary or visual aids. In Sponheuer's words: «However, the viable construction of such a wide-ranging musical coherence, as presented by the great symphonies, demands of the composer [...] a procedure of universalist scope, an all-pervading intention for the *whole*»[11].

---

[7]. See Oechsle 1992, pp. 40ff. and Kraus 2004, pp. 24ff. For the first time, the ninth symphony was heard in its entirety under his direction in Paris.

[8]. Oechsle 1992, p. 41.

[9]. Gauthier 1845, p. 76, quoted in Fauquet 1999, p. 123.

[10]. Strucken-Paland 2009, p. 356. Cadenbach compares Franck's Quartet in terms of its «symphonic orientation» with Bruckner (Cadenbach 1990, p. 490).

[11]. See Sponheuer 1978, pp. 27ff., «Die tragfähige Konstruktion eines so weit gespannten musikalischen Zusammenhangs aber, wie er von den großen Symphonien vorgestellt wird, verlangt vom Komponisten [...] eine

This cohesion and unity of the work overall, even in large-scale dimensions, could be achieved especially through the potent use of cyclically recurring elements. Through these, Franck provided listeners, especially in large concert audiences, with an aid for orientation, allowing them to participate in the development of the work. That it seemed important to bring the musical process closer to the audience is evident in a frequently observed custom that persisted at concerts of the Société nationale. For first performances of cyclically designed works, the Société nationale printed thematic overviews in its programmes that pointed out thematic affinities, as was the case for Franck's Symphony. Here Franck even specifies the recapitulation of the themes by means of musical examples in the programme for the premiere.

Franck's concentration on only a few cyclically recurring and recognisable themes proved a guarantor of unity even in his large-scale chamber works, such as the Piano Quintet in F minor of 1878/1879, the early Piano Trio in F-sharp minor Op. 1 No. 1 (c. 1839/1842), or his longest organ work, the *Grande pièce symphonique* Op. 17 (1863). The idea of large-scale form is closely linked to the principle of developing «[...] a musical discourse extending over hundreds of measures from seemingly minor thematic substance»[12]. For example, in his Violin Sonata, the *Variations symphoniques*, or even the String Quartet, Franck uses the technique of thematic transformation. This typical symphonic procedure fits particularly well with his themes, since they are characterised by cantabile-style melodies and closed period structure. Another typical feature of the symphonic style is a formal framework easily followed by the listener: for example, the first movement of the String Quartet uses salient tectonic points of orientation characterised by tempo and key changes. In the composition of his chamber music corpus, Franck refers to the principles of composition used by Beethoven in his fifth and ninth symphonies, and takes up procedures that were explicitly developed in symphonic music.

THE ROLE OF THE CENTRAL THEME IN THE STRING QUARTET

Throughout the String Quartet, Franck endeavours to relate the individual movements to one another by means of common motivic-thematic material and, as a result, brings them together into a unified whole — a technique that is designated by the term '*principe cyclique*'. This has become a buzzword in the literature and is always associated with Franck — since he used it systematically in all multi-movement instrumental works of his late period — and eventually lay at the heart of a seminal school in nineteenth-century France[13].

---

universalistisch orientierte Verfahrensweise, eine durchdringende Intention aufs *Ganze*».

[12]. See DAHLHAUS 1981, p. 37: «[...] einen musikalischen Diskurs, der sich über Hunderte von Takten erstreckt, aus scheinbar geringfügiger thematischer Substanz zu entwickeln».

[13]. See the author's study STRUCKEN-PALAND 2009.

The first main theme is introduced immediately at the beginning of the String Quartet's opening movement in the Lento section, which assumes a central function in the final movement; it runs cyclically through the entire work. The main theme of the Lento section, similar to the introductory theme of the Piano Quintet or certain themes of the Symphony, to which Peter Gülke attributes a «blatant directness»[14], imprints its mark on the piece right at the beginning. As in the opening of the Piano Quintet, there is a homophonic movement with a melody-bearing upper voice; it occupies a range of four octaves, clearly surpassing the norm in chamber music genres.

The characteristic triadic motive exposed at the beginning represents a stabilising element in relation to the rapidly progressing harmony. The forceful thematic beginning with its triad plays a very important role in marking out this central theme. A closer analysis exposes the fundamental cells that reveal the high structural density of the composition. Franck is working here with two simultaneous procedures, each touching a different level. On one hand, he uses the thematic opening as a quasi-leitmotivic idea, which is processed in the course of the first movement (in the fugato in F minor) and returns at the end of the work in a gesture of cyclical unity. On the other hand, he uses contrasting diastematic cells[15], which dominate the composition above all at the level of the sub-motif and, through their chromaticism, prepare the way for the complex harmonic constellations of the work.

GENESIS OF THE CYCLIC CENTRAL THEME

A look at the genesis of this opening, as documented in the surviving autograph, reveals the meticulousness with which Franck honed the cyclical main theme and developed it into its definitive form. It reveals that Franck composed the second movement, the Scherzo, very quickly: almost nothing is crossed out, and the period of composition from the completion of the first movement on 29 October 1889 to the Scherzo's completion on 9 November 1889 — only eleven days later — testifies to a «grande rapidité de gestation»[16]. But he experienced the greatest difficulty with the finale and especially with the first movement; consider the sketches and drafts contained in the autograph[17]. Apparently, Franck attached great importance to this figure for its cyclical function, so much so that he structured it extremely carefully. Franck's student Vincent d'Indy describes the difficult creation of this theme:

> The first movement, and above all the main idea, took him an infinite amount
> of time to get right; he often started over again, nervously erasing the next day what he

---

[14]. See GÜLKE 1971, «[...] eine knallige Direktheit».

[15]. The term 'diastematic' refers to the area/range of pitch (the range of rhythm is not included here).

[16]. JARDILLIER 1929, p. 184.

[17]. For more details, see EICH 2002, pp. 68ff.

Ex. 1: Facsimile – First page of the drafts for the opening movement prior to the autograph composition score of the D-major String Quartet, bb. 1ff. (Source: Sketch in pencil, Bibliothèque nationale de France, Département de la musique, shelf mark: Rés.Vma.ms.10.)

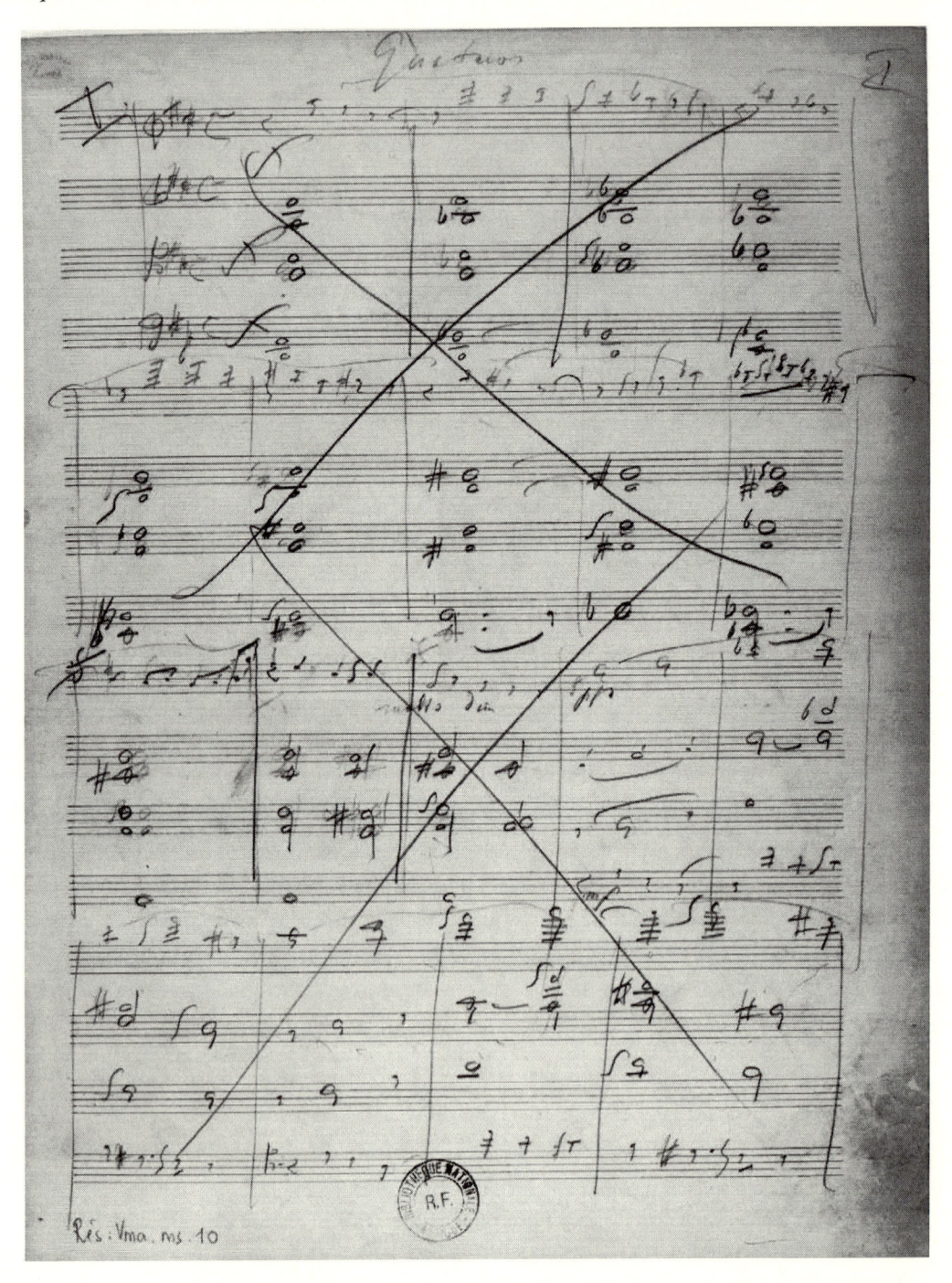

had thought definitive the day before. He even built a good third of the first piece on a
melodic idea, the framework of which he later had to modify almost entirely[18].

A rarity for Franck, the autograph contains three drafts of this central theme, which only gradually reveal the final fourteen-bar shape and the harmony of this central theme[19] (see Ex. 1).

Franck evidently attached great importance to the shape of the first main theme in context, painstakingly structuring it most thoroughly indeed in terms of the diastematic cells, harmonic 'motives', and 'crystallisation nuclei' constitutive of the work as a whole, and at the same time formulating the theme with melodic concision. Franck planned the head motive, which is used as a leitmotif throughout the work, from the beginning, but increasingly improved it over the course of the three versions[20]:

Ex. 2: First version of the main theme – first draft for the beginning of the first movement of the String Quartet, bb. 1ff. (Source: Sketch in pencil, Bibliothèque nationale de France, Département de la musique, shelf mark: Rés. Vma.ms.10.)

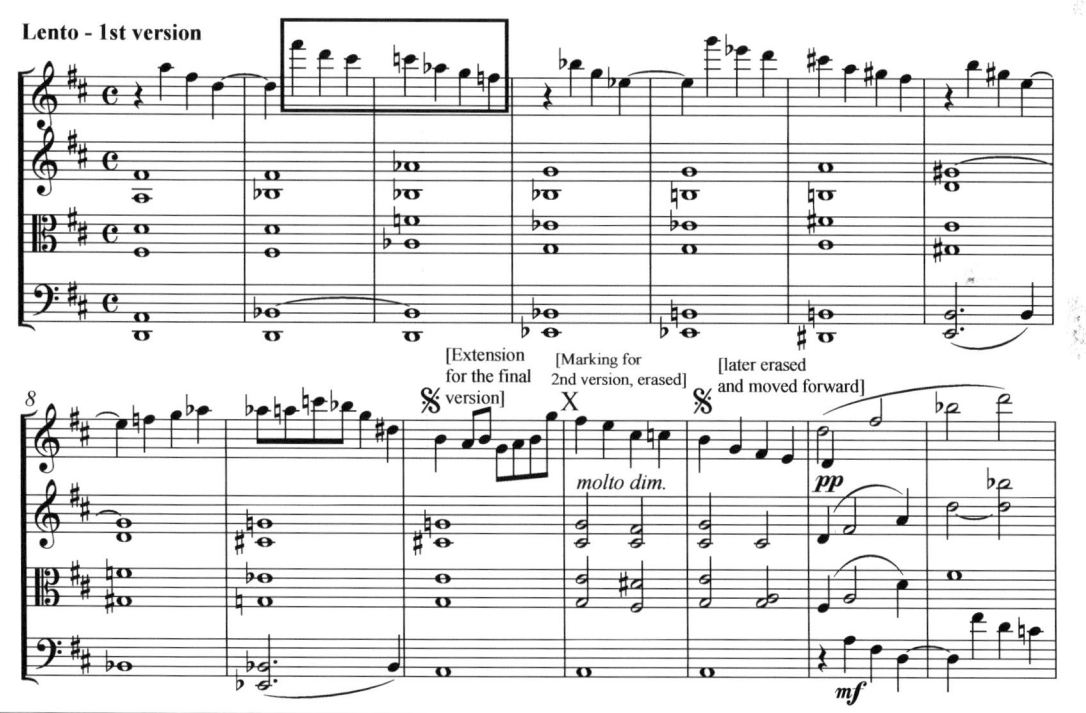

---

[18]. See D'Indy 1907, p. 166: «Le premier mouvement, l'idée mère surtout, lui coûtèrent des peines infinies à mettre sur pied; longtemps, souvent, il recommença, effaçant nerveusement le lendemain à grands coups de gomme ce qu'il croyait définitif la veille. Il édifia même un bon tiers du premier morceau sur une idée mélodique dont il fut amené ensuite à modifier presque entièrement l'ossature».

[19]. See Eich 2002, pp. 68ff.; Strucken-Paland 2009, pp. 271ff.

[20]. In the following, the term 'version' is used to describe the historical variation of a theme. See also Eich 2002, pp. 110ff. (But there are some errors in the musical examples.)

The first version (see Ex. 2) is the longest and includes the main theme — here still in twelve bars — as well as its repetition in the cello, identical to the final version, and the subsequent secondary theme (up to b. 37 in the final version), which already corresponds to that of the final version (only bb. 38-40 are still missing). This version already features the triad and the 'third-second constellation' as the basic diastematic cells and harmonic constellations that Franck uses as cycle-forming elements throughout the work. However, the rhythmic motive 'quarter + two eighths' is not yet present, and the melodic line is rhythmically monotonous, flowing without form.

Ex. 3: Second version of the main theme – second draft for the beginning of the first movement of the String Quartet, bb. 1ff. (Source: Sketch in pencil, Bibliothèque nationale de France, Département de la musique, shelf mark: Rés.Vma.ms.10.)

After ten bars, Franck continues the second version of the main theme (see Ex. 3) *dal segno* X with bars 11ff. of the first version. Here already, Franck shifts the first bars to the second half of the theme — probably to avoid jeopardising the tonic too quickly through premature modulation and to consolidate instead the tonic area for at least three more bars[21]. In this second thematic version, the outline of thirds filled with stepwise seconds and a rhythmic animation in bar 3 are already present, though here as a descent of a fourth. But still missing are the gradual introduction of the eighth-note motion and the acceleration of the harmonic rhythm.

---

21. But he now makes a tonic minor clouding in b. 5. (In the first version, the E-flat major region is already reached in bar 4, here only at the beginning of the second half.)

Ex. 4: Third version of the main theme – third draft for the beginning of the first movement of the String Quartet, bb. 1ff. (Source: Sketch in pencil, Bibliothèque nationale de France, Département de la musique, shelf mark: Rés. Vma.ms.10.)

Finally, the third version (see Ex. 4) already contains essential features that extend beyond the movement: it is melodically richer. Compared to the second version, the connection in bar 3 is more elegant, since the 'oscillating' insistence on a'' results in greater melodic suspense. This version is also harmonically mature: in bar 5, for example, the major tonality is confirmed before the far-reaching harmonic digressions.

A comparison of these three versions shows that, in terms of motives, Franck most carefully shapes the respective phrase openings after quarter rests; after all, these are most present to the attentive listener and must be recognised later on. In addition, while the melody repeatedly starts on the same notes[22], there is no real melodic development of new ideas. However, clear improvements may be observed within the three versions: the first version sequences the head motive only chromatically upward, whereas the second version constitutes an attempt to structure the theme and to hark back repeatedly to the beginning, in which it succeeds only to a limited extent, due to clouding by the tonic minor (b. 6). Only the third version is characterised by harmonic unity as well as structural cohesion, for Franck here changes the melodic line of b. 7 led downwards by seconds into the characteristic 'third-second constellation'.

---

[22]. Bars 1 and 3 correspond to each other; so do bars 7 and 9 as well as bars 11 and 13.

Ex. 5: Final version of the main theme with cello variant, beginning of the first movement of the String Quartet, bb. 1ff.

For the third version, Franck initially conceived a twelve-bar theme (see Ex. 4): at *dal segno* ℀, he prescribed skipping from b. 11 of the third version to b. 12 of the first version (see Ex. 2). Originally, he had not intended to extend the theme from twelve to fourteen bars; only much later did he change the conception for his final version (which might actually be called the fourth version) by moving the *segno* ℀ forward by two bars, now before bar 10 (of the first version), and then changing this b. 10 for the sake of a more fluid connection. Through this two-bar enlargement, he finally achieved a clear disposition of the second half, henceforth divided into two corresponding four-bar phrases, as well as a strengthening of the dominant A major, which leads to a harmonic calming: the main theme is perceived as self-contained.

In the final version of the introduction, the first 14-bar presentation of the central theme is followed by its repetition in the cello (see Ex. 5), but in the original 12-bar variant of the very first version. In the final version, Franck tellingly combines two thematic variants from chronologically different stages. But why does he retain this cello variant, which obviously points towards another version, and not change it according to the meticulously made modifications of the beginning? He was clearly intent on a forceful presentation to the listener of the characteristic interval constellations 'upbeat triad + syncopated upward leap of a tenth' and 'third-second constellation', identical in both versions. In addition, he could introduce this variant of thematic development, to which he later makes recourse, right at the beginning. Rathert interprets this cello development in a similar sense:

> The two-strophed thematic disposition (bb. 1-14, 15-26), in turn, is not to be understood as a re-affirmative repetition of the theme, but rather imparts a perspectival "rotation" that presents the identical (that of the repeated melodic contour) as the non-identical (that of a variation), but which draws it together into a unity: here already, an ambiguity is at work that must be understood as a characteristic, indeed archetypal trait of this musical thinking[23].

The Recurrence of the Cyclical Central Theme in the Other Movements

In the String Quartet, Franck not only resorts to the introductory theme in the form of isolated reminiscences, he also integrates it again and again in the form of adaptations to the

---

[23]. See RATHERT 1990, pp. 318ff: «Die doppelstrophige thematische Disposition (T. 1–14, 15–26) wiederum ist nicht bloß als bekräftigende Wiederholung des Themas zu verstehen, sondern prägt eine perspektivische "Drehung" aus, die das Identische (der wiederholten melodischen Kontur) als Nicht-Identisches (einer Abwandlung) ausgibt, aber zu einer Einheit zusammenspannt: Bereits hier ist eine Mehrdeutigkeit am Werk, die als charakteristischer, ja archetypischer Zug dieses musikalischen Denkens verstanden werden muß». However, Rathert does not discuss the different combined versions presented here.

musical process of the movements that follow. All the musical forms of the Quartet may be traced back to this central theme, exposed in the very first fourteen bars, which thus creates a double introductory function, for the first movement and for the entire work[24]. Already a strong presence in the opening movement, in the Trio of the Scherzo movement the central theme appears as an adaptation in the cello. It is now embedded in the movement's triple meter, quoted, but reduced to the first characteristic phrase (see Ex. 6).

Ex. 6: Cyclical central theme as adaptation in the Trio of the Scherzo movement (second movement) of the String Quartet, bb. 219ff.

This adapted theme is heard here in the key of its first appearance, D major, but is tailored to the new context of the movement by metrically embedding its phrase in the new ternary meter. In terms of tone colour, the cello's *senza sordino* playing clearly sets it apart from the other three voices playing *con sordino*. Characteristically, this playing instruction is immediately reversed at the end of the passage. The performance marking *molto cantabile* in bar 225, which applies specifically to the theme, also supports the special thematic status of the passage. If one considers the accompanying configuration in the three upper voices immediately preceding the

---

[24]. *Ibidem*, pp. 315ff.

cello entry, it is striking that the development stagnates at this point: in the two violin parts, a single two-bar motive is heard in insistent repetitions over a long sustained pedal point *d* in the viola. The beginning of the section (bb. 220-225), which is reduced to a minimum of musical action by a triple repetition of the motive, builds up in a special way the expectation of a new musical development, which is relieved by the entrance of the thematic quotation in the fourth voice. Significantly, it is only after the cello entry that the accompanimental voices begin to develop again.

Through this process of thematic adaptation, Franck succeeds in establishing a relationship between two outwardly highly contrasting movement characters — the lyrical emphasis of the opening Poco lento as the starting point of the work as a whole, and the eerie humour of the Scherzo — as two stages of one and the same musical process. The unity of the work is ensured by the fact that the cyclical theme exposed at the beginning passes through the various stages of formal development as a kind of musical protagonist, without relinquishing its identity.

Not surprisingly, the cyclic theme is also heard as a reminiscence in the finale, initially at the beginning (bb. 53ff.; see details below). Its appearance is very significant, especially as the finale itself is the goal of the entire cycle of the work and the whole Quartet is teleological, that is, directed toward the end. But fragmentary, directionless reminiscences often abruptly interrupt this tight sequence. In a new, subjective experience of time, which emerges here through the immediate incursion of the past, even that of the point furthest back in time, these moments of 'disconnection from time' afford the listener a simultaneous awareness of the past and present. Manfred Hermann Schmid characterised this feature, with regard to Beethoven's String Quartet in C-sharp minor, Op. 131, as a refraction and a change of musical perspective[25].

In the final section of the development (bb. 480ff.) the cyclic theme is largely undisguised apart from the initial reminiscences (bb. 53ff.) and slightly varied ***fff*** in the first violin and *Largamento recitando*. The key of F minor here possibly represents a reminiscence of the F minor of the fugato in the first movement. In addition to the prominent triad, the basic diastematic third-second cell is also brought out. The weaving of the cyclical Lento theme into the Scherzo and the final movement reveals its function of cyclically linking the movements of the work. In almost all movements, this theme appears as a unifying element — except in the third, slow movement, which, at best, has only latent cyclical connections to the other movements of the work and, according to tradition, was written first (perhaps the idea of the central theme had not yet been born at this point)[26]. Significantly, Franck quotes the third, final version of the Lento theme in the Scherzo, which, for the work's genesis, supports the conclusion that the

---

[25].   Schmid 1996, p. 325.

[26].   Franck may have tried to counteract this rather loose integration into the work's cycle by taking up the Andante theme in the finale. Especially in the surviving sketches for the finale, he explicitly indicates: «Here comes a reminiscence of the Andante theme!».

Ex. 7: Reminiscence of the cyclical central theme in the coda of the final movement of the String Quartet, bb. 836ff.

Scherzo (at least the quotation at this point in the Scherzo) must have been written after the final decision was made in favour of the third version.

Finally, at the end of the final movement (bb. 840ff., Ex. 7), the musical development of the coda heads toward the reminiscence of the central cyclic theme, which had previously fundamentally determined not only the entire work on a sub-surface level, but also through its positioning at key formal points. In the triple *forte* and *molto largamente*, it is recalled *recitando*, in a form similar to that found at the end of the development (bb. 480ff.). Harmonically, too, it refers back to the conclusion of the development, but at the same time it may also be constructively legitimised as a «retrospective return of the spectacular third displacement from the beginning of the quartet (first movement, bb. 10/11)»[27]. In the context of this thematic recurrence, Franck cites both interval sequences crucial to the work: the triad and the third-second constellation.

THE CYCLICAL CENTRAL THEME AS TRANSFORMATION

Franck also obtains the finale's main theme by transforming the third version of the central cyclic theme from the first movement (bb. 59ff., Ex. 8), using the first phrase largely unchanged diastematically and rhythmically as the starting point of the new theme, now shifted to an Allegro molto tempo. Although this follows the structure of the cyclical Lento theme in the first half, it extends the two phrases by one bar, from three to four. In addition, a four-bar sequence-like continuation is added to the model (bb. 67-70), creating a regular structure of 4+4+4 bars.

Ex. 8: Cyclical central theme as transformation, first and final movement of the String Quartet, I bb. 1ff., IV bb. 53ff.

Finally, Franck stresses the derivative character of this shape by having the underlying theme of the first movement sound as a reminiscence immediately before the first use of the main final theme (IV, bb. 53ff.). With the immediate adjacency of these two figures in the fourth movement, Franck thus seems to bring the latent diastematic network of relationships between the themes of the individual movements to the surface of the musical movement, in order to emphasise the substantial cyclical connection of the outer movements.

---

[27]. HINRICHSEN 2004, p. 99.

INNOVATION – FORM OVERLAY

The cyclical central theme is not only taken up again as a thematic variant in the later movements, but also plays a central role in the first movement as the functional bearer of the introduction. It is precisely in shaping the introduction of the String Quartet that Franck departs from tradition as to the function of the symphonic introduction as material preparation for the following Allegro. Instead, he develops a new formal dramaturgy applied to the connection between the introduction and the main movement. The main characteristic of the introduction could be its radical formal independence. It is therefore questionable whether this Lento section should still be considered as an introduction in the traditional sense. In the Poco Lento – Allegro sequence, Franck outwardly seems to follow the traditional convention of the introduction, yet a closer look reveals that this Poco Lento has detached itself from this function and developed into an autonomous formal entity. Even at face value, the eighty-bar opening section of the first movement is striking: no mere preparation for the following Allegro, it is rather a self-contained section that is clearly set apart from the minor key of the following Allegro by the key of D major — in contrast to the Symphony's introduction, whose inner development points toward the use of the main theme in the Allegro. The reinterpretation of function, from an introduction to a closed formal section, is particularly evident in the String Quartet: indeed, the final section of the Poco Lento (bb. 71-80) is repeated at the very end of the first movement as the only note-for-note repetition in the piece (bb. 364-373). This repetition of the Poco Lento after the conclusion of the recapitulation of the Allegro reflects the autonomy of the formal section in question, which is at odds with any traditional introductory function.

Here, in contrast to the Symphony's introduction with its progressive, developmental element, Franck — as in the Piano Quintet (1878/1879) — presents already 'elaborated' melodic and counter-themes in a clearly structured disposition[28], being first presented in fifths (the first theme in D major, the second in A major) and then directly repeated, i.e., recapitulated, in the principal key. Franck draws on the approach of thematic dualism within the introduction, already set forth in the Piano Quintet, and develops it by creating clear formal relationships between the two themes of the Poco Lento section and integrating them into a structured key plan that reveals sonata form as a traditional reference.

This outline of a sonata form in which the development section has been deleted is used by Franck only as a formal vehicle for his individual concept of form. This goes against that dramatic, forward-thrusting drive — a characteristic feature of sonata form. The String Quartet opens with an introspective formal section, of sorts, already taking on repetitive but at the same time 'retrospective' features through the immediately ensuing recapitulation, realising in the process the cyclical principle 'in miniature' at the beginning. The recapitulation of both

---

[28]. See further details in STRUCKEN-PALAND 2009, pp. 266ff.

themes, which immediately follows the exposition, avoids the character of the provisional and unfinished that is normally associated with this section of the form.

Probably also in order to avoid any process-like or teleological trait inherent in both a development and an introduction, Franck forgoes a development of the two exposed themes within the sonata framework of the Poco Lento. A solution to musical conflicts, as usually follows an exposition, is not intended, but also not necessary, since the themes are instead juxtaposed to be repeatedly illuminated differently over the course of multiple variations. In the lyrical expansion of the central theme, the Poco Lento competes with the third, slow movement as well. The fact that it does not appear there at all is possibly due to Franck's concern that it might overshadow the movement's own theme.

INTEGRATION INTO THE FIRST MOVEMENT

TABLE 1: DISTINCTIVE FORMAL CONCEPT OF THE *STRING QUARTET*, TWO FORMAL AREAS

Exposition		Development		Recapitulation	
Lento – exposition		**Lento – developement**		**Allegro – recapitulation**	
main theme	D maj.	fugato	F min.		
second theme	A maj.				
Lento – recapitulation		**Allegro – development**		**2nd Lento – recapitulation**	
main theme	D maj.			main theme	D maj.
second theme	D maj.			second theme	D maj.
Allegro – exposition					

In the String Quartet, Franck also develops a highly interesting, distinctive formal concept as to the integration of the introduction into the opening movement, combining simplicity and complexity with wilful abandon. Next to the development section of the Allegro itself, he places another development section (see TABLE 1), a fugato in F minor using the central theme of the Lento section (bb. 173-217, Ex. 9), the contrapuntal syntax clearly lifting this section out of context. In so doing, Franck also separates the two development sections through different techniques.

He uses counterpoint only for the development of the central theme — certainly also because its lyrical, cantabile character does not suggest dramatic development techniques. In addition, having already deployed the Lisztian technique of real sequence in the exposition, Franck now needs new techniques for the development. As Dahlhaus sees it[29], this fugato may also be interpreted as a solution to this compositional difficulty, in that Franck now resorts to counterpoint in the development, i.e., to a *qualitatively* new compositional technique, instead

---

[29]. DAHLHAUS 1980, p. 244.

Ex. 9: Fugato in F minor with the cyclical central theme in the first movement of the String Quartet, bb. 173ff.

of only *quantitatively* increasing the procedures already extensively used in the exposition. It is possible that Franck chose the fugue technique instead of a motivic-thematic treatment because it allowed the theme to be highlighted without any substantial change, only by alternating the added voices and counterpoints. Finally, Franck lets the first movement end as it were, redundantly, with a 'second recapitulation' or coda of this Lento section with the two Lento themes (bb. 340ff., TABLE 1). The result is that the recapitulation appears formally in a twofold manner, just as the Lento section fulfilled a dual function as the introduction to the movement and to the cycle as a whole. Beethoven had already attempted such thematic integration of the introduction into the main movement. In the String Quartet in C-sharp minor Op. 131, this type of thematic process of independence reached its climax: there, the introduction developed into an independent movement that may no longer be understood as an introduction in the traditional sense.

In this way, Franck weaves together two formal areas differing markedly in tempo and expression — the twice-repeated Lento sections and those sections of the opening movement belonging to the Allegro, each of which is conceived as a sonata form in its own right. Carl Dahlhaus calls this a «dual movement»[30]; Vincent d'Indy speaks trenchantly of permeation

---

30. *Ibidem*, p. 243: «Doppelsatz».

without flowing transitions and analyses the movement as, «the most astonishing symphonic movement written since the late String Quartets of Beethoven. The movement's essentially novel and original form consists of two pieces of music, each living its own life, each possessing a complete organism, and each mutually permeating the other without mingling, thanks to an absolutely perfect arrangement of their elements and sectional divisions»[31].

By inserting the Poco Lento sections as an independent sonata form into the structure, Franck's String Quartet suspends the original formal principle to the extent that its essential sections — exposition, development, and recapitulation — lose their own significance and relationship to one another because of duplication. Franck has the movement open with two expositions; a second, quasi external development occurs as a fugato before the 'main development', and instead of a coda, another recapitulation appears after the 'actual' recapitulation, namely that of the introduction. These functional doublings result in a characteristic paratactic structure of the movement[32], in which the formal sections seem to become independent from the overarching context.

At the same time, the separate sections of the two formal areas are linked by numerous structural relationships between the themes of the Lento and those of the Allegro. Thus, the first main theme of the Allegro is derived from the Lento secondary theme (both share the second-within-fourth)[33]. The formal disintegration of the Lento in the movement is offset by several subsurface links.

Why does Franck make such a peculiar permutation of the sections of the inner sonata structure, and why is the Lento exposition immediately followed by its recapitulation and then, only in the Allegro, by the development? Furthermore, why does Franck have the first movement end redundantly, with a 'second recapitulation' or coda? In this context, each of the two separate formal areas realises the sonata form, and their themes must be compared with each other. With respect to the overall formal dramaturgy, one can see that the thematic characters of these two interlocking formal areas complement each other: the themes of the Lento section, with their cantabile, lyrical character, do not lend themselves to the kind of strict, progression-oriented treatment traditionally characterising a sonata movement. Rather, the Lento section is based on melodically rich, firmly defined themes that preclude a developing formal process by clearly forming tonal centres of gravity and exhibiting a centripetal melodic progression that circles around central notes and ends in its own beginning. Frequently, direct

---

[31].   See ᴅ'Iɴᴅʏ 1907, p. 170: «Ce premier mouvement est, en effet, la plus étonnante pièce symphonique qui ait été construite depuis les derniers quatuors beethovéniens. Sa forme, essentiellement nouvelle et originale, consiste en *deux* morceaux de musique vivant chacun de sa vie propre et possédant chacun un organisme complet, qui se pénètrent mutuellement sans se confondre, grâce à une ordonnance absolument parfaite de leurs éléments et de leurs divisions». See the analysis in Sᴛʀᴜᴄᴋᴇɴ-Pᴀʟᴀɴᴅ 2009, pp. 307ff.

[32].   Rᴀᴛʜᴇʀᴛ 1990, p. 319.

[33].   See Sᴛʀᴜᴄᴋᴇɴ-Pᴀʟᴀɴᴅ 2009, pp. 310ff.

repetitions of motivic cells emerge, which are then combined with a half- or whole-tone shift and a harmonic modulation to initiate the harmonic process. Typical of this kind of theme formation is the central theme. Put succinctly, one could regard the melodic circling of the themes as a kind of cyclical principle *en miniature*. That the two themes, especially the central Lento theme, do not function as the mere starting point of a deliberate formal process, but rather as its constant centre of reference, is already shown in the first formal section by the repeated references back to the theme that opens the work. In no fewer than three complete passages, the central theme dominates the beginning, which places it at odds with the musical opening traditionally expected here. For Franck, too, the connection is valid between «a melodically richer theme and a temporal progression that resembles a circling movement rather than a teleological process», as noted by Dahlhaus in Beethoven's work[34]. The large-scale three-part superstructure of the movement, which again flows into its own beginning, lends the form the clarity necessary for coherence and compensates for the thematic and formal doublings and ambiguities. With these redundancies Franck suspends the sonata form and reconfigures the relationship between the introduction and the Allegro section.

ARRAY OF REMINISCENCES

At first glance, the formal structure of the finale appears based on traditional sonata form. The movement is divided into the following sections: introduction (bb. 1-58), exposition (bb. 59-281), development (bb. 282-505), recapitulation (bb. 506-704), and coda (bb. 705-881). But this rough structure is clouded and called into question by numerous formal ambiguities. On one hand, this is due to the ambiguous relationships between the thematic figures. On the other hand, in the course of the movement, the form is increasingly determined by retrospective moments and regressions, through which the musical process is interrupted and ultimately suspended. Franck, for example, develops the idea of the retrospective thematic review adopted from Beethoven and already tested in the *Grande pièce symphonique* by also taking up such an array of reminiscences within the definitive beginning of the String Quartet. Furthermore, he inserts another retrospective in the coda, neatly establishing an immanent connection to the beginning of the finale on one hand and building an overarching bridge to the preceding movements of the work on the other. In contrast to Beethoven, who almost programmatically overcomes the 'old state' at the beginning of the ninth symphony, Franck gives the past a new presence, especially with the reminiscences at the end of the work, which, as it were, overgrow the immanent musical events of the final movement.

---

[34]. See DAHLHAUS 2002, p. 123: «[...] einer melodisch reicheren Thematik und einem Zeitverlauf, der eher einer umkreisenden Bewegung als einem teleologischen Prozess gleicht».

The initially synthetic character of the finale as the outcome of a movement-spanning teleological process is called into question by an extended field of reminiscences at the beginning of the final movement (see Ex. 10).

Ex. 10: Array of reminiscences at the beginning of the final movement of the String Quartet, bb. 1ff.

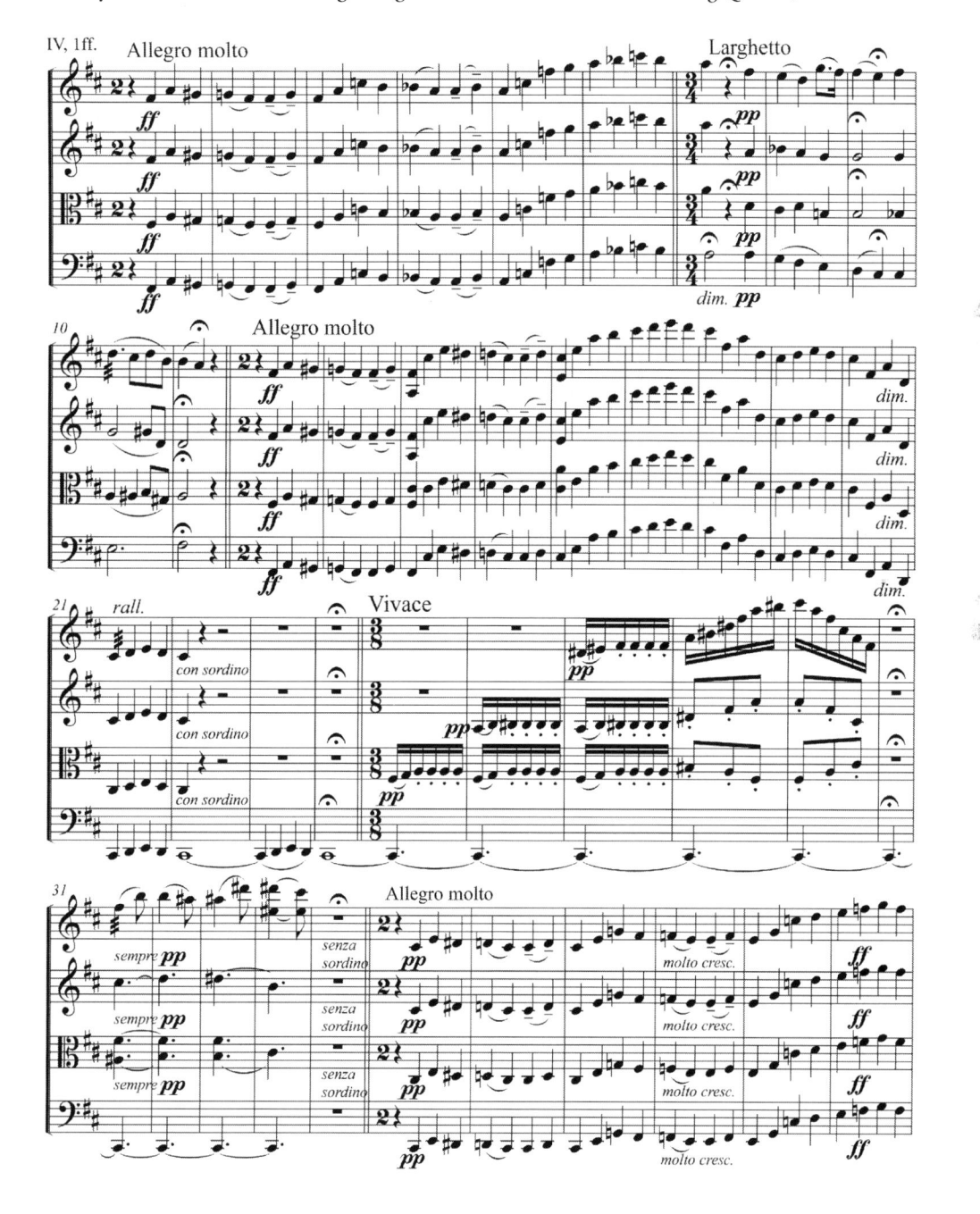

The opening successively recapitulates the main themes of the preceding movements in the manner of Beethoven's ninth symphony, usually in the form in which they first occur, each interlinked with the others by a brief 'refrain'. Unlike Beethoven, however, the themes appear in reverse order (see FIG. 1), proceeding from the slow third movement through the Scherzo with the trio theme, to the central theme of the opening movement. This latter theme contains what might be called the diastematic structure of the finale's main theme which immediately follows. As already shown, the finale's main theme derives from the central theme[35].

---

35. See the analysis in STRUCKEN-PALAND 2009, pp. 138ff. and 355ff.

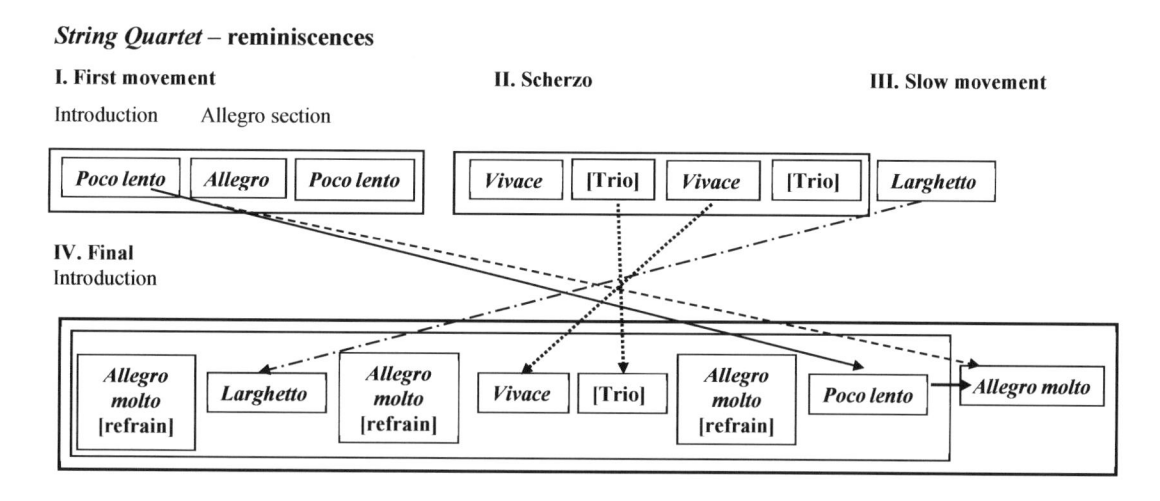

FIG. 1: Field of reminiscences at the beginning of the final movement of the String Quartet.

In this way, the introduction of the finale sums up the entire work up to that point. Franck himself remarked on the relationship to the Beethovenian precedent: «As in the Ninth, I start by recalling the ideas of the previous pieces, but then I don't abandon them, I use them in the developments»[36]. Only the short 'refrain', which is inserted between the reminiscence parts, has a dynamically driving gesture, though it slackens already after a few bars each time. First exposed *fortissimo* and in unison, it is taken up again three times in varied form. This refrain fulfils a function similar to that of the cello recitatives in the finale of Beethoven's ninth symphony, whose introductory principle Franck had already adopted in the final part of his *Grande pièce symphonique*. Whereas there the Allegro main theme itself acted as a link between the reminiscences, the refrain here in the String Quartet represents a new, as yet unheard theme that is about to play an important role within the finale.

The refrain connecting the reminiscences assumes the function of linking the recurrences and incorporating them into the finale. Further, within the finale itself, we find interspersed sections of the refrain that one could call 'tutti parts', given that their chromaticism and the quasi-orchestral tremolo effects cause them to stand out in harmonic and sonic contrast to the more stable passages dominated by themes and rendered by soloists in *concertante* alternation. Franck transfers to the refrain of the finale such scherzo-esque elements as the typical instrumental colour of tremolo (a characteristic sonority previously confined to the Scherzo), the entrance of parts in imitation, and staccato articulation, which, apart from the Scherzo, is likewise set

---

[36]. See BRÉVILLE 1925, p. 179, quoted in: EICH 2002, p. 129: «Comme dans la neuvième, je commence par rappeler les idées des morceaux précédents, mais ensuite je ne les abandonne pas, je m'en sers dans les développements».

aside exclusively for the refrain[37]. The different reminiscences are clearly distinguished from one another by double bar lines, fermatas, their own tempi, and metrical schemes (see Ex. 10). By adopting the original structure of the movement as well as the tempo, meter, dynamics, and timbre of the quoted passages, they seem to be standing next to each other without being linked.

After the introductory refrain of the last movement, the two opening phrases of the third movement are recapitulated first. The subsequent recapitulation of the first five bars of the Scherzo and the opening phrase of the Trio (bb. 25ff.) is linked to the refrain by the pedal point C-sharp in the cello; another intervention of the refrain (bb. 36-52) is followed by the recapitulation of the opening Lento section from the first movement. Due to the sixfold change of texture in only fifty-eight bars, no true musical progression occurs here at all; rather, the music surrenders almost without resistance to the uncontrolled memory of the fragments of the past. These fragments, of course, seem to represent not only themselves, but — like the reminiscences in Beethoven's ninth symphony — *pars pro toto* the movement itself. It is revealing for the dramaturgy of the final introduction that both the extension of the refrain and its position in relation to the inserted reminiscences change step by step: while the first reminiscence abruptly interrupts the refrain after only six bars, the second appearance — clearly related harmonically to D major — is significantly longer, and the last interpolation is melodically and tonally extended. Its gradual expansion should then be interpreted as a progressive immersion into the work's past. This manifests itself in reminiscences of musical events that are positioned further and further back in time. The fact that the introductory reminiscence area does not appear completely incoherent may be attributed to several factors. On the one hand, the refrain persistently recurs as an interpolating link. On the other hand, certain sub-motivic thematic affinities also ensure an underlying coherence, which is at least partially shown by the sequence of reminiscences Franck has chosen.

All in all, the introductory reminiscence area effects a kind of overview of the temporal dimension of the entire String Quartet, tracing in miniature the «changes of tone or character» accomplished in the sequence of the preceding movements by recalling fragmentarily the most important themes of the work. What is remarkable here, however, is the reversed arrangement of the reminiscences with respect to the sequence of movements: starting from the slow third movement (Larghetto) via the second movement representing the Scherzo (Vivace), the climax is reached in the first movement and here exclusively the main theme of the introductory Lento section, whose cantabile, almost lyrical character stands in striking contrast to the following, more agitated main theme of the finale. And yet, the finale's main theme represents a variant of the Lento's. The fact that these two opposing variants of the central theme immediately follow one another in the transition to the main section of the finale underlines the transformation of the theme and the concomitant change in thematic character. That Franck intended to

---

[37].   Except in the case of bb. 432-434; see STRUCKEN-PALAND 2009, p. 370.

emphasise the relationship between the two contrasting themes in this way is made particularly clear by his decision not to further interpolate the refrain at the end of the introductory section, which would have separated the final reminiscence from the exposition of the finale main theme. From the first movement, Franck quotes only the main theme of the Lento section and not the following Allegro theme (which is literally lost in the course of the work) — while he almost pedantically takes up both the Scherzo theme and the beginning of the Trio theme from the second movement. On one hand, this is probably related to his effort to make the «changes in tone» in the reminiscence feel even more vivid through corresponding tempo changes (slow – fast – slow); on the other hand, the first introductory theme as the central theme of the entire work is also highlighted by omitting a reminiscence of the 'competing' Allegro theme of the first movement.

While the introduction of the finale provides a time-lapse overview of the entire work up to that point, it is at the same time an anticipation of the coda[38]; in a further retrospective this coda again points back to the themes presented here as being a kind of development of this introduction. At the same time, the introduction, as Rathert notes, functions as a foil to the immense expanse of time in the ensuing sonata form of the Allegro, and thereby already at the beginning of the last movement focuses attention on the relationship of the events of the movement to temporally more distant stages of the musical discourse. In the coda, Franck develops this Beethovenian idea of thematic exposure by referring directly to the final introduction. All the thematic reminiscences occurring there are taken up again: the Scherzo figuration, the Larghetto theme, and finally, the central theme. In this way, Franck also builds an overarching bridge to the preceding movements of the work.

At the beginning of the coda, the augmented refrain theme (bb. 705ff.) is reduced to the first half — its basics — and subsequently interrupted by the Scherzo reminiscence. In a process of assimilation, Franck brings the refrain increasingly closer to the Scherzo theme in his interpolations during the movement, until it finally follows the Scherzo theme reminiscence in augmented form (bb. 715ff.). It is here indeed that one finds the psychological phenomenon of association that motivates and formally legitimises this incursion of the past into the beginning of the coda. Just as Franck has already twice emphasised the close connection between the cyclical Lento theme of the first movement and the main theme of the finale derived from it through their immediate succession, so in the coda does he ultimately place the two figures of the refrain theme and the reminiscence of the Scherzo theme, seemingly contrary at first, directly next to each other. The close diastematic relationship, already latent in the finale introduction, becomes unmistakably clear. With the Scherzo figure, all interpolations of the refrain share the gradually filled-in third motive. The gradual *rapprochement* of the refrain to the Scherzo theme reaches a term here because a direct association with past thematic material is now possible by

---

[38]. See Rathert 1990, p. 323.

means of the augmented refrain theme. The meticulous thematic changes therefore constitute a vehicle for reconnecting the ultimately psychologically-motivated resumption of past themes within the foreign context of the movement, mitigating the formal rupture that such an area of reminiscence represents according to traditional, inner-musical criteria.

At this point, the break from the underlying traditional form is irreversible. The entire coda is characterised by a tendency to regress in musical retrospectives of varying degrees. This gives the impression that the movement is becoming more and more caught up in an 'awakening of the past' from which the music is less and less able to escape. The main section of this finale had already demonstrated the transformation of the material essential to the String Quartet into new themes, but these largely took place at the most abstract level, that of the motive. Only in the introduction, as well as in the coda, does the finale draw directly on the themes of the preceding movements, demonstrating their substantive relationship. Thus, after two attempts and Scherzo borrowings (b. 705ff., 723ff. and 749ff.), the entire cantabile theme of the third movement is quoted as the climax (b. 808ff.). That the final apotheosis is conflated with the theme of the slow movement is characteristic for Franck, since these themes with their chordally accompanied cantabile upper voice are especially fitting for staging the emphatic-expressive culmination. Moreover, in the String Quartet's dramaturgy based on formal redundancy, the Larghetto — the only movement that does not quote the central theme — represents a kind of counterbalance to the lyrical emphasis of the introduction; the theme of this movement must therefore not be missing in the finale simply for the sake of cyclical balance.

As a logical consequence of the preceding retrospectives, the coda finally heads toward the reminiscence of the cyclical central theme (b. 840ff., see Ex. 7), which has fundamentally determined the work on a subsurface level, but also by its positions at significant places. It is recalled *fff*, *molto largamente*, and *recitando* in a form similar to the one that occurs already at the end of the development (see b. 480ff). Strikingly, Franck here quotes both interval sequences that are fundamental for the work, the triad and the third-second constellation, now chromatically coloured[39]. Finally, in its broken chords, the concluding refrain (bb. 868ff.), which sounds like a stretto in the Presto, also takes on the characteristic third-second constellation in all possible permutations. While the refrain at the beginning of the movement functioned as an impulse generator for the musical development, it presents a kind of musical *resumé* of the two form-constitutive levels at the conclusion of both the finale and the entire work.

Whereas Beethoven's Ninth Symphony served as a model for the finale of Franck's *Grande pièce symphonique*, insofar as the thematic reminiscences at the beginning of the finale (apart from the transformation of the refrain into the main theme of the final part) no longer

---

[39].   EICH 2002, p. 139.

play any role in the finale, in the String Quartet, a development may be observed in that the musical design now aims to integrate the reminiscences into the finale, and to work out their relationship through various assimilation processes, successive thematic associations and even thematic couplings. In contrast to Beethoven, who almost programmatically overcomes the 'former state of affairs' at the beginning of the finale of the Ninth symphony, Franck provides the past with a new presence, especially with the reminiscences at the end of the work, which, as it were, overlap the immanent musical events of the final movement. The finale thus no longer functions as the apotheosis of a teleological development that spans the entire movement, but rather, similarly to Beethoven's String Quartet in C-sharp minor, Op. 131, becomes a «reflection of the beginning»[40]. The weaving in and out of reminiscences and quotations within the formal development is oriented towards psychological mechanisms of experience such as associations or memories which obviously make temporal distance perceptible and paradoxically attempt to bridge it at the same time. In recalling the preceding movements, Franck exposes the close and substantial connection of the themes. In coupling originally successive themes, he also attempts to transfer what is initially non-simultaneous into simultaneity in the sense of an integrative culmination, and in so doing, break through the progression-based character of time as well. By time detaching itself from the teleology of form in this movement more radically than anywhere else in Franck's instrumental oeuvre, a non-teleological and — despite all dynamics — ultimately static concept of time emerges here.

BIBLIOGRAPHY

BRÉVILLE 1925
BRÉVILLE, Pierre de. 'César Franck (1822-1890)', in: *Encyclopédie de la musique et dictionnaire du Conservatoire. 2/1*, edited by Albert Lavignac and Lionel de la Laurencie, Paris, Delagrave, 1925.

CADENBACH 1990
CADENBACH, Rainer. 'Streichquartette, die zu Symphonien wurden, und die Idee des «rechten Quartettstils»', in: *Probleme der symphonischen Tradition im 19. Jahrhundert (Internationales Musikwissenschaftliches Colloquium Bonn 1989): Kongressbericht*, edited by Siegfried Kross and Marie Luise Maintz, Tutzing, Hans Schneider, 1990, pp. 471-492.

DAHLHAUS 1980
DAHLHAUS, Carl. *Die Musik des 19. Jahrhunderts*, Wiesbaden, Akademische Verlagsgesellschaft Athenaion, 1980 (Neues Handbuch der Musikwissenschaft, 6).

---

40. See RATHERT 1990, p. 313: «Reflexion des Anfangs».

DAHLHAUS 1981

ID. 'Liszts Idee des Symphonischen', in: *Referate des 2. Europäischen Liszt-Symposions, Eisenstadt 1978*, edited by Serge Gut, Munich-Salzburg, Katzbichler, 1981 (Liszt Studien, 2. Kongressbericht Eisenstadt 1978), pp. 36-42.

DAHLHAUS 2002

ID. *Ludwig van Beethoven und seine Zeit*, Laaber, Laaber-Verlag, 2002 (Große Komponisten und ihre Zeit).

EICH 2002

EICH, Katrin. *Die Kammermusik von César Franck*, Kassel, Bärenreiter, 2002 (Kieler Schriften zur Musikwissenschaft, 48).

FAUQUET 1999

FAUQUET, Joël-Marie. *César Franck*, Paris, Fayard, 1999.

GAUTHIER 1845

GAUTHIER, Gabriel. *Le Mécanisme de la composition instrumentale ou explication de toutes les productions de musique instrumentale*, Paris, Vinchon imprimeur, 1845.

GÜLKE 1971

GÜLKE, Peter. 'Wider die Übermacht des Thematischen. Zum Verständnis César Francks anhand seiner d-Moll-Sinfonie', in: *Beiträge zur Musikwissenschaft*, XIII (1971), pp. 261-271.

HINRICHSEN 2004

HINRICHSEN, Hans-Joachim. 'Individuelles Spätwerk und epochaler Spätstil. Zur harmonischen Konstruktion der «sonate cyclique» in César Francks Streichquartett', in: *César Franck. Werk und Rezeption*, edited by Peter Jost, Stuttgart, Franz Steiner, 2004, pp. 88-111.

D'INDY 1907

INDY, Vincent d'. *César Franck*, Paris, F. Alcan, 1907.

JARDILLIER 1929

JARDILLIER, Robert. *La musique de chambre de César Franck. Étude et analyse*, Paris, Mellotté, [1929].

KRAUS 2004

KRAUS, Beate Angelika. 'Komponieren im Schatten Beethovens: César Franck und das Pariser Musikleben seiner Zeit', in: *César Franck. Werk und Rezeption, op. cit.*, pp. 22-33.

OECHSLE 1992

OECHSLE, Siegfried. *Symphonik nach Beethoven. Studien zu Schubert, Schumann, Mendelssohn und Gade*, Kassel, Bärenreiter, 1992 (Kieler Schriften zur Musikwissenschaft, 40).

RATHERT 1990
RATHERT, Wolfgang. 'Form und Zeit im Streichquartett César Francks', in: *Neue Musik und Tradition. Festschrift Rudolf Stephan*, edited by Joesph Kuckertz *et al.*, Laaber, Laaber-Verlag, 1990, pp. 311-332.

SCHMID 1996
SCHMID, Manfred Hermann. 'Streichquartett cis-moll Op. 131', in: *Beethoven. Interpretationen seiner Werke. 2*, edited by Albrecht Riethmüller, Carl Dahlhaus, and Alexander L. Ringer, Laaber, Laaber-Verlag, [2]1996, pp. 217-326.

SPONHEUER 1978
SPONHEUER, Bernd. *Logik des Zerfalls. Untersuchungen zum Finalproblem in den Symphonien Gustav Mahlers*, Tutzing, Hans Schneider, 1978.

STRUCKEN-PALAND 2009
STRUCKEN-PALAND, Christiane. *Zyklische Prinzipien in den Instrumentalwerken César Francks*, Kassel, Bosse, 2009 (Kölner Beiträge zur Musikwissenschaft, 7).

STRUCKEN-PALAND 2010
EAD. *César Franck. Quatuor pour 2 Violons, Alto et Violoncelle*, edited by Christiane Strucken-Paland, Kassel, Bärenreiter, 2010 (Bärenreiter Urtext).

The Franck Quintet:
Dramatic Character, Style, and Relationship to the Beethoven Instrumental Tradition[1]

François de Médicis
(Université de Montréal - OICRM)

RECENT WORKS have presented César Franck as an influential figure in French musical life during the Third Republic, and leader of a preeminent school that helped to rehabilitate the major instrumental genres in France[2]. During the first third of the twentieth century, Vincent d'Indy published numerous Franck studies, weaving around his master a rich and complex historiographical narrative. Since then, our knowledge of Franck's life and works has been enriched by significant monographs such as VALLAS 1955, FAUQUET 1999, and STRUCKEN-PALAND 2009. Certain questionable interpretations proposed by d'Indy, however, have not always been subject to sufficient critical examination, and continue to exert influence in Franck studies[3]. For example, based on analyses of works by Franck and others, d'Indy asserts that Franck's cyclic writing is rooted directly in the works of Beethoven's third period, independently from any other European composer. In this chapter, I examine how Franck's Quintet relates to the nineteenth-century Beethovenian instrumental tradition (as established first by Beethoven's music and developed subsequently by other composers). To this end, I will first analyse the Quintet's significant stylistic features: cyclic form, topoi, development of contrasting ideas, variations in tension, and narrative trajectory across the movements. I will point to similar procedures in earlier works by Beethoven, Brahms, and Liszt. I will then review d'Indy's assertions about Franck's relationship to the Beethovenian tradition, underscoring where my analysis of the Quintet may add nuance to these claims, or call them into question.

[1]. I wish to thank Ariadne Lih for translating this article into English, Catrina Flint for her help in the final revisions of the text, and Stefan Keym for helpful suggestions. Earlier versions of this article were presented in 2021 at the conference *Chamber Music 1850-1918* based in Lucca (online), and in 2022 at the conference *César Franck and His Legacy*, at the London Royal College of Music.

[2]. See for example DUNSBY 2001, pp. 507-508 and TARUSKIN 2005, pp. 774-775.

[3]. See for example GUT 2004.

FRANÇOIS DE MÉDICIS

CYCLIC WRITING IN FRANCK'S QUINTET: GENERAL CONSIDERATIONS

Franck's Piano Quintet in F minor has three movements, fast-slow-fast, with neither scherzo nor character piece. Composed in 1878-1879, the work was premiered on 17 January 1880 at the Société nationale de musique, with composer Camille Saint-Saëns at the piano[4]. With the exception of a few minor works — the *Andantino quietoso*, Op. 6 (1843), the *Solo de piano avec accompagnement de quintette à cordes* (c.1844), and the *Duo concertant* (1844) — the Quintet constituted Franck's first return to chamber music in 37 years, that is, since 1842 and his four early trios (the three Trios, Op. 1 and the Trio, Op. 2). It also inaugurates the series of mature works written in the classical genres, for both chamber ensemble and orchestra (e.g., the *Variations symphoniques*, the Violin Sonata, the Symphony, and the String Quartet). Finally, the cyclic technique with which Franck experimented in his Trio No. 1 is applied here once again.

A close, but in no way exhaustive, review of salient manifestations of the cyclic principle in the Quintet, is a good place to begin. For this task, I often quote from the astute observations of STRUCKEN-PALAND 2009, including her contention that cyclic writing encompasses not only motivic and thematic relationships, but may also be extended into the harmonic organisation as well.

The overall form of the first movement contains a slow introduction followed by a sonata form[5]. One of the most audible cyclic elements resides in the recurrence of the first movement's subordinate theme in the rest of the Quintet (see Ex. 1, p. 78); Christiane Strucken-Paland, for example, highlights its return during the Quintet's slow movement (bb. 58-62). Here the cyclic theme, which was initially brimming with restrained passion, has become dreamy and ethereal, like a reminiscence[6]: rhythmic alterations create hesitancy in the piano melody, which floats over the sustained ***ppp*** notes played by the strings. Striking emotional transformations such as this are frequent when a cyclic theme is varied. But part of the scholarly literature tends to neglect this expressive dimension, focusing instead on the generative or unifying function of cyclic return. For his part, d'Indy never explicitly theorises the rhetorical role of cyclicism, although he is clearly sensitive to it and often describes its effects[7]. In his view, musical themes

---

[4]. Martin Marsick and Guillaume Rémy played violin, with Louis van Waefelghem on viola and Richard Loys on cello.

[5]. Following the slow introduction, the exposition (bb. 50-143) contains a short «motto» (bb. 50-51), the main theme (bb. 52-73), the transition (bb. 74-123), the subordinate theme in the relative major (bb. 124-143), and a short closing section (bb. 139-143). After the development (bb. 143-268), the recapitulation begins in b. 269. The reprise of the subordinate theme in the tonic (starting in b. 339) leads without pause into a powerful and substantial coda, which concludes the movement at b. 440.

[6]. STRUCKEN-PALAND 2009, p. 170.

[7]. For instance, d'Indy observes that when the cyclic theme (i.e., the subordinate theme of the first movement) reappears in the finale, the key is the same as it was in the slow movement, «but the expression is quite different. Soon

and motifs may be likened to characters and their various emotions, in the same ways as leitmotifs in operas[8]. Musically, he associates the transformations of cyclic themes with what he calls *variation amplificatrice* (amplifying variation), that is, a creative form of variation that goes beyond simple ornamental changes[9]. Somewhat surprisingly, he traces the most striking manifestations of this technique back to Johann Sebastian Bach's organ chorales[10]. A more recent musicological tradition has labelled the same technique 'thematic transformation', a practice strongly associated with Liszt, albeit with numerous precedents from the nineteenth century — the 'idée fixe' in Berlioz's *Symphonie fantastique*, for example, the reminiscence motifs in Carl Maria von Weber's operas, and beyond, from before 1800[11].

In addition, the first movement's subordinate theme contains harmonic progressions based on chromatic thirds, which escape common tonal practice. They may be described here as an accumulation of alterations to diatonic harmonies. Ex. 1b shows the VI chord that would have occurred in bar 333 had Franck written the passage diatonically; in Ex. 1c, this chord is altered via modal mixture (borrowing from minor); and in Ex. 1d, the third of the chord from 1c is lowered. Exs. 1e and 1f illustrate the same principle for the chord in b. 337. To a great extent, Neo-Riemannian theory has attempted to conceive a proper theoretical framework for addressing special chromatic third progressions such as these, and Franck's music proved a convenient source for testing its theories. In Ex. 1, the first third relation illustrates the H (hexatonic pole) transformation; the second shows the combined P and R (parallel and relative) transformations[12].

The first of these third progressions reappears throughout the Quintet. Strucken-Paland demonstrates that it operates on multiple levels of the work's structural hierarchy, thus serving a cyclic function. She therefore describes the progression as a harmonic motif (*Harmonische Motiv*) with surface manifestations such as the recurrences in bb. 147-155 and 163-171 of the final movement. The same type of progression appears in the second movement at a deeper level, with some additional chromatic inflexions: the first phrase prolongs the tonic from an

---

the calm disappears: the plaintive voice becomes stronger as it finds the main key once again; [...] its despairing cries continue to ring out over the brilliant peroration». My translation. «[M]ais l'expression est tout à fait différente. Bientôt le calme disparaît: la voix plaintive se fait plus forte en retrouvant le ton principal; [...] ses appels désespérés retentissent encore au-dessus de l'éclatante péroraison». D'INDY – SÉRIEYX 1909, p. 382.

[8]. According to d'Indy, Franck takes the *thème-personnage* (theme-as-character) approach, which originated with Beethoven. D'INDY – SÉRIEYX 1909, p. 377; STRUCKEN-PALAND 2009, pp. 98-99. Keym situates this filiation and Franck's opposition of dual cyclic materials with respect to nineteenth and twentieth-century developments in French and German conceptions of form. KEYM 2004, pp. 114-127.

[9]. D'INDY – SÉRIEYX 1909, p. 379; STRUCKEN-PALAND 2009, p. 102.

[10]. D'INDY – SÉRIEYX 1909, p. 447. See p. 85 in the same work for cyclic form in Bach's *St. Anne* fugue for organ, BWV 552.

[11]. See MACDONALD 2001.

[12]. See COHN 1998 for theoretical principles and COOK 2005 for their application to Franck.

Ex. 1: Franck, Quintet, first movement, bars 331-338.

A major chord to an A minor one (bb. 3-4); the second phrase sustains an F chord which goes from minor to major and then back to minor (bb. 5-8); after a retransition (bb. 8-11), the third phrase (bb. 12-16) brings back an A minor chord. Other manifestations of this progression worth highlighting are those that play a formal role. At the surface level, for instance, the harmonic motif sometimes occurs repeatedly rather than in isolation, signalling important articulations of form. Ex. 2a shows the progression in bb. 34-37, at the end of the introduction (shortly before the beginning of the exposition); Ex. 2b shows the progression in bb. 510-516 from the finale, at the end of the piece[13].

Ex. 2a: Franck, Quintet, first movement, bb. 34-37.

Ex. 2b: Franck, Quintet, third movement, bb. 510-516.

---

13. See also Strucken-Paland's other pertinent comments on these passages. STRUCKEN-PALAND 2009, pp. 239-240.

At a deeper level, another manifestation of the progression marks out the articulations of form in the first movement. This is highlighted by a short motto (comparable, for instance, to the 'fate motif' in Beethoven's Symphony No. 5). The motto appears three times in the first movement at different transpositions and at highly strategic points (see Ex. 3): in F minor in bb. 50-51, at the start of the exposition, in C-sharp minor in bb. 151-152, at the start of the development, and again in F minor in bb. 269-270, at the start of the recapitulation[14]. From this standpoint, the motto might be said to mark the expansion of the recurring third progression onto a deeper level, that is, onto the tonal pillars of the three major sonata form sections[15]. This expanded instance of the progression also occurs on significant pitches (F minor, D-flat/C-sharp minor, F minor)[16]: in a sense, this is the progression's most fundamental form, since the same notes can be found in the subordinate theme of the first movement when it recurs in the tonic during the recapitulation or when the progression appears in its repetitive guise at the end of the finale[17].

Ex. 3: Franck, Quintet, first movement, reduction.

---

[14]. In this instance, the harmonic motif is slightly altered, when the usual major form of the first and third chords are replaced by the minor form. The motto appears again near the end of the Quintet in bb. 427-428 of the finale, after the major climax that signals the end of the coda. This final occurrence has the same pitches as the one at the beginning of the recapitulation, however, and simply confirms the motto's final form.

[15]. This technique of creating «beginning – beginning associations» by using the same material at the onsets of different passages is described in ALEGANT – MCLEAN 2007, pp. 4-5.

[16]. This is a variant of the original progression (the same we saw earlier), where the major form of the first and third chords is replaced by the minor form.

[17]. In the latter two instances the progression reverts to original form, in which the F chord adopts a major third.

In more abstract terms, the triads underlying the keys of the Quintet's three movements — F minor, A minor, F major — could be regarded as an even more profound expansion of the harmonic motif. Strucken-Paland offers a slightly different interpretation that incorporates the key of D-flat major, which occurs at the heart of the slow movement and is signalled by the return of the cyclic theme[18]. Clearly, this harmonic motif repeatedly and pervasively regulates the harmonic and tonal parameters of the work as a whole. If the cyclic principle is defined as a fundamentally thematic phenomenon, however, then this aspect of the Quintet's cyclicism may well go unnoticed. D'Indy does not point out the structural role of the harmonic motif in his discussion of the Quintet; still, he makes clear elsewhere that the richest applications of the cyclic principle goes beyond mere thematic relationships in order to incorporate tonal organisation as well[19].

The technique of marking out sonata form sections, illustrated in Ex. 3 by the recurrence of the Quintet's motto, was already common during the Classical period and may be clearly heard in the works of the First Viennese School. Charles Rosen touches on this practice[20]. And indeed, prior to Franck's Quintet, one particularly striking example of a motto marking formal articulations occurs in the opening movement of Beethoven's Symphony No. 5, in which the famous 'fate' motif appears at the beginning of the exposition, development, and recapitulation of the first movement.

FRANCK'S QUINTET AND THE BEETHOVENIAN TRADITION: STYLISTIC CONSIDERATIONS

While articulating form through the recurrence of a motto constitutes a significant compositional technique that connects Franck to the Viennese and Beethovenian traditions, a deeper understanding of this connection may be had by turning our attention to the intertextual relationships between the Quintet and three other powerful and tempestuous works in the key of F minor. These are Beethoven's own Piano Sonata, Op. 57 (*Appassionata*) and two pieces by composers who followed in Beethoven's footsteps, namely Franz Liszt's *Funérailles* (the seventh piece in *Harmonies poétiques et religieuses*), and Johannes Brahms's Piano Quintet, Op. 34. Generally speaking, the stylistic attributes that make Franck's Quintet so robust and passionate also occur within these three pieces: expansive size, dense texture, and technical virtuosity[21].

---

18. STRUCKEN-PALAND 2009, p. 244.
19. D'INDY – SÉRIEYX 1909, p. 387 and D'INDY – SÉRIEYX 1933, p. 200.
20. ROSEN 1980.
21. TIERSOT 1917, p. 394; JARDILLIER 1929, pp. 89-90.

All four pieces, although *Funérailles* perhaps less so, also share another attribute, that is, pathos heightened to the extreme, underscored by brilliant climaxes and apotheoses[22].

Composed in 1864, the Brahms Quintet is about 42 minutes long. At more than 10 minutes longer than Schumann's 30-minute Quintet, Op. 44 (1842), and almost as long as Beethoven's colossal 44-minute *Hammerklavier* Sonata, Op. 106 (1819), the length of Brahms's piece stood out even at the time. Although all these works have four movements, Franck's Quintet only has three, and still runs about six minutes longer than Schumann's Op. 44[23]. The first movement of the Franck Quintet is also the longest of the four at 15 min 50 s; the opening movements of the Brahms Quintet, the *Hammerklavier*, and the Schumann Quintet run for 14 min 46 s, 11 min 17 s, and 8 min 37 s, respectively. The same trend holds true with respect to earlier French chamber works; Franck's Quintet is about 4 minutes longer than Saint-Saëns's 1855 Piano Quintet, Op. 14, which is also cyclic but has four rather than three movements[24].

The first and last movements of the Franck Quintet contain numerous climaxes and apotheoses, which are partly responsible for the work's overall heightened pathos and rich

---

[22]. Climaxes are one-off peaks of intensity, whereas apotheoses are peaks that last several bars. See MEYER 1989, p. 204.

[23]. Beethoven's Sonata Op. 106 (*Hammerklavier*) lasts 44 min 32 s on average, with performances ranging from 40 min 47 s to 52 min 44 s long (based on ten recordings from between 1991 and 2022 by pianists A. Schnabel, W. Backhaus, E. Gilels, S. Richter, R. Serkin, A. Brendel, V. Ashkenazy, M. Perahia, M. Uchida, and G. Sokolov). Schumann's Quintet lasts 29 min 19 s on average, with performances ranging from 27 min 53 s to 30 min 28 s long (based on ten recordings from between 1988 and 2017 by ensembles Pires, Dumay, R. Capuçon, Caussé, Jian Wang; Rubinstein, Paganini Quartet; R. Serkin, Budapest String Quartet; Zacharias, Cherubini Quartet; Vogt, Tetzlaff, Szulc, Masurenko, Rivinius; Ax, Cleveland Quartet; Argerich, Schwarzberg, R. Capuçon, Romanoff-Schwarzberg, Drobinsky; Bernstein, Juillard String Quartet; Hess, Stern, Schneider, Katims, Tortelier; and Malikova, Belenus Quartett). Brahms's Quintet lasts 41 min 52 s on average, with performances ranging from 37 min 7 s to 44 min 34 s long (based on ten recordings from between 1991 and 2022, with performers L. Fleisher, Emerson String Quartet; A. Rubinstein, Guarneri Quartet; B. Giltburg, Pavel Haas Quartet; L. Vogt, Eberle, Tetzlaff, Weinmeister, Steckel; S. Richter, Borodin Quartet; M. Pollini, Quartetto Italiano; E. Leonskaja, Alban Berg Quartet; A. Schiff, Takács Quartet; A. Yamamoto, Quatuor Ebene; G. Gould, Montreal String Quartet). Finally, Franck's Quintet lasts 35 min 20 s on average, with performances ranging from 30 min 48 s to 38 min 53 s long (based on ten recordings from between 1971 and 2020, with performers S. François, Quatuor Bernede; S. Richter, Borodin Quartet; P. Rogé, Ysaÿe String Quartet; J. Heifetz, I. Baker, W. Primrose, G. Piatigorsky, L. Pennario; Bingham, Medici String Quartet; M.-A. Hamelin, Bell, P. Frank, Nobuko Imai, Isserlis; Werner Bartschi, Amati Quartet; A. Cortot, International String Quartet; M. Dalberto, Novus String Quartet; W. Howard, Schubert Ensemble).

[24]. Saint-Saëns's Quintet lasts 31 min 17 s on average, with performances ranging from 29 min 25 s to 35 min 13 s long (based on ten recordings from between 1970 and 2021, with performers Cristina Ortiz, Fine Arts Quartet; Guillaume Bellom, Quatuor Girard; Andrea Lucchesini, Quartetto di Cremona; Ensemble musique Oblique; Pihtipudas Piano Quintet; Groupe Instrumental de Paris; Robin Wilson, Rachael Beesley, Simon Oswell, Daniel Yeadon, Neal Peres Da Costa; Bernardo Santos, Belem Quartet; Ian Brown, Marianne Thorsen, Benjamin Nabarro, Lawrence Power, Paul Watkins; Deniz Arman Gelenbe, Haydn Quartet).

instrumentation. In the first movement, during the development, two apotheoses highlight the return of material from the slow introduction, first in E minor (bb. 193-202) and then again in sequence, up a step to F-sharp minor (bb. 216-226). The strings play the melody in unison across three octaves, taking the first violin and cello into high, piercing registers while the piano adds breathless sixteenth-note and triplet figurations. The whole passage is *fff*. Lofty apotheoses such as these were not new within Franck's work; they often appeared in his earlier pieces, from the Trios to the oratorio *Les Béatitudes*. We will return to the topic of the musical parameters that contribute to the Quintet's climaxes and apotheoses, and highlight the role of one particular compositional technique which enhances their dramatic effect and which was in fact new within Franck's oeuvre.

Contemporary reactions reveal, and comparisons with contemporary repertoire confirm, that Franck's volcanic writing was in jarring contrast with the other French music of his time. For better or for worse, the Quintet's style attracted considerable notice. Liszt and Charles Bordes had reservations[25]. Léon Vallas, inspired by various reactions that he links in part to the intense fervour of the music, posits an amorous intrigue. He contends that the Quintet was an expression of Franck's feverish passion for his student Augusta Holmès (1847-1903), a striking and charming young composer. Holmès had already refused Saint-Saëns's hand in marriage, and according to Vallas, this backstory would explain both Félicité Franck's unfavourable opinion of her husband's piece and Saint-Saëns's irreverence towards the work even though it was dedicated to him, and even though he premiered the difficult piano part. At the conclusion of the concert, Saint-Saëns simply left the score cavalierly on the piano[26]. The grounds for Vallas's theory are somewhat shaky, and although the story is regarded with scepticism nowadays[27], it clearly illustrates the strong impression that the Quintet's impetuous passion left on its listeners. Two other mature, large-scale works by Franck also contain impassioned outbursts whose musical vigour is on par with the Quintet's: the operas *Hulda* (composed immediately after the Quintet) and *Ghiselle*. Premiered posthumously in Monte Carlo in 1894 and 1896 respectively, those works remain little-known today. Their violence was also met with condemnation at the time. Indeed, in this instance, far more so than for the Quintet, Franck's students and admirers considered the inspiration in these works to be less representative of Franck's true nature[28].

Although the Quintet had its detractors, as we have just seen, it was apparently quite well received by the general public. An anonymous author, likely one of Franck's students, says as much in his review of the premiere[29], and several subsequent articles hailed the Quintet as

---

25. Bréville 1935, p. 252; Bordes's opinion is described in Vallas 1955, p. 213.
26. This whole intrigue is recounted in *La véritable histoire de César Franck* (Vallas 1955, pp. 214-215).
27. Fauquet thoroughly dismantles Vallas's theory in Fauquet 1999, pp. 515-520.
28. *Ibidem*, pp. 769-774.
29. Anonymous, *Gazette musicale*, January 25, 1880, cited in Vallas 1955, p. 212.

one of Franck's greatest works, perhaps even the greatest[30]. The Quintet's obvious influence on Franck's student Ernest Chausson also speaks to its prestige[31]. Finally, the work commanded enough respect among the dignitaries of compositional officialdom to earn Franck the Prix Chartier in 1881; this prize was an annual distinction awarded by the Académie des Beaux-Arts to recognise significant contributions to the chamber music repertoire[32].

Laurence Davies and Joël-Marie Fauquet in greater depth, have already drawn parallels between the Franck and Brahms quintets[33]. Indeed, there is perhaps nothing in the piano quintet repertoire besides Brahms's Op. 34 that can compare to Franck's, at least in terms of length, rich texture, instrumental virtuosity, and heightened pathos; there are no suitable candidates among either earlier French works (such as the Saint-Saëns Quintet) or earlier German ones (such as Schumann's famous Op. 44). Fauquet also discusses Brahms's reception in late nineteenth-century France, and finds several indications that Franck may have encountered Brahms's piece[34]. Moreover, numerous studies have pointed to the striking formal and structural similarities between the Brahms Quintet and Beethoven's *Appassionata*[35]. The meaning and significance of these similarities between Franck and these earlier composers' works is beyond the scope of this essay[36].

The Franck Quintet may also be linked to its parallel Beethoven, Liszt, and Brahms pieces via comparison on other fronts. Take topical analysis, for example[37]. The opening measures of the Franck may be likened to a characteristic figure (see segment *x* in Ex. 4a, p. 86): their moderate tempi, duple metres, minor modes, and dotted rhythms all invoke the topos of the funeral march. This same topos also makes a striking appearance in the slow movement of Schumann's

---

[30]. COQUARD 1890, p. 16; DUKAS 1948, p. 37; BRUNEAU 1904, p. 2.

[31]. See MÉDICIS 2020, p. 437, Footnote 6 on the influence of Franck's Quintet within Chausson's Trio.

[32]. FAUQUET 1999, p. 528.

[33]. DAVIES 1970, p. 227; FAUQUET 1999, pp. 525-526.

[34]. FAUQUET 1986, pp. 162, 165, 171-172, 394-398, 412; FAUQUET 1999, pp. 385-386, 452-453.

[35]. FRISCH 1984, pp. 83-86; WEBSTER 1979, p. 68; SMITH 2005, pp. 143, 147, 150-153.

[36]. The *Appassionata*, the Brahms Quintet, and the Franck Quintet all contain effects wherein the boundaries of the recapitulation are strikingly blurred. In the first movements of both the *Appassionata* and the Brahms Quintet, the recapitulation begins with the main theme over a second-inversion tonic harmony, delaying the return of the root-position tonic. This separates thematic return from tonal return; see SMITH 1992, pp. 163-184. Similarly, in the third movement of the Franck Quintet, the main theme is recapitulated with the tonic harmony in second inversion (bb. 306 and following); the tonic is only truly re-established in m. 330. In the Quintet's first movement, however, the return of the tonic is anticipated rather than delayed. Most developments conclude with prolongations of the home-key dominant, but this one ends with a tonic pedal (bb. 234-245). The D-flat chord over this pedal, followed by the return of the tonic F chord at the beginning of the recapitulation (m. 271), creates a structural 6-5 movement over an F bass.

[37]. The study of musical topoi (or topics), which was inspired by the study of rhetoric, was first championed by RATNER 1980 and has remained a rich area for research; see MIRKA 2014, for example.

Piano Quintet, Op. 44. Within the parallel works considered here, however, Franck's funereal opening most closely resembles the opening theme of Liszt's *Funérailles*, which begins after the introduction in b. 24 (see melody *x* in Ex. 4d, p. 89). Both melodies descend almost identically and with similar rhythms from A-flat to C (and the *Funérailles* melody reappears later in the same register as Franck's). Liszt's piece lays clearly within the tradition of Chopin's *Marche funèbre* (which later became the slow movement of the Sonata in B-flat minor, Op. 35), with the contrast opposing the *x* material in the minor mode and the melancholy *y* material in the relative major. Moreover, the *y* material has a Chopinesque vocal line in the right hand, accompanied by widely spaced arpeggios that occasionally straddle the melodic line (see Ex. 4d)[38]. But Liszt distinguishes his piece from Chopin's by adding the *z* material (also shown in Ex. 4d): a heroic fanfare in the right hand with driving triplets in the left, more in line with the Beethovenian manner of the *Marcia funebre* from the Symphony No. 3, *Eroica*[39]. Franck's first movement also contrasts funeral march material (*x*) with a melancholy Chopinesque theme (*y*), in the form of a plaintive melody with very broad arpeggios (see Ex. 4a). Finally, during the finale, Franck breaks with the mournfulness of the first two movements by introducing *z* material in the same *topos* as Liszt's: a major-mode fanfare in the strings, accompanied by a galloping horseback ride figure from the piano[40].

The Franck, the Beethoven, and the Brahms all begin with the juxtaposition of two contrasting ideas that are then developed through fragments of decreasing length. In the *Appassionata* (Ex. 4b, p. 87), the alternation is relatively compact and concentrated within the main theme (bb. 1-16)[41]. First comes the *x* material, which monophonically outlines a widely spaced arpeggio; this then contrasts with the *y* material, a very tightly-spaced melody accompanied by block chords. This ceremonious, double-dotted opening recalls the style of the French overture, a *topos* frequently invoked at the beginning of classical sonatas, within

---

[38]. In Chopin's march (Op. 35), the melancholy major-mode passage occurs in bb. 31-55.

[39]. The funeral march from Beethoven's Symphony No. 3 illustrates the same three topics as Liszt's *Funérailles*. The first two, the funeral march and the expressive melody in major mode, are associated with the main two sections (section 1 in bb. 1-68, 105-157 and 173-247, and section 2, the *Maggiore*, in bb. 69-104). Dotted rhythms and fanfares add a touch of heroism and grandeur in the *Maggiore* section (bb. 76-79, 91-101); but a digression at the end of the developmental passage in bb. 158-172 announces more directly Liszt's *z* material, when a powerful fanfare is accompanied by running sixteenth triplets. The slow movement from Schumann's Piano Quintet Op. 44 (*In Modo d'una Marcia*) adopts a similar organisation. Following the first two topics, the third, animated one, adopts passionate and tragic accents instead of the heroic tone. (Section 1 is presented in bb. 1-29, 62-91 and 165-193; section 2 in bb. 30-61, 133-164; section 3, bb. 92-109; and a hybrid section that combines the themes from sections 1 and 3, in bb. 110-132.)

[40]. See Médicis 2020, p. 183 (including note 121) on Wagner's influence and the use of horseback-riding figures in works by the composers of Franck's circle.

[41]. Stefan Keym considers Beethoven's *Appassionata* Sonata an important precursor for the opposition of cyclic ideas found in Franck's music. See Keym 2004, p. 122.

Ex. 4a: Franck, Quintet, first movement, bb. 1-9, and third movement, bb. 73-76.

86

Ex. 4b: Beethoven, Sonata Op. 57 (*Appassionata*), first movement, bb. 1-13.

Ex. 4c: Brahms, Quintet, Op. 34, first movement, bb. 1-8.

THE FRANCK QUINTET

Ex. 4d: Liszt, *Funérailles*, bb. 24-29, 57-60, 110-115.

68

slow introductions especially. Beethoven uses similar contrasts in other minor-mode works to great dramatic effect[42].

The opening contrasts of the Franck and Brahms quintets are more expansive and thus more in line with Beethoven's works, such as the *Egmont* overture, Op. 84, or the slow movement of the Piano Concerto No. 4, Op. 58 (which Franck appears to echo closely at the beginning of his *Variations symphoniques*)[43]. The Brahms Quintet, like the *Appassionata*, contrasts the monophonic texture of its x material with the harmonised texture of its y material, at least in their initial forms; however, the opposition continues beyond the first eight bars shown in Ex. 4c (p. 88)[44]. In the Franck, both x and y are harmonised, but x has block chords while y has arpeggios (see Ex. 4a for the first instance of the contrast)[45]. Rhythm, dynamics, and instrumentation also heighten the contrast between x and y in both Franck and Brahms. In Franck's Quintet, x has dotted rhythms and is played *fortissimo* by the strings, whereas the fluid rhythms of y are played quietly by the piano[46]. The effect in Brahms's Quintet is almost the complete opposite: x is given softly, in unison tutti, with fluid rhythms, whereas y is played *forte*, with separate piano and string parts, and sudden rhythmic interruptions that create dramatic silences.

The shock generated by these contrasts builds anticipation, providing a sudden shearing force of sorts, like the pull-start on an engine, strongly driving the intensification to a climax. For Beethoven and Franck, these climaxes consist of extended sixteenth-note flourishes in the piano that occur towards the end of their respective structural units: the main theme in the *Appassionata* (bb. 14-15) and the slow introduction in the Quintet (bb. 48-49). The Quintet's slow introduction also ends with an acceleration that builds to the tempo of the Allegro and

---

[42]. Classical composers before Beethoven also used this contrasting-ideas technique to begin their minor-mode works. See for example Mozart's Violin Sonata in E minor, K. 304, Piano Sonata in C minor, K. 457, and Piano Quartet in C minor, K. 478. Here, however, I posit that nineteenth-century composers were primarily influenced by the oppositions found in Beethoven.

[43]. A number of authors have pointed out the similarity between Beethoven's Piano Concerto, Op. 58 and Franck's *Variations symphoniques*. See for example DAVIES 1970, p. 223. Many of Franck's initial themes (or opening measures) contrast monophonic musical ideas with harmonised ones; examples include the organ *Fantaisie*, Op. 16, *Rébecca*, and the 'Introduction' in *Rédemption, poème-symphonie*. But such contrasts do not normally suggest a reference to Beethoven, except in the case of the *Variations symphoniques*.

[44]. The first y continues until m. 11; x is reprised in bb. 12-17; and in bb. 18-22, a new version of y suggests a combination of the two ideas in diminution and close imitation, thus liquidating the material. The characteristic descending second of the y material dominates the cadence at m. 22 and generates the beginning of the transition in m. 23.

[45]. In the score, beyond Ex. 4a, the first y continues until m. 13; in the contrasts that follow, y's presence gradually diminishes in bb. 19-26, 40-41, and 43-44, allowing x to dominate the motto and the main theme (bb. 50-51 and 52-74).

[46]. STRUCKEN-PALAND 2009, pp. 254-257, discusses these contrast effects in Franck's Quintet.

merges into it without interruption. This is a typically Beethovenian tactic that appears, for example, in the *Egmont* overture, alongside the juxtaposition of contrasting ideas. Other Beethoven heirs also deployed acceleration to transition out of slow sections, as Schumann does in the opening movement of his Symphony No. 1, Op. 38, *Frühlingssinfonie*.

At the beginning of Franck's Quintet, x and y are part of a more specific formal procedure that I described in a previous study as, «development through dialectical opposition»:

> In its basic and more conventional form, this development consists of two differing musical ideas that are first contrasted with each other, then developed in tandem as the underlying tension grows (driven by factors such as increasing rhythmic energy, acceleration, higher registers, crescendi, and fragmentation). In its more developed and characteristic form, the development may have various outcomes: one idea might triumph over the other, or the conflict might be resolved by combining the two ideas. [...] This procedure was key for both Franck's arsenal of formal techniques and the broader French instrumental tradition of the late nineteenth century[47].

In the Quintet, the opposition between x and y becomes more intense as Franck alternates between increasingly short fragments in bb. 38-49, and the conflict is resolved at the beginning of the exposition (b. 50) only when y is completely eliminated, overcome by the typically x-like dotted material.

Ex. 5 shows another, shorter instance of this dialectical development technique in the Quintet. In this passage (bb. 259-271), Franck demonstrates his skill in coupling form with dramatic effect. Here, the ideas that produce the contrast are associated with significant formal elements: the motto, with dotted rhythms scored in octaves for the piano, and the beginning of the subordinate theme, with flowing rhythms played in octaves by the strings. After a dramatic pause, the two ideas are sequenced up a third (bb. 263-266), creating an intensification that leads to the shortening and alternation of ideas within a single measure (b. 267 and b. 268), heightening the tension even further. Finally, the motto, now sounding in all the instruments, 'defeats' and replaces the lyrical subordinate theme material (bb. 269-270). And, in a *tour de force*, this final instance of the motto arrives at the same transposition level as the instance that began the exposition, paving the way for the recapitulation of the main theme.

---

[47]. «Dans sa forme simple et relativement conventionnelle, deux idées musicales de caractères différents sont d'abord présentées en opposition, avant de faire l'objet d'un développement coordonné, sous-tendu par un accroissement de tension (résultant de facteurs tels que l'animation rythmique, l'accélération du tempo, une progression ascendante dans les registres, un crescendo ou de la fragmentation). Dans ses manifestations plus développées et plus caractéristiques, la lutte peut aboutir à différentes issues, comme la victoire d'une des idées sur l'autre, ou une forme de conciliation par la combinaison des deux idées. [...] Ce procédé constitue un outil important dans l'arsenal des techniques formelles franckistes et dans la tradition instrumentale française de la fin de siècle». MÉDICIS 2020, p. 419. Translation from the French original by Ariadne Lih.

Ex. 5: Franck, Quintet, first movement, bb. 259-271.

The first and final movements of Franck's Quintet both contain ongoing series of dramatic escalations wherein the intensification of various musical parameters leads to powerful climaxes or apotheoses. In the first movement, such escalations occur in the slow introduction (twice, at bb. 1-37 and 40-49), the main theme (bb. 52-64), the transition (bb. 74-103), the development (three times, at bb. 169-202, 203-225 and 242-270), and the coda — the beginning of which overlaps with the recapitulation of the subordinate theme (bb. 331-428). The apotheoses mentioned above (bb. 193-203 and 216-226), for instance, are part of major variations in tension during the development. These variations unfold in two rising waves, both of which begin at a very quiet dynamic level (*pp* and *molto dolce*) and conclude ***fff***. In terms of grouping structure, the preparation before the first peak begins with a five-bar grouping that is repeated sequentially (model bb. 169-173, sequence bb. 174-178). This unit is then fragmented into one-bar segments, beginning with a sequence (model b. 179, sequence b. 180). Finally, an expansion into two-bar groupings (bb. 185-186, 187-188, 189-190, and 191-192) leads into the first apotheosis (bb. 193-202). The second wave is more compact, beginning with four-bar groupings (bb. 203-206 and 207-210) that are then fragmented into increasingly shorter groupings from one to only a quarter of a bar. Finally, a brief expansion into one-bar groupings (bb. 214-215) leads into the second apotheosis (bb. 216-226). Parameters other than dynamics and grouping also contribute to these powerful passages of escalating tension: for example, during the two build-up phases, the melody gradually rises with a concomitant registral spread between melody and bass, with the highest point and greatest spread occurring during the apotheoses.

The instance of development through dialectical opposition shown in Ex. 5 underpins the development's third and more expansive build-up of tension (bb. 242-268). This longer passage provides a concrete example of how Franck coordinates various musical parameters to create his characteristic variations in tension. Dynamic levels gradually rise from ***ppp*** to ***fff***; rhythmic figures accelerate from continuous eighth notes to sixteenth notes (starting in b. 254); the ensemble begins with a very wide ambitus (F_{ii} in the piano's low register and f^{ii} in the first violin), which gradually converges onto the medium-low register of the motto during the climax (bb. 269-270). At the same time, the register of initially very wide-ranging melodic lines becomes increasingly condensed. Finally, groupings become shorter and shorter, from four-bar (bb. 242-245 and 246-249) to two-bar (b. 250-251, 252-253, 254-255 and 256-257) to one-bar units (b. 258). A brief return to four-bar groupings (bb. 259-262 and 263-266), each followed by a dramatic pause, creates a kind of respite or momentary plateau, followed finally by two, one-bar groupings (b. 267 and 268) that lead into the b. 269 climax.

Continuously high dramatic tension is one of the Quintet's distinctive features, made clear in its initial reception (see above). The various musical parameters we have observed that contribute to the intensification processes before peaks of intensity more than likely nourished that contemporary critical reaction. Among them, however, the technique of fragmentation in grouping structure is one of the most tangible markers of the stylistic watershed that occurs with the Quintet. This may be confirmed by comparing the Quintet to earlier works by Franck: the Trios, as examples of other large-scale chamber works, and *Les Béatitudes*, as an example of major works in other genres. We will return to these works at the end of this essay.

Another aspect of the Quintet that ties directly into Beethoven's legacy is its overall narrative trajectory. Several of Beethoven's tragic creations follow the so-called *per aspera ad astra* narrative trajectory, which encompasses all the movements. This narrative arc begins with minor-mode turbulence that gives rise to heroic struggle, but the tables eventually turn, and the piece ends with a glorious and resounding victory[48]. I would argue, however, that in at least one Beethoven piece, which would later give rise to a lesser-known tradition, the struggle against adversity has the opposite outcome. The *Appassionata* ends not only in defeat but in a kind of 'race to the abyss', as if the hero, spurred on by a sense of either sacrifice or self-destruction, were rushing ever more quickly towards his demise. These two types of trajectories are achieved through various musical means, which I will briefly mention here and discuss more concretely later in this essay. The path to victory is navigated through modal progression (minor to major) while the road to defeat is paved with modal invariance (minor to an even more implacable minor). Both types make use of transitions without pause between movements (emphasising continuity beyond internal movement structures); *topoi*, such as the funeral march and the triumphant fanfare; gradual rhythmic or tempo acceleration; and thematic transformation. Following this logic, Beethoven's Fifth and Ninth Symphonies may be considered examples of the *per aspera ad astra* trajectory while the *Appassionata* constitutes a race to the abyss. Single-movement works at times also encompass such narratives: the *Egmont* overture, for example, seems to portray a triumphant battle against grim fate. All the works involved in our intertextual comparison draw on these dramatic patterns to some extent. Although the end of *Funérailles* could be interpreted in various ways, the main sections of the piece (introduction, funeral march, lyrical section, hero's ride) clearly follow a positive trajectory towards affirmation and celebration. The final movements of the Beethoven and the Brahms, on the other hand, are examples of the race to the abyss.

Different elements of narrative strategy within Franck's Quintet echo different works in our comparison. Taken together, the three movements follow the *per aspera ad astra* narrative arc; the finale's horseback ride figure and breathless ostinato rhythm are not unlike the third section of *Funérailles*. In the same movement, however, Franck skilfully integrates his triumphant affirmation into a less straightforward trajectory than, say, the one in Beethoven's Fifth. Rather than proclaiming victory once and for all, Franck's fanfare must withstand several

---

48.   BRODBECK 1997, p. 2 and pp. 31-33; KEYM 2004, pp. 116-120; STRUCKEN-PALAND 2009, pp. 243-246, for this trajectory in the Franck Quintet.

more assaults once presented, and only triumphs over its assailants at the very end[49]. Likewise, back in the first movement, there is a climatic build-up of nervous energy in the coda, featuring several increases in tempo. And yet, at the last moment, a more peaceful atmosphere returns and creates a kind of respite. As we shall see, the coda's emotional arc and some of its pianistic features closely resemble the corresponding section in Beethoven's *Appassionata*.

The Franck Quintet and the Beethovenian Tradition: Historiographies

The stylistic similarities documented in the previous section raise important questions about Franck's relationship to the Beethovenian instrumental tradition. Vincent d'Indy's historiographical discourse on this topic remains the most thorough one available, even now. Recent studies have delved into the breadth and complexity of thought in d'Indy's writings, highlighting their importance in his time as well as their influence into the present day. These studies have also revealed prejudices within d'Indy's works that, in some cases, compromise their accuracy or impartiality[50]. D'Indy's assertions about Franck's relationship to the Beethovenian tradition, however, have not always been subject to thorough critical analysis. What follows is a critical revaluation of d'Indy's claims, in order to determine which elements hold true and which ones require greater nuance or correction.

---

[49]. The third movement of the Franck Quintet is in sonata form and contrasts the main theme material (bb. 73-118) with the transition and subordinate theme materials (bb. 119-146 and 147-198). The main theme material is spirited, triumphant, and in the major mode, with a melody featuring steadily rising arpeggios; the material from the transition and subordinate theme is more restrained, melancholy, and in the minor mode (or major and then minor for the subordinate theme), with a melody featuring steadily descending arpeggios. The subordinate theme also contains an ominous drumroll (see the repeated eighth notes in the pickups to m. 148, 152, and so on); this cyclic element, which is borrowed from the Quintet's slow movement and more generally from *Funérailles* or the funeral march in Beethoven's *Eroica*, gives the whole theme a sepulchral feeling. At the beginning of the development (bb. 199-230), the dialectical opposition between the major-mode main theme material and the minor-mode transition material leads to the temporary dominance of the minor-mode material (bb. 231-254). Then, during a long minor-mode section, the main theme material attempts to regain dominance (bb. 255-278), but the return to major presents the subordinate theme material first (bb. 279-305); finally, the main theme reappears as an apotheosis to usher in the recapitulation. The coda (bb. 400-528) is vast and continues the opposition between major and minor, incorporating the cyclic theme from the first movement as well. The Quintet ends in the victorious F major tonic (bb. 516-528), but ornamental notes borrowed from minor remain, like the scars from a bitter struggle. The whole finale contrasts descending minor-mode material with ascending major-mode material; this opposition, concentrated within a single movement, recalls the narrative arc of the *Egmont* overture.

[50]. Groth 1983, pp. 198-205; Campos – Donin 2005; Ellis 2006; Fauser 2006; Suchowiejko 2006; Campos 2013; Cathé 2020.

Vincent d'Indy wrote about Franck in many of his articles[51], as well as two of his large-scale works: the 1906 monograph *César Franck* and the *Cours de composition musicale*, specifically book two (two volumes published in 1909 and 1933) and book three (published in 1950), the latter two instalments being posthumous[52]. It would be reasonable enough for d'Indy to assert in these works that Franck's cyclic writing was indebted to Beethoven's, if not wholly then at least in part. But he goes much further. For example, in a 1903 article for *The Weekly Critical Review*, d'Indy wrote:

> The missing link in the chain connecting the grand methods of Beethoven to modern art — a link that none of the Germans could successfully form, and which perhaps only Liszt foresaw, without truly discerning its form — the work called upon to forge this link was the work of which I spoke earlier, the *Trio in F-sharp*[53].

This excerpt touches on a number of the recurring ideas in d'Indy's historiographical discourse on Franck. In 1904, for instance, he used almost exactly the same sentence as part of his speech to inaugurate a monument to César Franck[54]. His *César Franck* and *Cours de composition musicale* would later complete these ideas and expand upon them at length. Four main theses arise from these two texts:

1. The cyclic writing in Franck's Trio No. 1 was the basis for the cyclic writing that manifested 37 years later in the Quintet, and in Franck's other cyclic works as well;

2. Franck's cyclic writing in the First Trio and the Quintet continues not only the legacy of Beethovenian cyclicism but more specifically the compositional legacy of works from Beethoven's third period (1816-1827)[55];

3. Franck does not merely take up Beethoven's legacy. Instead, he develops it further;

4. Franck undertook this process in isolation, while other composers, French and German alike, remained blind to the same resources.

The first thesis is highly questionable. There are certainly elements of continuity between the First Trio and the Quintet, but the stylistic differences between them are difficult to ignore,

---

[51]. Most of which are reproduced in D'INDY 2019 and INDY 2021.

[52]. D'INDY – SÉRIEYX 1909 is book two, volume one; D'INDY – SÉRIEYX 1933 is book two, volume two (posthumous); D'INDY – LIONCOURT 1950 is book three (posthumous).

[53]. «Le point de suture entre la grande manière de Beethoven et l'art moderne, point que nul Allemand n'avait su effectuer et que, seul peut-être, Liszt avait entrevu sans lui donner de forme réelle, c'est le *trio en fa dièze* dont j'ai parlé plus haut qui était appelé à l'opérer». INDY 1903, reproduced in D'INDY 2019, pp. 562-563.

[54]. D'INDY 2021, p. 95.

[55]. This is d'Indy's own periodisation; see D'INDY 2019, p. 570.

given how much Franck's writing had matured by the time he wrote the Quintet, nearly four decades later. D'Indy was well aware of this and, in his 1906 book, readily acknowledges the weaknesses of Franck's early works. In his chapter on Franck's first period, he writes,

> [...] although Franck's first manner presents some extremely interesting particularities, it was far from foretelling all the grandeur, novelty, and sublimity that the master's art was eventually to bring forth[56].

D'Indy grants that, during these early years, Franck did not yet understand the «art of composition»; that he wrote pieces with no modulation whatsoever, which too often made his work regrettably monotonous. He further concedes that his approach to musical structure betrayed a surprising timidity[57]. This general assessment applies to all the works from the first period (1841-1858), including three of the four trios, but the First Trio appears to be an exception. D'Indy becomes suddenly indulgent whenever he discusses this work and even showers it with unexpected praise. Although he observes that only the final movement contains any modulation at all (!), he expresses admiration for the quality of the work's structure and cyclic writing, and links it to the tradition of Beethoven's last works. The only elements cited as grounds for this relationship are its cyclicism and the structure of its second movement, which «presents the type of the great *Scherzo* form, with two *Trios*, and follows step by step in the tracks of Beethoven's tenth and fourteenth quartets»[58]. Note that, according to d'Indy's periodisation[59], only the String Quartet No. 14 belongs to Beethoven's third period (1816-1827); the String Quartet No. 10, composed in 1809, falls into the second. I would add that many other second-period works use this same structure: the scherzi in Symphonies No. 4, 6, 7, and 8, for example, and the String Quartet, Op. 59 No. 2.

D'Indy seems aware that there is an element of exaggeration in this claim. At the very least, he makes a point of softening it on several occasions. The *Cours de composition* contains an analysis of the First Trio; although there is one passage taken verbatim from the 1906 monograph, the discussion also incorporates new reflections that recognise the immaturity of Franck's juvenilia in comparison with his later works:

---

56. D'INDY 1910, p. 104 (translation). «[...] [T]out en présentant certaines particularités infiniment intéressantes, fut loin de laisser présager tout ce que l'art du maître était appelé à produire par la suite de grand, de neuf, de sublime». D'INDY 1906, p. 81.

57. D'INDY 1910, pp. 119-120 and p. 105 (translation). D'INDY 1906, p. 97 and 81 for the original.

58. D'INDY 1910, p. 108 (translation). «[P]résente le type du *grand scherzo* à deux trios et suit pas à pas le tracé beethovénien des Xᵉ et XIVᵉ quatuors». D'INDY 1906, p. 84.

59. D'INDY 2019, pp. 569-570.

> Doubtless, the intrinsic quality of these themes was still far from foretelling the future mastery of the author of the *Quintet*, which we are about to examine; but already, Franck's assimilation of the construction principles applied by Beethoven in his last Quartets had reached a depth unknown to any of his predecessors and even to the majority of his contemporaries[60].

D'Indy also displays similar caution elsewhere in his writing, recognising the «naiveté» of the First Trio's cyclicism or emphasising the «very high degree of perfection» that separates the cyclicism of the final works from that of the first opus[61].

Despite d'Indy's insistence that the First Trio has an exclusive claim to the lineage of Beethovenian cyclicism, musicologists now generally agree that many of Beethoven's nineteenth-century successors also followed in his footsteps with respect to cyclic writing. According to Michael Puri, «It is mistaken and chauvinistic of [d'Indy] to exclude from this history [of cyclic form] the German composers — particularly Mendelssohn, Robert Schumann, and Brahms — who incorporated cyclicism into so many of their pieces»[62]. Surveying d'Indy's works reveals that he was indeed familiar with the cyclic achievements of Berlioz, Liszt, and Brahms[63]. As Renate Groth points out, however, within the consecrated genres — the sonata, the symphony, and the string quartet — d'Indy condemns these cyclic achievements for taking liberties with Beethovenian formal conventions, presumably with respect to formal layout and tonal organisation[64].

For example, d'Indy readily acknowledges the 'genius' of Berlioz and makes note of his experiments with cyclic writing in the 1830 *Symphonie fantastique*. This work predates Franck's

---

[60].   «Sans doute, la qualité intrinsèque de ces thèmes est encore bien loin de faire présager la maîtrise future de l'auteur du *Quintette* que nous allons examiner; mais l'assimilation des principes de construction appliqués par Beethoven dans ses derniers Quatuors atteint déjà, chez Franck, une profondeur insoupçonnée de tous ses devanciers et même d'un grand nombre de ses contemporains». D'INDY – SÉRIEYX 1933, pp. 199-200.

[61].   D'INDY 1922, p. xii, on Trio No. 1: «This is in fact the earliest work to plainly, one might say naively, establish, based on the principle laid down by Beethoven in his last quartets, the great *cyclic form*, which no musician since the composer of the Ninth Symphony had been able or dared to use». D'INDY 1923, p. 4: «This work was conceived in a form that the masters of the time did not employ. Through this work, César Franck introduced cyclic composition, which he later perfected to a very high degree of perfection». My translation. The two original quotations are: «Cette œuvre, en effet, est la première en date qui, partant du principe posé par Beethoven en ses derniers quatuors, établisse franchement, on pourrait dire naïvement, la grande *forme cyclique*, que nul musicien, depuis l'auteur de la IXe Symphonie, n'avait su ou osé employer». And: «Cette œuvre est conçue dans une forme que les maîtres de cette époque n'ont pas pratiquée. Par elle, César Franck inaugure la composition cyclique qu'il poussera plus tard a un très haut degré de perfection».

[62].   PURI 2011, p. 32.

[63].   For Brahms cyclicism, see D'INDY 1906, p. 63 and D'INDY – SÉRIEYX 1909, p. 418. D'Indy's comments on Liszt and Berlioz are discussed below.

[64].   GROTH 1983, pp. 202-204.

First Trio, but according to d'Indy, it «could not be any less like a symphony»[65]. Although d'Indy touches upon a large sample of Western works within the *Cours de composition musicale*, from the Middle Ages to the early twentieth century, he bases his historical outlook essentially on compositional models by a handful of canonical composers: Monteverdi, Bach, Beethoven, Wagner, Franck. He then defines form based on the conventions that seeded Franck's later works, borrowed from Beethoven, which creates circular reasoning: Franck's contemporaries made attempts at cyclic writing, but they shared an understanding of form that differed from the one later espoused by Franck, and for this reason they are deemed illegitimate. This applies not only to Berlioz but to other Romantics whose output includes the major Beethovenian instrumental genres and in whom d'Indy saw comparable shortcomings: Schubert, Schumann, and Brahms for example (again, as pointed out by Groth)[66]. But Franck's First Trio does not yet adhere to Beethovenian formal and tonal conventions either (the absence of modulation in the first three movements alone testifies to this).

Also excluded from d'Indy's discussions of cyclic organisation are works associated with the fantasy genre. For example, when discussing Liszt's *Après une lecture de Dante, Fantasia quasi Sonata* (composed in 1837, then revised and published in 1856 as part of the second volume of *Années de pèlerinage*), d'Indy explains:

> Franz Liszt published a kind of *Dramatic fantasy* for piano in 1837 [*recte* 1856], built upon a single theme and entitled *Sonata*; but this piece, which has none of the unique characteristics of the Sonata form, as it has been described and studied here, does not belong to the *cyclic* genre and will be examined in our chapter devoted to the Symphonic Poem and the Fantasy[67].

D'Indy adds key details about the fantasy and symphonic poem genres as part of his commentary on *variation amplificatrice*. When considering this technique in Franck's music, he writes:

> Between [cyclic writing] and Variation, the affinities are such that it is hardly possible to delineate their respective natures: the *Cyclic theme* that is transformed

---

[65]. In the French original, d'Indy recognizes that Berlioz is a «génie» but that the *Fantastique* «n'est rien moins qu'une symphonie» 'Discours de M. Vincent d'Indy', in: *Le Monde musical* (1904), reproduced in D'INDY 2021, p. 95.

[66]. Schumann, for instance, uses cyclic writing in his Quintet, Op. 44 (completed the same year as the Franck Trio) and his Symphony No. 4, Op. 120; Liszt uses cyclicism in his *Faust-Symphonie*.

[67]. «Franz Liszt publia en 1837 [*recte* 1856] une sorte de *Fantaisie dramatique* pour piano, construite sur un seul thème et intitulée *Sonate*; mais cette œuvre, qui n'a aucun des caractères propres à la forme Sonate, telle que nous l'avons décrite et étudiée, n'appartient pas au genre *cyclique* et sera examinée dans le chapitre consacré au Poème Symphonique et à la Fantaisie [...]». All translations from the *Cours de composition* are mine. D'INDY – SÉRIEYX 1909, p. 422, note 1. D'Indy does not in fact later examine Liszt's piece.

is in fact *varied* or even *amplified*; while the *Variation* that circulates between the component parts of a piece, ipso facto, serves a *cyclic* function[68].

D'Indy cites a generous sample of works by composers other than Franck, for once, in the process of establishing this intimate relationship between variation and cyclicism. In his view, the «return of the *leitmotif*» in Wagner, from *Tannhäuser* (1845) and *Lohengrin* (1850) onwards, all the way to:

> [...] certain dispositions used by Liszt in *Tasso* (1849), in the *Faust-Symphonie* and in the piano piece entitled *Sonate* (1853), might well also be described as Variations. But these applications, which incidentally postdate César Franck's *Trio* in F[-sharp], cited below (p. 422), do not constitute separate forms [...] indeed, they are not separable: for this reason, they are cited here for the record only, and we will reserve the possibility of returning to them, if necessary, later in this *Course*[69].

Although d'Indy recognises cyclic usage within these works, he seems to assign them to a different category from Franck's achievements based on the fact that they do not have separate movements; this is indeed true for practically all the works mentioned, except for the *Faust-Symphonie*. The *Cours de composition* section on fantasies and symphonic poems adds other elements to the definition that more clearly define the specificities of the two genres and distinguish them from the cyclic sonata. According to d'Indy, the basic principle of a symphonic poem lays in the, «[...] subordination of the music to an external idea (pictorial, poetic, literary)». Although this principle is «[...] as old as music itself, [...] if there were one era that proved exceptionally conducive to the emergence of these works that 'bypass the normal laws of composition', that era would most certainly be the Romantic era»[70]. D'Indy distinguishes between Beethoven's overtures, which continue to adhere to the rules of abstract composition, and the new genre that emerged afterwards.

---

68.   «Entre [l'écriture cyclique] et la Variation, il y a de telles affinités qu'un délimitation respective n'est guère possible: le *Thème cyclique* qui se transforme est véritablement *varié* ou même *amplifié*: la *Variation* qui circule dans les pièces constitutives d'une œuvre a, par cela même, une fonction *cyclique*». d'Indy – Sérieyx, 1909, p. 487.

69.   For d'Indy, the «rappel des *motifs conducteurs*» in Wagner, from *Tannhäuser* (1845) and *Lohengrin* (1850) onwards, all the way to «[...] certaines dispositions employées par Liszt dans Tasso (1849), dans la Faust-Symphonie et dans la pièce pour piano intitulée Sonate (1853) pourraient aussi bien être qualifiés de Variations. Mais ces applications, d'ailleurs postérieures en date au *Trio*, en *fa*[♯], de César Franck cité ci-dessus (p. 422) ne constituent point des formes séparées [...] ni même séparables: c'est pourquoi nous ne les citons ici que pour mémoire, nous réservant d'y revenir, s'il y a lieu, dans la suite de ce *Cours*». *Ibidem*, pp. 486-487.

70.   According to d'Indy, the basic principle of a symphonic poem lays in the «subordination de la musique à une idée étrangère (pittoresque, poétique, littéraire)». Although this principle is «aussi ancien que la musique elle-même [...] s'il y eut une époque particulièrement propice à l'éclosion de ces œuvres "échappant aux lois normales de la composition", ce fut à coup sûr l'époque du Romantisme». d'Indy – Sérieyx 1933, p. 314.

> Thereafter, [within the Symphonic Poem,] the symphonic equilibrium was disrupted, shifting the balance in favour of the poetic program, expressed or understood to varying degrees of clarity, that is, shifting the balance often to the detriment of composition strictly speaking. Just as the spectator cannot fully understand the Lyric Drama without attending the performance, that is, without witnessing the action upon which the music commentates, the listener cannot fully penetrate the meaning of the symphonic poem without, in addition, knowing something besides the music[71].

For d'Indy, works that fall under the heading of fantasy can be folded in with the symphonic poem because they, too, bypass the rules of composition:

> In any event, these fairly disparate works, whose thematic and tonal order can be justified by nothing except an extra-musical idea, expressed or unexpressed, for this very reason invoke the *Symphonic Poem* type, insofar as one may call such an indeterminate composition a «type»[72].

Franck's 1863 *Grande pièce symphonique* for organ, Op. 17, elicits comments from d'Indy that are highly revealing with respect to this imposed gulf between the fantasy and the cyclic sonata. This organ work occupies a position about halfway between the First Trio and the Quintet, both chronologically and in terms of compositional maturity, and is one of the few works from this middle period of Franck's career cast in sonata form[73]. Unlike the composer's early works, the *Grande pièce* contains abundant and fluid modulation, softening the edges of the work's foursquare framework and enhancing its musical language with the help of harmonic colour changes. Furthermore, whereas the Trio and the Quintet have independent movements, the *Grande pièce* adopts one unified form with movements that are played *attaccati*, culminating in a final-movement fugue. Similar structures can be found in two Schubert pieces that end in fugues, the *Wandererfantasie* for piano, D. 760, and the Fantasy for piano duet, D. 940, as well as in some of Liszt's symphonic poems[74]. The structural parallels with two of Liszt's organ works are perhaps even more immediately obvious, simply by virtue of instrumentation; these

---

[71]. «Désormais, [dans le Poème symphonique,] l'équilibre symphonique sera rompu en faveur du programme poétique, plus ou moins nettement exprimé ou connu, c'est-à-dire le plus souvent au détriment de la composition proprement dite. De même que le spectateur ne peut comprendre entièrement le Drame lyrique sans assister à sa représentation, c'est-à-dire à l'action dont la musique est le commentaire, ainsi, l'auditeur du *Poème Symphonique* n'en peut pénétrer le sens s'il ne connaît pas, par ailleurs, autre chose que sa musique». *Ibidem*, p. 298.

[72]. «Quoi qu'il en soit, ces œuvres assez disparates, dont l'ordre thématique et tonal ne peut se justifier par rien, sinon par une idée extra-musicale exprimée ou non, se réclament, pour ce motif même, du *Poème Symphonique*, dans la mesure où l'on peut appeler "type" une composition aussi indéterminée». *Ibidem*, p. 300.

[73]. The others are two of the *Six pièces* for organ: *Prière*, Op. 20, and *Final*, Op. 21.

[74]. VANDE MOORTELE 2009.

two works are the *Praeludium und Fuge über den Namen B-A-C-H* (composed 1855, published 1856, revised 1870) and especially the *Fantasie und Fuge über den Choral Ad nos, ad salutarem undam* (composed 1850, published 1852), for which Franck owned the score[75].

Towards the end of the *Grande pièce*, Franck includes a passage that quotes fragments of themes from earlier movements (bb. 423-471), followed by the final section and the brilliant return of the first cyclic theme. This technique appears to be directly inspired by the beginning of the final movement in Beethoven's Ninth Symphony, Op. 125 (and the same effect appears in the finale of Franck's String Quartet). In this respect, the work does indeed refer to something from Beethoven's third period. But the Ninth is sort of an exception among Beethoven's late works, because of its enthusiastic reception throughout the nineteenth century (as opposed to the hostility or indifference that greeted the final quartets for most of that era)[76].

Despite the features that seem to tie the *Grande pièce* into the tradition of the Romantic fantasy, d'Indy compares the piece to a true symphony[77]. It is subjected to a brief analysis in the *Cours de composition musicale* chapter on the cyclic sonata, and the joined movements are said to «adhere to the usage of the ancient Italian Sonata» (that is, the Baroque violin sonatas of Vitali, Corelli, Tartini or Locatelli), rather than following in the footsteps of Schubert's or Liszt's fantasies[78]. In other words, d'Indy makes an exception for Franck; he discusses the cyclic form of the *Grande pièce symphonique*, even though he refuses to do so for similarly structured nineteenth-century works, which he categorises as fantasies. This shows a lack of consistency in d'Indy's reasoning and suggests partiality in his judgement. His approach also erases the ways in which Franck resembled and, plausibly, emulated this particular Romantic Beethovenian tradition, and the creative appropriation of Beethoven's oeuvre that emerged as a result.

FRAGMENTATION, CLIMAX, AND APOTHEOSIS

As far back in his output as we may observe, Franck consistently exhibits a fondness for powerful climaxes and brilliant apotheoses. Within his aesthetic, such effects were tried and true methods for marking out the articulations of form and highlighting the return of cyclic material. This is already apparent, for example, in the First Trio. As d'Indy indicates[79], the Trio's

---

[75]. FAUQUET 1999, p. 945. In the first movement of Franck's Quintet, the sixteenth-note figure in the transition from the slow introduction into the sonata form seems to be calqued on the figure that transitions into the fugue in Liszt's *Fantasie und Fuge über den Choral Ad nos, ad salutarem undam*.

[76]. KNITTEL 1998, p. 57, fn. 27 and p. 61.

[77]. D'INDY 1906, pp. 112-114.

[78]. See D'INDY – SÉRIEYX 1909, p. 423 for the analysis. D'Indy deals with the order of movements in the Baroque violin sonata on pp. 178-183 of the same volume.

[79]. D'INDY 1906, p. 64.

first movement contains two cyclic themes, the first one of which (bb. 83-114) is more lyrical and always played softly within the first movement. The conclusion of the last movement, however, brings back this theme as an apotheosis (bb. 536-566). Franck prepares this triumphant return by gradually building tension, using various musical parameters: a gradual crescendo, rising melodic movement, and an acceleration of rhythmic figures within the melody wherein half notes are replaced by quarter note triplets. Unlike the intensifications in Franck's later cyclic works, however, this build-up does not involve fragmentation.

Integrating fragmentation as a technique for creating variations in tension would allow Franck's pre-climax and pre-apotheosis build-ups to become considerably more flexible. The movements of Franck's oratorio, *Les Béatitudes*, contain an abundance of powerful climaxes and apotheoses, expertly conceived to highlight the grandeur of the subject. These peaks are prepared by passages of increasing tension, and these passages now include fragmentation, although they are somewhat weighed down by their extreme length. These intensification processes serve to articulate the oratorio's rather simplistic formal design, in which binary forms map onto the libretto's binary opposition between good and evil[80]. For example, in the third *Béatitude*, the first part depicts the suffering and endless torment inflicted upon humans, while the second part (starting in b. 377) depicts Christ and his promise of consolation: «Heureux ceux qui pleurent / Car ils seront consolés!» («Blessed are those who mourn, / For they shall be comforted», Matthew 5:4.) The first part ends with an apotheosis (bb. 345-376) that coincides with the return of the theme from the beginning of the part; this apotheosis is prepared by 141 measures of mounting tension, beginning with the Animato quasi Allegro in b. 204. The build-up spans a number of sections that combine fragmentation with other intensification factors (crescendo, accumulating voices, rising registers)[81]. In the last of these sections (bb. 313-345), after the orchestral introduction (bb. 313-316), the rising slope of intensity features a very gradual fragmentation effect in which four four-bar groupings (bb. 317-332) become four two-bar groupings (bb. 333-340), and finally four one-bar groupings (bb. 341-344).

Les Béatitudes represents an important stage in the development of Franck's oeuvre. It was composed over the course of a decade (1869-1879) and completed around the time the Quintet was composed. Although the oratorio already contains fragmentation as a technique for producing intense climaxes and apotheoses, in the Quintet, this same technique evolves to become more malleable. This evolution is even more striking in light of the contrasting forms of these two pieces. After the sectional structure of *Les Béatitudes* comes the sonata form of

---

[80]. D'INDY – LIONCOURT 1950, pp. 304-307; FAUQUET 1999, pp. 536-540.

[81]. The first six sections can be described as follows: an orchestral introduction (bb. 204-223), a minor-mode fugato that presents a new theme (bb. 224-262), an imitative episode (bb. 263-283), the theme's return in major (bb. 284-294), an imitative interlude (bb. 295-302), and a modulating version of the theme that concludes with a D major cadence (bb. 303-313).

the Quintet's first movement. Sonatas require significant continuity across complex structures, but Franck, with great responsiveness, adapts the fragmentation technique to its new formal context without compromising its integrity. Furthermore, the heightened dramatic tension to which fragmentation contributes resembles the style of certain works from Beethoven's heroic period or Brahms's early maturity.

More specific similarities come to light upon close examination of the first-movement codas in Beethoven's *Appassionata* and Franck's Quintet. The two works have different overall narrative arcs: as detailed above, the *Appassionata* is a race to the abyss whereas the Quintet is *per aspera ad astra*. The two finales thus have different outcomes, but the two first movements end on similar notes: a dizzying rush to their doom, cut short by a kind of respite or temporary remission. In the *Appassionata*, this respite enables Beethoven to save the feeling of irreparable defeat for the finale.

Peaks of intensity are often associated with codas, and the coda in the first movement of the *Appassionata* (bb. 204-261) contains several, including two climaxes (bb. 231-233 and 257), in addition to an impetuous flourish that comes as a surprise in order to mark a cadence (bb. 218-240). In the first movement of the Quintet, meanwhile, the recapitulation of the subordinate theme overlaps with the beginning of the coda (bb. 331-383). A series of equivalent effects or gestures can be found in both works (for the Quintet, these equivalencies are concentrated within the piano part). In Beethoven's Piano Sonata, the series consists of the following elements. First, a virtuosic passage consisting of wide-ranging, climbing arpeggios in the manner of a concerto cadenza (bb. 227-239). Second, an acceleration in tempo (the *più Allegro* starting in b. 239). Third, an idiomatic piano composition technique in which tonic and dominant chords are passed from hand to hand (bb. 249-56), maintaining a pace of three onsets per beat and ending with a rapid rise in register (bb. 254-256). Fourth and finally, a kind of remission, brought about by a sudden *p* dynamic and gradual diminuendo (*p*, *pp*, *più pp*, and finally *ppp*), immediately after the resolution of a phrase in a *f* dynamic. The right hand maintains a simple minor third tremolo (A-flat – C) during this fourth stage.

The elements of the coda in the first movement of Franck's Quintet correspond quite closely to the ones in the first movement of the *Appassionata*, although Franck changes the order slightly. First, the piano plays a cadenza, which is made even more concerto-like by suddenly *tacet* strings (bb. 396-399). Second, there is an even more pronounced acceleration in tempo, with an *Animato* starting in b. 400 and a *Più presto* in bb. 412-426. Third, the piano plays the same tonic-dominant, hand-to-hand alternation (bb. 384-395 and 412-426), again ending with a rapid registral ascent. The chordal similarities between b. 384 of the Franck and b. 251 of the Beethoven are particularly striking. Fourth and finally, a remission of sorts occurs in bb. 429-440. The volume falls from *fff* to *p* and then decreases even further (from *p* to *pp* and finally *estinto*), and at the very end (bb. 437-440), the piano steadily repeats a simple harmonic third (F – A-flat). In this case, the remission is underscored by a return to *Tempo 1*. There is no tremolo figure in this final passage, but one does occur earlier, in bb. 406-411.

D'Indy insists that Franck's mature works, including the Quintet, form a direct continuity with the works of Beethoven's final period, and indeed that Franck's final period in some ways surpasses Beethoven's. D'Indy does not demonstrate these claims in any way. Perhaps he feels that his eloquence renders demonstration unnecessary? This study has opened up some lines of reasoning to tackle this question, although to do so with all the attention it deserves would be beyond the scope of this chapter. Here I have established that the Quintet's characteristic features include its length, textural richness, and passionate nature or volcanic style, due at least in part to major variations in tension leading to plentiful climaxes and apotheoses. Such peaks of intensity are crucial for the two narrative arcs addressed in this essay: *per aspera ad astra* and the race to the abyss. Starting in his second period, Beethoven traces this trajectory in a number of his works, as do some of his nineteenth-century disciples (such as Liszt and Brahms). The importance of climaxes and apotheoses within them has clear repercussions on Franck's Quintet and on other of his late instrumental works. Moreover, there exist direct parallels between certain passages in Franck's Quintet and Beethoven's Piano Sonata, Op. 57 (*Appassionata*). In and of themselves, these observations call into question any attempt to link Franck's Quintet and other late works to Beethoven's third, or 'mature' period, and provide sufficient grounds to place Franck's chamber oeuvre within the legacy of the second, 'heroic' era.

BIBLIOGRAPHY

ALEGANT – MCLEAN 2007
ALEGANT, Brian – MCLEAN, Don. 'On the Nature of Structural Framing', in: *Nineteenth-Century Music Review*, IV/1 (2007), pp. 3-29.

BRÉVILLE 1935
BRÉVILLE, Pierre de. 'Les *Fioretti* du père Franck', in: *Mercure de France*, 1 September 1935, pp. 244-263.

BRODBECK 1997
BRODBECK, David. *Brahms Symphony No. 1*, Cambridge, Cambridge University Press, 1997 (Cambridge Music Handbooks).

BRUNEAU 1904
BRUNEAU, Alfred. 'César Franck', in: *Courrier de l'orchestre*, III/35 (1 November 1904), pp. 1-3.

CAMPOS 2013
CAMPOS, Rémy. 'Le Cours de composition de Vincent d'Indy', in: *Théories de la composition musicale au XXe siècle. 1*, edited by Nicolas Donin and Laurent Feneyrou, Lyon, Symétrie, 2013, pp. 67-92.

CAMPOS – DONIN 2005
ID. – DONIN, Nicolas. 'La maîtrise artistique de Vincent d'Indy: de quelques relations nouvelles entre composition et analyse au début du XXᵉ siècle', in: *Schweizer Jahrbuch für Musikwissenschaft, Annales suisses de musicologie, Annuario svizzero di musicologia*, XXV (2005), pp. 155-216.

CATHÉ 2020
CATHÉ, Philippe. 'Pratique cyclique et liberté compositionnelle dans l'œuvre de Vincent d'Indy', in: *Musurgia*, XXVII/2 (2020), pp. 7-26.

COHN 1998
COHN, Richard. 'Introduction to Neo-Riemannian Theory: A Survey and a Historical Perspective', in: *Journal of Music Theory*, XLII/2 (1998), pp. 167-180.

COOK 2005
COOK, Robert C. 'Parsimony and Extravagance', in: *Journal of Music Theory*, XLIX/1 (2005), pp. 109-140.

COQUARD 1890
COQUARD, Arthur. 'César Franck 1822-1890', in: *Le Monde musical*, 1890; offprint, Imp. F. Levé, Paris, s.d. [1891].

DAVIES 1970
DAVIES, Laurence. *César Franck and His Circle*, London, Barrie & Jenkins, 1970.

DUKAS 1948
DUKAS, Paul. 'Les séances du Quatuor Ysaÿe-Salambo' [1892], in: *Les écrits de Paul Dukas sur la musique*, Paris, Société d'éditions françaises et internationales, 1948, pp. 31-39.

DUNSBY 2001
DUNSBY, Jonathan. 'Chamber Music and Piano', in *The Cambridge History of Nineteenth-Century Music*, edited by Jim Samson, Cambridge, Cambridge University Press, 2001, pp. 500-521.

ELLIS 2006
ELLIS, Katharine. 'En route to Wagner. Explaining d'Indy's Early Music Panthéon', in: *Vincent d'Indy et son temps*, edited by Manuela Schwartz, Sprimont, Mardaga, 2006 (Musique-Musicologie), pp. 111-121.

FAUQUET 1986
FAUQUET, Joël-Marie. *Les sociétés de musique de chambre à Paris, de la Restauration à 1870*, Paris, Aux amateurs de livres, 1986.

FAUQUET 1999
ID. *César Franck*, Paris, Fayard, 1999.

FAUSER 2006
FAUSER, Annegret. 'Archéologue malgré lui: Vincent d'Indy et les usages de l'histoire', in: *Vincent d'Indy et son temps*, *op. cit.*, pp. 123-133.

Frisch 1984
Frisch, Walter. *Brahms and the Principle of Developing Variation*, Berkeley (CA), University of California Press, 1984.

Groth 1983
Groth, Renate. *Die französische Kompositionslehre des 19. Jahrhunderts*, Wiesband, F. Steiner, 1983.

Gut 2004
Gut, Serge. 'Beethovens Fünfte und Francks Symphonie', in: *César Franck. Werk und Rezeption*, edited by Peter Jost, Stuttgart, F. Steiner, 2004, pp. 34-49.

d'Indy 1903
Indy, Vincent d'. 'César Franck: Le premier des Symphonistes français', in: *The Weekly Critical Review*, 5 March 1903, pp. 1-3.

d'Indy 1906
Id. *César Franck*, Paris, Alcan, 1906.

d'Indy 1910
Id. *César Franck*, translated by Rosa Newmarch, London, John Lane, The Bodley Head, 1910.

d'Indy 1922
Id. 'César Auguste Franck and His Compositions for Piano (1822-1890)', in: Franck, César. *Selected Piano Compositions*, edited by Vincent d'Indy, New York, Oliver Ditson, 1922 (The Musicians Library).

d'Indy 1923
Id. 'La première manière de César Franck', in: *Revue de musicologie*, iv/5 (February 1923), pp. 2-7.

d'Indy 2019
Id. *Écrits de Vincent d'Indy. 1: 1877-1903*, edited by Gilles Saint Arroman, Arles-Venice, Actes Sud-Palazzetto Bru Zane, 2019.

d'Indy 2021
Id. *Écrits de Vincent d'Indy. 2: 1904-1918*, edited by Gilles Saint Arroman, Arles-Venice, Actes Sud-Palazzetto Bru Zane, 2021.

d'Indy – Lioncourt 1950
Id. – Lioncourt, Guy de. *Cours de composition musicale, 3ᵉ livre*, Paris, Durand, 1950.

d'Indy – Sérieyx 1909
Id. – Sérieyx, Auguste. *Cours de composition musicale, 2ᵉ livre, 1ᵉʳᵉ partie*, Paris, Durand, 1909.

d'Indy – Sérieyx 1933
Id. – Id. *Cours de composition musicale, 2ᵉ livre, 2ᵉ partie*, Paris, Durand, 1933.

JARDILLIER 1929
JARDILLIER, Robert. *La musique de chambre de César Franck: Étude et analyse*, Paris, Mellottée, 1929.

KEYM 2004
KEYM, Stefan. 'César Francks Violinsonate und ihre Stellung in der Geschichte des zyklischen Sonate', in: *César Franck. Werk und Rezeption, op. cit.*, pp. 112-130.

KNITTEL 1998
KNITTEL, K. M. 'Wagner, Deafness, and the Reception of Beethoven's Late Style', in: *Journal of the American Musicological Society*, LI/1 (1998), pp. 49-82.

MACDONALD 2001
MACDONALD, Hugh. 'Transformation, Thematic', in: *Grove Music Online*, 2001, <www.oxfordmusiconline.com/grovemusic>, accessed December 2023.

MÉDICIS 2020
MÉDICIS, François de. *La maturation artistique de Debussy dans son contexte historique (1884-1902)*, Turnhout, Brepols, 2020 (Speculum Musicae, 38).

MEYER 1989
MEYER, Leonard B. *Style and Music: Theory, History, and Musicology*, Philadelphia, University of Pennsylvania Press, 1989.

MIRKA 2014
MIRKA, Danuta. *The Oxford Handbook of Topic Theory*, Oxford-New York, Oxford University Press, 2014.

PURI 2011
PURI, Michael. *Ravel the Decadent: Memory, Sublimation, and Desire*, Oxford-New York, Oxford University Press, 2011.

RATNER 1980
RATNER, Leonard G. *Classic Music: Expression, Form, and Style*, New York-London, Schirmer Books-Collier Macmillan, 1980.

ROSEN 1980
ROSEN, Charles. *Sonata Forms*, New York, W. W. Norton, 1980.

SMITH 1992
SMITH, Peter H. *Formal Ambiguity and Large-Scale Tonal Structure in Brahms's Sonata-Form Recapitulations*, unpublished Ph.D. Diss., New Haven (CT), Yale University, 1992.

SMITH 2005
ID. *Expressive Forms in Brahms's Instrumental Music: Structure and Meaning in His Werther Quartet*, Bloomington, Indiana University Press, 2005.

STRUCKEN-PALAND 2009

STRUCKEN-PALAND, Christiane. *Zyklische Prinzipien in den Instrumentalwerken César Francks*, Kassel, Bosse, 2009 (Kölner Beiträge zur Musikwissenschaft, 7).

SUCHOWIEJKO 2006

SUCHOWIEJKO, Renata. 'Du «métier à l'art»: L'enseignement de Vincent d'Indy', in: *Vincent d'Indy et son temps*, *op. cit.*, pp. 101-110.

TARUSKIN 2005

TARUSKIN, Richard. *The Oxford History of Western Music. 3: The Nineteenth Century*, Oxford, Oxford University Press, 2005.

TIERSOT 1917

TIERSOT, Julien. 'Un demi-siècle de musique française entre les deux guerres (1870-1917) [III César Franck]', in: *La Revue*, 1-15 May 1917, pp. 383-396.

VALLAS 1955

VALLAS, Léon. *La véritable histoire de César Franck*, Paris, Flammarion, 1955.

VANDE MOORTELE 2009

VANDE MOORTELE, Steven. *Two-Dimensional Sonata Form: Form and Cycle in Single-Movement Instrumental Works by Liszt, Strauss, Schoenberg, and Zemlinsky*, Leuven, Leuven University Press, 2009.

WEBSTER 1979

WEBSTER, James, 'Schubert's Sonata Form and Brahms's First Maturity (II)', in: *19th-Century Music*, III/1 (1979), pp. 52-71.

Challenging Tradition: All-Female String Quartets of the Late Nineteenth and Early Twentieth Centuries

Nancy November
(University of Auckland)

The string quartet was firmly located in the male domain throughout most of the eighteenth and nineteenth centuries. A 'strong genre', associated with technical mastery and the highest compositional achievements in this time, the string quartet was composed by men (including, notably, the main exponents of the Viennese Classical canon), performed by men (in both public and private settings), and written about by men. Women were largely excluded from its sphere, except as audience members at concerts, which started to flourish in the early and mid-nineteenth century. This chapter explores changes to this paradigm that occurred during the nineteenth century, especially in the late nineteenth century. I consider three female performers who led successful professional string quartets during this period: Wilma Norman-Neruda (Lady Hallé, 1838-1911), Nora Clench (Lady Streeton, 1867-1938), and Edith Robinson (1867-1940). I also consider ideas and ideals associated with female participation in string quartets that persist to the present day.

The String Quartet as a 'Masculine' Genre

Several factors kept women away from string quartets, at least as performers, in the late eighteenth century and most of the nineteenth. These factors may be classified as specifically music-cultural, largely socio-political, and ideological. Starting with the music-cultural factors, the public-sphere activities of music publication and reviewing were almost exclusively male-dominated in the nineteenth century. One might expect that more gender equality was achieved in private-sphere chamber music-making. After all, the domestic sphere was generally much

ILL. 1: Johann Carl Arnold's watercolour *Quartettabend bei Bettina con Arnim* (1855). Courtesy of Almy images.

more open to women than other areas of musical life. However, this was not always the case during the period in question. In particular, men dominated the performance of string chamber music around 1800.

Evidence of this male dominance is found in iconography of the time, in memoirs, accounts of musical life and musicians, and in period descriptions of music-making. Iconography indicates that, in the sphere of the string quartet, women were admitted as listeners, and could be engaged in 'serious listening'. But the performance of string quartets was depicted as an almost exclusively male activity. A prime example is ILL. 1, Johann Carl Arnold's watercolour *Quartettabend*

ILL. 2: August Borckmann, *Beethoven und das Rasumowsky'sche Quartet* (photographic reproduction from 1880-1890 of the original 1827 painting). Courtesy of Beethoven-Haus, Bonn.

bei Bettina con Arnim (1855)[1]. At this time, artists almost invariably depicted women playing piano, singing, and playing what were then-acceptable instruments (notably guitar, harp, lute, and mandolin), in the then-acceptable settings (chiefly the home)[2]. The exceptions prove the rule: where a woman is shown taking part in a string quartet, supposedly the 'Rasumovsky Quartet', in a retrospective view of Beethoven's time from the late nineteenth century, she plays the piano (see ILL. 2)! As Michaela Krucsay notes, in the period between the French Revolution and the beginning of World War I (1798-1914), there were rigid social restrictions on female musical performance in public. However, in private homes in Berlin, Paris, and Vienna in particular, women could take part as musical and literary leaders in middle-class salons, which remained important centres of female cultural activity well into the twentieth century[3].

Men dominated string quartet performance in Vienna in the time of celebrated classical string quartet composers Joseph Haydn, Wolfgang Amadeus Mozart, and Ludwig van

[1]. NOVEMBER 2013, p. 14; NOVEMBER 2004.
[2]. LEPPERT 1993, Chapter 4.
[3]. KRUCSAY 2018.

Beethoven — both in public and in private. Accounts by Eduard Hanslick, Ignaz von Mosel, Johann Ferdinand Schönfeld, and Leopold von Sonnleithner indicate the predominance of men among amateur performers of stringed instruments at this time, and the predominance of string chamber music over other kinds[4]. The *Address Book* of Anton Zeigler (1823) is instructive[5]. It includes musicians, institutions, instrument makers, and composers in Vienna around the time of the eminent Schuppanzigh Quartet's public performances of Beethoven's late string quartets. In the list of composers and 'Dilettanten', female pianists (168) outnumber male pianists (147) and are slightly fewer in number than male violinists (171). Piano is very clearly the preferred instrument among women, singing taking second place. Only two female violinists are listed, and there are no female violists or cellists. These proportions are typical of Europe more generally at this time. An exception was Louis Spohr's pupil Elisabeth Filipowicz (c.1790-1841) in Braunschweig. She was one of the very few women violinists who was able to perform in public in the early nineteenth century[6]. Others who made the cut were exceptional performers, and often Italians, where female virtuosity on the violin had something of a tradition: Maddalena Laura Lombardini Sirmen, Regina Strinasacchi, Luigia Gerbini, and also Mariane von Berner[7].

Larger social and political factors also help explain the traditional gender association of instruments and the predominance of string chamber music in the early nineteenth century. In Vienna under the Metternich System, for instance, with its strict surveillance and censorship of male group activities, men, and particularly educated middle-class men, required leisure pursuits that would not attract the suspicion of the authorities or suggest that they were potential incubators of political uprising. The popularity of string quartets and quintets, especially in Vienna but also Europe-wide, was driven by a particular need for male (or masculine) leisure activities that would be perceived as politically innocuous[8]. The playing of 'Quartettmusik' with one's family or in a small group of close friends apparently allowed politically safe male sociability.

More generally, accounts of string chamber music-making from the period, and of its subsequent development in concert series, show that men also wanted their group activity to be distinct from feminine pastimes (like playing piano and singing) and perceived as useful for (male) education and self-development (*Bildung*). In this spirit, the Protestant theologian Wilhelm Conrad Petiscus claimed hopefully in 1810: «the quartet table will soon replace the bar»[9]. At that time the string quartet was also capable of fulfilling an arguably larger need felt

---

[4]. NOVEMBER 2017, pp. 133-134.
[5]. ZIEGLER 1823.
[6]. TIMMERMANN 2015; TIMMERMANN 2017.
[7]. WASMER 1997, pp. 73-93.
[8]. See LOTT 2015.
[9]. PETISCUS 1810, p. 514: «Der Quartetttisch wird bald den Schenktisch verdrängen».

by male participants, who otherwise lacked a socio-political voice. Construed as a particularly German cultural artefact, the 'true' string quartet could be held up as an emblem of the cherished ideals of democracy and unity, used to help establish a sense of national identity. Evidence for this may be found in the mid-century writings of Adolph Bernhard Marx, who distilled this ideal into a new vision of the string quartet in performance, which embodied the new *Kunstreligion* (art religion) of the Romantics: «No more do we have four jolly brothers-in-art who make music for their own, and our, pleasure; we have four deeply stirred creative spirits, who soar in glorious freedom and wonderful sympathy in a quadruple brotherly embrace»[10]. The metaphor of quartet conversation was adapted to take on elements of Kantian philosophy, particularly Kant's conceptions of extended sympathy and universal brotherhood; people were to learn — chiefly by means of public-sphere discussion — to pursue the 'common good', ultimately uniting in a world community[11]. Like the Kantian philosophy, the new quartet ideology was based on what was in reality a hegemonic, Germano-centric worldview, a way of celebrating and constructing German identity — and cultural, social and religious 'unity' — through art. This worldview was also essentially masculine.

In mid-nineteenth-century German discourse about, and iconography relating to, string quartets, male proponents of this culture constructed their chosen genre with a growing sense of nationalist pride, as well as of masculine identity. Richard Wagner's vignette of string quartet playing in the bourgeois home encapsulates this stance:

> Go and listen one winter night in that little cabin: there sit a father and his three sons, at a small round table, two play the violin, a third the viola, the father the 'cello. What you hear so lovingly and deeply played, is a quartet composed by that little man who is beating time [...]. Again I say, go to that spot, and hear that author's music played, and you will dissolve in tears; for it will search your heart and you will know what German Music is [...][12].

Wagner's vignette was directed at a French readership. French and German writers promote somewhat contrary conceptions of the string quartet and its place in musical culture at this time[13]. Germans, which is to say, German middle-class intellectual men, became increasingly interested in establishing 'true' quartets (that is, string quartets composed by selected Austro-German composers) as score-based, cerebral works requiring serious study and

---

[10]. MARX 1828, p. 467: «Es sind nicht mehr vier heitre Kunstbrüder, die uns zu ihrer und unsrer Freude Musik machen; es sind vier tief ergriffne schöpferische Geister, die in herrlicher Freiheit und wunderbarer Sympathie in vierfach geschlungener Bruderumarmung aufschweben».

[11]. NOVEMBER 2013, p. 103.

[12]. WAGNER 1840. Translated in LOTT 2015, pp. 17-18.

[13]. NOVEMBER 2004; NOVEMBER 2013, pp. 9-17.

attentive listening; they promoted themselves as the main composers, performers, listeners, and judges of such works. French conceptions were more grounded in performance and the body. But there, too, the idea was tied up with masculinity, the militaristic and 'heroic' embodiments encouraged by the performance and compositional styles of members of the French Violin School[14]. In England the situation was much the same in the early nineteenth century. As Bella Powell notes, the taboo on violin-playing women was based on the virile kind of virtuosity associated with the instrument, its repertoire and playing style, which was considered unseemly for women not only in terms of physicality (bodily positions and contortions) but also in terms of the level of accomplishment they would need to demonstrate, which would detract heavily from their household duties[15].

String quartet composition — especially that emanating from Vienna, or from composers inspired by the Viennese classicists — was considered to involve considerable skill, even 'genius', and was in that sense widely constructed as 'masculine'. To express this 'genius' required a genius in performance that (early nineteenth-century writers found) required a performer (or ensemble) to 'step back' and allow the voice of the composer to be clearly heard. Two German writers of the time summarised the selflessness required of string quartet performers. The first, a Protestant theologian by the name of Wilhelm Conrad Petiscus, wrote in general about 'Quartet Music' and its performance in Leipzig in 1810: «[A] primary duty of all quartet performers is to cultivate a *clear*, *beautiful* tone from their instruments. [...] The effect of [string] quartet music is based in part on the beautiful euphony of the four instruments»[16]. The second, writing in Vienna in 1824, was reviewing Schuppanzigh's quartet, at the time considered the first exponents and champions of Beethoven's string quartets:

> These four gentlemen appear to have but one soul when they perform their quartet and nobody can boast to have heard an ensemble of greater perfection. [...] Each of these four artists is so complete in his place that he seems irreplaceable[,] and Mr. Schuppanzigh knows the enthusiasm that flows through him, so fully honouring his collaborators, that one does not know whether he moves them or they him[17].

---

[14]. See KAWABATA 2004.

[15]. POWELL 2022.

[16]. PETISCUS 1810, p. 520: «Eine Hauptpflicht aller Quartettisten ist daher, sich eines *klaren, schönen* Tons auf ihrem Instrumente zu befliessigen».

[17]. *WIENER THEATER-ZEITUNG* 1824, p. 71: «Diese vier Herren schienen nur eine Seele zu haben, wenn sie ihr Quartett ausführen und niemand kann sich wohl rühmen, ein vollkommeneres Ensemble gehört zu haben. [...] Jeder dieser vier Künstler ist auf seinem Platz so vollständig, daß er unersetzbar zu seyn scheint, und Hr. Schuppanzigh weiß die Begeisterung, welche ihn durchströmt, so vollg[e]istig in senimen Mitwirken zu ehren, daß man nicht weiß, wirket er auf sie oder sie auf ihn».

Challenging Tradition

The creative act of composition in general, and string quartets in particular was considered something best left to men. That remained firmly the case, into the era of Amy Beach, and arguably even today. Eduard Hanslick (in *On the Musically Beautiful*, published in 1854), for example, considered women too emotional to create coherent works of musical art, let alone string quartets[18]. But certain string quartets, notably those of Schubert, and those by composers outside the Austro-German quartet tradition, became acceptable for female string quartet performers to play in the later nineteenth century. Below I shall explore why this was so.

Three Drivers of Change

Women were still largely barred from performing in professional orchestras well into the twentieth century. But, as Christina Bashford shows, in the later nineteenth century they increasingly took up string instruments and string quartet performance in the domestic environment[19]. Starting around the 1870s, the social taboo against women learning string instruments eased, and women started to participate not only in private string quartets but also in public ones. This was partly a function of changing access to conservatoire training for women and notable female performers, including the Czech violinist Norman-Neruda and the Canadian violinist Clench. Both of these women had access to the Austro-German tradition through teachers and repertoire, which helped them to establish their reputations and their string quartet leadership, in a still almost exclusively male arena. But the women themselves should also be given credit for their pioneering spirit, which led them to confront tradition and try new repertoire. The American Maud Powell is a classic example of such a pioneer violinist in the era under consideration, discussed in detail by Judith Tick[20].

England became a particularly fertile place for concerts involving all-female or part-female string quartets[21]. Female quartet players who made a name in London as professional musicians helped to pave the way for others[22]. These included foreigners Norman-Neruda, Marie Soldat-Roeger, Gabriel Wietrowetz, Powell, and Clench; and British violinists Jessie Grimson, Marie Hall, May Harrison, and Beatrice Langley. All-female quartets were formed by Clench, Beatrice Langley, and Emily Shinner (Mrs. A. F. Liddell). Grimson's quartet was otherwise comprised of men. Lady Radnor was a key proponent for women learning and performing string instruments, founding an all-female string orchestra[23]. But the craze for playing instruments of the violin

---

18. Hanslick 1854, p. 53.
19. Bashford 2010.
20. Williams 2012; Tick 1973.
21. Bashford 2016.
22. McVeigh 2010.
23. Rudd 2017.

family in late-nineteenth-century Britain was also driven by commercial factors, which helped pave the way for professional women's success. Inexpensive factory fiddles brought instruments into the hands of working-class adults and school children, aided by a strong infrastructure for violin playing that included violin magazines and advertisements. Paula Gillett identifies further socio-economic factors that facilitated the breakthrough in acceptance of female violinists: the increasing use of music by philanthropic organisations and the democratisation of the piano[24].

Norman-Neruda, born in Brno in 1838, was a child prodigy. Her father was a composer, and, seeing her natural talent, allowed her to study violin. She studied with Leopold Jansa in Vienna, a concession made in view of her prodigious talent. She made her solo debut at the age of eleven with London Philharmonic Orchestra playing the de Beriot Concerto, and together with her siblings performed regularly in either a trio or quartet. At the encouragement of Henri Vieuxtemps, she joined a Monday Popular Concert series in London with a string quartet, where she led from the first violin except when Joseph Joachim was visiting. During the winter season of 1879-1880, Norman-Neruda performed with Hans von Bülow, who subsequently published an essay about her. He called her a «violin fairy», described her as a «female Joachim», and emphasised her outstanding position in English musical life: «The miracle girl Wilma Neruda has become a miracle woman and in England she reigns as violin queen by Apollo's grace and with the approval of all music connoisseurs and music lovers»[25]. She performed regularly in Europe and toured throughout the world: Australia (1890-1891), South Africa (1895), the United States (1899)[26].

Clench was also a child prodigy, likewise supported by her father. Backing by authoritative men was vital for a woman who wished to move forward in a career as a violinist around 1900. She entered the Leipzig Conservatory at the age of fifteen and studied under Russian violinist Adolph Brodsky, continuing her training thereafter with Joachim in Berlin in 1895. She formed the Nora Clench Quartet in 1904, with Lucy Stone as second violin, Cecilia Gates on viola, and May Mukle on cello. Their first concert in June 1904 included works by Mozart and Borodin. The quartet was short-lived, ending in 1907, although they received good reviews and large audiences. Clench retired in 1908 when she married Australian painter Arthur Streeton. By the time she died in Toorak, Australia in 1938, she was only known for her relationship to Streeton.

British female performers of stringed instruments, and female professionals who visited Britain, were uniquely able to lead the way. This was perhaps partly because they were not directly involved in the Austro-German quartet tradition, which as we have seen was strongly masculine in its conception and ideology. But, in order to gain acceptance in the first place, some ties to that quartet playing tradition were still necessary. For Edith Robinson, this included her studies

---

[24]. GILLETT 2000.
[25]. BÜLOW 1880, p. 243.
[26]. HELSE 2017.

ILL. 3: Wilma Norman-Neruda as a first violin of the string quartet at The Monday Popular Concerts in St James's Hall, London; also pictured Louis Ries (violin 2), Ludwig Straus (viola) and Alfredo Piatti (cello). Engraving by Frederick Wentworth. *London Illustrated News*, 1872.

with Brodsky at the Leipzig Conservatoire. She then returned to Manchester and taught at the Royal Manchester College of Music from 1907, where Brodsky was principal and leader of the Brodsky Quartet. She formed the all-female Edith Robinson Quartet in response to the all-male Brodsky group, and the quartet emphasised the performance of new music.

How were these female quartet players and all-female string quartets received, and how did this change? In reviews of their time we find references to the purity, uniformity, and invisibility of female performers, which seem to be an effort to contain the covert voyeurism evident elsewhere, for example in iconography. ILL. 3 shows 'Madam' Norman-Neruda in a quartet recital at St James's Hall in London, in 1872. Here the spotlight is on the performers, but especially Norman-Neruda: «Perhaps no lady violinist has ever equalled Madam Norman-Neruda in calm repose of manner and graceful use of the bow arm. Certainly no player of her sex has commanded a *purer* tone, a *truer* intonation, or more *neat* and *finished* mechanism»[27]. That is, Norman-Neruda succeeded where other women had failed thanks to her self-effacing

---

[27]. SCHWAB 1971, p. 160. My emphasis.

performance style (which, as we have seen, was an important ingredient in 'true quartets' from around 1800) — her ability to direct listeners to the contemplation of the quartet as a sequence of 'true', 'pure', and unified tones.

Other aspects of reception help to explain Norman-Neruda's particular success, which included acceptance as an exponent of Beethoven[28]. Her sex still presented a problem that needed to be explained away. Some critics reached for the 'exception to the rule' argument:

> The quartet party was led by a woman; and the leader played with such power, force, dignity, and fire as few indeed of the most gifted men are endowed withal. There is a strong and scarcely unnatural prejudice against a female fiddler. Men, and women too, for that matter, are somewhat unwilling to believe that one of the gentler sex can conquer all the technical difficulties of the most arduous of instruments, and they are quite ready to affirm that to shoulder a violin is an unladylike proceeding. How in a single eight-bar phrase Mdme. Norman-Neruda scattered all prejudices to the winds must be fresh in the recollection of every subscriber to last season's Philharmonic Concerts[29].

The same British newspaper writer made further comments specifically on Norman-Neruda's quartet performances with Alfredo Piatti, Louis Ries, and John Baptiste Zerbini: «Madame Neruda, we must hasten to explain, needs no special consideration on account of her sex. Classed among the finest quartet players in Europe, she must take all but the very highest place»[30]. The writer all but admits to the prejudices that, he notes, are widely held and suggests that Neruda succeeds where other women (and even some «most gifted men») fail because she has the necessary power and technical skill (understood to be primarily masculine traits) for string quartet performance. In other words, the critic did indeed give her, «[...] special consideration on account of her sex», to explain her skill by making her into an honorary man.

A neater way of doing the same thing, which also made Norman-Neruda into an honorary German, was to claim that she was the female Joachim — as Hans von Bülow and others did. In this way she was understood to have a fitting lineage as a performer. One obituary writer even heralds her as the last of this particular line:

> She shared with Dr. Joachim the honour of being among the last exponents of a school of violin playing which is unfortunately disappearing under the blast of impatient modernity. It is not the least tribute to her playing to say that she never for a moment allowed her mastery of technical matters to stand in the way of the composer's intentions. With such attributes it was only natural that her conception

---

28. HELSE 2011.
29. *MUSICAL WORLD* 1869.
30. *Ibidem.*

of Beethoven's work should be a thing never to be forgotten [...] as an interpreter of Beethoven, Mozart, and Brahms and much later of Bruch, her style and finish were unrivalled[31].

Norman-Neruda herself clearly understood the value of a violin performance pedigree. In an interview late in her life, she reinforced the idea that she was part of a larger school, and one closely linked to the canonic string quartet repertoire she played:

> I have never studied under any others than my father and Jansa. I thoroughly disapprove of the system of changing schools so prevalent just now. One master only should develop and train the flexible, impressionable growth of interpretation, so that the young shoots in the form of impressions may not wander adrift and lose themselves in the ocean of infinity. Is it not better to adopt one particular manner of expression and express one's self well than to try several methods and interpret these indifferently[32]?

Another reception motif, which helped with Norman-Neruda's acceptance as a quartet performer, was to place her above reproach, as artist-royalty:

> But of all the manifold attractions of the Dublin Musical Society's recent concerts, perhaps none succeeded in literally electrifying the public to such an extent as the playing of Lady Hallé, *the queen of lady violinists*. Quiet, unostentatious, but thoroughly ladylike in manner, and magnificently robed, Lady Hallé [...] holds her violin with a grace and ease which our young players might well imitate. The pose of her right hand and arm, in particular, is wonderful. The right curve elicited universal admiration, and the marvel to many violinists was that, although holding the arm higher than is the perhaps ordinary custom, the distinguished performer thereby got a command of expression and power from her instrument which was little short of marvellous[33].

An obituary recapitulates this idea of the 'violinist queen', recounting an anecdote in which the King of Denmark makes an exception for Norman-Neruda in allowing her to bring her dog into his country. One who was considered above and beyond the string quartet ideology was freely allowed, by the critics, to perform virtuoso feats such as Giuseppe Tartini's 'Devil's Trill' and Antonio Bazzini's *Scherzo fantastique*, requiring far more unladylike contortions than Beethoven's late quartets. But this virtuoso repertoire was anyway not subject to the same German nationalist ideology as canonical string quartets — especially those of Beethoven.

---

[31]. *MANCHESTER* 1911.
[32]. *CASSEL's* 1894, pp. 780ff.
[33]. *PATTERSON* 1901. My emphasis.

The all-female Nora Clench Quartet had difficulty getting their performances of Beethoven past the critics[34]. The Special Correspondent from the 1908 Hereford Musical Festival found that the quartet was not up to this more 'masculine' repertoire:

> The performance by Miss Nora Clench's Quartet did not seem to me satisfactory. It certainly lacked virility of tone and energy in the phrasing, and it was at times dangerously near carelessness. The same may be said of their playing of Beethoven's noble Quartet in F (opus 135). It was not sufficiently earnest. It lacked grip, although the technical difficulties were fairly well mastered[35].

Success for this quartet seemed to depend on repertoire: less mainstream Austro-German repertoire was praised in roughly the same terms as the criticism levelled at the Beethoven performance. Earnestness, precision, and even a 'masculine vigour of expression' became apparent when the repertoire was Haydn, George Walker, Ernő Dohnányi, and Claude Debussy, as noted in this review in the *Irish Times* (1907):

> Yesterday one of the best-known London chamber music parties, the Norah [*sic*.] Clench Quartet, including Miss Clench, Miss Stone, Miss Gates, and Miss Mukle, made a peaceful invasion of our old music town and won a complete victory. It was a pleasure merely to see the way in which these four ladies played — their fire, their strict sense of rhythm, their certainty and warmth of attack. They combine in the happiest manner a masculine vigour of expression with just and sane sensibility. Their programme was full of interest. It comprised a capitally played Haydn, Walker fantasies, representing young England very attractively, Dohnanyi's serenade trio, and, as the main item of interest, Debussy's string quartet. [...] May this quartet visit us every year, bringing their cornucopia of novelties. We need them[36].

A slightly later review in *The Irish Times* (1907) notes the first performance of an all-female string quartet at the Royal Dublin Society, and observed the careful selection of repertoire for this occasion: «(1) quartet in G major, Op. 34 (Peter's Edition) (Haydn); (2) quartet in G minor, Op. 10 (Debussy); (3) quartet, C minor, Op. 18, No. 4 (Beethoven)»[37]. So Beethoven was present on the programme, but an early quartet rather than the more canonical middle and late quartets. With this repertoire the quartet apparently largely achieved the requisite «sonority and purity of tone» required for the performance of 'true' quartets:

---

34. *Manchester* 1906.
35. *Ibidem*.
36. *Irish Times* 1907A, p. 6.
37. *Irish Times* 1907B, p. 5a.

> The andante scherzo and the menuetto, were the best played movements in
> a performance of somewhat uneven merit, but it was at the same time evident that
> the whole reading was the result of thoughtful care. [...] One and all of the artists
> exhibited marked sonority and purity of tone, sound artistic perception, and a keen
> feeling for colour and expression, if with, perhaps, an occasional tendency to lapse
> into the sentimental, which had better be avoided[38].

The Dublin, Hereford, and Manchester audiences clearly felt that the time was right to move beyond the old chestnuts of the string quartet repertoire and give some fresh voices an airing, particularly local composers. Another review the following year shows the Nora Clench Quartet playing more new music, this time a quartet by Cyril Scott, whose work was poorly received but with praise for the quartet's performance[39]. Shortly thereafter they performed James Franklin's quartet for piano and strings, again with positive reception of their performance: «This clever and capable organization certainly does its best in the matter of production of native novelties»[40]. So all-female quartets of the time found a way to work around the demands that came with the Austro-German string quartet tradition: avoiding the key repertoire around which the quartet ideology developed meant that the ensemble could be judged at least somewhat according to its own merits, even if the terms originally associated with that canonical repertoire (power, purity, vigour, virility) were still applied.

The Edith Robinson Quartet rose to the challenge of middle- and late-period Beethoven, with some success. But they were still not masculine enough (here «drastic» enough) for some reviewers:

> The readings of the three quartets — in F major, opus 18, in E minor, opus
> 59, and in E flat, opus 127 — were admirable examples of a finished Beethoven style.
> If we may suggest that for the three lower instruments a more drastic handling of the
> composer would yield even a fuller satisfaction it is not in the way of fault-finding
> [sic][41].

However, another reviewer refers to this group's ability to bring off, 'a real type of quartet playing', which again seems to refer to a kind of selflessness — a style that is not artificial nor showy, but apparently 'true' to the nature of stringed instruments:

> The playing of Miss Robinson and her colleagues lives most in this essential
> warmth of string playing. In the deviations from this normal style they are somewhat

---

38. *IRISH TIMES* 1907, p. 5.
39. *MANCHESTER* 1908.
40. *OBSERVER* 1909.
41. *MANCHESTER* 1920.

too loth to leave what is essential to their instruments and to adopt an artificial precision for brilliant or fanciful ends [regarding Schumann's F major Quartet] [...]. The slow movement of Haydn's Quartet in C and the daring minor trio of its minuet were equally fine. These things were the real type of quartet playing, and they gave a deep satisfaction to the listener[42].

Again, though, reviewers had difficulty separating the 'real type of quartet playing' from what they consider to be the 'real type of quartet', and uncoupling both from conceptions of masculinity (here power and vigour):

> Most musicians would agree that [...] the music, say, of Brahms, Handel, or Beethoven would demand a powerful handling, while that of Schubert, Mozart, or even the broader tones of Schumann are more effective when more tenderly handled, and demand more of sensibility than power. The music of Schubert, for instance, is probably poised on the whole a little higher than that of Brahms, and on that account, among others, has a more easy flexibility. The Schubert movement yesterday seemed to be given with a perfect poise and stress, while the music of Brahms hardly seemed to have all its effectual vigour [...][43].

One might conclude that the Edith Robinson Quartet tended to settle for Schubert, and gave a series of Schubert concerts to critical acclaim. In this context they were even praised for their own interpretation. It is notable, though, that only when a male performer joined the group was his own particular 'voice' in performance praised:

> The playing last night lent to Schubert a most likeable substantiality, even roughness. Too much Schubert-playing nowadays is merely suave and comfortable. Mr. Carl Fuchs joined the Edith Robinson Quartet in the C major Quintet, and his full, broad 'cello was unmistakably his own[44].

Regarding the Edith Robinson Quartet's performance of Schubert's G major String Quartet, one critic did single out Robinson, but for her particular realisation of Schubert's idea rather than her own playing style: «It would not be fair to pass over without mention Miss Robinson's poignant treatment of the strange ejaculations for the first violin in the andante. These notes and the broken phrases that succeed them are almost physical in effect — veritable cries of pain»[45]. More typical praise came for the cellist of the Nora Clench Quartet, for helping

---

[42]. Manchester 1921.

[43]. Manchester 1923.

[44]. Manchester 1928a.

[45]. Manchester 1928b.

to achieve the balance and blend required of the 'true' quartet: «a word must be said for Miss Edith Evans, who contributed not a little to the balance by her judicious playing of the 'cello part [Schubert's D minor String Quartet, D810, "Death and the Maiden"], which is often rather aggressive in a string quartet»[46].

Why was the performance of Schubert's string chamber music any more acceptable for female performance than that of Beethoven, who, after all, lived contemporaneously in Vienna? The answer is rooted at least partly in the fact that the string quartet ideology, mentioned above, developed strongly around the public performance of Beethoven's middle and late string quartets. Schubert was known then, and still in the early twentieth century, as a composer of songs — and one who lived a more sheltered, less heroic, less canonical life largely in the domestic sphere. His music was, precisely, well suited to women.

After Clench, Shinner led an all-female quartet with Stone, Cecilia Gates and Florence Hemmins; later Wietrowitz became the leader. And the Lucas Quartet, comprising four sisters, played octets with the Rosé ensemble in the years leading up to the First World War[47]. The 1930s witnessed the second and third generation of professional female string musicians, and the employment of other chamber ensembles led by women. The Macnaghten-Lemare concerts were a major milestone, a London concert series run by the violinist Anne Macnaghten and the conductor Iris Lemare for six seasons in the 1930s, with the help of the composer Elisabeth Lutyens. These performances were noteworthy for showcasing the work of emerging British composers like Benjamin Britten and Elizabeth Maconchy, and for the central roles played by women[48]. More to the point, Macnaghten led her own quartet in London from 1932. It originally consisted entirely of women and gave concerts and broadcasts until 1939. It was reorganised in 1947 with a focus on concerts for schools, and on teaching and coaching, especially in Hertfordshire.

Persistent Ideals

What persists and changes today in the ways we understand the all-female string quartets of our time? First of all, the idea of 'selflessness' in performance persists in discourse about string quartet playing in general. With respect to the Brentano Quartet (a 'mixed' ensemble of two men and two women), one critic writes: «[...] the Brentanos are a magnificent string quartet

---

46. *Irish Times* 1909, p. 8; see also Deserno 2018.
47. Potter 2003, p. 50.
48. Fuller 2013.

[...]. This was wonderful, selfless music-making»[49]. This is just one example drawn from many in which the idea persists that string quartet players must bow to the genius of the composer and leave their own personalities out of the performance. More subtly, the iconography and discourse around female string quartet performers tends to draw attention to their sex, as it had done around 1900. This is obvious in a 2020 Artemis publicity photograph, taken at a time (post-1994) when this group's ratio of women to men had peaked at three to one. Gregor Sigl (viola since 2016) literally fades into the background[50]. In a review for *The Strad* we read: «Under the fingers of the new-look Artemis Quartet, Op. 20 No. 2 had all its airs and graces [...]. [Suyoen] Kim and [Harriet] Krijgh joined less than a year ago, yet they fit seamlessly within the 30-year-old Artemis aesthetic»[51]. Just as in the case of the review of Norman-Neruda, there is an oblique reference to the unusual presence of women in this quartet — the references to «airs and graces» doesn't quite fit Haydn's Op. 20, No. 2 (which references the Baroque trio sonata at the beginning and fugue at the end, and is arguably more quirky than graceful, throughout); but these 'features', especially the «graces», could be references to the three women. And there is the idea, too, that the two «new» women (Kim and Kriigh) fit nicely into the quartet aesthetic because they weave themselves in «seamlessly» — another code word for selfless performance.

A table helps to contextualise the Artemis quartet, which we see (in the third column) is still highly unusual in terms of its high female-to-male ratio. This table shows at least some of the 'world-class' string quartets. In practice 'world-class' is very difficult to measure, but could include, for example, an active career of around fifty concerts per annum (pre-COVID-19), existence for more than twenty years, recordings on major labels, and regular international tours. Although the table shows only a sample of the quartets that fit into these categories, it nonetheless provides an approximate idea of how the music industry views women in professional string quartets today. The Lark Quartet, an all-female quartet formed in 1985 and based in New York, is the only one to make it into the last column of this table, but it terminated in 2019. Rather like the Nora Clench Quartet, it was highly acclaimed; but when one crucial member left (the cellist, Caroline Stinson, got a job at Duke), the ensemble decided that it was not appealing to re-form the group. It is no accident that these quartets often tend to focus on the more modern and non-Austro-German repertoire — Aleksandr Borodin, Debussy, and Maurice Ravel.

---

49. Brentano 2021; *Gramophone* 1991.
50. Quantrill 2020.
51. *Ibidem.*

TABLE 1: SAMPLE OF TWENTIETH- AND TWENTY-FIRST-CENTURY STRING QUARTETS
SHOWING GENDER RATIOS

Original gender ratio (female:male)	0:4	1:4	2:4	3:4	4:4
Quartet (date founded)	Alban Berg (1971) Amadeus (1947) Arditti (1974) Borodin (1945) Budapest (1917) Busch (1919) Danish String Quartet (2020) Emerson (1976) Fine Arts (1946) Guarneri (1964) Jerusalem (1993) Kolisch (1920s) LaSalle (1946) Orford (1965) Tokyo (1969) Vermeer (1969)	Cleveland (1969) Quartetto Italiano (1945) Ebene (2017) Kronos (1978) Kus (2002) Brodsky (1972)	Belcea (1994) Borromeo (1989) Brentano (1992) Hagen (1981) Juilliard (2016) Pacifica (1994) Takács (2005)	Artemis (1994) New Zealand String Quartet (1987) Galimir (1927)	Lark (1985)

Why is this table so ill-balanced in terms of gender, even more than 250 years after the era in which string quartets first started to be composed and then flourished? The answer resides partly in the ideological and social factors, which persist to the present day. We have seen how the string quartet, early on, was linked to connoisseurship and related to expression of the composer's genius through selfless performance. We have seen how women made a real entry into the sphere of string quartet performance only in the late nineteenth century, as professional performers, and only when they were highly exceptional. But women have arguably never attained a normative position in the string quartet. Just as Norman-Neruda had to be 'made to disappear' in performance, so that she could count as a real quartettist, so too modern-day female performers must execute a similar disappearing act, at least according to mainstream critics.

Despite all of this, if we make a more or less random selection from a quick Google search, and scroll through the imagery attached to all-female quartets today, we see that the 'all-female' nature of the quartet is usually brought visually to the foreground — more or less overtly. These groups are dressed in white, pink, and glitter, not the traditional black. In other words, these groups are marketing themselves first of all as being 'All Women' and only secondarily as 'string quartet ensembles'. This visual highlighting of gender, in a stereotypical way, does not help to normalise the phenomenon of women performers in string quartets. Nor does the self-governed 'buddy system' by which quartets tend to be formed and maintained. There are many other factors that lead to the imbalance in the table — including the general lag in female presence in professional orchestras. This persistent gender imbalance is perhaps mainly due to our still persistent need to hear the great 'Masterworks' of the string quartet tradition performed as 'absolute music' — as pure sonority uncluttered by bodies and bows.

BIBLIOGRAPHY

BASHFORD 2010
BASHFORD, Christina. 'Historiography and Invisible Musics: Domestic Chamber Music in Nineteenth-Century Britain', in: *Journal of the American Musicological Society*, LXI/2 (2010), pp. 291-360.

BASHFORD 2016
EAD. 'Art, Commerce and Artisanship: Violin Culture in Britain, c.1880-1920', in: *The Idea of Art Music in a Commercial World, 1800-1930*, edited by Christina Bashford and Roberta Montemorra Marvin, Woodbridge, Boydell and Brewer, 2016 (Music in Society and Culture), pp. 178-201.

BRENTANO 2021
Brentano Quartet Website, 2021, <https://www.brentanoquartet.com/about/>, accessed December 2023.

BÜLOW 1880
BÜLOW, Hans von. 'Wilma Norman-Neruda', in: *Signale für die musikalische Welt*, XXXVIII/16 (1880), pp. 242-244.

CASSEL'S 1894
'A Chat with Lady Hallé', in: *Cassel's Family Magazine*, 1894.

DESERNO 2018
DESERNO, Katharina. *Cellistinnen: Transformationen von Weiblichkeitsbildern in der Instrumentalkunst*, Cologne, Bölau, 2018.

FULLER 2013
FULLER, Sophie. '«Putting the BBC and T. Beecham to Shame»: The Macnaghten-Lemare Concerts, 1931-7', in: *Journal of the Royal Musical Association*, MXXXVIII/2 (2013), pp. 377-414.

GILLET 2000
GILLETT, Paula. *Musical Women in England, 1870-1914: «Encroaching on All Man's Privileges»*, Basingstoke, Palgrave Macmillan, 2000.

GRAMOPHONE 1991
'Simpson String Quartets', in: *Gramophone*, 1991, <https://www.gramophone.co.uk/review/simpson-string-quartets-0>, accessed December 2023.

HANSLICK 1854
HANSLICK, Eduard. *Vom Musikalisch-Schönen: Ein Beitrag zur Revision der Aesthetik der Tonkunst*, Leipzig, Weigel, 1854.

HELSE 2011
HELSE, Jutta. 'Wilma Neruda, verw. Norman, verh. Hallé, gen. Lady Hallé (1838-1911): Wilma Neruda – «Groß und rein wie Joachim»', in: *«...mein Wunsch ist, Spuren zu hinterlassen...»: Rezeptions- und Berufsgeschichte von Geigerinnen*, edited by Carolin Stahrenberg and Susanne Rode-Breymann, Hannover, Wehrhahn, 2011 (Beiträge aus dem Forschungszentrum Musik und Gender, 1), pp. 44-63.

HELSE 2017
EAD. *Die Geigenvirtuosin Wilma Neruda (1838-1911): Biografie und Repertoire*, unpublished Ph.D. Diss., Hildesheim, Universität Hildesheim, 2017.

IRISH TIMES 1907A
'Royal Dublin Society', in: *The Irish Times*, 11 December 1907.

IRISH TIMES 1907B
'Royal Dublin Society', in: *The Irish Times*, 14 December 1907.

IRISH TIMES 1909
'Royal Dublin Society's Recitals', in: *The Irish Times*, 26 January 1909.

KAWABATA 2004
KAWABATA, Maiko. 'Virtuoso Codes of Violin Performance: Power, Military Heroism, and Gender (1789-1830)', in: *19th-Century Music*, XXVIII/2 (2004), pp. 89-107.

KRUCSAY 2018
KRUCSAY, Michaela. '«Alleinherrscherin aller Tasten und Herzen»: Musikkulturelles Handeln von Frauen des langen 19. Jahrhunderts zwischen Rollenstereotyp und Rebellion', in: *Stereo-Typen: Gegen eine musikalische Mono-Kultur*, Innsbruck, Universitätsverlag Wagner, 2018, pp. 72-81.

LEPPERT 1993
LEPPERT, Richard D. *The Sight of Sound: Music, Representation, and the History of the Body*, Berkeley (CA), University of California Press, 1993.

LOTT 2015
LOTT, Marie Sumner. *The Social Worlds of Nineteenth-Century Chamber Music*, Urbana-Chicago-Springfield, University of Illinois Press, 2015.

MANCHESTER 1906
'Hereford Musical Festival', in: *The Manchester Guardian*, 15 September 1906.

MANCHESTER 1908
'Music in London: Mr. Cyril Scott's New Works Mr. F. Kell's Recital a Delightful Concert', in: *The Manchester Guardian*, 26 March 1908.

MANCHESTER 1911
'Lady Halle', in: *The Manchester Guardian*, 17 April 1911.

MANCHESTER 1920
'Beethoven Commemoration Concerts: The Quartets', in: *The Manchester Guardian*, 20 November 1920.

MANCHESTER 1921
'The Edith Robinson Quartet Concert', in: *The Manchester Guardian*, 24 December 1921.

MANCHESTER 1923
'Edith Robinson Quartet Concert', in: *The Manchester Guardian*, 28 April 1923.

MANCHESTER 1928A
'The Edith Robinson Schubert Concerts', in: *The Manchester Guardian*, 14 January 1928.

MANCHESTER 1928B
'Edith Robinson, Quartet Concerts', in: *The Manchester Guardian*, 21 January 1928.

MARX 1828
MARX, Adolph Bernhard. 'Quatuor für zwei Violinen, Viola und Violincell von Beethoven...', in: *Berliner Allgemeine musikalische Zeitung*, V (1828), pp. 467-468.

MCVEIGH 2010
MCVEIGH, Simon. '«As the sand on the sea shore»: Women Violinists in London's Concert Life around 1900', in: *Essays on the History of English Music in Honour of John Caldwell: Sources, Style, Performance, Historiography*, edited by Emma Hornby and David Maw, Woodbridge, Boydell Press, 2010, pp. 232-258.

MUSICAL WORLD 1869
'Monday Popular Concerts', in: *The Musical World: A Weekly Record of Musical Science, Literature and Intelligence*, XLVII/47 (1869), p. 797.

NOVEMBER 2004
NOVEMBER, Nancy. 'Theater Piece and Cabinetstück: Nineteenth-Century Visual Ideologies of the String Quartet', in: *Music in Art: International Journal for Music Iconography*, XXIX/1-2 (2004), pp. 134-150.

NOVEMBER 2013
EAD. *Beethoven's Theatrical Quartets: Opp. 59, 74 and 95*, Cambridge, Cambridge University Press, 2013 (Music in Context).

NOVEMBER 2017
EAD. *Cultivating Chamber Music in Beethoven's Vienna*, Woodbridge, Boydell Press, 2017.

OBSERVER 1909
'Music: The Nora Clench Quartet', in: *The Observer*, 14 November 1909.

PATTERSON 1901
PATTERSON, Annie. 'Music and the Drama', in: *Weekly Irish Times*, 16 November 1901, p. 5.

PETISCUS 1810
PETISCUS, Wilhelm Conrad. 'Über Quartettmusik', in: *Allgemeine musikalische Zeitung*, XII (1810), cols. 513-523.

POTTER 2003
POTTER, Tully. 'From Chamber to Concert Hall', in: *The Cambridge Companion to the String Quartet*, edited by Robin Stowell, Cambridge, Cambridge University Press, 2003 (Cambridge Companions to Music), pp. 39-59.

POWELL 2022
POWELL, Bella. 'Notions of Virtuosity, Female Accomplishment, and the Violin as Forbidden Instrument in Early-Mid Nineteenth-Century England', in: *The Routledge Handbook of Women's Work in Music*, edited by Rhiannon Mathias, Abingdon-New York, Routledge, 2022 (Routledge Handbooks), pp. 241-249.

QUANTRILL 2020
QUANTRILL, Peter. 'Concert review: Artmis Quartet', in: *The Strad*, 27 March 2020, <https://www.thestrad.com/reviews/concert-review-artemis-quartet/10448.article>, accessed December 2023.

RUDD 2017
RUDD, Philip Christopher. *Countess, Conductor, Pioneer: Lady Radnor and the Phenomenon of the Victorian Ladies' Orchestra*, unpublished Ph.D. Diss., Iowa City (IA), University of Iowa, 2017.

SCHWAB 1971
Musikgeschichte in Bildern. 4/2: Musik der Neuzeit. Konzert, edited by Heinrich W. Schwab, Leipzig, VEB, 1968.

TICK 1973
TICK, Judith. 'Women as Professional Musicians in the United States, 1870-1900', in: *Anuario Interamericano de Investigacion Musical*, IX (1973), pp. 95-133.

TIMMERMANN 2015

TIMMERMANN, Volker. '«Sie könnte eben so gut auf einem Spinnfaden geigen»: Die Spohr-Schülerin Elisabeth Filipowicz – Karriere als Folge von Emigration', in: *Louis Spohr Symposium Braunschweig 2014: Musik und Politik – Politische Einflüsse auf Musikerbiografien und kompositorisches Schaffen von 1784 bis heute*, edited by Anja Hesse, Bernhard Weber and Hendrik Bartels, Kassel, Merseburger, 2015 (Braunschweiger kulturwissenschaftliche Studien, 5), pp. 142-154.

TIMMERMANN 2017

ID. *«...wie ein Mann mit dem Kochlöffel». Geigerinnen um 1800*, Oldenburg, Bis-Verlag der Carl von Ossietzky Universität Oldenburg, 2017.

WAGNER 1840

WAGNER, Richard. 'De la musique Allemande', in: *Revue et gazette musicale*, VII (1840), p. 376.

WASMER 1997

WASMER, Marc-Joachim. 'Primadonna der Violine Maddalena Laura Lombardini Sirmen', in: *Annäherung: An sieben Komponistinnen*, Kassel, Furore, 1997 (Annäherung an sieben Komponistinnen, 8), pp. 73-93.

WIENER THEATER-ZEITUNG 1824

'Schuppanzigh's Quartetten', in: *Wiener Theater-Zeitung*, 10 February 1824.

WILLIAMS 2012

WILLIAMS, Catherine C. *«The Solution Lies with the American Women»: Maud Powell as an Advocate for Violinists, Women, and American Music*, unpublished M.Mus. Diss., Tallahassee (FL), Florida State University, 2012.

ZIEGLER 1823

ZIEGLER, Anton. *Addressen-Buch von Tonkünstlern, Dilettanten, Hof-Kammer-Theater-und Kirchenmusikern, Verreinen, Lehr- und Pansions-Instituten, Bibliotheken zum Behufe der Tonkunst; k.k. privil. Kunst- und Muiskalien-Handlungen, Instrumentenmachern, Geburts- und Sterbtagen vorzüglicher Tonkünstler &c. in Wien*, Vienna, Ziegler, 1823.

PRIVATE AND PUBLIC:
BLURRING THE BOUNDARIES

Reportage of Chamber Music in the Paris Daily Papers, 1860-1914[1]

Sylvia Kahan
(The Graduate Center and College of Staten Island,
City University of New York)

The French have never stinted when it comes to lionising their artistic heroes in the press. In the nineteenth and early twentieth century, one did not have to read the specialized journals and magazines devoted to music, theatre, literature, or the visual arts to be well informed about cultural matters: the activities of major artistic figures were routinely splashed across the front pages of Paris daily newspapers such as *Le Figaro*, *Le Gaulois*, and *Le Temps*. A summary of the season's top theatrical and operatic events was front-page news in *Le Figaro* of 2 April 1854. The upcoming publication of George Sand's letters was the main headline in *Le Gaulois* on 22 October 1896, as was the heated debate around the commission of a statue to honor Balzac — a proposition first made by Alexandre Dumas in 1851, which, by 1857, had become a target of satire and, decades later, was still a hotly contested issue[2]. The death of Victor Hugo (22 May 1885) occupied the entirety of *Le Figaro*'s front page. And, similar to the present day, the activities (artistic or otherwise) of superstars always made headlines. Sarah Bernhardt, for example, received constant media attention, for both her storied performances at the *Comédie française* as well as her publicity-attracting 'eccentricities'. While not born French, cosmopolitan figures like Richard Wagner and Nicolò Paganini — and later, Sergey Diaghilev — were considered 'honorary' Frenchmen by virtue of their prestige, and their comings and goings were always worthy of press coverage.

[1]. I presented portions of this topic at the *Chamber Music 1850-1918* conference sponsored by the Centro Studi Opera Omnia Luigi Boccherini (virtual conference, 10-12 December 2021) and the annual conference of *France: Musique, Cultures* (Venice, Italy, 11-13 July 2022). I am grateful to Michel Duchesneau, Katharine Ellis, and Jann Pasler for their insightful comments and useful suggestions, which aided me in the preparation of this text.

[2]. See *Le Figaro*, 9 July 1857 and later *Le Gaulois*, 5 December 1894.

Native-born composers were hailed in the Parisian press for their important contributions to French cultural patrimony. The premiere of Charles Gounod's *Faust* was treated to a lengthy front-page review[3]. A similarly in-depth article covered the upcoming premiere of Léo Delibes' *Lakmé*[4]; no less attention was paid to the first performance of Jules Massenet's *Manon*[5]. And it was not just opera composers who made headlines: a lengthy homage to César Franck, who had died in 1890, was the lead article in *Le Gaulois* fourteen years later (19 October 1904).

The Paris daily newspapers regularly heralded the musical activities of opera divas, international conductors, violin and piano virtuosos, and composers, and occasionally featured articles about operas, ballets, and symphonies. But, curiously, the coverage of chamber music and chamber musicians was a mixed bag — this, despite the fact that chamber-music societies, especially string-quartet societies, were multiplying and prospering, occupying an increasingly large place in concerts and soirées[6]. For *Le Figaro* and *Le Gaulois*, the favoured papers of the aristocracy and upper-bourgeoisie, the genre was rarely deemed worthy of coverage: performances by instrumental duos, trios, and string quartets were relegated to the back pages, where the week's 'Spectacles et Concerts' were listed. On the other hand, the music journalists of the more liberal *Le Temps* were indefatigable champions of both the genre and the instrumentalists who devoted themselves to the repertoire.

This study aims to give an overview of chamber music coverage by the three daily newspapers. *Le Figaro* and *Le Gaulois*, whose approach to coverage of musical events is similar, will be considered together, while the reportage of *Le Temps* will be examined separately. Press coverage of three of the most popular chamber-music ensembles, the Société philharmonique, the Société de musique de chambre pour instruments à vent, and the Quatuor Capet will serve as case studies. The conclusion addresses the disparity in press coverage and the questions raised as a result of this journalistic mixed bag: what, according to reporters and critics, was the value ascribed to chamber music as a genre, and what stature did it deserve in French cultural patrimony? Was chamber music an elitist commodity, a remnant of a bygone era — or was it a form of entertainment that deserved to be brought to the attention of broader concert audiences? Did this repertoire — including chamber music by young contemporary composers — merit the stature of opera and symphony, and should it be more widely and enthusiastically embraced by the musical public?

---

[3]. See *Le Figaro*, 24 March 1859.

[4]. See *Le Figaro*, 13 April 1883 [front page].

[5]. See *Le Figaro*, 20 January 1884 [front page]; *Le Gaulois*, 20-26 January 1884 [multiple articles]; and *Le Temps*, 29 January 1884.

[6]. WEBER 1862D.

Reportage and Criticism of Chamber Music in *Le Gauolis* and *Le Figaro*

Founded in 1854, *Le Figaro* dubbed itself a 'non-political' newspaper, whereas *Le Gaulois*, founded in 1868 by the royalist Arthur Meyer, adopted a conservative editorial stance. Both papers catered to aristocratic and upper-bourgeois readerships. The respective approaches to arts-related reporting was remarkably similar, and, frequently, notices of upcoming musical and theatrical events employed identical or nearly identical language[7]. Reporting of most musical events was relegated to the back pages of the papers, where lists of upcoming performances in theaters and concerts halls were published; some brief 'reviews', usually of an uncritical nature and written in flowery prose, also appeared in these pages. The exceptions involved reporting of major premieres of operatic works (as discussed above) or brief mentions on the front page of musical performances in the homes of ambassadors, political figures, or at prominent aristocratic salons.

The first mentions of chamber music (*musique de chambre*), in both newspapers, appeared in 1869: both short articles made reference to the violinist Jean-Pierre Maurin, who, along with cellist Pierre Chevillard[8], had co-founded a string quartet, the Société des Derniers Quatuors de Beethoven (Society of Late Beethoven Quartets), in 1835[9]. The first official ensemble to promote this unusual repertoire, previously considered unplayable and unfathomable, the Société des Derniers Quatuors de Beethoven indefatigably championed these masterworks in public concerts, first in Paris and subsequently in Germany and Switzerland. In its article, *Le Figaro* recalled that the four French string players had been summoned at the behest of King Ludwig II of Bavaria, to Lucerne, Switzerland, where the French musicians performed a surprise recital of late Beethoven quartets on the occasion of Wagner's birthday[10]. This event will be referenced again further on.

Aside from these concert listings, chamber music received no extensive reporting until the opening of the 1878 Exposition universelle (World's Fair) in Paris. Twenty-six concerts of art music featuring French composers (especially living composers) and performing artists were programmed for the Exposition, in keeping with the desire of the Exposition's organisers to celebrate the French nation and the finest examples of its cultural production[11]. The chamber-

---

[7]. See, for example, the identical announcements reporting the two performances of the Quatuor Capet at the Salle du Conservatoire: Delilia 1906 and Nicolet 1906.

[8]. Prével 1877. When Pierre Chevillard died, in 1877, Jules Prével wrote that «he contributed greatly to the creation of chamber-music societies, which have since become so numerous among us. It was several years ago, thanks to his initiative and artistic zeal that the *Société des derniers quatuors de Beethoven* was founded, which allowed us to get to know a whole series of masterworks».

[9]. Un Domino 1869; Lafargue 1869.

[10]. Jullien 1885. Jullien's anecdote was reprinted *verbatim* in Nicolet 1885.

[11]. For a discussion of music at the 1878 Exposition universelle, see Chapter 4 (especially pp. 275-284) of Pasler 2009.

music works performed on the programme of 2 August 1878 were the Piano Trio in G by Paul Lacombe, Camille Saint-Saëns's Piano Quartet, Op. 41, and George Onslow's Quintet in D minor. Ignoring Lacombe's trio altogether, the critic for *Le Gaulois* characterised the latter two works as *œuvres d'élite* (superior works) and praised the utility of the Exposition's programming of French works: «If these concerts have no other result than to acquaint our generation with these fine artists about whom they know nothing [...] then we'd have to declare the institution [i.e., the Exposition universelle] excellent»[12]. As for *Le Figaro*, the first mention of a chamber music ensemble — in this case, a string quartet (*quatuor à cordes*) — also signaled a shift in gender norms. In 1875, *Le Figaro* had posted a brief announcement of upcoming performances by the all-female Quatuor Sainte-Cécile, founded by an up-and-coming young violin virtuoso, Marie Tayau[13]. Three years later, when the quartet performed at the 1878 Exposition Universelle, *Le Figaro* reported that the curiosity of hearing an all-female ensemble drew an audience of nearly six hundred to the first of its three performances[14].

During the 1880s, the two columns devoted to concert and theatrical activities, 'Courrier des Spectacles' (*Le Gaulois*) and 'Courrier des Théâtres' (*Le Figaro*), rarely, if ever, mentioned chamber music, except to list performances and give brief information about repertoire and certain artists. Indeed, the term *musique de chambre* appeared almost exclusively in connection with satirical political writing. It is curious that the term should be disparaged by journalists whose readership came from the upper classes. Nonetheless, the pejorative use of the term is pervasive, as demonstrated by the following examples, such as these two front-page 'dictionary' entries in *Le Gaulois*: «A definition: *Chambre des députés*: National Academy of Chamber Music»; «Election: a cacophony of voices, destined to produce an even more discordant chamber music»[15]. Often, *musique de chambre* served as code for 'infighting' or 'useless discussions'. When the president of the Chamber of Deputies, gave a large banquet, to which were invited representatives of groups from both the political right and left, the satirist from *Le Gaulois* quipped that: «the quartet of Republican groups — the radical Left, the Republican Union, the Democratic Union and the extreme Left — will create detestable chamber music»[16]. And, in 1901, *Le Figaro* described the «edifying spectacle» of a «brawl» that took place among

---

[12]. Georges 1878: «Quand ces concerts n'auraient d'autre résultat que de faire connaître à notre génération ces fins artistes qu'elle ignore, [...] il faudrait en déclarer l'institution excellente».

[13]. Lafargue 1875. Earlier that year, Marie Tayau had given the first performance of Gabriel Fauré's A-major Violin Sonata, Op. 13.

[14]. *Le Figaro* 1878a, *Le Figaro* 1878b.

[15]. Un Domino 1885: «Une définition: *Chambre des députés*: Académie nationale de musique de chambre». Un Domino 1881: «Petit dictionnaire [...] Election. – Cacophonie de voix, destinée à produire une musique de chambre encore plus discordante».

[16]. Taverny 1882: «j'ai, pour ma part, la conviction que le quatuor des groupes républicains: Gauche radicale, Union républicaine, Union démocratique et extrême gauche, fera de détestables musiques de chambre».

the members of Paris's municipal council: «Blows were exchanged, then they started throwing the inkwells, the paper cutters, and the office furniture. To this 'chamber music' was attached lyrics that, out of respect for my readers, I will not reproduce here»[17].

The rare serious reportage or critiques of chamber-music performances were generally well-written. One such column, written by *Le Gaulois*' music critic, Louis de Fourcaud, appeared in January 1880: it was a critique of a concert presented by the Société nationale de musique (which had been in existence for nearly a decade). «There are hardly any concerts [by the Société] in which modern quartets or quintets are not performed», wrote Fourcaud, who praised established composers like Saint-Saëns, Franck, and Édouard Lalo for, «setting the example and the tone» for up-and-comers like Gabriel Fauré, Henri Duparc, André Messager, Camille Benoît, Vincent d'Indy, and Octave Fouque[18]. Franck's 1879 Piano Quintet, performed by Saint-Saëns and the Quatuor Pierre Marsick, was singled out for its harmonic novelty and for its «severe, solid, marvelously pure composition and from every standpoint of superior order. The author can be assured of the fate of his new work: it is fashioned to be admired for all times»[19].

The fate of chamber music reportage began to change in the 1890s, when musical salon culture represented the height of elegance. The growth of salon culture coincided with a marketing ploy by the daily newspapers to increase sales by satisfying their respective readership's insatiable curiosity about the goings-on in high society. To that end, in 1891, *Le Gaulois* created a special column called 'Mondanités: Chronique d'élégance' ('Society Life: Chronicle of Elegance'); *Le Figaro* followed suit in 1895 with a counterpart called 'Le Monde et la Ville' ('High Society and the City'). The columns broke down into categories of *mondain* activity: 'Social Information', 'Clubs', 'Charity Events', 'Hunting', 'Vacation Spots', 'Marriages', and 'Deaths'. But by far the greatest amount of newsprint was devoted to the section entitled 'Salons', in which the musical entertainment offered by the various hostesses was reported in meticulous detail, as were the names of those in attendance. A reader could track the daily movements of the Duchesse de X by reading that the lady in question had attended the Marquise de Brou's

---

[17]. UN DOMINO 1901: «Avant-hier nos édiles ont donné aux tribunes publiques l'édifiant spectacle d'une rixe entre conseillers. Des gifles ont été échangées, puis l'on a jeté à la volée des encriers, des coupe-papiers, des fournitures de bureau; sur cette musique de chambre, on a plaqué des paroles que, par respect pour mes lecteurs, je me garderai de reproduire ici».

[18]. FOURCAUD 1880: «Il n'y a guère que [les concerts de la Société nationale de musique] où l'on exécute des quatuors et des quintettes modernes [...] Des maîtres, tels que MM. Saint-Saëns, César Franck, E. Lalo, y donnent l'exemple et le ton à des jeunes gens qui seront des maîtres aussi, tels que MM. Gabriel Fauré, Duparc, Messager, Camille Benoît, Vincent d'Indy et Octave Fouque».

[19]. *Ibidem*: «Ce quintette, divisé en trois mouvements, nous a surpris par sa nouveauté harmonique et son ample ordonnance. C'est une composition sévère, solide, merveilleusement pure et de tout point hors ligne. L'auteur peut être rassuré sur le sort de son nouvel ouvrage: il est fait pour être admiré de tout temps».

musical matinee on Monday, a string quartet recital at the Princesse Murat's on Tuesday, a dinner followed by a vocal recital in honour of the Queen of Spain on Wednesday, the first performance of a work by Saint-Saëns at the home of the Comte de Ganay on Thursday, and a *five o'clock* hosted by the Comtesse Greffulhe on Friday.

And, in these reports, chamber music took pride of place. Eminent international ensembles were regularly engaged to perform both standard quartet repertoire by Joseph Haydn, Wolfgang Amadeus Mozart, Ludwig van Beethoven, Robert Schumann, and Felix Mendelssohn, as well as lesser-known and new works by Aleksandr Borodin, Johannes Brahms, Claude Debussy, and Antonín Dvořák. Some salons offered 'festivals' paying homage to a particular composer: Dr. and Madame Châtellier, for example, offered a multi-part 'Schumann' cycle, featuring the Quatuor Parent[20]. Young composers in particular benefitted from the salon and the financial and social support of forward-thinking hostesses. Fauré, Franck, d'Indy, and Saint-Saëns, all of whom wrote major pieces of chamber music, were able to hear their chamber works performed in intimate surroundings before appreciative audiences. Pieces like Fauré's A-major Violin Sonata, Op. 13 and the C-minor Piano Quartet, Op. 15, for example, which had received scant press notice at the moment of their premieres (in 1881 and 1884, respectively), garnered substantially more attention in the society columns. By the end of the 1890s, 'all-Fauré' programmes were performed with increasing frequency, often with the composer at the piano[21].

Such a coincidence may not be ascertained, but as coverage of salon performances of chamber music in the society columns increased, so did serious reportage and critiques of the repertoire and its performances in public venues in specifically music columns. One such full-length article appeared in *Le Figaro* on 16 May 1892, when music critic Charles Darcours devoted a full column to several concerts given by the Quatuor Ysaÿe — a thoughtful discussion both of the genre and of new works by French composers. Darcours stressed the intimate interplay necessary among the players: «The pleasure of listening [to chamber music] comes from its intimate disposition, which should not, however, be left constantly unexpressed, for the performers need to feel that their conviction is understood and shared [...]. Underneath its apparent simplicity, the execution of a quartet is thus a more complex artistic act than one can imagine». He continued:

> Chamber music, having so long been neglected, has, however, regained its standing among us, and today Paris possesses several quartet societies with loyal audiences [made up of] serious connoisseurs. [...] For many years, only the marvelous repertoire of foreign masters was admired, but our young [French] school — for

---

[20].   Boisfleury 1907.

[21].   See, for example, reports of performances 'all-Fauré' programs in the salons of Gaston Berardi (Gant de Saxe 1894), pianist Léon Delafosse (Ferrari 1896a), Princesse Hélène Bibesco (Ferrari 1896b; Chéron 1899), and Princesse Edmond de Polignac (Ferrari 1908).

whom so few paths are open! — are beginning to have their works performed, and these compositions have, in a short amount of time, conquered a legitimate place.

So the arrival of the Belgian quartet created by Monsieur Ysaÿe is fortunate for Parisians; it should be even more welcome because, in an act of rare delicacy, M. Ysaÿe's concert programs consist of works exclusively by French composers. [...]

I'd hardly know how to express what impressions caused such an explosion of enthusiasm for [Vincent d'Indy's] superb [String Quartet]. [...] Long acclamations made the walls of the Salle Pleyel tremble, and the composer and his interpreters had to return to the stage several times to confront the thunderous applause of the audience[22].

Ironically, the success of the Ysaÿe concerts led to a popularisation of the genre that belied its inherently intimate nature. By the end of the century, established symphonic societies like the Concerts Colonne began to incorporate chamber music into the programming of their 'concerts populaires' in an effort to attract a wider public. For its inaugural concert of its 'Popular-Music Thursdays' (*Jeudis populaires*), the Concerts Colonne engaged no less of a musical eminence than international violin virtuoso Pablo de Sarasate to perform a Haydn string quartet along with members of the Quatuor Parent[23]. The newspapers stressed the attractive prices of the tickets, ranging from two francs for the orchestra seats to fifty *centimes* for seats in the upper balconies, as much as the music itself.

It's well known that the *Jeudis populaires* intend to do for chamber music (quintets, quartets, trios, solos, *mélodies*) what the grand Sunday concerts have done for the symphony. [...]

---

[22]. DARCOURS 1892: «[L]a jouissance que cause cette audition [de la musique de chambre] provient donc d'une disposition tout intime et qui ne doit cependant pas demeurer constamment inexprimée, car les exécutants ont besoin de sentir leur conviction comprise et partagée [...] / L'exécution d'un quatuor, sous son apparente simplicité, est donc un acte artistique plus complexe qu'on ne se l'imagine [...] / La musique de chambre, après avoir été longtemps négligée, a toutefois repris son rang parmi nous, et Paris possède aujourd'hui plusieurs sociétés de quatuors qui comptent de nombreux fidèles et de sérieux connaisseurs. [...] Le merveilleux répertoire des maîtres étrangers y a été pendant nombre d'années uniquement admiré, mais notre jeune école — à laquelle si peu de voies sont ouvertes! — a commencé à s'y produire, et ses compositions y ont acquis en peu de temps une place légitime. / La venue du Quatuor belge créé par M. Ysaÿe était donc une bonne fortune pour les Parisiens; elle devait être d'autant mieux accueillie que, par une rare délicatesse, M. Ysaÿe n'a inscrit sur le programme de ses séances que des œuvres de compositeurs français. [...] / On ne saurait dire quelle impression a produite et quel enthousiasme a fait éclater [le premier quatuor de M. Vincent d'Indy...] [...] De longues acclamations ont fait trembler les murs de la salle Pleyel, et le compositeur et ses interprètes ont dû revenir plusieurs fois affronter les tonnerres d'applaudissements du public».

[23]. NICOLET 1897A. Sarasate returned the following to play chamber music with the Quatuor Parent in the Concerts Colonne's 'Popular Thursdays' series, this time performing a Beethoven String Quartet. See *Le Gaulois*, 31 October 1898.

> We can say at present that the celebrated quartet of the Beethoven
> Foundation (Quatuor Geloso) will participate to these interesting afternoons, which
> seem to be destined for a success at least as great as that of the Poetry Saturdays of
> the Odéon[24].

The practice of including serious chamber music at popular music venues even trickled down to café-concerts: those managers, too, hoped that the 'something for everyone' approach would increase its customer base — a practice that led to some journalistic amusement.

> The most recent incarnation of musical taste in Paris: it's the present
> custom whereby every café and brasserie has "musical performances", in which,
> for the thirty centimes spent for all the beer you can drink, everyone may satisfy
> their music-maniacal appetites. [...] All the passers-by have in their hearts a sleeping
> community chorister [orphéoniste] and they come in as families, adding to their
> modest repast the treat of a string quartet, under the direction of Monsieur X...
> "from the Opéra"[25]!

REPORTAGE AND CRITICISM OF CHAMBER MUSIC IN *LE TEMPS*

As discussed, coverage of chamber music in *Le Figaro* and *Le Gaulois* was, for the most part, spotty and, with rare exceptions, superficial in nature. This was not the case with another important French newspaper, *Le Temps*. The paper's liberal philosophy and moderate politics resulted in a smaller readership than its aforementioned competitors, but it was highly regarded for its serious reportage. From its very inception (1861), the paper showed an avid interest in the arts and afforded ample space for its coverage. *Le Temps*'s first music critic, Johannes Weber, wrote for the paper for thirty-four years (1862-1895). His weekly column, 'Critique musicale', occupied the bottom third of both the front page and the second page, with article lengths averaging a generous five thousand words. Weber, a thoughtful musician and superior writer about music, used his bully pulpit to inform and educate the paper's readership on musical matters of all kinds.

---

[24]. NICOLET 1897b: «On sait que les jeudis populaires se proposent de faire pour la musique de chambre (quintettes, quatuors, trios, soli, mélodies) ce que les grands concerts du dimanche ont fait pour la symphonie [...] Nous pouvons dire dès à présent que le célèbre quatuor de la Fondation Beethoven (quatuor Geloso) prêtera son concours à ces intéressants après-midis, qui paraissent destinés à un succès au moins aussi grand que celui des samedis poétiques de l'Odéon».

[25]. LE MASQUE DE FER 1891: «La dernière incarnation du goût musical à Paris. C'est l'usage à présent que tout café, toute brasserie ait ses "auditions musicales" où, pour les trente centimes d'un bock qui s'éternise, chacun puisse satisfaire ses mélomaniaques appétits [...] Les passants ont tous dans leur cœur un orphéoniste qui sommeille, et ils entrent en famille, joindre à leur consommation modeste le régal d'un quatuor à cordes, sous la direction de Monsieur X... "de l'Opéra!"».

From the onset, Weber indefatigably promoted both the string-quartet repertoire and its artists. His favorite *société de quatuor* was comprised of violinists Jules Armingaud and Léon Jacquard, violist Édouard Lalo, and cellist Joseph Mas. Formed in 1855, a period during which there was little audience for chamber music, the group had for years presented «popular» public series (i.e., with tickets offered at reduced prices) devoted to the quartets of Haydn, Mozart, Beethoven, and Mendelssohn. Weber praised these performances:

> These works are the foundation of chamber music. To play the compositions of different masters is, besides, the best means to acquire the variety and the necessary perfection of style to interpret each one with the deep intelligence, sureness of execution, and richness of sound that Messieurs Armingaud, Jacquard, Lalo and Mas possess to such a high degree[26].

In almost every column, Weber averred that classical concerts filled a «public need». In 1863, the success of Armingaud's quartet had inspired the founding a new 'popular' chamber music society, the *Séances populaires de musique de chambre*, conceived by Charles Lamoureux and Émile Rignault: «To put within reach of every pocketbook chamber music by Boccherini, Haydn, Mozart, Beethoven, and Mendelssohn — there you have a useful, practical, and artistic idea that will be welcomed by everyone, no doubt about it, with the favour that it deserves»[27]. Weber sold the 'popularity' of Lamoureux's chamber music series with the pitch that «the programme is always put together with perfect taste in order to interest the listeners so that their attention will not flag and they will get tired»[28]. With the founding of the Société des quatuors français in 1864, Weber championed the cause of French music, declaring that the best way to programme chamber music was «to start with standard repertoire as a base, without excluding [established] French composers — and then to add good pieces by living composers, even those who are yet little known»[29]. He lamented that the chamber music of Henri Reber

---

[26]. WEBER 1862C: «ces œuvres sont, en effet, le fondement de la musique de chambre. Jouer des compositions de différents maîtres est, d'ailleurs, le meilleur moyen d'acquérir la variété et la perfection nécessaires du style, pour les interpréter chacune avec cette intelligence profonde, cette sûreté de jeu, cette richesse de la sonorité que MM. Armingaud, Jacquard, Lalo et Mas possèdent a un degré si éminent».

[27]. LEGAULT 1863: «Mettre à la portée de toutes les bourses les œuvres de musique de chambre de Boccherini, Haydn, Mozart, Beethoven, Mendelssohn, voilà une pensée utile, pratique, artistique, qui sera accueillie de tous, nous n'en doutons pas, avec la faveur qu'elle mérite».

[28]. WEBER 1863: «Le programme est toujours composé avec un goût parfait pour intéresser les auditeurs sans que leur attention [ne] languisse jamais ni se fatigue».

[29]. WEBER 1864: «la meilleure manière de composer le programme d'une séance de musique symphonique ou de musique de chambre, c'est de prendre pour base les belles œuvres des musiciens regardés comme les maîtres du genre, sans en exclure les compositeurs français, puis d'y ajouter de bons ouvrages de compositeurs vivants, ne fussent-ils encore que peu connus».

(best known as a teacher of harmony at the Conservatoire) was not better known: «We heard a trio [that was] wise and deep, mysterious [yet] altogether clear, which shares so much kinship with the chamber music of the great masters, and our emotions were absolutely similar to what the landscapes of Corot arouse in us»[30].

Weber was the first French critic to write extensively about the chamber music of Brahms. In 1869, he praised the A-major Piano Quartet, Op. 26 (in its first performance in Paris) as «a magisterial creation, of consummate skill and astonish verve; the first movement is a masterpiece, from every point of view»[31]. He was less enthusiastic about the Clarinet Quintet, Op. 115, which received its Paris debut in 1893: «The skill of the writing is never in doubt with Brahms; but, like Schumann, when he is boring, he doesn't do it halfway»[32]. Between 1879 and 1895 (the year of his retirement), the majority of Weber's chamber-music-related columns were devoted to the founding and the performances of the Société de musique de chambre pour instruments à vent, which will be discussed further on.

In 1898, *Le Temps* engaged Pierre Lalo (son of composer Édouard Lalo) to succeed Johannes Weber as music critic, a position in which he served for fifteen years (1899-1914). Trained in literature, languages, and the classics, Lalo had previously contributed articles to the *Journal des débats* and the *Revue de Paris*. His writing was erudite and witty, although his musical tastes were more conservative than that of his predecessor, and when he didn't like something, his rapier-sharp wit could devolve into meanness. Having grown up with a father who played in a string quartet, Lalo devoted many of his columns to the chamber music repertoire and to the ensembles that played it. The first such column, written in 1899, was about Eugène Ysaÿe and his quartet. Lalo praised the group for bringing to the standard repertoire «an original and new tendency, whose revolutionary spirit should not be concealed»[33]. Lalo had nothing but praise for the performance under the auspices of the Société nationale de musique of d'Indy's String Quartet No. 2, declaring it «one of the noblest and strongest works of the current time»[34]. His assessment of a new string quartet of Saint-Saëns prompted a rumination on writing for a quartet and on chamber music in general that is worth quoting at length:

---

[30]. WEBER 1870: «nous écoutions un trio de Reber, un de ces trios savants et profonds, mystérieux et clairs tout ensemble, qui ont tant de parenté avec la musique de chambre des grands maîtres, et notre émotion était absolument semblable à celle que nous procurent les paysages de Corot». For additional columns in which the critic praises Reber's chamber music, see WEBER 1862A, WEBER 1862B and WEBER 1880D.

[31]. WEBER 1869: «une création magistrale d'une habileté consommée, d'une verve étonnante; le premier morceau est un chef-d'œuvre à tous les égards».

[32]. WEBER 1893: «L'habileté de la facture ne fait jamais de doute chez M. Brahms; mais, comme Schumann, quand il est ennuyeux, il ne l'est pas à demi».

[33]. LALO 1899A: «une tendance originale et neuve, et dont il ne faut pas se dissimuler l'esprit révolutionnaire».

[34]. LALO 1899B: «l'une des œuvres les plus nobles et les plus fortes de ce temps».

[The Saint-Saëns String Quartet] was played with intelligence, vivacity, and perfect unity by four young people [...]. I can only say with what happiness I would see these artists manage to give us, finally, a chamber music society comparable to the illustrious societies that exist in various cities in Germany and whose equivalent cannot be found in France. To be sure, we have a number of societies comprised of excellent musicians who perform the works of the masters in a satisfying fashion. [...] [But] it rarely happens that they have in their interpretation the absolute sense of ensemble that is the supreme object of all interpretations of chamber music. You'll understand that, by the word "ensemble", I'm not alluding to material qualities. I'm talking about unity of expression, of an intellectual and almost moral quality, thanks to which, in hearing Beethoven played by the Quatuor Joachim, or by the Quatuor Ysaÿe, we had the impression of hearing them played not only by a single instrument, but by a single *spirit*, so much do the four players have the same manner of feeling and translating the music of the master. Such communication cannot be obtained by artists united only by the occasion; something else completely is necessary. They must be assembled by deep affinities, brought together by similar tastes and manners of thinking: an exceptional encounter, no doubt, but it is a condition necessary in every good chamber music society. They have to like to work together, they must put their personal glory and their pride aside to reveal, in all their beauty, the illustrious works that they interpret; their musical association must be the essence of their lives. They must arrive at the most direct, the most natural artistic familiarity; they must "stick together" at every moment; spontaneously, without effort, each of them must take on and maintain his rank and his place in the ensemble; all of them must function as a single person. And, too, they must take on the task of penetrating the thoughts of the masters right up to their inmost depths; it must never be enough to play correctly, to the letter, Beethoven or Schumann; they must seek to play them faithfully, according to their spirit; they must take the care and the pain to study them with passionate attention; to find and make appreciable the result of their ideas, the logic of their developments, the requirements of their musical architectures; to express all the intensity of emotion, all the lyrical or dramatic power that is contained in the written text.

You see that the qualities required by chamber music are not small in number, nor mediocre, nor easy. [...] To possess a beautiful and good quartet society, that's one of the happiest fortunes that I could wish for French music[35].

---

35. Lalo 1900: «Ce quatuor a été joué avec une intelligence, une vivacité et une unité parfaites par quatre jeunes gens, MM. Jacques Thibaud, Stanley Mosès, Henri Casadesus et Francis Thibaud. Je ne puis dire avec quel contentement je verrais ces artistes s'efforcer de nous donner enfin une société de musique de chambre comparable aux sociétés illustres qui existent en diverses villes d'Allemagne, et dont l'équivalent ne se retrouve point chez nous. Assurément, nous possédons un certain nombre de sociétés composées de musiciens excellents, et qui exécutent de façon très satisfaisante les œuvres des maîtres. [...] [Mais] il arrive rarement qu'ils aient dans leur interprétation l'ensemble absolu qui est l'objet suprême de toute interprétation de musique de chambre. Vous entendez assez que par ce mot d'ensemble, ce n'est point à des qualités matérielles que je fais allusion. Je veux parler de l'unité

Lalo's yearning to discover a quartet that achieved the superiority of the German string quartet established by Joseph Joachim will be discussed in the next section of this chapter. Lalo had much to say about contemporary quartet repertoire. In his view, Albéric Magnard's String Quartet, which received its premiere under the auspices of the Société nationale de musique, was difficult to penetrate, but worth the effort: «We feel strongly the astonishing vitality, energy, and originality stimulated by this music, so lively and so strong, animated by a movement so vehement; no doubt, we are struck by the lively force, and the depth and gravity of the emotion in the musical ideas; the rhythm strikes us with its richness, its diversity and its novelty»[36]. Also receiving its premiere that night was Ravel's String Quartet, which Lalo described as symptomatic of «a new musical epidemic» that he found «deplorable».

> It is often pleasant to listen to. [...] But this quartet is all about exterior effects, some picturesque and some almost dramatic. There is nothing of the intimate character that [defines] chamber music [...]. And there is yet another fault, even more disturbing and unfortunate: in its harmonies, in the chord progressions, in its sonority, in its form, in all the sensations that it evokes, it offers an incredible resemblance to the music of M. Debussy. [...] Here is the evil of which I spoke; here is the imminent epidemic[37].

---

d'expression, de cette qualité intellectuelle et presque morale grâce à laquelle, en écoutant Beethoven joué par le quatuor Joachim, ou encore par le quatuor Ysaÿe, on avait l'illusion de l'entendre jouer, non pas seulement par un seul instrument, mais par un seul *esprit*, tant les quatre interprètes avaient la même façon de sentir et de traduire la musique du maître. Une telle communion ne saurait être obtenue par des artistes que l'occasion seule réunit; il y faut tout autre chose. Il faut qu'ils soient assemblés par des affinités profondes, rapprochés par des goûts et des manières de penser pareilles: rencontre exceptionnelle, sans doute, mais condition nécessaire de toute bonne société de musique de chambre. Il faut qu'ils aiment à travailler en commun, qu'ils mettent leur gloire et leur orgueil à révéler dans toute leur beauté les œuvres illustres qu'ils interprètent; il faut que leur association musicale soit l'essentiel de leur vie. Il faut qu'ils arrivent à la plus étroite, à la plus naturelle familiarité artistique; qu'ils se "serrent les coudes" à tout moment; que, spontanément, sans effort, chacun d'eux prenne et garde son rang et sa place dans l'ensemble; qu'à eux tous ils ne soient qu'une seule personne. Et il faut encore qu'ils aient le souci de pénétrer la pensée des maîtres jusque dans ses plus intimes profondeurs; qu'ils ne se contentent point d'exécuter correctement, selon la lettre, Beethoven ou Schumann; il faut qu'ils cherchent à les exécuter fidèlement, selon l'esprit; qu'ils se donnent le soin et la peine de les étudier avec une attention passionnée; de retrouver et de faire apercevoir la suite de leurs idées, la logique de leurs développements, l'ordonnance de leurs architectures musicales; d'exprimer toute l'intensité d'émotion, toute la force lyrique ou dramatique qui est contenue dans le texte écrit. [...] / Vous le voyez, les qualités qu'il faut à la musique de chambre ne sont pas en petit nombre, ni médiocres, ni faciles. [...] Posséder une belle et bonne société de quatuors, c'est une des plus heureuses fortunes que je souhaite à la musique française».

[36]. Lalo 1904b: «on éprouve fortement l'étonnante impression de vitalité, d'énergie et d'originalité que suscite cette musique si vivace et si ferme, animée d'un mouvement si véhément; sans doute les idées frappent par leur force vive, par la profondeur et la gravité de leur émotion; et le rythme par sa richesse, sa diversité et sa nouveauté».

[37]. *Ibidem*: «Le quatuor de M. Maurice Ravel [...] montre le cas le plus notable d'une épidémie musicale assez nouvelle encore [...] qui me paraît tout à fait déplorable. [...] il est souvent fort plaisant à écouter [...] Mais

Three Case Studies

In this section, we will examine the reportage by *Le Figaro*, *Le Gaulois*, and *Le Temps* of the activities of three different chamber-music ensembles and reviews of their performances in order to demonstrate more clearly the editorial priorities of the three newspapers and the musical priorities of their music writers. In some cases, there are notable similarities in the reporting and the critical assessments; in others, there sharp differences. In any case, there is sufficient material in these case studies to assess the extent to which the various newspapers inform, educate, and entertain their respective readerships. The three case studies focus on:

1. Ludovic (Louis) Breitner, virtuoso Italian-Austrian pianist and former student of Anton Rubinstein, who founded and directed two Paris chamber music societies: La Gallia (1887-1889) and the Société philarmonique (1895-1898);

2. The Société de musique de chambre pour instruments à vent, a.k.a. Société des instruments à vent (1879-1893; 1896-1914). Founded by flutist Paul Taffanel, this important and highly-esteemed ensemble presented over one hundred fifty works in concert, including fifty-odd first performances;

3. The Quatuor Capet (1893-1928), founded by violinist Lucien Capet, one of the most important French quartets of the nineteenth and early twentieth centuries. The other personnel changed fairly often across the thirty-five years of the group's existence; in its first iteration, the quartet's other three players were André Touret, 2nd violin; Henri Casadesus, viola; and Louis Hasselmanns, cello. (Note: for the sake of clarity, I use the French *quatuor* to designate a performing ensemble; 'quartet' refers either to the genre or to the name of a piece of music.)

Breitner's Chamber-Music Ensembles

Ludovic (Louis) Breitner (1852- 194?) was a student of Anton Rubinstein. Even at a young age he was hailed as a true piano virtuoso, who played with power and musicality in the big Romantic repertoire. At age 23, Breitner embarked on an international career. On the occasion of his first Paris performances, Johannes Weber of *Le Temps* wrote: «Not only does he possess a perfect mechanism, he also draws a beautiful sound from the instrument»[38]. By

---

ce quatuor est tout en effets extérieurs, tantôt pittoresques et tantôt presque dramatiques; il n'a rien du caractère intime qui est celui de la musique de chambre [...] Et il a un autre défaut encore, plus incommode et plus fâcheux: il offre dans ses harmonies, dans l'enchaînement de ses accords, dans sa sonorité, dans sa forme, dans tous les éléments qu'il contient et dans toutes les sensations qu'il éveille, une ressemblance incroyable avec la musique de M. Debussy. [...] Voilà le mal dont je parlais tout à l'heure; voilà l'épidémie imminente».

[38]. WEBER 1875: «non seulement il est en possession d'un mécanisme parfait, il tire un beau son de l'instrument».

1880, Breitner was playing regularly in Paris as a concerto soloist and recitalist and was hailed by *Le Gaulois* as ranking «among the premier virtuosos of the piano»[39]. He quickly formed connections in the city's top freelance circles and, in addition to his solo appearances, was soon performing regularly with Paris's most eminent chamber musicians. Breitner appeared to have possessed both boundless energy and a savvy sense of how to publicize his career in the papers. Both *Le Figaro* and *Le Gaulois* reported regularly on Breitner's chamber-music activities and included detailed notices of the repertoire. The 'review' of one such performance by *Le Gaulois'* music reporter, Nicolet, is written in a style typical of the period and of this newspaper, combining press-release-style factual information with lavish, uncritical praise.

> The performance of classic and modern music given in the Salle de la Société d'Horticulture [...] by M. Breitner, assisted by MM. Marsick and Bürger, was crowned with complete success. It's one of the most interesting [concerts] that we have heard in a long time.
> The Schumann Trio, Op. 110, was interpreted with the rarest perfection, as was the Trio, Op. 26 of Monsieur Édouard Lalo, who brings such honor to the new French school. We know the Sonata, Op. 69, of Beethoven for piano and cello: it would be difficult for anyone to play it better than M. Breitner and M. Bürger. The Sonata [Op. 13] by M. Grieg for piano and violin earned unanimous applause for M. Marsick and M. Breitner.
> We keenly wish that this beautiful performance will be only the first of a series[40].

Nicolet's wish was fulfilled: in 1887, Breitner formed a chamber-music society, La Gallia, to:

> [...] allow the public to hear, in the most artistic conditions, the masterworks of classical music and modern repertoire. [...] The programmes of the society will include an instrumental part and a vocal part. [Audiences] will hear beautiful works, from early music to the most recently written [pieces], from every school, with the participation of the most brilliant virtuosos from every country[41].

---

[39]. ORDONNEAU 1883: «M. Breitner, qui a pris rang parmi les premiers virtuoses du piano».

[40]. NICOLET 1884: «La séance de musique classique et moderne donnée dans la salle de la Société d'horticulture [...] par M. Breitner, avec le concours de MM. Marsick et Bürger, a été couronnée d'un plein succès. C'est l'une des plus intéressantes auxquelles nous ayons assisté depuis longtemps. / Le trio de Schumann (Op. 110) a été interprété avec la plus rare perfection, ainsi que le trio (Op. 26) de M. Édouard Lalo, qui fait tant d'honneur à la nouvelle école française. On connaît la sonate (Op. 69) de Beethoven pour piano et violoncelle: il est difficile de la mieux jouer que M. Breitner et M. Bürger. La sonate (Op. 69) [*sic*: Op. 13] de M. Grieg, pour violon et piano, a valu d'unanimes applaudissements à M. Marsick et à M. Breitner. / Nous souhaitons vivement que cette belle séance ne soit que le commencement d'une série».

[41]. NICOLET 1887: «Il vient de se former une nouvelle société musicale, la Gallia, sous la direction de l'éminent pianiste Ludovic Breitner, pour faire entendre au public, dans les conditions les plus artistiques, les chefs-d'œuvre

Breitner presented two brilliant seasons of performances, but when his international touring increased, he was forced to halt La Gallia's activities in 1889. In 1895, the pianist resumed his chamber-music performances with a four-concert series presented in tandem with his wife Bertha, an excellent violinist, and with distinguished colleagues. The four programmes included violin sonatas by Beethoven and Saint-Saëns; cello sonatas by Rubin Goldmark and Rubinstein; the 13th, 14th, and 15th string quartets by Beethoven; piano trios by Schumann, Brahms, and — in its first Paris performance — Dvořák's 'Dumky' Trio; Breitner also programmed the Dvořák Piano Quintet, the Saint-Saëns Septet, and the first performance of a suite by Danish composer Eduard Schütt[42].

By the end of the year, Breitner had launched a new chamber-music society, the Société philharmonique, which presented a full season of twenty biweekly concerts. In *Le Gaulois*, Louis de Fourcaud praised the «charming ingeniousness» of the Dvořák Quintet, the «rich and diverse sonority» of the Sextet by Giulio Alary, and the «exquisite» Variations for Two Pianos by Christian Sinding; Fourcaud went on to laud Breitner and his colleagues with fulsome praise: «This is a sure and valiant company [...] to whom we keenly wish success as a form of justice and as a gauge of the musical state of the public»[43]. *Le Figaro* sang Breitner's praises as well — not in the music section of the paper, but in the society column 'Le Monde et la Ville', writing in a manner intended to attract the paper's upper-class readership:

> The most elegant audience [attended] the fourth concert of M. Breitner's Société philharmonique. On the programme: the Dvořák Quintet, the Sonata by E. Sjögren; a Beethoven [Piano] Quartet played by MM. Breitner, Marsick, Hayot, Bailly and Loëb. Their great success was shared by Madame Eléonore Blanc, who sang in a ravishing manner the *Ballade de Barberine*, *Mignonne*, and *Chanson d'un Vanneur de Bled* by M. G. de Saint-Quentin, who received great ovations. Recognized in the hall: Princesse A. Bibesco, Baronne Caruel de Saint-Martin, Comte de Saussine, the ministers of Sweden, Norway, the Netherlands, etc.[44]

---

de la musique classique et du répertoire moderne. [...] / Les programmes de la société comprendront une partie instrumentale et une partie vocale. / On se propose de faire entendre les belles œuvres les plus anciennes comme les plus récentes de toutes les écoles, avec le concours des plus brillants virtuoses de tous les pays».

42. Fourcaud 1895a.

43. Fourcaud 1895b: «Le concert auquel il m'a été donné d'assister, comprenait un *Quintette* fort brillant, plein d'ingéniosités charmantes du compositeur bohémien Antoine Dvorak, [...] et un *Sextuor à cordes*, d'un style pur et soutenu, d'une sonorité riche et diverse, de M. Alary. J'y ai entendu, encore, des *Variations* exquises pour deux pianos [...] / Il y a là [...] une compagnie sûre et vaillante, de laquelle les musiciens peuvent beaucoup attendre et dont nous souhaitons vivement le succès comme une justice et comme un gage de l'état musical du public». See also Fourcaud 1896 and Fourcaud 1898.

44. Ferrari 1897: «Assistance des plus élégantes au 4e concert de la Société philharmonique de M. Breitner. Au programme: Quintete [*sic*], de Dvorak; Sonate, d'E. Sjögren; Quatuor, de Beethoven, exécutés par MM.

Le Temps continued to announce all of the Société philharmonique's performances but did not provide extensive reportage or criticism — except once, in 1899, when Pierre Lalo wrote, «A few interesting performances. One was given by M. Breitner, who is one of the best pianists of our time and who, I don't know why, is never heard at the Châtelet or at the Cirque d'Été»[45]. In the first decades of the twentieth century, Breitner continued his breakneck schedule of international performances up through the advent of World War I. On 6 March 1911, he participated in a chamber music concert with German musicians at the French Embassy in Berlin, performing a Schumann trio and the Franck Piano Quintet[46]; three years later, in the same venue, he performed with German musicians in a programme featuring Fauré's C-minor Piano Quartet and the Violin Sonata of Saint-Saëns[47]. It is not clear if Breitner ever sought French citizenship, but it seems that both of his children were French citizens. His son served as an infantryman in the French army and was killed in battle in 1915. After the war, the Breitners settled definitively in Paris. The pianist devoted more of his time to teaching (including at the Lausanne Conservatoire) and to home salon performances with his wife and a long list of eminent colleagues. He was still performing as he approached his eightieth year: in 1931, *Le Figaro* announced his recital at the Salle Gaveau[48]. His performances continued to be listed in the papers until 1939, after which his name disappears from the press altogether. To date, no obituary has been found in any print source.

The Société de Musique de Chambre pour *Instruments à Vent*

It was, once again, *Le Temps*' 'Critique musicale' column that was the first to announce the founding of an important new chamber-music ensemble, the Société de Musique de Chambre pour instruments à vent (for convenience's sake, henceforth referred to as Société d'instruments à vent). On 4 February 1879, Johannes Weber wrote a long column explaining the origins of the group. In 1873, a 'Société Classique' had created an ensemble comprised of both strings and winds; their performances had been well-reviewed. But the wind players felt that they were they were playing a secondary role, and the artists did not play regularly in the Société's concerts. «Now», wrote Weber,

---

Breitner, Marsick, Hayot, Bailly et Loëb. Leur grand succès a été partagé par Mme Eléonore Blanc, qui a chanté à ravir le ballade de *Barberine, Mignonne* et *Chanson d'un Vanneur de Bled*, de M. G. de Saint-Quentin, auquel on a fait de grandes ovations. Reconnu dans la salle: Princesse A. Bibesco, baronne Caruel de Saint-Martin, comte de Saussine, les ministres de Suède et Norvège, des Pays-Bas, etc.».

[45]. Lalo 1899c: «Quelques séances intéressantes. L'une a été donnée par M. Breitner, qui est un des meilleurs pianistes de ce temps et que, je ne sais pourquoi, l'on n'entend jamais au Chat ni au Cirque d'été».

[46]. Delaroche 1911.

[47]. Bonnefon 1914.

[48]. Crémone 1931.

> In order for wind music to have a performance worthy of the great classical works, it requires a group composed of very good artists — but these artists must also be in the habit of playing together regularly [...] in order to obtain, to the extent possible, the fusion of instrumental sonority, in which, because of the diversity and strength of their respective timbres, even the smallest errors stand out and become detrimental to the ensemble.
>
> These difficulties were perfectly understood by a well-known group of artists who have worked hard to overcome them. [...] The new society consists of a flute, two oboes, clarinets, two horns, and two bassoons[49].

And, thus, the new group, co-founded by flutist Taffanel and clarinetist Charles Turban, was born. The first performance of the Société des instruments à vent took place on 6 February 1879 in the small hall of the Salle Pleyel; the programme consisted of the Beethoven Octet, Op. 103, the B-minor flute and keyboard sonata of J. S. Bach, and two works for wind quintet: one by Anton Rubinstein and a second, entitled *Aubade*, by Adrien Barthe. While Weber enjoyed the music, he felt that the acoustics of the hall caused the piano to drown out the other instruments[50]. Following Weber's advice, the Société moved its subsequent performances to the large hall of the Maison Pleyel[51]. In his third review of the group, Weber wrote that «the performances are followed assiduously by music-lovers and artists, not only because of the excellent interpretations, but because most of the works played are little-known or entirely new»[52]. After the concluding concert of its inaugural season, Weber wrote, «Definitely, the new Société has had more success than its excellent constituent artists dared to dream of, and we will see them again with great pleasure next winter»[53]. Over the next decade, Weber would go on to write more than a dozen reviews of the group, not only praising the excellent performances but also educating his readership about the new works introduced in the programmes[54]. During its

---

[49]. WEBER 1879A: «Or, pour qu'une musique d'instruments à vent, surtout s'ils sont en petit nombre, puisse avoir une exécution parfaitement digne des grandes œuvres classiques, il faut non-seulement qu'elle soit composée de très bons artistes, mais encore que ceux-ci aient l'habitude de jouer ensemble, [...] afin d'obtenir autant que possible la fusion de la sonorité d'instruments, chez lesquels, grâce à la diversité et à la force de leur timbre, les plus légères erreurs font saillie et deviennent préjudiciables à l'ensemble. / Ces difficultés ont été parfaitement comprises par une réunion d'artistes tous bien connus et ayant sérieusement travaillé à les vaincre; [...] La nouvelle société comprend ainsi une flûte, deux hautbois, deux clarinettes, deux cors et deux bassons».

[50]. WEBER 1879B.

[51]. WEBER 1879C.

[52]. WEBER 1879D: «les auditions sont suivies assidûment par les amateurs et les artistes, non-seulement à cause de l'excellente interprétation, mais aussi parce que la plupart des œuvres exécutées sont peu connues ou entièrement nouvelles».

[53]. WEBER 1879E: «En définitive, la nouvelle Société a eu plus de succès que n'osaient l'espérer les excellents artistes qui la composent, et nous la reverrons avec grand plaisir l'hiver prochain».

[54]. See for example, WEBER 1880A, WEBER 1880B, WEBER 1880C, WEBER 1881A, WEBER 1881B, WEBER 1882A, WEBER 1882B, WEBER 1882C, WEBER 1883, WEBER 1884, WEBER 1885, WEBER 1886, WEBER 1890.

eminent career, the Société performed over one-hundred-fifty works, including several dozen first performances, and Weber followed the group's success with evident delight.

To put it mildly, *Le Figaro* and *Le Gaulois* did not keep up a similar pace in their respective coverage of the Société. *Le Figaro* never wrote anything about the Société d'instruments à vent beyond concert listings in its 'Concerts et Spectacles' column. Not until 1884, a full five years after the Société's founding, did *Le Gaulois'* Louis de Fourcaud write his first substantial review of the group:

> There was a huge crowd at this concert, and it is right that people are rushing [to hear] such curious performances. We rarely have the occasion to hear a quantity of chamber-music compositions where the instruments are mixed. Thanks to this association of virtuosos, there's a whole repertoire that has begun to come out of the shadows and could become larger. What composer wouldn't be happy to have as interpreters artists like Messieurs Taffanel, Gillet, Turban, Espaignet, Grisez, and their peers? We cannot conceive of a more perfect performance. [...]
> I can only praise the performers as a whole. It must be said, however [...] that the flutist Taffanel stood out by virtue of his precision and the delightful spirit of his virtuosity[55].

Le Gaulois listed the Société's performances once or twice a year; occasionally, the titles of the works to be performed were included, but even these diminished over time. In 1893, the group temporarily disbanded. For many years, Taffanel had pursued a conducting career in addition to his work as a soloist and chamber musician. In 1892, he won the coveted post of the conductor of the Orchestre de la Société des concerts du Conservatoire, stepping down from the distinguished chamber-music ensemble that he had co-founded. With Taffanel gone, the Société ceased its activities, playing one last concert together on 4 May 1893. After Taffanel died in 1895, the Société des instruments à vent regrouped, launching a three-concert series in 1896 with its new personnel[56]. From 1898 until the advent of World War I, the group maintained an active concert schedule. None of the performances of the reconstituted group were reviewed in the daily newspapers.

---

[55].　FOURCAUD 1884: «Il y avait foule à ce concert, et c'est justice que l'on s'empresse à d'aussi curieuses auditions. On n'a que rarement l'occasion d'entendre quantité de compositions de musique de chambre, où les instruments à cordes sont mêlés essentiellement. Grâce à cette association de virtuoses, c'est tout un répertoire qui a commencé à sortir de l'ombre et qui peut s'augmenter. Quel compositeur ne serait heureux d'avoir pour interprètes des artistes comme M. Taffanel, Gillet, Turban, Espaignet, et leurs pairs? On ne saurait concevoir de plus parfaite exécution. [...] / Je ne puis que faire en bloc l'éloge des exécutants. Il convient de dire, néanmoins, que [...] le flûtiste Taffanel s'est principalement distingué par la précision et le délicieux entrain de sa virtuosité». The program consisted of the Dvořák *Serenade*, Op. 44, the Beethoven *Quintet*, Op. 16, and an unspecified *Divertimento* by Mozart for winds and strings.

[56].　NICOLET 1896.

The last mention of the Société was published on 17 December 1900, after Taffanel was promoted to Officier de la Légion d'honneur. The snooty tone of the article in *Le Gaulois* announcing Taffanel's honour perfectly sums up the paper's approach to music reporting.

> Who would have thought that Taffanel, the little flutist of the Opéra, would one day be armed with a conductor's baton? A quarter-century ago, Taffanel seemed to have limited his ambition to virtuosity on the piccolo or the flute. [...] In this little man, however, there was, after all, a very legitimate ambition. He founded the Société des instruments à vent, which the salons snapped up. His reputation as an orchestral leader increased to that of high-society virtuoso. Already in possession of a pretty fortune, living in his townhouse, he gave very popular soirees. The Opéra made him one of their conductors, preparing the road that led him to the head of the phalanx of the Conservatoire. The struggle was heated. However, Taffanel prevailed. He has just carried off the rosette [of the Legion of Honour] with flying colours. It will be well-placed on the lapel of the maestro of the flute and the orchestra[57].

The Quatuor Capet; Other French String Quartets

In 1900, Pierre Lalo of *Le Temps* had yearned for the formation of a French string quartet that could rival the superiority of the best German quartets, especially the Joseph Joachim Quartet. In 1904, it seemed his wish had come true: «Will we finally have a quartet? It seems that way — and it's high time». And what were the qualities necessary to produce an ensemble that would meet the highest standards of music-making exemplified by the Joachim Quartet?

> This quartet not only possesses almost complete perfection and sense of absolute ensemble in its execution; but [it also] attains the unity of expression, the intellectual and almost moral feeling of communion, thanks to which one has the impression of hearing the music played, even more than by a single instrument, by a single spirit, so much do its members have the same manner of understanding, feeling, and translating what they feel; or, better yet, hearing the music express

---

57.   P. R. 1900: «Qui aurait pu croire que Taffanel, le petit flûtiste de l'Opéra, serait un jour armé du bâton de chef d'orchestre? Il y a un quart de siècle, Taffanel semblait devoir borner son ambition à la virtuosité de la petite ou de la grande flûte. [...] Dans ce petit homme, pourtant, il y avait une ambition très légitime après tout. Il avait fondé la Société des instruments à vent que les salons s'arrachaient. Sa réputation de chef de pupitre s'accrut de celle de virtuose mondain. Possesseur déjà d'une jolie fortune, habitant son hôtel, il donnait des soirées très recherchées. La direction de l'Opéra en fit un chef d'orchestre, lui préparant le chemin qui devait le conduire à la tête de la phalange du Conservatoire. La lutte fut chaude. Cependant, Taffanel l'emporta. Il vient d'emporter de haute main sa rosette. Elle sera bien placée sur le revers de l'habit du maëstro de la flûte et du chef d'orchestre». Taffanel's promotion was awarded in the category of Public Education and Fine Arts.

itself, directly, as if without intermediary — that is how deeply and intimately the players penetrate the thought of the [composer]. [...] It's this depth and simplicity, this sobriety and nobility, all combined; this disdain for empty effect, this almost religious devotion to the music; and this naturalness, flexibility, and ease, through which the most diverse nuances, motions, and feelings effortlessly move and join and mix; this infallible sense of the relation of the parts to the ensemble that gives to each detail exactly the importance and the eloquence that it should have in the expression of the total idea: it's always one of the most magnificent examples of musical interpretation that has ever been realized[58].

It so happened that the Joachim Quartet and the Quatuor Capet performed within one week of each other, both groups offering a performance of Beethoven's String Quartet No. 12, Op. 127, on their respective programmes, and Lalo opined that, in some movements, the young French artists very nearly approached the level of their glorious elders:

> I won't say that the Quatuor Capet can [yet] equal the Quatuor Joachim. It lacks the forty years of familiarity with each other and with the composers that makes it unique [...] [but] we feel that they have in M. Capet a true leader [...] [and] they have the highest ambition of grasping the work and manifesting its thought. [...] Let the young musicians of the Quatuor Capet persevere as they began; let them continue to work in the same spirit; let them make their collective work the focus of their life and their art; they will create in this country a quartet equal to the best German quartets. A half-century ago, when the exiled Wagner lived in Zurich [*sic*: Lucerne] and when his friends wanted to offer him a party according to his wishes, they had come from Paris, to play some of the late quartets of Beethoven for him, the society whose leader was Maurin. It was not then in Germany, but in France that one found the best quartet players[59].

58. Lalo 1904a: «Aurions-nous enfin un quatuor? Il semble. Et c'est grand temps [...]».

59. *Ibidem*: «Je ne vous dirai point que l'on puisse égaler au quatuor Joachim le quatuor Capet. Il lui manque les quarante années de familiarité avec soi-même et avec les maîtres qui donnent à l'autre cette profondeur simple par laquelle il est unique. [...] on sent qu'ils ont en M. Capet un chef véritable [...] [et] ils ont l'ambition plus haute d'en saisir et d'en manifester la pensée; [...] Que les jeunes musiciens qui composent le quatuor Capet persévèrent ainsi qu'ils ont commencé; qu'ils continuent de travailler dans le même esprit; qu'ils fassent de leur œuvre collective l'essentiel de leur vie et de leur art; ils créeront chez nous un quatuor égal aux meilleurs quatuors allemands. Il y a un demi-siècle, quand Wagner exilé habitait Zurich [*sic*: Lucerne], et que ses amis lui voulaient offrir une fête selon son souhait en jouant quelques-uns des derniers quatuors de Beethoven, la société dont le chef était Maurin: ce n'était pas alors en Allemagne, c'était en France que se rencontraient les meilleurs quartettistes». The longest and most detailed version of this anecdote was published by Adolphe Jullien (Jullien 1885; see note 10). In Jullien's telling, «Wagner had retained the most vivid memory of this unexpected celebration, and a few years before his death he was still saying [...] that he had never heard the late Beethoven quartets better played than by these four French artists». («Wagner avait conservé le souvenir le plus vivace de cette fête inattendue, et quelques années

Lalo wrote about the Quatuor Capet, often at length, in numerous articles published between 1904 and 1912[60]; no other French string quartet or chamber-music ensemble received as much of his attention. The Quatuor Capet was the subject of much press in all three papers in 1905 and 1906, when the quartet played the complete cycle of seventeen Beethoven string quartets. *Le Gaulois'* Georges Pelca wrote of the Capet's performance of the 13th quartet, Op. 130: «One cannot express [its] deep and troubling beauty. Audacities swarm about in this work: rhythmic and harmonic audacities, brusque changes of tempo, surprising designs and modulations. One can conceive of the astonishment that it provoked in earlier times! — The Quatuor Capet already plays it marvelously. No doubt that it will soon play it with all the precision and finesse dreamed of. Unanimous applause»[61]. Shortly thereafter, the Quatuor Capet received an exceptional authorisation to perform the late Beethoven string quartets in the Salle du Conservatoire[62]. *Le Figaro's* critic Robert Brussel wrote, «I wouldn't know how to express in these brief lines the perfection of this interpretation, in which Beethoven's ideas were understood, transmitted, and lived, with the sole feeling necessary for such works: piety. The quartet didn't so much play as officiate: and there existed between the audience and these interpreters a truly religious communion»[63]. In subsequent years, when the critics wrote of the Quatuor Capet, they often evoked the memory of Joseph Joachim, who died in 1907. When the Capet was engaged to perform in 1910 at the Beethoven Festival in Bonn, *Le Gaulois'* Nicolet wrote, «We note this news with pride, for, since Joachim's death, no quartet has been judged

---

avant sa mort il disait encore, à l'un de mes amis, qu'il n'avait jamais entendu mieux jouer les derniers quatuors de Beethoven que par ces quatre artistes français»).

60.   LALO 1904C; LALO 1904D; LALO 1905; LALO 1906A; LALO 1906B; LALO 1907A; LALO 1907B; LALO 1911; LALO 1912.

61.   PELCA 1906: «on ne peut exprimer la profonde et troublante beauté. Les audaces fourmillent dans cette œuvre, audaces rythmiques, harmoniques, brusques changements de mouvements, dessins et modulations surprenants. On conçoit l'étonnement qu'elle provoquait jadis! – Le quatuor Capet la joua déjà à merveille. Nul doute qu'il ne la joue, bientôt, avec toute la précision et le fini rêvés. Applaudissements unanimes».

62.   Normally, use of the Salle du Conservatoire, a hall with exceptionally fine acoustics, was reserved only for use by its own faculty and students. All three papers wrote at length about the exceptional measures taken, thanks to special pleading by Conservatoire director Gabriel Fauré, for the Quatuor Capet to perform the late Beethoven quartets in the jealously guarded concert hall. Pierre Lalo noted wryly in his column, «The sky didn't tremble; the walls didn't crumble; the sacrilege was consummated without any sign of celestial fury [...]. To the contrary, [the quartet] achieved such a striking success that M. le Under-Secretary of Beaux-Arts, without fear of wearing out divine patience by repeating and aggravating his crime, immediately promised them the hall for the following year» (LALO 1906B).

63.   BRUSSEL 1906: «Je ne saurais dire dans ces courtes lignes la perfection de cette interprétation, où la pensée de Beethoven fut comprise, transmise, vécue, avec le seul sentiment qui convienne à de telles œuvres: la piété. Ils ont moins joué qu'officié: et ce fut entre le public et ces interprètes une communion vraiment religieuse».

worthy of taking part in this grand artistic solemnity. The Quatuor Capet, thus, finds itself officially invested as the successor of the Quatuor Joachim»[64].

The first decade of the twentieth century was, in fact, a golden age for string-quartet playing in France: in addition to the Quatuor Capet, eminent quartets led by violinists Jules Delsart, Albert Geloso, Maurice Hayot, Pierre Marsick, Armand Parent, and the Belgian Eugène Ysaÿe performed regularly in Paris. But it would be hard to judge either the interpretive prowess or the popularity of these ensembles based on reportage in the three newspapers discussed here, for they were rarely accorded the critical attention they deserved. Most mentions of these groups and their concert programs are found either in terse concert listings at the back of the paper or in the society columns. For example, before the advent of the Quatuor Capet, the Quatuor Geloso offered, for many years, its own traversals of late Beethoven quartets. After one such concert performed under the auspices of the Concerts Colonne, Charles Joly of *Le Figaro* noted the «extreme polyphony, the range and the complexity of the developments» in the 14th Quartet, Op. 131, and congratulated the Geloso Quartet on its «perfect understanding of the work», and «the efforts that it makes every year to initiate us into Beethoven's mysterious beauties»[65]. That glowing review was written in 1902 — and it was the last that the Quartet would receive in the dailies: the group would henceforth be more frequently associated with its appearances in the salon of the Princesse Edmond de Polignac[66]. Although the Quatuor Parent gave forty-two performances of the Debussy String Quartet over a ten-year period, *Le Figaro* never wrote a review of what it deemed to be a «very curious» work that had been «popularised» by the group's repeated performances[67]. While the paper's music critic Alfred Delilia did laud the group for «putting its talent in the service of the French School»[68], he never wrote anything substantive about the contemporary music championed by the quartet. *Le Gaulois* did not even deign to publicise the new-music events. But it was a different story when the Quatuor

---

64. NICOLET 1910: «Nous enregistrons cette nouvelle avec fierté car, depuis la disparition de Joachim, aucun Quatuor n'avait été jugé digne de prendre part à cette grande solennité artistique. Le Quatuor Capet se trouve donc, de ce fait, officiellement investi de la succession du Quatuor Joachim».

65. JOLY 1902: «Ces derniers quatuors de Beethoven diffèrent en effet des précédents par leur extrême polyphonie, par l'étendue et la complication des développements [...] Il faut féliciter le quatuor Géloso [...] des efforts qu'il fait chaque année pour nous initier à ces mystérieuses beautés de Beethoven [...] étant donné qu'une pareille exécution exige, non seulement une parfaite connaissance de l'ouvrage, mais encore une longue et minutieuse préparation».

66. FERRARI 1901, FERRARI 1906; DELAROCHE 1912.

67. DELILIA 1907: «Le quatuor Parent donnera après-demain vendredi, salle Æolian, sa septième séance [...]. Le programme, entièrement moderne, comprendra [...] le très curieux Quatuor à cordes de Debussy. N'oublions pas que c'est le quatuor Parent qui a vulgarisé cette dernière œuvre en en donnant quarante-deux auditions en dix années».

68. DELILIA 1904: «On verra que l'admiration des classiques n'empêche pas le Quatuor Parent de mettre son talent au service de l'école française».

Parent performed in the salon of Dr. and Madame Châtellier — who, keeping up with the trend, presented their own salon series devoted to the complete Beethoven string quartets: *Le Gaulois* reported that «[their] performance was perfect and the marvelous Adagio of the 10th quartet, with its deep emotion, thrilled the very artistic audience»[69]. And, for all its renown, the Quatuor Capet also performed in music salons and high-society venues: both the Comtesse Joachim Murat and Comtesse Élaine Greffulhe, president of the Société des Grandes Auditions de France, capitalised on the reputation of the Quatuor Capet, presenting their own Beethoven-quartet performances, thus burnishing their own social standing[70]. The article on the front page of *Le Gaulois* informed its readership that, in the Beethoven performances in the Église du Gésu performed by the Quatuor Capet and organised by the Comtesse Greffulhe, «the work of Beethoven, which has found in the Quatuor Capet the ideal interpreter, has *finally* [emphasis mine] found the atmosphere and the milieu in which it should be heard»[71].

CONCLUSION

This study has given an overview and assessment of coverage of chamber-music ensembles and their performance activities in the three largest of the Paris daily newspapers — *Le Figaro*, *Le Gaulois*, and *Le Temps* — in the years between 1860 and 1914. The results reveal a complex, often frustrating mixture of reportage and criticism. Thanks to the erudition and the sincere passion for chamber music of its two music critics, Weber and Lalo, the readership of *Le Temps* was treated to lengthy, well-written, and highly detailed articles about the major goings-on and trends in chamber-music performance in Paris up until World War I. Even when this reader found reasons to disagree with Weber's or Lalo's assessments, it was always a pleasure to read such informative and beautiful prose. In contrast, the writings about chamber music by the music reporters and critics of *Le Figaro* and *Le Gaulois* during the same period were often spotty and inconsistent. While it is possible to glean a fair idea of the repertoire being performed in the concert halls, the superficiality of the 'reviews' in the Music columns — by Alfred Delilia for *Le Figaro* and Nicolet for *Le Gaulois* — leaves much to be desired: the superficially adulatory language of these reporters is strikingly bereft of nuance and critical distance; most of the time,

---

69. FERRARI 1904B: «Le quatuor Parent [...] a donné avant-hier soir, chez le docteur et Mme K. Châtellier, la deuxième séance de l'audition intégrale des dix-sept quatuors à cordes de Beethoven. L'exécution a été parfaite et le merveilleux adagio du dixième, d'une émotion profonde, a enthousiasmé le très artistique auditoire». See also FERRARI 1904A; FERRARI 1904C; FERRARI 1904D; FERRARI 1904E; FERRARI 1904F.

70. VALFLEURY 1911; UN DOMINO 1912A.

71. UN DOMINO 1912B: «L'œuvre de Beethoven, qui avait trouvé dans le quatuor Capet l'interprète idéal, a rencontré enfin l'atmosphère et le milieu où elle devait être entendue». See also UN DOMINO 1912C.

it would appear that the artists themselves had written fulsome praise into their press releases, and the reporters published these puff pieces verbatim. Actual reviews of chamber-music performances by the papers' music critics — Darcours and Brussel for *Le Figaro*, Fourcauld and Pelca for *Le Gaulois* — are, for the most part, knowledgeable and insightful. But, unfortunately, these critics did not give chamber music the attention that was devoted to opera and symphonic concerts. For the most part, it is easier to ascertain trends in chamber-music performance during the *Belle Époque* by reading the society columns, which describe the repertoire and performers in private salon performances in copious detail.

Several trends stand out: The outsized interest in the Beethoven's late string quartets during this period seems to have been something akin to a mania. These works were programmed constantly, to (if the papers can be believed) capacity crowds. Sometimes two different ensembles would be performing Beethoven's magnificent last works in the same week — as was the case, as per Pierre Lalo's article, when the young Quatuor Capet was playing the E-flat String Quartet, Op. 127 within days of a performance by the venerable Quatuor Joachim. And the craze for this music was not limited to the concert halls: numerous upper-class salon hostesses programmed 'Beethoven Festivals' in their homes or in the societies they sponsored because the late quartets were all the rage.

In general, most chamber music programming centered around the string quartets, piano trios, and piano quartets or quintets of Haydn, Mozart, Beethoven, and Mendelssohn. 'The New French School' of chamber-music composers meant, primarily, Fauré, Franck, d'Indy, Lalo, and Saint-Saëns. There existed a clear mistrust of the music of Debussy, and his String Quartet, written and premiered by the Société nationale de musique in 1893, it received no reviews at all in the daily newspapers. It was mentioned only in passing in 1897, when *Le Gaulois*, announcing an upcoming performance for a 'Popular Thursdays' concert, referred to the composer as «Claude Bussy»[72]. And, as of 1907, the same paper was still unaware of the forty-two performances of the work, to which I referred earlier, that had been given by the Quatuor Parent. In contrast, *Le Figaro*'s Alfred Delilia was more broad-minded when it came publicising works by the progressive branch of contemporary French music: in announcing the Quatuor Parent's upcoming twelve-concert chamber-music series, he lauded the group for promoting young French composers; the Debussy String Quartet and Ravel's 'new' String Quartet were explicitly named in a lineup that also included works by Franck, d'Indy, and Chausson[73]. While the Debussy Quartet received no critical comment in the follow-up article, Delilia described Ravel's Quartet as «[...] a little marvel. This work, extremely difficult, was

---

[72]. NICOLET 1897c: «Au programme du prochain jeudi populaire de musique de chambre ancienne et moderne [...] un Quatuor de Claude Bussy».

[73]. See fn 68. DELILIA 1904.

interpreted by the Quatuor Parent in a remarkable manner»[74]. Despite the aforementioned invective of Pierre Lalo, who had qualified the Ravel Quartet one year earlier as «deplorable», the work proved so popular with audiences that the Quatuor Parent decided to give it a second hearing on a subsequent concert programme[75].

Several weeks after the repeat performance of the Ravel Quartet, Fauré, an occasional music writer for *Le Figaro*, published a lengthy encomium tracing the illustrious career and influence of Joseph Joachim. With sad irony, Fauré noted that «[Joachim] knew that Paris venerates great talents as it venerates great works. He knew all that as well, or better, perhaps, than do we ourselves, [the French], who either don't always know it or feign to forget it»[76]. At the conclusion of his column, Fauré recalled the command performance in Lucerne of late Beethoven string quartets by the Société des Derniers Quatuors de Beethoven.

> Who remembers that, on three different occasions, in 1856, 1859 and 1866, the quartet composed of violinists Maurin and Sabatier, violist Mas and cellist Chevillard [...] obtained, in the Rhineland, an enormous success? that — in the words of Fétis — "Cologne, Frankfurt, Darmstadt, Hanover, Leipzig, and Berlin resounded with prodigious praise and applause for the most perfect interpretations that they had ever heard in the most difficult [chamber]-ensemble music that existed?"
>
> Will this memory, at least, make us more attentive to the efforts made, in our midst, by other French artists who are close to attaining, in the same order of ideas, supreme perfection[77]?

---

[74]. DELILIA 1905A: «De Maurice Ravel, [...] un Quatuor à cordes qui est une petite merveille. Cette dernière œuvre, extrêmement difficile, fut interprétée par le quatuor Parent d'une manière remarquable».

[75]. DELILIA 1905B. The repeat performance of the Ravel Quartet took place on 24 February 1905.

[76]. FAURÉ 1905: «Il sait que Paris a le culte des grands talents comme il a le culte des grandes œuvres. Il sait tout cela aussi bien et mieux, peut-être, que nous-mêmes qui ne le savons pas toujours, ou qui feignons de l'oublier».

[77]. *Ibidem*: «Qui se souvient qu'à trois reprises, en 1856, 1859 et 1866, le quatuor composé des violonistes Maurin et Sabatier, de l'altiste Mas et du violoncelliste Chevillard [...] obtint, au-delà du Rhin, un immense succès? que "Cologne, Francfort, Darmstadt, Hanovre, Leipzig et Berlin — ainsi que l'a écrit Fétis — retentirent des éloges et des applaudissements prodigués à l'interprétation la plus parfaite qu'on eût jamais entendue de la musique d'ensemble la plus difficile qui existe?" / Ce souvenir, du moins, nous rendra-t-il plus attentifs aux efforts que tentent, au milieu de nous, d'autres artistes français bien près d'atteindre, dans le même ordre d'idées, la suprême perfection?».

Bibliography

Boisfleury 1907
Boisfleury. 'Mondanités', in: *Le Gaulois*, 16 January 1907.

Bonnefon 1914
Bonnefon, Charles. 'Figaro en Allemagne: La Cour et la Ville', in: *Le Figaro*, 12 March 1914.

Brussel 1906
Brussel, Robert. 'Les Concerts', in: *Le Figaro*, 5 February 1906.

Cheron 1899
Chéron, Raoul. 'Mondanités', in: *Le Gaulois*, 9 March 1899.

Cremone 1931
Crémone, L. de. 'Courrier musical', in: *Le Figaro*, 19 November 1931.

Darcours 1892
Darcours, Charles. 'Notes de musique: le Quatuor Ysaÿe', in: *Le Figaro*, 16 May 1892.

Delaroche 1911
Delaroche, E. 'Le Monde et La Ville', in: *Le Figaro*, 11 March 1911.

Delaroche 1912
Id. 'Le Monde et La Ville', in: *Le Figaro*, 25 February 1912.

Delilia 1904
Delilia, Alfred. 'Spectacles et concerts', in: *Le Figaro*, 29 November 1904.

Delilia 1905a
Id. 'Spectacles et concerts', in: *Le Figaro*, 11 February 1905.

Delilia 1905b
Id. 'Spectacles et concerts', in: *Le Figaro*, 16 February 1905.

Delilia 1906
Id. 'Spectacles et concerts', in: *Le Figaro*, 17 January 1906.

Delilia 1907
Id. 'Spectacles et concerts', in: *Le Figaro*, 13 February 1907.

Fauré 1905
Fauré, Gabriel. 'Joachim', in: *Le Figaro*, 13 March 1905.

FERRARI 1896A
FERRARI. 'Le Monde et la Ville', in: *Le Figaro*, 18 January 1896.

FERRARI 1896B
ID. 'Le Monde et la Ville', in: *Le Figaro*, 13 April 1896.

FERRARI 1897
ID. 'Le Monde et la Ville', in: *Le Figaro*, 10 January 1897.

FERRARI 1901
ID. 'Le Monde et la Ville', in: *Le Figaro*, 29 May 1901.

FERRARI 1904A
ID. 'Le Monde et la Ville', in: *Le Figaro*, 26 January 1904.

FERRARI 1904B
ID. 'Le Monde et la Ville', in: *Le Figaro*, 11 February 1904.

FERRARI 1904C
ID. 'Le Monde et la Ville', in: *Le Figaro*, 7 March 1904.

FERRARI 1904D
ID. 'Le Monde et la Ville', in: *Le Figaro*, 22 March 1904.

FERRARI 1904E
ID. 'Le Monde et la Ville', in: *Le Figaro*, 24 April 1904.

FERRARI 1904F
ID. 'Le Monde et la Ville', in: *Le Figaro*, 3 May 1904.

FERRARI 1906
ID. 'Le Monde et la Ville', in: *Le Figaro*, 23 January 1906.

FERRARI 1908
ID. 'Le Monde et la Ville', in: *Le Figaro*, 6 April 1908.

FOURCAUD 1880
FOURCAUD, Louis de. 'Les Grands Concerts: Salle Pleyel: Concert de la Société nationale de musique', in: *Le Gaulois*, 18 January 1880.

FOURCAUD 1884
ID. 'Courrier des spectacles', in: *Le Gaulois*, 15 February 1884.

FOURCAUD 1895A
ID. 'Courrier des spectacles', in: *Le Gaulois*, 18 February 1895.

FOURCAUD 1895B
ID. 'Musique', in: *Le Gaulois*, 10 December 1895.

FOURCAUD 1896
ID. 'Musique', *Le Gaulois*, 30 November 1896.

FOURCAUD 1898
ID. 'Musique', in: *Le Gaulois*, 9 April 1898.

GANT DE SAXE 1894
GANT DE SAXE. 'Mondanités', in: *Le Gaulois*, 20 February 1894.

GEORGES 1878
GEORGES [pseudonym for Louis de Fourcaud]. 'Musique: Salle du Trocadéro. – Les concerts de la semaine', in: *Le Gaulois*, 6 August 1878.

JOLY 1902
JOLY, Charles. 'Spectacles et concerts', in: *Le Figaro*, 10 January 1902.

JULLIEN 1885
JULLIEN, Adolphe. 'Revue musicale', in: *Le Français*, 10 August 1885.

LAFARGUE 1869
LAFARGUE, Gustave. 'Courrier des théâtres', in: *Le Figaro*, 25 May 1869.

LAFARGUE 1875
ID. 'Courrier des théâtres', in: *Le Figaro*, 31 December 1875.

LALO 1899A
LALO, Pierre. 'La Musique', in: *Le Temps*, 7 January 1899.

LALO 1899B
ID. 'La Musique', in: *Le Temps*, 24 January 1899.

LALO 1899C
ID. 'La Musique', in: *Le Temps*, 2 May 1899.

LALO 1900
ID. 'La Musique', in: *Le Temps*, 18 January 1900.

LALO 1904A
ID. 'La Musique', in: *Le Temps*, 14 April 1904.

LALO 1904B
ID. 'La Musique', in: *Le Temps*, 19 April 1904.

LALO 1904C
ID. 'La Musique', in: *Le Temps*, 28 June 1904.

LALO 1904D
ID. 'La Musique', in: *Le Temps*, 6 December 1904.

LALO 1905
ID. 'La Musique', in: *Le Temps*, 5 December 1905.

LALO 1906A
ID. 'La Musique', in: *Le Temps*, 6 February 1906.

LALO 1906B
ID. 'La Musique', in: *Le Temps*, 21 February 1906.

LALO 1907A
ID. 'La Musique', in: *Le Temps*, 9 April 1907.

LALO 1907B
ID. 'La Musique', in: *Le Temps*, 20 August 1907.

LALO 1911
ID. 'La Musique', in: *Le Temps*, 1 August 1911.

LALO 1912
ID. 'La Musique', in: *Le Temps*, 12 March 1912.

LE FIGARO 1878A
'À l'Exposition', in: *Le Figaro*, 8 October 1878.

LE FIGARO 1878B
'À l'Exposition', in: *Le Figaro*, 11 October 1878.

LE MASQUE DE FER 1891
LE MASQUE DE FER. 'Échos: Instantanés: Le Concert à six sous', in: *Le Figaro*, 7 September 1891.

LEGAULT 1863
LEGAULT, L. 'Chroniques et faits divers: Lettres, sciences et beaux-arts', in: *Le Temps*, 10 November 1863.

NICOLET 1884
NICOLET. 'Courrier des spectacles', in: *Le Gaulois*, 21 November 1884.

NICOLET 1885
ID. 'Courrier des spectacles', in: *Le Gaulois*, 10 August 1885.

NICOLET 1887
ID. 'Courrier des spectacles', in: *Le Gaulois*, 11 December 1887.

NICOLET 1896
ID. 'Courrier des spectacles: Spectacles divers', in: *Le Gaulois*, 14 January 1896.

NICOLET 1897A
ID. 'Courrier des spectacles: Spectacles divers', in: *Le Gaulois*, 4 November 1897.

NICOLET 1897B
ID. 'Courrier des spectacles', in: *Le Gaulois*, 10 December 1897.

NICOLET 1897C
ID. 'Courrier des spectacles', in: *Le Gaulois*, 19 December 1897.

NICOLET 1906
ID. 'Courrier des spectacles: Spectacles divers', in: *Le Gaulois*, 17 January 1906.

NICOLET 1910
ID. 'Courrier des spectacles', in: *Le Gaulois*, 26 December 1910.

ORDONNEAU 1883
ORDONNEAU, Maurice. 'Concerts et spectacles', in: *Le Gaulois*, 12 April 1883.

P. R. 1900
P. R. 'Les Décorés d'hier: M. Paul Taffanel, Officier', in: *Le Gaulois*, 17 December 1900.

PASLER 2009
PASLER, Jann. *Composing the Citizen: Music as Public Utility in Third Republic France*, Berkeley-Los Angeles, University of California Press, 2009.

PELCA 1906
PELCA, Georges. 'Concerts: Aux soirées d'art', in: *Le Gaulois*, 2 January 1906.

PREVEL 1877
PRÉVEL, Jules. 'Courrier des théâtres', in: *Le Figaro*, 22 December 1877.

Taverny 1882
Taverny. 'Autour du Parlement', in: *Le Gaulois*, 26 February 1882.

Un Domino 1869
Un Domino. 'Ce qui se passe', in: *Le Gaulois*, 4 February 1869.

Un Domino 1881
Id . 'Nos Échos: Nouvelles à la main', in: *Le Gaulois*, 4 August 1881.

Un Domino 1885
Id . 'Nos Échos: Nouvelles à la main', in: *Le Gaulois*, 23 December 1885.

Un Domino 1901
Id. 'Ce qui se passe: La Politique, comme à la future chambre', in: *Le Gaulois*, 10 July 1901.

Un Domino 1912a
Id. 'Échos de partout', in: *Le Gaulois*, 26 June 1912.

Un Domino 1912b
Id. 'Échos de partout', in: *Le Gaulois*, 29 June 1912.

Un Domino 1912c
Id. 'Échos de partout', in: *Le Gaulois*, 2 July 1912.

Valfleury 1911
Valfleury. 'Mondanités', in: *Le Gaulois*, 16 June 1911.

Weber 1862a
Weber, Johannes. 'Critique musicale', in: *Le Temps*, 25 February 1862.

Weber 1862b
Id. 'Critique musicale', in: *Le Temps*, 19 March 1862.

Weber 1862c
Id. 'Critique musicale', in: *Le Temps*, 22 April 1862.

Weber 1862d
Id. 'Critique musicale', in: *Le Temps*, 2 December 1862.

Weber 1863
Id. 'Critique musicale', in: *Le Temps*, 1 December 1863.

Weber 1864
Id. 'Critique musicale', in: *Le Temps*, 9 February 1864.

Weber 1869
Id. 'Critique musicale', in: *Le Temps*, 27 April 1869.

Weber 1870
Id. 'Critique musicale', in: *Le Temps*, 23 April 1870.

Weber 1875
Id. 'Critique musicale', in: *Le Temps*, 20 April 1875.

Weber 1879a
Id. 'Critique musicale', in: *Le Temps*, 4 February 1879.

Weber 1879b
Id. 'Critique musicale', in: *Le Temps*, 18 February 1879.

Weber 1879c
Id. 'Critique musicale', in: *Le Temps*, 18 March 1879.

Weber 1879d
Id. 'Critique musicale', in: *Le Temps*, 15 April 1879.

Weber 1879e
Id. 'Critique musicale', in: *Le Temps*, 30 April 1879.

Weber 1880a
Id. 'Critique musicale', in: *Le Temps*, 3 February 1880.

Weber 1880b
Id. 'Critique musicale', in: *Le Temps*, 30 March 1880.

Weber 1880c
Id. 'Critique musicale', in: *Le Temps*, 11 May 1880.

Weber 1880d
Id. 'Critique musicale', in: *Le Temps*, 7 December 1880.

Weber 1881a
Id. 'Critique musicale', in: *Le Temps*, 1 March 1881.

Weber 1881b
Id. 'Critique musicale', in: *Le Temps*, 15 March 1881.

Weber 1882a
Id. 'Critique musicale', in: *Le Temps*, 14 March 1882.

Weber 1882b
Id. 'Critique musicale', in: *Le Temps*, 28 March 1882.

Weber 1882c
Id. 'Critique musicale', in: *Le Temps*, 9 May 1882.

Weber 1883
Id. 'Critique musicale', in: *Le Temps*, 8 May 1883.

Weber 1884
Id. 'Critique musicale', in: *Le Temps*, 20 May 1884.

Weber 1885
Id. 'Critique musicale', in: *Le Temps*, 4 May 1885.

Weber 1886
Id. 'Critique musicale', in: *Le Temps*, 4 October 1886.

Weber 1890
Id. 'Critique musicale', in: *Le Temps*, 24 February 1890.

Weber 1893
Id. 'Critique musicale', in: *Le Temps*, 20 February 1893.

Constructing and Re-Mediating the Ethos of a Music Lover: The Case of Marguerite de Saint-Marceaux[1]

Isabelle Perreault
(Université de Montréal / OICRM)

To admit you to the "little nucleus", the "little group", the "little clan" at the Verdurins', one condition sufficed, but that one was indispensable: you must give tacit adherence to a Creed one of whose articles was that the young pianist whom Mme Verdurin had taken under her patronage that year and of whom she said, "Really, it oughtn't to be allowed, to play Wagner as well as that!", licked both Planté and Rubinstein hollow [...]. The Verdurins never invited you to dinner; you had your "place laid" there. There was never any programme for the evening's entertainment. The young pianist would play, but only if "the spirit moved him", for no one was forced to do anything [...]. Evening dress was barred, because you were all "good pals" and didn't want to look like the "boring people" who were to be avoided like the plague[2].

In the opening pages of *Swann in Love*, Marcel Proust introduces the Verdurin salon and caricatures its *salonnière*, with passages depicting ivory tower soirées, carefully designed to be exclusive and socially distinguished, with admittance requiring most of all a taste for the musical avant-garde and intimate knowledge of the avant-garde's inner circle. Although amplified for comic effect, the Verdurin way corresponds, more or less, to the prevailing customs of

[1]. The research presented here is part of a project entitled *Une histoire des publics du concert à Paris: 1870-1939* (A history of Parisian concert audiences, SSHRC 2018-2022), led by Michel Duchesneau (OICRM, Université de Montréal) and funded by the Social Sciences and Humanities Research Council of Canada, and to some extent, by the Fonds de recherche du Québec – société et culture. I am grateful to Ariadne Lih for her translation of this chapter.

[2]. Proust 1987 [1913], pp. 185-186 (original), pp. 205-206 (translation).

Marguerite de Saint-Marceaux's famous 'Fridays', which she hosted in her Paris *hôtel particulier* on boulevard Malesherbes. Only artists, regardless of discipline, were allowed as Friday dinner guests at the Saint-Marceaux; wives were seldom invited unless they displayed true artistic sensibilities. Society notables were automatically excluded from Friday meetings and visited on Thursdays instead, the day Madame de Saint-Marceaux reserved for the fulfilment of her worldly obligations. Only a select few among the aristocracy and *grande bourgeoisie* earned exceptions to this rule: those who, like the Princesse de Polignac, practised music and had true feeling for it. The honour of being among such cannily chosen guests compounded the feeling of familiarity that prevailed at the ostensibly intimate Saint-Marceaux soirées, and arriving in evening dress was consequently out of the question. This casual dress code was intended as a riposte to aristocratic formalities, but it also enhanced the *artistic* prestige of the Saint-Marceaux salon; rather than glorifying status or wealth, the custom served as an absolute — but nonetheless absolutely performative — rejection of snobbery, although no one was truly fooled by this rejection. Ricardo Viñes writes, «Ravel told me that the Saint-Marceaux were snobbish, but he was wrong, they're very snobbish»[3] and even Fauré, who was close friends with the couple, proclaimed, «Without a doubt, [...] she will die of a fit of snobbery!»[4]. Small wonder that Madame de Saint-Marceaux is among the foremost 'keys' cited as inspiration for the famous fictional *salonnière* in Proust's *roman à clefs* — in *In Search of Lost Time*, Madame Verdurin stakes her social status on her avant-garde musical convictions and her exclusive and fiercely guarded artistic relationships. Proust himself is nowhere to be found in the long list of guest names that Madame de Saint-Marceaux recorded in her *Journal* — a diarist's archive of a vast web of privileged connections; a few days before the beginning of *Journal*, however, Proust's presence at 100 boulevard Malesherbes was noted by the now-forgotten author Jean de Tinan, who was struck by the strangeness of Proust's diffident and awkward manner alongside other guests at the salon. Regardless, it seems highly unlikely that Proust only ever attended this one reception at the Saint-Marceaux. The editor of *Journal*, Myriam Chimènes, notes in her introduction that Madame de Saint-Marceaux's correspondence contains a long letter from Proust, dated May 1922, in which he apologises for being unable to attend an exhibition by Monsieur de Saint-Marceaux to which Madame de Saint-Marceaux had invited him, and fondly recalls a conversation between himself and the *salonnière* on a train trip. This message implies considerable familiarity, and the two would certainly have been attendees at the same events, especially the ones hosted by Madeleine Lemaire and the Princesse de Polignac. There are thus reasonable grounds to believe that Proust rubbed elbows with the Saint-Marceaux enough to

---

[3].   Ricardo Viñes, *Journal inédit*, cited in CHIMÈNES 2007, p. 58: «Ravel m'a dit que les Saint-Marceaux étaient snobs, mais il se trompe, ils sont très snobs». Unless otherwise noted, all translations are Ariadne Lih's.

[4].   *Ibidem*: «Certainement, [...] elle mourra d'une attaque de snobisme».

know about the peculiar habits of their salon, and at the very least he would have heard reports from his close companion Reynaldo Hahn, a Saint-Marceaux Friday regular.

On the one hand was the musical devotion of Marguerite de Saint-Marceaux, née Jourdain, authoritarian *salonnière* and self-proclaimed musical patroness; on the other, the hypersensitivity of the exuberant (and laughable) Madame Verdurin. One may easily discern the connection between them, as Lucien Daudet did in a letter to Proust: «I saw at the Lyon's what one may call [...] a Verdurin who was far more Verdurin than my old friend, and who was Mme de Saint-Marceaux, peering down from atop her nose, informed, "*au courant*", "well aware", familiar yet supercilious, "knowing all about", "being much inclined to think"»[5]. Habitual readers of *In Search of Lost Time* may even be tempted to compare the two figures in appearance: the piercing features of Madame Verdurin, with her «bird-like eyes», aquiline nose, and haughty demeanour, perching «[...] on her high seat like a cage-bird»[6], and the striking portrait of Marguerite de Saint-Marceaux, who was described by Colette as «[...] a hostess quick of wit and tongue, basically intolerant, with beaked nose and roving eye»[7]. The perspicacity of Daudet and Colette being beyond reproach, these two contemporary accounts from outside observers seem to point towards the *salonnière*'s musical tastes being avant-garde as a matter of *tactics*, in an effort to accumulate symbolic capital. These *sotto voce* accusations of snobbishness are nonetheless worth verifying using the texts that have come down to us, so that we can evaluate whether the configuration of an existence entirely devoted to music does indeed reveal an undertaking in self-enhancement as well as, *a fortiori*, an incipient attempt at *active* integration into the musical field.

Looking beyond the immortal figure of Proustian satire, we come to examine the role played by Marguerite de Saint-Marceaux in the promotion of French music — promotion in the sense of dissemination, but also promotion in the sense of facilitating musical creation, especially by forging connections between musicians who crossed paths in her salon. Marguerite, nicknamed 'Meg', was an inescapable figure in worldly Parisian life under the Third Republic, and she became the apparent epicentre for various networks containing the musicians, artists, and critics who forged musical modernity. Her orbit included such illustrious regulars as Fauré, Debussy, Ravel, d'Indy, Willy, and Colette, as well as other notable figures from both the artistic avant-garde and the major musical institutions, such as the Conservatoire de Paris and the Institut de France. Her *Journal*, which she maintained from 1894 to 1927, comprises an exceptional archive of private activities, meetings between creators, and inner circles, all situated

---

5. Lucien Daudet, letter to Marcel Proust, 3 July 1922, in: PROUST 1993 [1922], p. 334: «J'ai vu chez les Lyon ce qui s'appelle [...] une Verdurin beaucoup plus Verdurin que ma vieille amie, et qui était Mme de Saint-Marceaux, dressée sur son nez, entendue, "au courant", "avertie", familière et hautaine, "en sachant long", "n'en pensant pas moins"».

6. PROUST 1987 [1913], p. 205 (original), p. 221 (translation).

7. COLETTE 2004 [1950], p. 107 (original), p. 19 (translation).

at the margins of musical activity but nevertheless exerting crucial influence on the music scene. The day-to-day life described within the journal was, moreover, organised entirely around music: days went by to the rhythm of vocalise, sight-reading, Friday evening performances where Meg's composer friends played their latest creations, opera rehearsals among enlightened amateurs, concerts to attend, and so on. Meetings, works seen, works heard, places visited, deaths, births, and marriages were all chronicled without dwelling on their circumstances and without bothering to include narrative detail. The resulting accumulation effect creates the impression that music was Meg's vocation, that is, her journal reads as if music were the only thing she deemed worthy of interest — or rather, more likely, as if this were the portrait of herself that she wanted to immortalise in the eyes of her descendants. Passages in which she made disparaging comments about friends or family were often censored or crossed out; this practice, notes Myriam Chimènes, suggests that Meg actually «[...] censored herself *a posteriori*, out of concern for bequeathing to her children and grandchildren, without running the risk of wounding them, this document conveying to them their family history»[8]. This prospective awareness may explain Marguerite de Saint-Marceaux's self-figuration within the *Journal* as an enlightened music lover, whose society parties were mere self-sacrifice in service of a pure and seemingly selfless passion for musical creation.

Madame Verdurin's caricatural intensity should not be automatically mapped onto Meg's daily writings, in which the stresses of everyday life — illnesses, aches and pains, melancholy musings on how time flies, births, deaths, marriages, and the like — commingle with narration of the author's busy schedule, monopolised as it always was by music. But despite the inclusion of these everyday occurrences, which are recounted somewhat drily, sparingly, almost *pro forma*, the *Journal* comes across more as an antechamber of sorts onto public representation than as a *lieu de mémoire* or a device for introspection. Meg's journal, like her salon, essentially functioned as a *continuum* uniting the private and public spheres, and in this sense, carved out an intermediate or even hybrid space for itself. The space was intimate, because the writing process was not governed by an intention to publish in the immediate future, but was nevertheless *addressed* to posterity, hence the author's *a posteriori* censorship, if not pre-emptive exclusion, of the derogatory remarks that she let slip from time to time. Journalling was one of the only writing practices encouraged for women at the time, and indeed, keepers of journals and keepers of salons gained access to similar means of acting upon the world; both endeavours allowed for an underground influence, marginal in appearance but not in nature, on the development of contemporary musical life. For Meg, journalling was primarily an arena for formulating opinions and weighing competing values and behaviours against each other, but it also provided an opportunity for her to portray herself as an exemplary listener, receptive

---

8. CHIMÈNES 2007, p. 20: «[...] qu'elle effectua elle-même *a posteriori* cette censure, soucieuse de léguer à ses enfants et petits enfants, sans risquer de les blesser, un document leur livrant une histoire de leur famille».

to all things being done in music, from the avant-garde to the academy. The 'stagecraft' behind this enlightened listener persona took the form of discursive choices that were axiologically conditioned and therefore emblematic of Meg's time and milieu; that is, the French bourgeoisie at the turn of the twentieth century. Meg was of her time, but also took full advantage of her time, using her own unique resources to consolidate her symbolic authority. With more than thirty years of notes made almost daily, the *Journal* provides historians with valuable insight into the society customs associated with concert life, and pulls back the curtain on the activities that took place at the sidelines of musical creation and reception — such activities being deeply embedded within domestic socialities. Meg's *Journal* as a historical document, moreover, sheds light on the crucial, albeit confidential, role played by *salonnières*, not only in establishing creative nuclei among composers and artists who moved in the same circles, but more broadly in the development of musical language, which was inevitably shaped by such fortuitous and fruitful encounters as were orchestrated by the organisers of salons.

The journal and the salon occupy an intermediate position encompassing elements of both the public and the intimate spheres, or rather — better — act as an articulation between them. This makes the dual salon-journal apparatus an ideal crucible for the stagecraft[9] behind the exemplary listener persona, which was nourished by a socially connotative lexicon and by musical preferences that were purposefully put forward to support a personal ethics of distinction. Such postural strategies were tested within the private space of the journal, but still spread outward onto the sites of the socialities wherein they were actualised and exerted direct influence on concert life — initially on a domestic scale, and eventually, thanks to the unique channels pertaining to the domestic sphere, on the scale of more official musical societies. Essentially, we are tasked with identifying the means of acting upon the world that were contained within apparatuses reserved for women and therefore shunted to the margins of public life, keeping in mind that such apparatuses also gave women the capacity to act and to influence within the limited frameworks available to them. In other words, we can observe how barriers imposed upon women were reclaimed and made to support direct action both upon the world and, in this instance, upon the musical politics unfolding in the margins of concert life.

---

[9]. The concept of stagecraft here is based on the idea of *scénographie auctoriale* (authorial stagecraft), which has been explored by José-Luis Diaz in particular, after the works of Dominique Maingueneau. This idea can be defined as a set of postures, images of self, and representations, which are put forward «in accordance with the repertoire of existing postures [...] [and which] suggest both ways of writing and ways of living» (AMOSSY – MAINGUENEAU 2007, par. 5). Transposed into the field of concert history, this idea signifies that listening, when it takes place within society events, has an intransigent performative element at its core, that is, listening produces signs that are addressed to the audience as a whole and that signal social status and symbolic capital. This is true even though hegemonic discourse at the time was uniquely disposed to value absolute music, for which listening was supposed to be scrupulous and contemplative, and not a pretext for theatricalising oneself and the world, as was implicitly encouraged in earlier periods.

ISABELLE PERREAULT

MUSICAL DOMESTICITIES AND PUBLICISED ACTS OF LISTENING

Discussions of the latter third of the nineteenth century often allude to a radical change in the relationship between concert audiences and musical (or indeed theatrical) performances, one that affected institutional, rustic, and private concerts alike; such discussions are wont to imply that performance — which had long served as an excuse to increase sociability and engage in court intrigue — henceforth triumphed over all trifling society and even political matters, instead inviting listeners to embrace the righteous spirit of contemplation. But this outlook tends to ignore the fact that the imperative to contemplate musical works religiously — so as to experience the slightest aesthetic sentiment with the power of an emotional stroke of lightning — arose owing more to discourse among Wagner-saturated composer-theorists, poets, and music critics than to any socially observable phenomenon within bourgeois audiences, or at least more to this discourse than to any truly sincere aesthetic affect. As James H. Johnson demonstrates in his works on Parisian music audiences, the idea that post-*ancien ré*gime concert spaces were not opportunities for sociality *above all* is false. In fact, musical taste acquired a political function, because certain aesthetic conducts were prescribed, and the public display of musical taste became a symbolic apparatus through which to convey one's social status — even more so, perhaps, than in the eighteenth century, when «[...] to be seen was a higher priority»[10]. The change that actually took place in the nineteenth century was an axiological one: music rose to the top of the hierarchy of arts where it had previously been relegated to the bottom. But there persisted around music, even after this displacement, a political economics of visibility in which certain visible elements acted as social markers and thus became integrated into the process of behaviour normalisation. These visible elements included not only opinions held and tastes displayed, but also bodily postures, somatic reactions, and gestures occasioned by the music. The domestication of concert situations, which blurred the lines between public and private, displaced this political economics of auditory practices once again. The general adoption of darkness in the concert hall, under the influence of Wagnerism, seems to have relocated spectators' 'theatre at the theatre' into the private spaces of bourgeois salons, where their postural figurations became even more outwardly *addressed* given the presence of fewer addressees, and given the space, which was shared among the various activities proposed (conversation, games, performance) and therefore unlikely to be plunged in darkness. Within such a space, music listeners could be perceived at any time, which conditioned them to display attention according to the normative expectations of their milieu (as in Jeremy Bentham's panopticon). The resulting manifestations of listening, private and yet outwardly expressive, reflected an awareness of the perpetual potential gaze of others; within communication situations, these manifestations advertised the listener's refined tastes and acute artistic comprehension rather

---

[10]. JOHNSON 1995, p. 16.

more than they genuinely embraced the mimicked introspective trance. Performing music and listening to music thus became two parallel semiotically productive activities, and in the case of listening, the boundaries between being outwardly reserved and being outwardly sensational became more permeable. This induced the prerogative of eighteenth-century socialities — that is, the reigning indistinctness between private and public — to persist into the nineteenth century. Anne Martin-Fugier reminds us that private socialities extended into the Republican era without undergoing rupture or revolution[11]. Certainly, the role of the *salonnière* remained unchanged, since the hostess's notoriety and the success of her soirées depended entirely on her personality. As the hearts of their salons, such women inevitably came to occupy a median or even transitional space between the private sphere and public, or political, affairs.

Bourgeois women were trained to keep house and to make charming conversation; still, they were encouraged to know their place and to be modest both in general and *a fortiori* with respect to their (male) guests, who were to be given precedence as far as opportunities to shine were concerned. Voice and piano skills were subject to the same modesty imperative. Educated young women could certainly show themselves to be charming piano players who were conversant with *solfège*, but as a general rule, such aptitudes were to be developed as sources of amusement, not sources of artistic creation. As a result, displaying virtuosity, or betraying too much familiarity with harmony and composition, ran the risk of discrediting bourgeois women within their milieu. Most salons did not even feature music as an object of attentive listening, since most guests were not aesthetically motivated to attend; on the whole, they were more interested in the diplomatic benefits of rubbing elbows with lady such-and-such at one of her 'evenings'. The fact nevertheless remains that, regardless of whether any specific *salonnière* professed herself to be a great lover of music, the musicians who performed at a salon were major factors in its prestige and thus in determining the hostess's reputation.

These contextual elements illustrate the uniqueness of Marguerite de Saint-Marceaux's persona and salon, given the societal and gender norms of her time; this uniqueness did, however, remain controlled and was established firmly within social codes. Meg's agency, which she derived specifically from the in-betweenness of the space she occupied, serenely assimilated these social codes while also pushing at them. She was evidently highly skilled at navigating the expectations of her milieu while drawing on the full extent of the resources provided by her education, and it was this skill that allowed her influence to act directly upon the public sphere, transcending the private sphere in which she operated. Although moderate musical skill and regular voice and piano practice were by no means exceptional among women of the haute bourgeoisie, the young Marguerite Jourdain displayed exceptional passion for her music education, and according to Jean-Michel Nectoux, teachers also found Meg's strong personality

---

[11].   See MARTIN-FUGIER 2003.

quite striking, being «[...] both charmed and impressed during the lessons that they gave her»[12]. Prominent music teachers noted Marguerite's abilities from a young age and encouraged her to pursue her musical interests. She studied first with Antoine-François Marmontel, whose studio at the Conservatoire included Bizet, Debussy, and d'Indy; then with François Seghers, founder of the Union musicale and the Société Sainte-Cécile concerts; and finally with Romain Bussine, who taught voice at the Conservatoire and was president of the Société nationale de musique from 1871 to 1886. Throughout her training, she applied herself to both performance (piano and voice) and music theory, and the solid theoretical knowledge she obtained would make her a formidable score reader. All her instructors made plain that they held her musical talents and rigorous study habits in high esteem, and in one letter, François Seghers went so far as to compare her artistic sensibilities — and by extension her aptitude for composition — to Beethoven's: «In the meantime, continue to rest from working as you contemplate the splendid nature that lies before your eyes. Endeavour to steal one of nature's secrets, as our Beethoven did; study nature, and you will find the strength to more fully embrace the art for which you are so dearly designed!»[13]. Although such praise indubitably influenced the development of Meg's identity as a music lover, neither she nor her instructors really had any illusions as to whether her love of music could be professionalised: for women of her station, musical activity was strictly reserved for the domestic sphere. Rather, this precocious entry into Conservatoire circles — where she briefly became involved with Camille Saint-Saëns — seems to indicate *a posteriori* Meg's destined vocation, as well as providing the opportunity to become familiar with the ways of musical composition 'initiates'.

Meg put this privileged musical education to use. Not only did her musical vocation serve her worldly objectives; she also invested all her erudition into making her salon, as well as her conversation, into a participatory space for musical creation and dissemination. In this way, Meg exerted real influence on compositional activity: she connected the composers in her inner circle with sites of reception and with her broad network, and her impact was such that those who frequented the *hôtel particulier* on boulevard Malesherbes, faubourg Saint-Honoré, stood to gain a whole host of professional head starts: funding opportunities, 'aye' votes for nominations to prestigious institutional directorships or to the Institut de France, chances to collaborate with up-and-coming librettists, and even favourable critical reception, which could be pre-emptively secured by making sure that works not yet premiered and works in progress fell on the right ears, through performances by both professionals and talented amateurs. These

---

[12]. NECTOUX 1992, p. 62: «[...] personnalité si forte que ses maîtres étaient à la fois charmés et impressionnés lors des leçons qu'ils lui donnaient».

[13]. François Seghers, cited in CHIMÈNES 2007, p. 15: «En attendant continuez à vous reposer du travail en contemplant la belle nature que vous avez sous les yeux. Tâchez de lui voler un de ses secrets, comme a fait notre Beethoven: étudiez-la, vous puiserez des forces pour mieux étreindre l'art pour lequel vous êtres précieusement organisée».

were the avenues by which Marguerite de Saint-Marceaux involved herself with contemporary musical creation, and this involvement undeniably had a hand in musical composition, despite being apparently situated at the outskirts of the composition world. Meg's contributions from the shadows invite us to broaden the implications of the phrase 'chamber music'. That is, to understand the term both in its usual sense — music for small string ensembles — and as an evocation of conditions for the development of said music: certain sets of preliminary steps, collections of opposing forces, and adjuvants to creation that are essential to the flourishing of creative activity, despite their reliance on salon socialities. Madame de Saint-Marceaux was thus a chamber music collaborator even though she was barred from the inner sanctum of chamber music composition; through society reception and mediation, she found compensatory activities that surreptitiously conferred upon her true creative power.

Chamber Musics and Musical Antechambers

Saint-Marceaux's *Journal* reads, in places, like the society section of a Third Republic newspaper, simply by dint of the dizzying array of still-renowned artists, writers, and performers who were chronicled as Friday guests. Looking closely at this long list of names reveals some that are featured only once, putting the *salonnière*'s alleged familiarity with the leading lights of French music somewhat into perspective. Debussy, for instance, is listed only once as a Friday attendee, even though his works were often performed at the salon, and even though Meg tried in vain to secure him as a guest at the Saint-Marceaux's once more:

> Debussy afternoon at the Princesse de Cystria's. The *Quartet* that prefigures *Pelléas* so well, the first piano pieces, *Pagodes* very well played by Blanche Selva. Two *Proses lyriques* sung well enough by Bagès, then *Mandoline* with amusingly excessive movement. A charming hour. Debussy was there [...]. I am trying to get him to come to our home again, it will be difficult[14].

Other guests were led to the salon by exceptional happenstance — Isadora Duncan, for instance, who was introduced by Meg's son, or Puccini, who accompanied Giovanni Boldini to dinner, Boldini being a painter within the artistic circle of sculptor René de Saint-Marceaux, Meg's husband. Indeed, despite the assiduity of regulars like Fauré, Messager, Viñes, Henry Février, and Reynaldo Hahn, a sizeable portion of the guests was subject to change — a good indicator that the salon was something of a hub and that befriending the Saint-Marceaux came with significant power of influence. According to Colette, who for years « [...] never missed

---

[14]. 16 January 1904, Saint-Marceaux 2007, p. 329.

a Friday»[15], «Mme de Saint-Marceaux did not appear to seek anyone out and the favour of becoming a familiar of those Fridays had to be solicited»[16]. The salon was thus genuinely capable of revealing new talents, while the persistent attendance of exceptional or in-demand artistic figures and creators ensured the salon's prestige. As Jean-Michel Nectoux notes, «[...] as soon as she discovered a new gem, Meg put to use her rare skill for attracting such gems to herself and setting them anew within the royal crown of her Fridays»[17]. Isadora Duncan, for one, seems to have been propelled by her contacts with the Saint-Marceaux: she appeared in the *Journal* for the first time in 1901 as «the little American dancer»[18], and eight years later, on 19 February 1908, Meg summed up her Friday reception as follows: «Beaunier and Jeanne and the charming Isadora, the darling of Paris, who is wanted by all the duchesses, whose grace no one knew about nine years ago»[19]. Isadora's glory, of course, radiated onto the Saint-Marceaux salon as well, highlighting the *salonnière*'s clairvoyance in hosting the dancer as early as 1901. Similarly, Maurice Ravel was first received at the salon thanks to Fauré, in 1898. Colette would later remember meeting Ravel at the Saint-Marceaux's in an atmosphere that was infused with creative complicity: «It was in this setting, echoing but responsive to meditation [...] that I first met Maurice Ravel»[20]. *L'Enfant et les Sortilèges* was thus the direct result of the Friday evenings that the two spent on boulevard Malesherbes. Ravel would later attend with pianist Ricardo Viñes in tow, and Viñes in his turn would become a Friday regular.

These examples are emblematic of a larger system of visibility and recognition to which the Saint-Marceaux salon belonged, and this system extended to musical compositions — that is, the phenomenon surrounding people who were 'introduced' at the salon is analogous to the one surrounding works that were first heard there and subsequently rose to fame. Boulevard Malesherbes was a place for unpublished or previously unheard works to be debuted, refined, or even workshopped by means of performances from both veteran composers and amateur players, often both at once. In one significant instance, Meg heard Debussy perform the first sketches of *Pelléas et Mélisande* in piano reduction, on the only evening that the *Journal* records his presence. An entry from February 1894 reads, «In the evening, dinner at home and music with Debussy. He had me sing *La Damoiselle élue*. [...] The next day, he played me everything that has been completed so far of *Pelléas et Mélisande*. A revelation. Everything is new. The

[15]. Février 1948, p. 218: «[...] ne manqu[a] pas un vendredi».

[16]. Colette 2004 [1950], p. 105 (original), p. 18 (translation).

[17]. Nectoux 1992, p. 79: «[...] [a]ussitôt découvert [*sic*] une perle nouvelle, Meg déployait une habileté rare pour l'attirer à elle et à le sertir derechef sur la couronne royale de ses vendredis».

[18]. 20 January 1901, Saint-Marceaux 2007, p. 234: «la petite danseuse américaine».

[19]. 19 February 1909, Saint-Marceaux 2007, p. 533: «Beaunier et Jeanne et la charmante Isadora, la coqueluche de Paris, celles dont veulent toutes les duchesses, celle dont tout le monde ignorait la grâce il y a neuf ans».

[20]. Colette 2004 [1950], p. 108 (original), p. 20 (translation).

harmony, the writing, and everything still musical»[21]. André Messager would also play whole sections of the *Pelléas* score on piano at Saint-Marceaux society gatherings. When the opera was finally produced, with Messager as conductor, Meg again described her experience of the work in terms connoting both rapture and special discernment: *Pelléas* was an «enchantment», «wholly new», an «absolute masterpiece» about which «the public understood nothing», «the purest art ever to be written in music»[22]. A similar process occurred and was well documented for Bréville's *Éros vainqueur*, given Meg's close relationship with the composer; the opera was very often performed by small ensembles on Fridays. Déodat de Séverac's *Cœur du moulin* and Henry Février's *Monna Vanna* are also worth mentioning in this vein (although Meg considered the latter to be completely unmusical): like *Pelléas* and *Éros*, they were opportunities for guests to add their voices or instrumental talents to performances of works in progress, usually arranged for voice and piano. These early contributions to musical works in progress demonstrate that *salonnières* had significant resources at their disposal, with respect to both the dissemination and the creation of the latest music. In Marguerite de Saint-Marceaux's case, they underscore the fact that she participated actively in French music, and indirectly — from the margins, as it were — contributed to its composition, by giving it centre stage.

There was no shortage of chamber music on the programmes that came together from Friday regulars, even though Meg herself showed more enthusiasm for French art song and opera. This preference for vocal music reflected both the spirit of the time and Meg's personal performance abilities; she continued her singing lessons into adulthood, studying diligently under Pauline Roger, Reynaldo Hahn, Gabrielle Krauss, and Berthe Kohl. However, her *Journal* also includes several mentions of Meg playing an unspecified Fauré quartet in an arrangement for piano four hands, which she called a «merveille»[23] (marvel), as a duet with her musical partner Marthe Mathey[24]. Mathey and Meg also played a Beethoven quartet (presumably either No. 10 or No. 12)[25] and the Franck Violin Sonata in four-hands arrangements, and even arranged a small performance for enlightened amateurs. The programme reveals general familiarity with chamber music piano arrangements: «First session of the year on two pianos. Marthe and I played the 2nd Fauré *Quartet*, the Bach *Concerto in F*, the Albéniz

---

21. February 1894, SAINT-MARCEAUX 2007, p. 77: «Le soir dîner chez moi et musique avec Debussy. Il m'a fait chanter *La Damoiselle élue*. [...] Le lendemain il m'a joué tout ce qui est fait de *Pelléas et Mélisande*. C'est une révélation. Tout est neuf. L'harmonie, l'écriture, et tout reste musical».

22. 28 April 1902, SAINT-MARCEAUX 2007, pp. 270-271: «enchantement»; «nouveauté en tout»; «chef-d'œuvre absolu»; «[le] public [ne] comprend rien»: «l'art le plus pur qui ait jamais été écrit en musique».

23. For very short descriptors in the following passage, I have provided the French to aid readers in scanning the text. 14 January 1904, *ibidem*, p. 328.

24. Marthe Mathey was the daughter of painter and salon regular Paul Mathey. She herself became a frequent attendee due to her exceptional musical abilities as a singer and sight reader.

25. 20 février 1905, SAINT-MARCEAUX 2007, p. 379.

Rondo espagnole»[26]. As for violin, Meg admired violinist Eugène Ysaÿe's skill in performing the Franck Sonata, a Bach violin sonata, and the *Kreutzer Sonata*. The *Kreutzer*, however, she found «démodée» (old-fashioned), whereas she wrote of the Franck Sonata that she had «[...] never felt more emotion»[27]. This evaluative comparison must be understood in light of Meg's marked inclination for French music and her subtle but unmistakable anti-Germanic tendencies, in line with the anti-Germanism of the time. Hence, she described Ravel's Quartet as a «chef-d'oeuvre»[28] (masterpiece) and Franck's as a «belle œuvre»[29] (beautiful work); d'Indy's Violin Sonata earned the epithet «bien belle»[30] (very fine) on several occasions; Chausson's *Concert* for piano, violin, and string quartet, performed by the Parent Quartet, she deemed «admirable»[31]; the Franck Sonata — a «marvel, marvellously performed» by Ysaÿe — made a Bach chaconne seem «ennuyante» (dull) by comparison, despite the current fashion, as Meg saw it, for «[...] finding everything amusing in Bach»[32]; Franck's *Quintet* elicited her praise as an «œuvre géniale et passionnante»[33] (brilliant and captivating work); Magnard's Violin Sonata she considered to be «une belle chose»[34] (a beautiful thing). Such assessments, made in passing, abound within *Journal* and are mostly complimentary for French chamber pieces, suggesting a notable partiality for French style in composition and performance, as well as an implicit profession of nationalist faith that aligned with Meg's anti-Dreyfusism. And indeed, the *salonnière* took frequent jabs at German taste:

> Richard Strauss's *Symphonie domestique* at the Châtelet. Himself conducting. A dense work with many charms, betraying Liszt's influence, but with a true artist's nature emerging from the piece. [...] One feels how little regard he has for French music. He knows nothing of Fauré, speaks of Charpentier as if he were a great artist, knows almost nothing of Debussy and d'Indy. German bad faith felt here as elsewhere[35].

---

[26]. 26 December 1905, *ibidem*, p. 417: «Première séance de l'année à deux pianos. Nous jouons Marthe et moi le 2ᵈ *Quatuor* de Fauré, le *Concerto en fa* de Bach, le *Rondo espagnol* d'Albéniz».

[27]. 8 May 1896, *ibidem*, p. 136: «[...] n'[a] jamais ressenti plus grande émotion».

[28]. 5 March 1912, *ibidem*, p. 693.

[29]. 9 January 1912, *ibidem*, p. 326.

[30]. 21 February 1912, *ibidem*, p. 689.

[31]. 8 June 1912, *ibidem*, p. 545.

[32]. 19 May 1896, *ibidem*, p. 137: «[...] de trouver tout amusant dans Bach».

[33]. 28 May 1914, *ibidem*, p. 810.

[34]. 1 July 1914, *ibidem*, p. 816.

[35]. 25 March 1906, *ibidem*, p. 430: «Au Châtelet la *Symphonie domestique* de Richard Strauss. Il conduit lui-même. Œuvre touffue pleine d'attraits, se ressentant de Liszt mais d'où ressort une vraie nature d'artiste. [...] On sent la petite estime en laquelle il tient la musique française. Il ignore Fauré, parle de Charpentier comme d'un grand artiste, ignore presque Debussy et d'Indy. La mauvaise foi allemande se sent là comme ailleurs».

After attending a Salle Gaveau performance of Ravel's Trio and Fauré's latest songs, Meg also wrote that chamber programmes were «[...] made for a salon and too long in a large hall»[36]. In her comments on Debussy's quartet, she described her preferred venue, writing that works «[...] made for this intimate setting» should be played where they would be listened to best, that is, «[...] by the light of a lamp»[37]. In other words, the best listening was the kind that was reintegrated into everyday life — the implication being that this day-to-day setting was when the *salonnière* truly listened, for herself.

Let us single out one final occurrence as a measure of Marguerite de Saint-Marceaux's role as a facilitator who expanded the reach of musical life and thus *a fortiori* the reach of chamber music. The *Journal* entry for 6 May 1904, reads as follows:

> Musical evening. *Trio* and *Sonata* by Henry Février, the *Trio* performed by Viñes, Mlle de la Bouglise and Maurice de Crépy. Charming work, full of youth, well written. Mediocre performance. Enesco played the *Sonata* masterfully. Admirable sonority, deep feeling. An imprecise attack that adds charm to his playing. Many musicians, a vibrant audience, which I plunged into darkness so that they would understand and feel. Very musical evening[38].

The conditions surrounding this private performance, which once again brought together professional musicians and ordinary amateurs, deserves comment, especially as regards Meg's orchestrated dimming of the lights to encourage listening without looking; in the early twentieth century, 'blind' listening was still experienced as a deeper and paradoxically more 'enlightened' experience[39]. (Recall the auditory practices of Madame Verdurin, for instance, who would dramatically bury her face in her hands or on Princess Sherbatoff's shoulder in order to relish the music better, as she claimed, though she neglected to stifle her snores.) Meg highlighted the musical superiority of this particular experience twice, writing, «Musical evening [...] Very musical evening», and the quality of listening received by the evening's programme clearly played a key role in this superiority. This is the sense in which the *salonnière*'s somewhat tyrannical interference — Colette called her «basically intolerant»[40] — assumed the role of an adjuvant to musicians and to musicians' creative activity. «The mistress of the

---

[36]. 28 January 1915, *ibidem*, p. 843: «[...] fait[s] pour un salon et trop long dans une grande salle».

[37]. 19 January 1915, *ibidem*, p. 842: «[...] faites pour ce cadre intime»; «[...] à la clarté d'une lampe».

[38]. 6 May 1904, *ibidem*, pp. 342-343: «Soirée musicale. Le *Trio* et la *Sonate* d'Henry Février, le *Trio* exécuté par Viñes, Mlle de La Bouglise et Maurice de Crépy. Œuvre charmante et pleine de jeunesse, bien écrite. Exécution médiocre. Enesco joue la *Sonate* en maître. Sonorité admirable, sentiment profond. Attaque imprécise qui ajoute un charme à son jeu. Beaucoup de musiciens, public vibrant que je plonge dans l'obscurité pour qu'il comprenne et sente. Soirée très musicale».

[39]. Kaltenecker 2010, pp. 293-341.

[40]. Colette 2004 [1950], p. 107 (original), p. 19 (translation): «intolérante au fond».

house», recalled Colette, «maintained an atmosphere of "ordered liberty". She did not insist that one listened to the music but *suppressed the slightest whisper*»[41]. From a music historical point of view, moreover, the phenomenon of silent, attentive listening is fairly recent, and was amplified by the Wagnerian stage and stance on listening. The fact that Meg valued such listening clearly shows that, for her, the aesthetic experience came first, and socialities came second. At least, she claimed as much, and railed against society settings in which musical performances were met with relative indifference. In 1912, she wrote of an evening at the Princesse de Polignac's, «Everyone was talking. People who call themselves well-bred behaved like boors, without so much as lowering their voices to listen to the artists»[42].

We must understand such dealings in concert scenography as integral to Meg's self-appointed role as an artistic accelerator. This role was not solely a matter of gathering composers and performers around the piano, such that they might later be recruited into vocal ensembles or asked to perform in upcoming matinees, nor can Meg's participation be reduced to encouraging players to bring out their latest compositions, although such encouragement cannot be discounted. Rather, Meg's power of influence specifically resided in her deliberate provision of the best possible settings for the dissemination and reception of musical works. This power of influence was added onto the *salonnière*'s moderately significant effect on the political dealings surrounding Fauré's nomination to the Institut de France or Messager's rise to the head of the Opéra de Paris, which she bore in mind when curating her Friday guest lists.

Creating the appropriate conditions for brand-new works to be heard called upon Meg's musical erudition, fine-grained musical comprehension, and excellent command of the codes and behaviours pertaining to listening within her milieu. At the time, in an era of post-Wagnerism, these codes and behaviours still prized contemplation in opposition to the exuberance displayed by certain society audiences. Meg scorned such hyperbolic enthusiasm or ignorant enjoyment, particularly in this account of a Gounod opera and Mascagni's *Cavalleria Rusticana*: «The audience jumped up and down for joy. The crowds are idiotic, art speaks only to a small number, and one needs the approval of this small number only»[43]. When narrating the musical experiences that made up her day-to-day, Meg took care to differentiate herself from these audiences by focusing on certain elements of the score, for instance, or by highlighting specific performance choices as worthy of either praise or reprobation. Qualitative comments of

---

[41]. *Ibidem*, pp. 105-106 (original), p. 18 (translation): «[...] la maîtresse de maison»; «[...] entretenait une atmosphère de "liberté surveillée". Elle n'obligeait personne à écouter la musique, mais *réprimait le moindre chuchotement*». My emphasis.

[42]. 10 March 1912, SAINT-MARCEAUX 2007, p. 693: «[...] [t]out le monde parle. Les gens soi-disant bien élevés se conduisent comme des goujats et ne baissent même pas la voix pour écouter les artistes».

[43]. 15 November 1902, *Ibidem*, pp. 284-285: «Le public trépignait de bonheur. La foule est imbécile, l'art ne s'adresse qu'à un petit nombre, et c'est de ce petit nombre seulement qu'il faut avoir les suffrages».

this nature abound in the *Journal*, bearing witness to its author's musical erudition and technical knowledge; succinct and specifically focused on various aspects of the works encountered, this incipient enterprise in empirical criticism prevents Saint-Marceaux's *Journal* from reading like a mere catalogue. Although Meg had neither the opportunity nor the intention to develop this enterprise, her informed critical remarks played an important role in asserting her credibility as an enlightened music lover. They also made the artistic vacuity of society gatherings seem even greater in comparison. Meg consistently cast aspersions on the quality of the music at such gatherings, as attested by the following *Journal* entries: «Evening at Mme Bouwens's. Mlle Cesbron sang badly. Evenings in society are very dull»[44] (dated 3 February 1904); and «Delicious afternoon at Suzette Lemaire's. Some young girls sang some mediocre Massenet pieces perfectly well. [...] Very bad music that does well in a salon. Everyone understands, which makes people cheerful, since the public can scarcely be educated»[45] (dated 25 May 1906). Thus, when Madame de Saint-Marceaux congratulated herself on successful Fridays filled with guests of high intellectual quality, she was also presenting herself in opposition to her *salonnière* counterparts, whom she deemed artistically superficial and uninterested in music. Indeed, Jean-Michel Nectoux advances the idea that when Meg attended the evenings of her «Parisian competitors» — Winnie de Polignac, Madeleine Lemaire, the Princesse de Cystria, the Comtesse de Béarn, Ninette Gandrax, and company — she did so «without indulgence» in order to secure that most worldly satisfaction of prevailing over her competitors, and «with panache»[46]. As for the numerous distinguished interlocutors frequenting her salon, she attributed their presence to her own artistic temperament rather than to the fact that composers in her orbit gained access to certain special advantages. At least, this is what her *Journal* implies. In January 1909, for instance, she wrote: «In the evening Poujaud, the Brévilles, Labey, J[ean]-Louis Vaudoyer, Billotte came and talked about all the things of interest to our people, *our purely artistic milieu*»[47]. (Ricardo Viñes did refute this *idée reçue* in his own journal: «I went to dinner at Debussy's, with the Laloys and Mme Charpentier. Naturally, we did not play any music and we hardly spoke of it, as is the

---

[44].   3 February 1904, *ibidem*, p. 333: «[S]oirée chez Mme Bouwens. Mlle Cesbron chante mal. C>est très ennuyeux une soirée dans le monde».

[45].   25 May 1906, *ibidem*, p. 436: «Matinée délicieuse chez Suzette Lemaire. De jeunes filles chantent tout à fait bien des œuvres médiocres de Massenet. [...] De la très mauvaise musique qui fait bien dans un salon. Tout le monde comprend et cela amène de la gaîté, car l'éducation du public ne se fait guère».

[46].   NECTOUX 1992, p. 81: «concurrentes parisiennes»; «sans indulgence [d]es soirées»; «[...] toute mondaine, de l'emporter avec panache».

[47].   15 January 1909, SAINT-MARCEAUX 2007, pp. 529-530. «Le soir Poujaud, les Bréville, Labey, J[ean]-Louis Vaudoyer, Billotte viennent et causent de tout ce qui intéresse notre monde, *notre milieu purement artistique*». My emphasis.

way among TRUE artists»[48].) Although the constraints associated with Meg's gender and status precluded the possibility of professional musical practice, she was active among artists and well aware of the magnitude of her role in shaping artistic creation — through the gatherings over which she presided, the curation of her guest lists, and the quality of the experience provided. Indeed, she assumed these responsibilities fully and intentionally, which supports the hypothesis proposed earlier in this essay: that Madame de Saint-Marceaux's operations (which were not truly peripheral, despite their appearance) contained inherently creative elements, even though professionalising these elements was impossible. She vouched for aesthetic views that revealed the nature of the discernment she possessed; in the words of Marc Fumaroli, this discernment was neither more nor less than an «[...] art of judgement [...] that would in all circumstances worthily reflect on the patron's quality and shine a light on the patron himself»[49]. In other words, the reflected glory from Meg's discernment as a patroness was also apt to illuminate her personal strengths.

On Distinction and Distance: Intimate Figurations and Self-Representations

Meg's displays of familiarity with the preeminent composers of her day could sometimes be exaggerated, or nearly ostentatious; she directed these displays towards her actual close relations as well as towards composers who only occasionally stopped by on Fridays. But she combined this form of musical devotion with another one. At first glance, the other form appears to have unfolded privately, unobserved by others, but Meg's daily writing helped to record her devotion for posterity, as discussed earlier in this essay. Her *Journal* thus conveyed the musical devotion of a life suffused with music, daily practice, and solo and small ensemble piano-playing; in all likelihood, this interior vocation had no effect on Meg's established, outward-facing posture, but it should nonetheless be understood as an integral part of the self-portrait that she herself created by journalling about her sustained musical endeavours. Often these endeavours received no more than a passing mention, such as «Music with Marthe [Mathey]»[50] (May 1909) or «Sang with the Marthes [Mathey and Jacot]»[51] (February

---

[48]. Ricardo Viñes, 23 January 1912, in: *Le journal inédit de Ricardo Viñes*, cited in CHIMÈNES 2004, p. 39: «Je suis allé dîner chez Debussy, ainsi que les Laloy et Mme Charpentier. Naturellement, on n'a pas fait de musique et on en a à peine parlé, comme cela se passe entre artistes VÉRITABLES».

[49]. FUMAROLI 1985, p. 10: «[...] art du jugement, [...] propr[e] à refléter dignement, en toutes circonstances, la qualité du mécène et à le mettre en lumière».

[50]. 27 May 1909, SAINT-MARCEAUX 2007, p. 544.

[51]. 7 February 1910, *ibidem*, p. 577.

1910); still, the number of entries that contain daily summaries of this nature is enormous. This creates an equivalence within the *Journal* between the trivial aspects of everyday life on one hand — recorded through comments on the weather, people's illnesses, the ever-shifting political landscape, and so on — and Meg's deeply ingrained, everyday musical habits on the other. Saint-Marceaux's *Journal* can scarcely be called 'intimate', given that Meg hardly talked about herself: instead, she focused on music, as though methodically listing her musical tasks would allow her to recompose herself. Meg's writing also creates the impression that all her activities were governed by the same selflessness, such that the very fabric of her life seemed to be woven from various musical pastimes: «wildly amusing» meetings where she «played on two pianos with Marthe in a little ensemble»[52], musical matinées, and private singing lessons, for instance, taken purely for the «satisfaction» of singing: «I am satisfied by my voice. Poor old resuscitated thing»[53].

The selflessness in the *Journal* was a dramatisation of Meg's true musical passion, but it also manifested within the public sphere: details about remuneration for artists invited to perform at the Saint-Marceaux's are almost systematically excluded, and an implicit silence surrounded both the capital and the increased visibility that they stood to gain, the implication being that other factors were enough to justify their presence — artistic devotion, the pleasure of impromptu music-making, and Meg's sparkling conversation. Material detachment was assigned moral value while also serving as a sign of social distinction, a staged performance wherein musical practice and musical thought arose from naturally music-loving temperaments, and wherein the enthronement of music was elevated to the level of an existential comportment. In this context, musical performance, when undertaken with taste and artistic sensitivity, emerged as a sign of not only social but moral distinction:

> Saint-Saëns afternoon at Madeleine Lemaire's. Reynaldo Hahn sang the master's songs wonderfully well, accompanied by the man himself. Clément the tenor, Gaubert the flutist, Mme Kinen sang too. *Delicious ensemble, highly elegant people, artists.* It is the gayest salon in Paris[54].

It should be noted that the idea of taste and artistic sensitivity implicitly excluded the working classes as well as the greater Parisian public — an audience that, according to Meg,

---

52. 21 November 1904, *ibidem*, p. 369: «follement amusants»; «[...] jou[e] à deux pianos avec Marthe en petit comité».

53. 21 December 1909, *ibidem*, p. 568: «satisfaction»; «Ma voix me satisfait. Pauvre vieille chose rajeunie».

54. 15 June 1906, *ibidem*, p. 441. «Matinée Saint-Saëns chez Madeleine Lemaire. Reynaldo Hahn y chante merveilleusement bien des mélodies du maître accompagnées par lui-même. Clément le ténor, Gaubert le flûtiste, Mme Kinen chantent également. *Ensemble délicieux, des gens fort élégants, des artistes.* C'est le salon le plus gai de Paris». My emphasis.

swooned before uninteresting music even though they had been «inundated with the best music by such interesting concerts which were given all winter in Paris»[55]. In sum, financial matters and other base material interests were erased and firmly separated from pure aesthetic sentiment — such sentiment being «rooted in an ethic, or rather, an ethos of elective distance from the necessities of the natural and social world»[56], in the words of Pierre Bourdieu.

Nevertheless, in terms of adjusting to institutional contexts and influencing institutional membership through confidential dealings, the Saint-Marceaux salon was second to none. Soirées drew a wide audience, but dinner guests were selected more strategically, because nominations to institutional bodies were discussed around the table:

> Intimate supper where Fauré's election to the Institut [de France] was much discussed. He was with us, [André] Messager as well. Saint-Saëns returning from Las Palmas to influence his colleagues who are much enthralled by the smiles of Mme Max, who wants Widor to be nominated. What will prevail, talent or intrigue[57].

And in the case of René Saint-Marceaux's 1905 accession to the Académie des Beaux-Arts as a sculptor, the permeability between domestic spaces and the political scene cannot be denied. Myriam Chimènes arrives at this conclusion as well, noting that «contrary to conventional wisdom, Parisian salons remained closely linked to the workings of musical life, and the music historical role of salon hostesses during this period was much more than anecdotal»[58].

When others took advantage of their contacts to favour competitors of the Saint-Marceaux's inner circle, however, Meg condemned the strategy severely. With Messager poised to become director of the Opéra de Paris, for instance, she scoffed at manoeuvring in support of other candidates: «Directorship of the Opéra still unresolved. There is talk of bribing Clémenceau, of Mme Roussel giving money for Carré to succeed. It's an appalling

---

55.   23 June 1910, *ibidem*, p. 598: «[...] [qu'a]breuvé de la meilleure musique par les concerts si intéressants donnés tout l'hiver à Paris, [...] se pâme en écoutant [de la] musique [...] inintéressante».

56.   BOURDIEU 1979, p. iv (original), p. xxviii (translation).

57.   4 March 1909, SAINT-MARCEAUX 2007, p. 535: «Dîner intime où l'élection de Fauré à l'Institut [de France] est fort discutée. Il est des nôtres, [André] Messager aussi. Saint-Saëns revient de Las Palmas pour influencer ses confrères très conquis par le sourire de Mme Max qui veut faire nommer Widor. Qui l'emportera, du talent ou de l'intrigue».

58.   CHIMÈNES 2004, p. 14: «[...] [c]ontrairement aux idées reçues, les salons parisiens demeurent étroitement liés au fonctionnement de la vie musicale et le rôle de ceux qui les animent n'est pas anecdotique dans l'histoire de la musique de cette époque».

quagmire, as is everything that has to do with government»[59]. Here, the monetary element, which Meg deemed vulgar, no doubt accounts for her indignation, seeing as she herself kept mum on financial issues as a point of honour. We know nevertheless that financial capital exerted influence on the decision-making of official artistic bodies just as symbolic capital did, and consequently altered the course of compositional history. Economic fluctuations affect all art histories, setting their courses and their limits, and music history is no exception — despite music's enthronement in the nineteenth century as the purest and most spiritualistic of all the arts, and therefore by nature the furthest removed from the material interests that motivated the greater public. Music, as Bourdieu reminds us, «represents the most radical and most absolute form of the negation of the world, and especially the social world, which the bourgeois ethos tends to demand of all forms of art»[60]. Small wonder that Madame de Saint-Marceaux, her genuine musical inclinations notwithstanding, drew upon music as a catalyst for her own moral distinction.

Working at the limits, within intermediate zones with porous boundaries between private and public, Marguerite de Saint-Marceaux found in the *continuum* between these spaces ways to *actively* insert herself into her musical milieu — which was still, at the turn of the twentieth century, an exclusively masculine domain. She used methods that were intimate *a priori* (the bourgeois salon, the intimate journal) for the purposes of agency; she availed herself of artistic forms without explicit meanings, which were consequently perceived as politically inoffensive (although this perception is of course patently untrue). And in doing, so she revealed mechanisms for self-figuration, nourished by incipient attempts at distinction and the reflex to cultivate worldly dominance, under the surface of her musical vocation.

Far be it from the author of this essay to dispute the authenticity of Marguerite de Saint-Marceaux's musical passion. Rather, my goal has been to reiterate the crucial role of mediation in the making of history, thanks to the unique perspective arising from this *situated* gaze, immersed in an artistic crucible as both participant and witness. Within this crucial mediation, there is interpersonal mediation, certainly, the kind that invigorates interpersonal networks. But there is subjective mediation also, linked to the elements of creation, confabulation, and embellishment that are inherent to any witness's account and indeed to any historical narrative — these accounts and narratives being forever one version among many.

---

[59].   11 January 1907, SAINT-MARCEAUX 2007, p. 468: «La direction de l'Opéra est toujours en suspens. On parle de pot-de-vin donné à Clémenceau, de Mme Roussel donnant l'argent pour la réussite de Carré. C'est un micmac écœurant, et tout ce qui touche au gouvernement est ainsi».

[60].   BOURDIEU 1979, p. 18 (original), p. 11 (translation).

Bibliography

Amossy – Maingueneau 2007

Amossy, Ruth – Maingueneau, Dominique. 'Autour des «scénographies auctoriales»: entretien avec José-Luis Diaz, auteur de *L'Écrivain imaginaire* (2007)', in: *Argumentation et Analyse du Discours*, iii (2009), <http://journals.openedition.org/aad/678>, accessed December 2023.

Bourdieu 1979

Bourdieu, Pierre. *La Distinction. Critique sociale du jugement*, Paris, Les Éditions de Minuit, 1979 (Le sens commun); English translation by Richard Nice, *Distinction: A Social Critique of the Judgement of Taste*, London, Routledge & Kegan Paul, 1986.

Chimènes 2004

Chimènes, Myriam. *Mécènes et Musiciens. Du salon au concert à Paris sous la iiie République*, Paris, Fayard, 2004.

Chimènes 2007

Ead. 'Introduction', in: Saint-Marceaux 2007, pp. 13-60.

Colette 2004 [1950]

Colette. 'Un salon en 1900', (1950), in: *Journal à rebours*, Paris, Fayard, 2004, pp. 105-112; English translation by David Le Vay, 'A Salon in 1900', in: *Looking Backwards*, Bloomington-London, Indiana University Press, 1975, pp. 18-22.

Février 1948

Février, Henry. *André Messager, mon maître, mon ami*, Paris, Amiot-Dumont, 1948.

Fumaroli 1985

Fumaroli, Marc. 'Quelques réflexions liminaires sur le mécénat d'Ancien Régime', in: *L'Âge d'or du mécénat (1598-1661)*, edited by Jean Mesnard and Roland Mousnier, Paris, Éditions du CNRS, 1985, pp. 1-12.

Johnson 1995

Johnson, James P. *Listening in Paris: A Cultural History*, Berkeley-Los Angeles, University of California Press, 1995.

Kaltenecker 2010

Kaltenecker, Martin. *L'Oreille divisée. Les discours sur l'écoute musicale aux xviiie et xixe siècles*, Paris, Musica Ficta, 2010 (Répercussions).

Martin-Fugier 2003

Martin-Fugier, Anne. *Les Salons de la iiie République. Art, littérature, politique*, Paris, Perrin, 2003 (Tempus).

NECTOUX 1992

NECTOUX, Jean-Michel. 'Musique et beaux-arts: le Salon de Marguerite de Saint-Marceaux', in: *Une famille d'artistes en 1900. Les Saint-Marceaux*, Paris, Réunion des musées nationaux, 1992 (Les Dossiers du Musée d'Orsay 49), pp. 62-90.

PROUST 1987 [1913]

PROUST, Marcel. *À la recherche du temps perdu. 1*, (1913), edited by Jean-Yves Tadié, Paris, Éditions Gallimard, 1987 (Bibliothèque de la Pléiade); English translation by C. K. Scott Moncrieff and Terence Kilmartin, *In Search of Lost Time. 1*, New York, The Modern Library, 2003.

PROUST 1993 [1922]

ID. *Correspondance. 21*, (1922), edited by Philip Kolb, Paris, Plon, 1993.

SAINT-MARCEAUX 2007

SAINT-MARCEAUX, Marguerite de. *Journal 1894-1927*, edited by Myriam Chimènes, Paris, Fayard, 2007.

THE MUSICAL ART QUARTET, ALICE WARDER GARRETT, AND AMERICAN MUSICAL DIPLOMACY IN THE EARLY TWENTIETH CENTURY

Kathryn M. Fenton
(STEPHEN F. AUSTIN STATE UNIVERSITY)

To THE READERS OF *Time* magazine's issue of 21 July 1930, the music columnist offered the following origin story concerning an emerging young string quartet, known as the Musical Art Quartet (1926-1944):

> Critics agree that each is a virtuoso in his own right. The Quartet's origin was as casual as its playing has been brilliant. The four friends, students in the Institute of Musical Art at Manhattan, had long been wont to meet of an afternoon or evening and beguile the hours with music for their own entertainment. Often, they played at the home of Efrem Zimbalist and his wife Alma Gluck, or for Jascha Heifetz. Sometimes, with one of these three the quartet would become temporarily a quintet. Admirers prevailed on them to give a series of recitals. They did so and found themselves famed. Such great virtuosos and maestros as Zimbalist, Heifetz, Arturo Toscanini verbally crowned the young artists with laurel, forecast shining futures. Singer Gluck created a fund to aid them, received contributions from Manhattan's music-loving Warburgs, Kahns, Guggenheimers, Lewisohn[1]. Thus

---

[1]. The writer most likely refers to two internationally-renowned virtuosi, violinists Efrem Zimbalist (1889-1985) and Jascha Heifetz (1901-1987). Alma Gluck (1884-1938) had been a leading soprano who had performed with the New York Metropolitan Opera Company and concertised around the United States. Following her 1925 retirement, she was well known for her musical patronage and activities supporting musicians in the United States, including serving as Vice President of the American Guild of Musical Artists, of which she was one of the founders. Her husband was the celebrated violinist, composer, and conductor Efrem Zimbalist. Italian conductor Arturo Toscanini (1867-1957) was well ensconced in New York City's musical circles, having directed both the Metropolitan Opera Company and the New York Philharmonic Symphony Orchestra. Otto Hermann Kahn (1867-1934) was the president of the Metropolitan Opera Company and sat on its board of directors (1908-

blessed, they went forth as the Musical Art Quartet, and for four seasons have passed
from fame to fame[2].

In this chapter, I demonstrate how an emerging American string quartet — The Musical
Art Quartet — was used to validate American cultural and musical achievements for Italian
audiences in the early 1930s, not in an official capacity by the U.S. State Department (as was
the case for jazz musicians or composers like Aaron Copland during in the postwar period), but
in an unofficial capacity by a private citizen with strong ties to the American Embassy in Rome:
Alice Warder Garret (1877-1942).

Current scholarship on musical diplomacy tends to focus on the Cold War era, with
substantial projects undertaken by Emily Ansari, Lisa Davenport, and Penny Von Eschen
among others[3]. Yet except for Jessica C. E. Gienow-Hecht's masterful volume on pre-World
War I musical exchange between the U.S. and Germany, very few scholars examine instances
of cultural diplomacy in the years prior to the Cold War Era[4]. Moreover, like Gienow-Hecht's
work, most musical diplomacy scholarship emphasises the transatlantic relationship between
the U.S. and either Germany or Russia.

The case of the Musical Art Quartet and Alice Warder Garrett brings to light an instance
of American musical diplomacy in Italy during the inter-war period. As such, it fills in the
chronological gap between Gienow-Hecht's work and scholarship centered on the Cold War
Era, while expanding the geographical boundaries to include Italy. I begin by describing the
quartet and its connection to Alice Warder Garrett before addressing Garrett's connection to
Italy via the American Embassy in Rome. I conclude with an analysis of the reception of the
quartet as American musical ambassadors.

Although the 1930 *Time* article suggests that all four members of the Musical Art
Quartet went to school together at the Institute, only the quartet's first violinist, Aleksander
'Sasha' Jacobsen (1895-1972) and cellist Marie Roemaet-Rosanoff (c.1896-1967) met while

---

1931). He was also vice-president of the New York Philharmonic and treasurer for the American Federation of
Arts. Felix M. Warburg (1871-1937), the Guggenheim family, and Samuel Adolph Lewisohn (1884-1951) were all
well-known philanthropists and patrons of the arts in New York City at the time. For a first-hand account of the
quartet's early beginnings and first public concerts, see KAUFMAN 1996.

    [2].   *TIME* 1930.

    [3].   See for example, ANSARI 2011, ANSARI 2014, ANSARI 2018; DAVENPORT 2009; FOSLER-LUSSIER 2015;
GIENOW-HECHT 2012; ROSENBERG 2010; ROSENBERG 2014; VON ESCHEN 2004. This concentration on the
U.S. and Germany or Russia is not particular to musicology. In a recent critique of diplomatic history scholarship,
researchers have argued that the attention paid to the U.S.-Russian relationship during the Cold War has resulted
in an unbalanced view of international diplomacy history, and have called for new relationships to be explored. See
OSGOOD – ETHERIDGE 2010.

    [4].   GIENOW-HECHT 2009. See also, RATHBERGER 2014.

classmates at the Institute of Musical Art — known today as The Juilliard School[5]. Jacobsen had been a rising star with an international concert and recording career when he accepted a teaching position at the Institute in 1926, replacing his own teacher Franz Kneisel (1865-1926) who had died[6]. Cellist Roemaet-Rosanoff studied with Wilhelm Willeke (1879-1950) and with Pablo Casals (1876-1973) after graduation. She too had a bourgeoning career as an international soloist and teacher of growing renown[7]. The quartet's original second violinist, Bernard Ocko (1901-1972), had just won the International Naumberg Competition (1926—) and was playing with the New York Philharmonic (1842—) and the Hartman String Quartet. Ocko was replaced early on by Paul Bernard (c.1907-c.1990) who had studied at the Institute with Paul Stassévitch (1894-1968) and possibly Leopold Auer (1845-1930). The quartet had some difficulty locating a suitable violist, in part because the Institute lacked a viola professor at that time. In his memoire about Jacobsen, the quartet's violist Louis Kaufman (1905-1994) explained that Jacobsen had looked to his own violin students at the music school for volunteers who might be willing to practice viola. Kaufman won the position and played with the quartet until 1933 when he left to pursue a career as an orchestral musician and soloist[8]. All the members of the quartet played on Stradivarius instruments loaned to them by Felix Warburg (1871-1937) beginning in 1926 or 1927[9].

Three years after forming, the quartet had established itself among the leading American chamber ensembles of the day, variably seen as the heirs to the Kneisel Quartet (1886-1917) or the Flonzaley Quartet (1902-1928). Reviews of public concerts regularly held at the Institute of Musical Art, Dumbarton Oaks, The Town Hall, and Kneisel Hall, constantly credited their success to a uniquely warm and uniform sound that elevated listeners[10]. Walter Damrosch

---

[5]. For a history of The Institute of Musical Art and its 1928 merger with the Julliard Graduate School, see OLMSTEAD 1999. Frank Damrosch (1859-1937) and James Loeb (1867-1833) founded the school, modelling it upon the national conservatories of several European countries. See also DAMROSCH 1936.

[6]. For reflections on Jacobsen's life and career during the years he played in the quartet, see KAUFMAN 1996 and KIEVMAN 1996. For a brief biography of Jacobsen, see WALLACE 1996. For more on the string quartet's history, see POTTER 1997.

[7]. POTTER 1997; OLMSTEAD 1999.

[8]. Kaufman was replaced by Louis Kievman (1910-1990). See KAUFMAN 1996, KAUFMAN 2003, and POTTER 1997.

[9]. While newspaper articles from the period are vague about when the quartet began playing on the Warburg instruments, Andrea Olmstead suggests that they began to do so in 1936. See OLMSTEAD 1999, p. 106. However, by 1937 Felix Warburg was dead and, according to the archivist at Dumbarton Oaks, the set of instruments was returned to his estate. A group of patrons (including Alice Warder Garrett) banded together to purchase more Stradivarius instruments for the ensemble. See DUMBARTON OAKS ARCHIVES 2017, KAUFMAN 1996, KAUFMAN 2003.

[10]. Alice Warder Garrett collected reviews of the quartet's American concerts beginning in 1929 from the following papers: *Baltimore Sun, New York Herald Tribune, New York Sun, New York Telegram, New York World, New York Evening World, Philadelphia Public Ledger, Washington Herald*. See GARRETT SCRAPBOOK n.d.

ILL. 1: West Elevation. Evergreen, 4545 North Charles Street, Baltimore, Independent City, MD. ID: No. 1, HABS MD-1167, Historic American Buildings Survey, Library of Congress Prints and Photographs Division Washington, D.C.

(1862-1950) once declared that they sounded as if «four well-bread and high-minded people had come together to discuss the mysteries of life»[11]. Their concert success led to recording contracts with Columbia records in the late 1920s[12].

While the quartet performed at some of the leading chamber music venues in and around New York City, they also offered private concerts in the homes of wealthy patrons as was customary at the time[13]. Newspaper articles sometimes reported on these private concerts and mentioned the names of the illustrious guests in attendance. In his memoire, violist Louis Kaufman recalled that the quartet played at «many elegant homes of his and Marie's friends: the Efrem Zimbalists, the Warburgs, and, once at the large apartment of Dr. Walter Damrosch when Arturo Toscanini and Pablo Casals were guests [...]»[14]. It was during this 1926 gathering at Damrosch's apartment that the quartet first met Alice and John Work Garrett (1872-1942). The couple would become one of their most significant patrons.

---

[11].   GARRETT *MUSIC IN AMERICA*, n.d.
[12].   SUEBERT n.d.; MUSICAL ART QUARTET 2022.
[13].   POTTER 2003.
[14].   KAUFMAN 1996, p. 117.

ILL. 2: View Looking East in the Baskt Theater, Evergreen, 4545 Charles Street, Baltimore, Independent City, MD. ID: No. 138, HABS MD-1167, Historic American Buildings Survey, Library of Congress Prints and Photographs Division Washington, D.C.

The next summer, the Garretts invited the quartet to stay at their Baltimore estate 'Evergreen' for six weeks. Evergreen was a large property, with several smaller houses and buildings on the estate in addition to the main mansion. The home was acclaimed for its library, both the room itself and extensive collection of over 35,000 rare and priceless books[15]. The Garretts would sometimes host small concerts in the famous library, but by and large, most were presented at the small private theatre that Alice Garrett had commissioned Leon Baskt to design and furnish with sets and costumes[16]. Every evening (except Sundays), the quartet performed in the theatre, playing the standard quartet repertoire of the Classical and Romantic eras, and exploring a few contemporary French and Italian works.

John W. Garrett (1872-1942) inherited the estate from his parents, and he worked for a time as a banker in the family firm, Robert Garrett and Sons (1896-1934). The family money

---

[15]. ABBOTT ET AL. 2017; GARRETT 1944.
[16]. ABBOTT ET AL. 2017; KELLY 2004; WOODS 1938.

came from his grandfather, who had been president of the Baltimore and Ohio Railroad, the oldest railroad company in the United States. John met Alice Warder while she was living in Berlin in 1905 studying voice[17]. Raised in Washington D.C. and hailing from a very wealthy family, Alice travelled to Europe for extended periods of time, studying art, music, literature, and dance. Throughout her life, she corresponded with some of the leading European and American figures in the fine and performing arts, whom she met during her sojourns in Europe and visits to New York City, where she kept an apartment. Her correspondence includes letters from composers like Maurice Ravel (1875-1937) and Giacomo Puccini (1858-1924)[18]. Best known today as a visual art patron and collector, Warder was also a passionate musical benefactor as well[19]. In addition to her support of the Musical Art Quartet, she was deeply involved in the Baltimore Symphony Orchestra Guild and self-published an essay — almost a manifesto — calling for more substantial financial support from the American private sector for composers and performers[20].

Alice's decision to assume patronage of the quartet was carefully researched. She began collecting reviews shortly after meeting the group at Damrosch's party and wrote to established musicians such as Alma Gluck and Walter Damrosch for advice[21]. In a letter dated 12 May 1929 from Samuel Chotzinoff — Jascha Heifetz's accompanist, music critic for the *New York World* and music director for the National Broadcasting Corporation (NBC) — the Garretts received some background information about the quartet and the players' musical training[22]. Chotzinoff endorsed them highly, explaining:

> In my opinion the Musical Art Quartet is a unique ensemble because it unites, for the first time I believe, the qualities of the Kneisels and the Flonzaleys. The first violin and cellist have under the tutelage of the late Mr. Kneisel become imbued with the Classical spirit while their own instincts tend toward the Romantic. Yet another feature is the extreme youth of the Quartet. Ensembles are usually formed after the players have reached the age of discretion with the consequent decline in technical ability. The Musical Art Quartet have agile fingers, youthful imaginations, musical culture, enthusiasm all working in a beautiful relation because of the classical background of their pupilage. The amazing thing is that the Quartet is entirely unlike the Kneisel, which it might excusably have resembled, but has its own artistic individuality. To my mind, and I have heard almost every ensemble, the Musical Art

---

17. ABBOTT *ET AL.* 2017.
18. Letters to Alice from other composers include those from Ernst Bloch (1880-1959), Manuel de Falla (1876-1946), and Ottorino Respighi (1879-1936). See GAR 0035 Ser. 1. Box 1. Fol. 54.
19. QUERCI 2004.
20. DISHAROON 1980; GARRETT *MUSIC IN AMERICA* n.d.
21. GARRETT *SCRAPBOOK* n.d.
22. CHOTZINOFF 1929.

Quartet, by reason of all its virtues is the only string quartet for which one does not
have to make any allowances. I consider it the finest string ensemble playing today[23].

The 1927 concerts at Evergreen were such a success that the Garretts decided to permanently
host the Musical Art Quartet for regular, in-house concert series. Recital programmes in Garrett's
scrapbook suggest that each series lasted six-weeks and consisted of eighteen concerts[24]. They
hosted two series every year — the first in May and June, the second in September and October.
Concerts took place on Thursday and Sunday evenings at 5:00pm and on Friday and Saturday
evenings at 9:30pm[25]. The repertoire consisted of works by Wolfgang Amadeus Mozart, Joseph
Haydn, Ludwig van Beethoven, Johannes Brahms, Antonín Dvořák, César Franck, Darius
Milhaud, Maurice Ravel, Dmitry Shostakovich, and others. The Garretts often included
a banquet in tandem with the concerts[26]. In return for the quartet's services, the Garretts
offered room and board at small cottage on the estate, including a travel allowance. Account
records show that the Garretts spent about 2,750 US dollars per season on the ensemble[27].

The Garrett concerts were essentially private. In addition to close friends and colleagues,
the couple invited statesmen, foreign ambassadors, senators, writers, and prominent
Baltimoreans[28]. There could be as many as fifty people invited to attend one concert. Surviving
letters document the views of individual audience members. One such attendee recalled, «Last
night we went to town [...] to one of Mrs. John W. Garrett's [...] concerts. Each year they hire
the Musical Arts [*sic*] Quartet to play [...]. A chosen few are invited [and] we happily were
chosen»[29]. Despite the private nature of these recitals, local and national newspapers reviewed
them. One such review praised the quartet as «probably the best of those playing in the United
States today», and noted its debt to the patronage of the Garretts claiming that «it could not
keep itself intact were it not for the enthusiasm of patrons like Mr. and Mrs. Garrett»[30].

In 1930, the quartet's path took a decidedly international turn. In January the Garretts
moved to Rome, Italy. They did so because, in addition to being a banker, John W. Garrett
also had a career in the American diplomatic corps. He had served terms in various places
throughout the years following his marriage to Alice[31]. In fact, when he first met Alice, he was

---

23. *Ibidem.*
24. GARRETT *SCRAPBOOK.*
25. ABBOTT *ET AL.* 2017.
26. KAUFMAN 1996.
27. ABBOTT *ET AL.* 2017.
28. KAUFMAN 1996.
29. ABBOTT *ET AL.* 2017, p. 44.
30. *BALTIMORE SUN* 1930B.
31. His main appointments included: second secretary to the Ambassador in Berlin, first secretary to the
Ambassador in Rome, 1908-1911; special assistant to the Ambassador in Paris, 1914-1917; envoy extraordinary

ILL. 3: Left to right: Sascha Jacobsen, John Work Garrett, Alice Warder Garrett, Marie Roemat-Rosanoff, Paul Bernard, Louis Kaufman. Garden of *Villa San Michele* 1932. ID: JHU_coll-0002_15087, Johns Hopkins University Graphic and Pictorial Collection.

the second secretary to the American Ambassador in Berlin[32]. Between the time they were married and their first encounter with the Musical Art Quartet, the couple had lived abroad in many places, including Buenos Aires, Paris, Rome, and The Hague. It was during their visits home to Baltimore that they offered the concert series. When Garrett accepted his appointment as American Ambassador to Italy in 1931, he and Alice brought the quartet with them[33].

Nonetheless, the quartet did not permanently reside in Rome. Accounts of their activities in the American press suggests the ensemble travelled back and forth between New York and Rome while the Garretts were stationed in Italy. They played for select audiences at

and minister plenipotentiary to Venezuela, 1910-11; and envoy extraordinary and minister plenipotentiary to Argentina, 1911-1914. For more on John W. Garrett's diplomatic career, see for example, HOLLAND 1996.

[32]. President Herbert Hoover brought Garrett out of retirement unexpectedly in the summer of 1929, with Garrett's mission officially beginning on November 20, 1929 and lasting until May 22, 1933. Garrett's familiarity with Rome and Italian customs combined with his reputation as a skilled statesman proved a valuable an asset in negotiating U.S.-Italian relations during the interwar period. See ABBOTT *ET AL.* 2017.

[33]. *Ibidem.* Republican Herbert Hoover (1874-1864) served as President of the United States from 1929 to 1933. His secretary of state was Henry Lewis Stimson (1867-1950). Benito Mussolini (1883-1945) was the Prime Minister of Italy from 1922-1943.

the temporary American Embassy quarters in the Antico Palazzo Rospigliosi in Rome and at the Garrett's temporary summer home Villa San Michele on the Isle of Capri[34]. While in Capri, the quartet performed at various functions organised by Alice. Each afternoon — around four o'clock — they also performed exclusively for the couple in an ancient chapel near the Garrett's villa in Anacapri.

While there was little news coverage of the quartet's spring visit to Italy, there was quite a bit more coverage of their summer one[35]. Reports focused on the quartet's status as a representative for all American musicians and on its continued sponsorship by the newly-minted Ambassador and his wife[36]. Even though the trip was privately funded by the Garretts and born out of a previous private arrangement between them and the Quartet, the American press shaped the trip as a case of musical diplomacy. *Time* magazine reported that «last week this group hobbed up in the nation's diplomatic news [...]», specifying that at «Garrett receptions, teas, [and] soirées, the Quartet will play Debussy, Bach, Schumann, Franck, Brahms, Beethoven, for whomever Mrs. Garrett bids attend. Later they will play in Naples, then return to Manhattan in time for a November concert, the first of their next season's series at Town Hall»[37].

Nationalist rhetoric frequently found its way into the assessment of the quartet's performances. In his praise of the ensemble, William J. Henderson of the *New York Sun* wrote that «the Quartet has assumed a commanding position in the artistic life of this city and is rapidly becoming a national institution»[38], and the critic of the *Philadelphia Evening Public Ledger* wrote that the quartet was «undoubtedly one of the best organisations of its kind on the American concert stage today»[39]. Critics and other musicians not only viewed the quartet as best the country had to offer, but also as the first American chamber music ensemble of international calibre. Discussions fashioned it as symbol of American musical development and exceptionalism. Conductor and composer Walter Damrosch, for instance, wrote that «America is at last taking a prominent place in the music of the world. Our symphonic orchestras are considered the most perfect. Many of our pianists, violinists, and

---

[34]. Villa San Michele was owned by Swedish physician and writer Axel Munthe who gained international success with his book *The Story of San Michele,* MUNTHE 1929. See also JANGFELD 2008. For correspondence between the Garretts and Munthe arranging their accommodations at San Michele and the quartet's visit, see MUNTHE n.d. Louis Kaufman vividly recounts his time at San Michele, KAUFMAN 2003.

[35]. Alice collected close to twenty newspaper clippings documenting the Quartets Italian activities and reception from various American newspapers. See GARRETT SCRAPBOOK n.d.

[36]. *WASHINGTON HERALD* 1929.

[37]. *TIME* 1930.

[38]. HENDERSON 1930.

[39]. From an unidentified clipping attributed to the Philadelphia *Public Ledger* 1929 found in GARRETT SCRAPBOOK n.d.

singers are considered the most perfect. Many of our pianists, violinists, and singers have achieved world-wide distinction and now we have a string quartet which is equal to the best Europe can produce — The Musical Art Quartet»[40].

While the seeds had been sown for the image of the quartet as an American national institution and as a symbol of American musical achievements well before the group's Italian engagements, period press coverage of the quartet's Italian visits amplifies this trope. One article suggests that the Italian performances «will probably do more to acquaint Italians with the high degree of excellence of American musical performances than any single event [...]»[41]. This article goes on to describe the Capri concerts and to argue that the quartet would receive international exposure at those events, despite the relatively private nature of the performances. The author concludes that «[...] through the munificence of one individual hundreds will be afforded an opportunity of judging for themselves the place the United States occupies in the musical world»[42].

This assessment that the quartet would elevate the image of American musicians and musical culture abroad was not entirely spontaneous on the part of the press. The American embassy took part in crafting this image. A press release issued by the embassy concludes by claiming that the quartet would be «certain to be a definitive factor in presenting cultural America to Europe»[43]. A promotional pamphlet from the Quartet's artist agency was framed with the title: 'Musical Art Quartet: American Ambassadors of Chamber Music'[44]. Articles bearing headlines such as 'Cites U.S. Cultural Triumphs in Italy' and 'Mrs. Garrett Hostess at Concerts in Rome. Many Voices Delight in Programs [*sic*] by American Quartet at Ambassador's Home' echoed language from the embassy's press release and other promotional materials[45]. It seems to the American press, at least, that Alice Garrett's American-Italian cultural exchange was a success.

The image of the Musical Art Quartet as musical ambassadors for the United States persists throughout newspaper coverage in 1930 and 1931. Even reviews of New York City concerts drew reference to the Italian visit. These 1930 concerts in Italy were so well received they yielded another set of invitations for a more extensive tour of several major Italian cities in the spring of 1931, including: Florence, Naples, Milan, Parma, Rome, Turin, and Venice[46]. The

---

[40]. For more on Damrosch, see DAMROSCH 1923 and MARTIN 1983.

[41]. *CALL* 1930.

[42]. *Ibidem.*

[43]. GARRETT *SCRAPBOOK* n.d.

[44]. ENGLES n.d.

[45]. *BALTIMORE SUN* 1930A. Both 'Cites U.S. Cultural Triumphs in Italy' and 'Mrs. Garrett Hostess at Concerts in Rome. Many Voice Delight in Programs by American Quartet at Ambassador's Home' are unidentified newspaper clippings found in GARRETT *SCRAPBOOK* n.d.

[46]. KAUFMAN 2003.

Garretts provided a car and driver, and paid for all expenses, with proceeds donated to charity, specifically the National Committee of Mothers and Children for Prevention of Childhood Tuberculosis. In 1930, there is some indication that Italians were initially skeptical of the quartet when they first performed in Italy, but by 1931 had embraced the ensemble. One family friend recalled that some Italians complained about the favouring of the American quartet over Roman musicians. To counter this, Alice Garrett hired a local Roman orchestra to perform at the embassy on Monday evenings[47].

Whether or not Italians ultimately interpreted the quartet as representing a new era of American cultural development remains to be seen. Alice collected only a couple of Italian reviews for her scrapbook: 'Un quartetto americano' and 'Il Quartetto d'arte di New York', both published in *Il Messaggero*. The tour did spark an interest in American musical life, and Alfredo Casella published a series of articles called 'La vita musicale negli Stati Uniti'[48]. Evidence suggests, however, that Italians did come to view the quartet as highly accomplished, at least according to American members of press. Following the end of the 1931 tour, one U.S. paper printed a translation of a laudatory Italian review of the quartet's recitals. It recognized both the exquisite musicianship of the performers and Alice Garrett's role in bringing the quartet to Italy. The discussion of the quartet's final recital in Rome concludes by asserting that «four jewels (quartets by Mozart, Schubert, Brahms, and Franck at the embassy) come providentially at the end of the season to compensate us for all the ugly performances listened to during the year»[49]. At home, the quartet from that point on was frequently marketed as not only an American ensemble, but one with an international reputation.

Perhaps the highest Italian praise of Alice's cultural diplomacy came from Benito Mussolini himself, writing upon the couple's return to the U.S.: «I take this opportunity to renew to you our thanks for your valuable effort in fostering the friendship between Italy and the United States [...]. I wish to tell you how much we appreciated the interest you took to all Italian activities especially in the social and artistic field, and how much we regret that you and Mr. Garrett are leaving Italy»[50]. In a time when the U.S. was confirming its place on the world stage as a political equal to Europe, it comes as no surprise to see efforts to promote American culture as also on par with that of Europe. In the first quarter of the twentieth century, it was commonplace to find discussions in American music magazines and newspaper articles addressing the 'development of American music' always with an eye toward how it would measure up against its European counterpart. What is unusual to see is a private local patron assume responsibility for the international promotion of an ensemble intended to represent

---

47. BALDWIN 1974; BALDWIN – GARDINE 1985.
48. GARRETT *SCRAPBOOK* n.d.
49. HALL 1931.
50. SOTTOSEGRETARIO 1933, English translation in ABBOTT *ET AL*. 2017.

the nation. The case of the Musical Art Quartet's tour of Italy opens the door for further considerations about the nature of American musical diplomacy and Italian-American cultural relations during the interwar years.

BIBLIOGRAPHY

Archival Sources and Documents

CHOTZINOFF 1929
CHOTZINOFF, Samuel. Letter to John Work Garrett, 12 May 1929, in: GARRETT *SCRAPBOOK* n.d.

ENGLES n.d.
ENGLES, George. *Musical Art Quartet: American Ambassadors of Chamber Music*, New York, National Broadcasting Company Artists Service, n.d., in: GARRETT *SCRAPBOOK* n.d.

GARRETT 1944
GARRETT, John Work. *John Work Garrett and His Library at Evergreen House*, Baltimore, Privately Printed, 1944.

GARRETT *MUSIC IN AMERICA* n.d.
GARRETT, Alice. *The Development of Music in America*, Baltimore, Privately Printed, n.d. MS.GAR.035. Ser. Box 1. Fol.3.

GARRETT *SCRAPBOOK* n.d.
GARRETT, Alice. *Musical Art Quartet Scrapbook*, Alice Warder Garrett Papers, MS.GAR.035, The Evergreen Foundation (on deposit at the Johns Hopkins University), n.d.

MS.GAR.035
Alice Warder Garrett Papers, MS.GAR.035, The Evergreen Foundation (on deposit at The Johns Hopkins University).

MUNTHE n.d.
Letter from Axel Munthe to Alice Garrett, n.d. MS.GAR.035 Series 1, Box 1 Folder 112.

SOTTOSEGRETARIO 1933
Letter from Sottosegretario di Stato per gli Affari Esteri to Alice Warder Garrett, 19 May 1933, in: GARRETT *SCRAPBOOK* n.d.

WOODS 1938
WOODS, Helen. *Music in the Library*, Baltimore, Privately Printed, May 1938. MS.GAR.035 Ser. 7 Box 1. Fol. 13.

THE MUSICAL ART QUARTET

Secondary Sources

ABBOTT *ET AL.* 2017
Evergreen: The Garrett Family, Collectors and Connoisseurs, edited by James Archer Abbott, Earle A. Havens, Bodil Ottesen and Susan G. Tripp, Baltimore, Johns Hopkins University Press, 2017.

ANSARI 2011
ANSARI, Emily Abrams. 'Aaron Copland and the Politics of Cultural Diplomacy', in: *Journal of the Society for American Music*, V/3 (August 2011), pp. 335-364.

ANSARI 2014
EAD. 'Musical Americanism, Cold War Consensus Culture, and the U.S.-U.S.S.R. Composer's Exchange, 1958-1960', in: *The Musical Quarterly*, XCVII/3 (Fall 2014), pp. 360-389.

ANSARI 2018
EAD. *The Sound of a Superpower: Musical Americanism and the Cold War*, Oxford, Oxford University Press, 2018.

BALDWIN 1974
BALDWIN, Billy. *Billy Baldwin Remembers*, New York, Harcourt-Brace-Jovanovich, 1974.

BALDWIN – GARDINE 1985
ID. – GARDINE, Michael. *Billy Baldwin: An Autobiography*, New York, Little, Brown, 1985.

BALTIMORE SUN 1930A
'Cites U.S. Cultural Triumphs in Italy', in: *Baltimore Evening Sun*, Friday, 6 June 1930.

BALTIMORE SUN 1930B
'Noble Music', in: *Baltimore Evening Sun*, 10 July 1930.

CALL 1930
'Mrs. Garrett's Quartet', in: *San Francisco Call*, 26 August 1930

DAMROSCH 1923
DAMROSCH, Walter. *My Musical Life*, New York, Charles Scribner's Sons, 1923.

DAMROSCH 1936
DAMROSCH, Frank. *History of the Institute of Musical Art*, 1905-1926, New York City, Julliard School of Music, 1936.

DAVENPORT 2009
DAVENPORT, Lisa E. *Jazz Diplomacy, Promoting America in the Cold War Era*, Jackson, University Press of Mississippi, 2009.

DISHAROON 1980
DISHAROON, Richard Alan. *A History of Municipal Music in Baltimore, 1914-1947*, unpublished Ph.D. Diss., College Park (MD), University of Maryland, 1980.

DUMBARTON OAKS ARCHIVES 2017
DUMBARTON OAKS ARCHIVES. 'The Musical Art Quartet and the Bliss Stradivarius Viola', in: *Seventy-Fifth Anniversary Blog*, 15 June 2017, Dumbarton Oaks Research Library and Collection, <https://www.doaks.org/research/library-archives/dumbarton-oaks-archives/historical-records/75th-anniversary/blog/the-musical-art-quartet-and-the-bliss-stradivarius-viola>, accessed December 2023.

FOSLER-LUSSIER 2015
FOSLER-LUSSIER, Danielle. *Music in America's Cold War Diplomacy*, Oakland, University of California Press, 2015.

GIENOW-HECHT 2009
GIENOW-HECHT, Jessica C. E. *Sound Diplomacy, Music and Emotions in Transatlantic Relations, 1850-1920*, Chicago, University of Chicago Press, 2009.

GIENOW-HECHT 2012
EAD. 'The World Is Ready to Listen, Symphony Orchestras and the Global Performance of America', in: *Diplomatic History*, XXXVI (2012), pp. 17-28.

HALL 1931
HALL, Raymond. 'New York Musical Art Quartet', in: *New York Times*, 12 July 1931.

HENDERSON 1930
HENDERSON, William J. [No title], in: *New York Sun*, 15 April 1930.

HOLLAND 1996
HOLLAND, Fait. 'What a Difference a Year Made, John Work Garrett Finds a Diplomatic Career', in: *Maryland Historical Magazine*, XCI/3 (1996), pp. 277-297.

JANGFELD 2008
JANGFELD, Bengt. *Axel Munthe, The Road to San Michele*, English translation by Harry Watson, London, I. B. Tauris and Company, 2008.

KAUFMAN 1996
KAUFMAN, Louis. 'Memories of Sascha Jacobsen and the Musical Art Quartet', in: *Journal of the Violin Society of America*, XIV/13 (1996), pp. 116-121.

KAUFMAN 2003
ID. *A Fiddler's Tale, How Hollywood and Vivaldi Discovered Me*, Madison, University of Wisconsin Press, 2003.

KIEVMAN 1996
KIEVMAN, Louis. 'Sascha Jacobsen and the Musical Art Quartet (1932 to 1937)' in: *Violin Society of America*, XIV/13 (1996), pp. 121-124.

KELLY 2004
KELLY, Cindy. *Léon Baskt at Evergreen House, A Collection Built Around a Friendship*, Baltimore, Evergreen House-Johns Hopkins University, 2004.

MARTIN 1983
MARTIN, George. *The Damrosch Dynasty, America's First Family of Music*, Boston, Houghton Mifflin, 1983.

MUNTHE 1929
MUNTHE, Axel. *The Story of San Michele*, New York, Dutton, 1929.

MUSICAL ART QUARTET 2022
Musical Art Quartet, Complete Columbia Recordings, Biddulph 85017-2 August 19 2022 CD, recorded c.1928-1829.

OLMSTEAD 1999
OLMSTEAD, Andrea. 'The Institute of Musical Art, A European Tradition', in: ID. *Julliard: A History*, Urbana-Chicago, University of Illinois Press, 1999, pp. 30-57.

OSGOOD – ETHERIDGE 2010
The United States and Public Diplomacy: New Directions in Cultural and International History, edited by Kenneth A. Osgood and Brian C. Etheridge, Leiden, Martinus Nijhoff, 2010.

POTTER 1997
POTTER, Tully. 'Success in High Society', in: *The Strad*, CVIII/1282 (1997), pp. 154-159.

POTTER 2003
ID. 'The Concert Explosion and the Age of Recording', in: *The Cambridge Companion to the String Quartet*, edited by Robin Stowell, Cambridge, Cambridge University Press, 2003 (Cambridge Companions to Music), pp. 60-93.

QUERCI 2004
QUERCI, Eugenia. 'Alice Warder Garrett, una ambasciatrice per l'arte', in: *Storia dell'Arte*, CVIII (1 January 2004), pp. 125-157.

RATHBERGER 2014
RATHBERGER, Andreas. 'The «Piano Virtuosos» of International Politics, Informal Diplomacy in the Late Nineteenth and Early Twentieth Century Ottoman Empire', in: *New Global Studies*, VIII/1 (2014), pp. 9-29.

ROSENBERG 2014
ROSENBERG, Jonathan. '«The Best Diplomats are Often the Great Musicians»: Leonard Bernstein and the New York Philharmonic Play Berlin', in: *New Global Studies*, VIII (2014), pp. 65-86.

ROSENBERG 2010
ID. 'Fighting the Cold War with Violins and Trumpets, American Symphony Orchestras Abroad in the 1950s', in: *Winter Kept Us Warm, Cold War Interactions Reconsidered*, edited by Sari Autio-Sarasmo and Brendan Humphreys, Helsinki, Kikimora Publications, 2010, pp. 23-43.

SUEBERT n.d.
'Musical Art Quartet', in: *Discography of American Historical Recordings*, edited by David Suebert, <https://adp.library.ucsb.edu/names/107490>, accessed December 2023.

TIME 1930
'Diplomatic Notes', in: *Time*, 21 July 1930.

VON ESCHEN 2004
VON ESCHEN, Penny M. *Satchmo Blows Up the World: Jazz Ambassadors Play the Cold War*, Cambridge (MA), Harvard University Press, 2004.

WALLACE 1996
WALLACE, David. 'Sascha Jacobsen, A Master Violinist Remembered', in: *Violin Society of America*, XIV/13 (1996), pp. 111-116.

WASHINGTON HERALD 1929
'Garretts Named as Patrons for Music Arts Tour', in: *Washington Herald*, 9 July 1929.

CHAMBER MUSIC AND NATIONHOOD

Evaluating Dvořák's 'Niche': The 1892 Farewell Tour, the *Dumky* Piano Trio Op. 90, and Perceptions of Dvořák as Chamber Music Composer

Eva Branda
(Wilfrid Laurier University)

IN HIS SCATHING REVIEW of Antonín Dvořák's *Rusalka* (1900) penned after the work's premiere in 1901, critic Zdeněk Nejedlý (1878-1962) makes this statement: «In the name of Dvořák's true followers, we have to ask the master most earnestly not to be taken off course by flattery, which leads him to paths that are fateful for him and to return to the domain where he reigns supreme in the world: chamber music»[1]. Known for his rather severe criticism of Dvořák as an opera composer, Nejedlý was nevertheless willing to acknowledge Dvořák's skill in the realm of chamber music; indeed, this was the one area in which Dvořák's Czech critics seemed to be somewhat in agreement, as confirmed by another contemporary critic Josef Boleška (1868-1914), who — some ten years later — would go so far as to claim that enthusiasm in Prague for Dvořák's chamber works had reached cultish levels[2].

This paper explores Dvořák's Czech reception as a chamber music composer — an area that was identified early on as his niche. Specifically, it will delve into a circumstance when Dvořák's chamber music was featured prominently in his homeland. In 1892, Dvořák embarked on a five-month-long 'farewell tour'[3] of the Czech lands ahead of his American sojourn, which would begin later that year[4]. Along with violinist Ferdinand Lachner (1856-1910) and cellist

---

[1]. Nejedlý 1901, p. 209: «Ve jménu pravých ctitelů Dvořákových musíme mistra prosit co nejsnažněji, aby se nedal svést lichocením, jež ho vede na dráhy jemu v budoucnosti osudné a vrátil se tam, kde je dnes neomezeným pánem světa, k hudbě komorní. Jeho symfonické básně a jeho zpěvohry vždy budou Dvořákovi ujímat v historii na veliké slávě, již si pojistil svými výtvory absolutně hudebními».

[2]. Boleška 1912, p. 171.

[3]. Šupka 2020.

[4]. Dvořák left for the United States on 1 September 1892.

Hanuš Wihan (1855-1920), Dvořák toured various parts of Bohemia and Moravia, thereby allowing his chamber works to reach a wide audience. The centrepiece of the tour programme was Dvořák's *Dumky* Piano Trio, Op. 90, completed in 1891. Much like the *Slavonic Dances* that had kickstarted Dvořák's career — and with the added nostalgia that comes from being pitched as a kind of 'farewell' to Czech audiences — the *Dumky* Piano Trio proved an ideal vehicle for affirmations of Dvořák's 'Czechness' and his chamber music prowess. Using the *Dumky* Trio as a case study, this paper seeks to tease out broader discourses on Dvořák's chamber music works and to understand why, relative to other genres, his reception in this area was comparatively uncontroversial.

«Instrumental music is his true home»: Exploring Issues of Genre

Perceptions of Dvořák were largely predicated on issues of genre; that is, critical assessments of his work were often dependent on a certain set of expectations, both for the given genre and for Dvořák himself. As early as 1873, absolute instrumental music had been designated by the Czechs as Dvořák's domain. In an article for the music journal *Dalibor* dated 4 April 873, Václav Juda Novotný (1849-1922) reflects on the recent performance of Dvořák's orchestral composition *May Night* [*Májová Noc*] with the following words:

> We can expect great things from Dvořák in the future, which can only be to the glory of the Czech name, not so much in the realm of dramatic art — since, (thus far), Dvořák lacks deeper aesthetic studies, defter treatment of the human voice, and finally, true expression in declamation that would befit the Czech language — but mainly in *the field of instrumental music*, as we can judge based on everything that we have heard from the composer so far. *Instrumental music is his true home* [...][5].

Novotný seems to offer a somewhat backhanded compliment here, leading with a *critique* of Dvořák's work as a dramatist and assigning instrumental music to Dvořák, almost by default. These ideas were echoed by critic Ludevít Procházka (1837-1888), who carved out an even narrower niche for Dvořák. Writing for the Prague daily newspaper *Národní listy* within a few

---

5. [Novotný] 1873, p. 113: «Od Dvořáka smíme již pro budoucnost očekávati činy velké, jaké jen k oslavě sloužiti mohou jménu českému, ani ne tak na poli dramatického umění — schází zde (dosud) Dvořákovi hlubších esthetických studií a obratnějšího zacházení s hlasem lidským a konečně pravého výrazu při deklamaci přiměřené duchu jazyka českého — nýbrž hlavně *na poli hudby instrumentální*, jak souditi můžeme dle všeho, co jsme dosud od skladatele našeho slyšeli. Hudba instrumentální jest jeho pravým domovem; neboť mysliti tak čistě orkestrálně, v tak vznešeném slohu polyfonním není věru každému popřáno». (The emphasis is mine.)

days of Novotný and commenting on the same orchestral piece, Procházka declares that «the extraordinary loveliness pouring forth in [Dvořák's] instrumentation points especially to his true calling *in the realm of absolute instrumental music*»[6]. The swiftness with which these critics seem to be willing to dismiss Dvořák's dramatic works is remarkable, considering that no Dvořák opera had yet been performed in the Czech lands[7]. Perhaps even more surprising is the degree of confidence that the writers place in Dvořák's instrumental compositions, which likewise had been given little exposure to that point. Though it would appear that these conclusions were reached after a very limited sampling of Dvořák's output, the composer's alleged area of expertise was established in the press quite early on in his career, and on some level — as long as Dvořák conformed to these expectations in terms of genre — he was able to escape negative scrutiny[8].

This sort of 'pigeon-holing' would continue to inform Dvořák reception in later decades. A Dvořák compendium was published in Prague in 1912, with chapters divided up by genre. The task of providing an overview of Dvořák's chamber music fell to Josef Boleška, who, apart from working as a critic, was a concert organiser, publicist, and former Dvořák pupil[9]. Boleška opens his study by stating unequivocally that «out of Dvořák's rich output, first prize is awarded to chamber music»[10]. He backs this statement up, first by pointing to the ease with which Dvořák's chamber works had become entrenched in the permanent international repertory[11] as well as the frequency with which these works are performed, especially in comparison with Dvořák's operas, his choral compositions, and even his symphonies. What follows is an attempt to pinpoint the essence of Dvořák's approach to chamber music, and Boleška claims that Dvořák ultimately had a kind of 'symphonic' conception of the genre. Whereas Brahms' symphonies were basically chamber pieces writ large, Dvořák, in Boleška's view, took the opposite approach

---

[6]. [Procházka] 1873, p. 2: «Půvabnost nevšední, která rozlívá se nad instrumentací jeho, poukazuje zejmena k pravému jeho povolání v říši *absolutní hudby instrumentální*». (The emphasis is mine.)

[7]. Beveridge 2009, p. 75.

[8]. For a detailed discussion of Dvořák's reception as a symphonist (i.e. in another absolute music genre), see Branda 2017, pp. 109-111.

[9]. Boleška 1912; Jitka Ludvová provides a biographical sketch: <http://biography.hiu.cas.cz/Personal/index.php/BOLE%C5%A0KA_Josef_1.6.1868-16.(17.).8.1914>, accessed December 2023.

[10]. *Ibidem*, p. 170: «z bohaté tvorby Dvořákovy připisuje se první místo komorní hudbě».

[11]. Dvořák's chamber music had been performed abroad since at least the late 1870s. For instance, his String Quartet in E-flat major, Op. 51, the *Slavonic*, was premiered in 1879 by Joseph Joachim's quartet at a private event in honour of the composer, and within months of its premiere and publication (also in 1879), it made its rounds on the public concert platform, primarily in German-speaking Europe, with performances in Magdeburg, Prague, Hamburg, Vienna, Halle, Hannover, Hildesheim, Kassel, and Stuttgart. The *Dumky* Trio itself became widely available after its publication in 1894 by Simrock in Berlin.

and was able to infuse his chamber works with an orchestral sweep, contributing in large part to their effectiveness and by extension, their popularity.

Considerations of genre have a unique bearing on discussions of the *Dumky* Piano Trio. Given Dvořák's identification with absolute instrumental music, it is curious that, when addressing Dvořák's Trio, many writers borrow from the language of other genres, but before these discourses can be analysed, some observations on the roots of the 'dumka' genre are in order. 'Dumka' is the diminutive form of the term 'duma' — a term that has Ukrainian, rather than Bohemian, roots[12], meaning, «to meditate, ponder or brood» as well as «to think»[13]. Jarmil Burghauser uses several terms and phrases to describe the 'dumka', including «lyrical or lyric-epical» and a piece in a «plaintive mood», to be played at a «restrained pace»[14]. Apart from its broadly meditative qualities and the melancholic connotations that it typically carries, the 'dumka' has no specific programmatic element, and critics and scholars are seemingly more at ease speaking of the 'dumka' in terms of its mood or character, rather than providing a laundry list of concrete musical features. The genre has also developed and changed throughout its history. Initially, the slow 'dumka' was conceptualised, by such Ukrainian composers as Mykhaylo Zavadsky (1823-1900) and Mikola Lysenko (1842-1912), as an introduction and counterpart to the fast-paced 'shumka'[15]; however, Dvořák seems to have conflated the two. In fact, this conflation is the only consistent feature present in all of Dvořák's 'dumky', which have a sectional construction, alternating between slow, melancholic material, on the one hand, and cheerful, dancelike material, on the other (see TABLE 1 for a summary of the movements in Dvořák's Op. 90, with tempo designations). Other composers to cultivate the genre included Chopin, Liszt, Mussorgsky, Tchaikovsky, and Janáček; however, Dvořák wrote more 'dumka' movements than any other composer, with no fewer than eleven pieces that bear this designation in his oeuvre. This includes two individual pieces for piano entitled *Dumka* (Op. 12 and Op. 35, respectively), the second movement of his String Sextet in A major (Op. 48), the second movement of his String Quartet No. 10 in E-flat major, the *Slavonic* (Op. 51), the second movement of his Piano Quintet No. 2 in A major (Op. 81) as well as the six movements of Op. 90. This brief survey shows that Dvořák especially turned to the «dumka» idiom in his chamber music, and — it was often reserved for slow movements in particular.

---

[12]. It is closely related to the Czech verb 'dumat', which literally also means «to muse», «to brood», or «to think (deeply)».

[13]. CLAPHAM 1966, p. 105.

[14]. BURGHAUSER 1991, pp. 86-89.

[15]. TYRRELL 2001.

Table 1: Overall Structure of Dvořák's *Dumky* Trio, Op. 90

Mvt.	Tempo	Key
1	Lento maestoso – Allegro quasi doppio movimento	E minor
2	Poco adagio – Vivace non troppo	C♯ minor
3	Andante – Vivace non troppo	A major
4	Andante moderato (quasi tempo di marcia) – Allegretto scherzando	D minor
5	Allegro – Meno mosso, quasi tempo primo	E♭ minor
6	Lento maestoso – Vivace	C minor

Even though the precise definition of the 'dumka' is far from clear, and it has ambiguous extra-musical associations, if any at all, early commentators tended to pepper their discussions of the *Dumky* Trio with concrete programmatic imagery, especially with descriptions of nature and rural life. Boleška engages in this; in reference to the second movement of the Trio, for example, he offers the following pictorial images: «with its harmony of colours, alternating shadow and light, [Dvořák] conjures up the magic of a moonlit night, wrapped in the translucent veil of a blue fog». Boleška continues: «in the *vivace* second section, it is as if fireflies suddenly emerge in a shimmering swarm, and a water nymph (rusalka), in the exuberant C-sharp-minor melody, throws herself into a whirling dance to the sounds of the high staccato tones in the piano»[16]. Karel Hoffmeister's description is even more vivid in its detail. Here is how *he* characterises the piece as a whole:

> Profound grief and sparkling gladness; melancholy monotony and earnest prayer; the silvery, bell-like rhythm of the dance; the moonlight overspreading the broad plain, and dreamy, drowsy moods by the banks of rushing streams; [...] wild drunken [revelry] among the village lads; the slow, stumbling footsteps of a dark funeral procession crossing the hills; the whirlwind flight of red elemental joy — the *Dumky* Trio speaks to us in these contrasts[17].

The pictorial images offered by Boleška and Hoffmeister are remarkably similar and striking in their specificity.

Apart from offering programmatic readings, Czech writers tended to describe the *Dumky* Trio in vocal, and specifically operatic, terms. The cello, in particular, is often likened to the voice in these discourses, and many writers highlight the instrument's 'singing qualities'. The writing

---

[16]. Boleška 1912, p. 183: «Svým sladěním barev, střídáním stínu a jasu unáší v kouzla měsíční noci, zahalená průsvitným závojem lehkých, modravých mlh. Z nich rázem, ve vivace druhé části, jakoby se vyrojily světlušky v mihotavém roji a jakoby rusalka v bujné melodii, Cis-moll, pustila se ve vírný tanec za zvuku vysokých tónů staccato klavíru».

[17]. Hoffmeister 1928, p. 67.

of Dvořák's early Czech biographer Otakar Šourek illustrates this trend. In his description of the opening movement, Šourek uses operatic terminology, like «recitative» in reference to the cello's lines and «cantilena» for the piano part, as well as imbuing the instruments with certain human attributes, with phrases like «the piano would like to soothe the pain» and «the cello continues to lament»[18]. Admittedly, the 'dumka' had originally been a vocal genre, but by the late nineteenth century, the term appears to have shed any vocal connotations. This kind of language is surprising, not just because of Dvořák's reputation as a composer with a natural proclivity for purely instrumental music, but also because both the nineteenth-century programmatic genre *par excellence*, the symphonic poem, and opera were genres in which Dvořák had struggled to achieve universal acceptance. In general, these more public genres served as the primary aesthetic battlegrounds in the Czech press, forcing critics to work out their positions on issues of nationalism and modernity in the face of encroaching New German influences. Meanwhile, the arena of chamber music did not seem to yield comparable debates or stir contentions in the same way.

INTIMACY, DISCERNMENT, AND SINCERITY: VENUES FOR CHAMBER MUSIC PERFORMANCE

Another factor that set chamber genres apart in *fin-de-siècle* Prague was their performing contexts. Smaller in scale than theatre or orchestral performances, chamber concerts tended to draw less of an eclectic crowd. In a detailed article from 1879 on concert venues in Prague, critic Otakar Hostinský (1847-1910) observes a superficiality among concert goers at the larger Žofín Hall, and he places the space in contradistinction to the chamber music venue Konvikt Hall, a small concert space which in his view was likely to draw a more discerning — albeit narrower — circle of listeners[19]. Though the concerts in this space were not organised by any particular music society, Konvikt Hall was affiliated with the Prague Organ School. In particular, Hostinský speaks of a core group of enthusiasts, who show a genuine interest in music rather than viewing concerts merely as 'society' events, and these were precisely the kinds of listeners that populated the smaller venues at which Dvořák's chamber works were usually performed. That these audiences had a certain level of interest and expertise in music does not necessarily guarantee that they were favourably disposed towards Dvořák. However, such listeners *were* likely to give his works a fair hearing — more so than audiences at the city's larger venues, where attendance was primarily «dictated by fashion», to quote another critic for *Dalibor*[20].

---

18. ŠOUREK 1930, pp. 11-12: «klavír, jako by chtěl bolest konejšiti» – «violoncello žaluje však dál».

19. This perhaps led to a greater unanimity of opinion. [HOSTINSKÝ] 1879, pp. 101-102.

20. This critic reiterates some of Hostinský's ideas and provides a telling portrait of concert life in Prague: «It is true that concerts in Prague are well-attended, sometimes very well-attended, especially when there is an artist

In keeping with the intimate nature of these performing spaces, discourses on Dvořák's chamber music, especially retrospective discussion from the early twentieth century, emphasise the *intimacy* of the music. This is evident in the writing of Boleška from 1912. When attempting to account for the success of Dvořák's chamber works, Boleška argues that Dvořák's skills in this area are instinctive and innate. He asserts:

> [...] the answer [to why Dvořák chamber music is well-liked] is easy. [Dvořák's chamber output] is not only valuable, but also rewarding. It is rewarding not because of any concessions made to the wider audience, but because of a characteristic that is inherent to Dvořák's creative nature: its beautiful sound. [...] [Dvořák] would not be capable of writing something soundless or a poorly sounding instrumental combination, even if he wanted to do so, since every idea comes from his *inner-being* (*nitro*)[21].

Similar language appears in Šourek's discussion of the *Dumky* Trio, including the exact same term — «nitro», meaning *inner-being* or *core*. Šourek claims that this piece was deeply personal for Dvořák[22]. Rather than conceptualising the work as broadly nationalist, he speaks of it as having sprung from the composer's soul, and he draws connections between the changing moods of the music and Dvořák's own temperament. In his words:

> [Dvořák's] dumky are nothing but an extremely spontaneous expression of the whimsical changeability and impetuosity of the *inner-being* (*nitro*), which was

from abroad, who has been praised by foreign newspapers — someone who just happens to come to Prague, plays a few pieces, and then hurries to continue his career elsewhere. To attend such a concert is dictated by fashion and this is determined by the wide circles of those who are interested in art [...]. But a loyal audience of people who regularly attend good concerts of home-grown artists and societies because of the thing itself, because of art, there are few of those»; «Pravda sice, že koncerty pražské bývají dosti četně, někdy i velmi četně navštěvovány, zejména dostaví-li se nějaký umělec z ciziny, jenž vychválen novinami zahraničými, do Prahy jen tak mimochodem zavítá, zde své kusy odehraje a opět dále za svým povoláním spěchá. Navštiviti takovýto koncert káže moda a dobrý ton, a to v nejšírších kruzích přátel umění rozhoduje... Ale stálého obecenstva, jež pravidelně dobré koncerty domácích umělců a spolků k vůli umění navštěvuje, toho jest velice pořídku». DB 1882, p. 57.

[21]. BOLEŠKA 1912, p. 171: «Na otázku proč je komorní hudba Dvořákova oblíbena, možno dáti odpověď snadno. Je nejen cenna, ale zároveň vděčná. Ale tato vděčnost není vykoupena u ní koncessemi širokému kruhu činěnými, nýbrž vlastností, jež srostla již s celou povahou Dvořákova tvoření: krasným zvukem svým... Jemu nepodařilo by se, ani kdyby tomu chtěl, napsati nic bezzvučného nebo špatně zvučného v instrumentální kombinaci, poněvadž každá myšlenka vychází z jeho nitra již v konkrétním obrnění nástrojového sprostředkovatele».

[22]. In a playful letter to his family (dated 5 February 1895), Dvořák suggests that he would like to play the piece one day in his homeland with his eldest daughter Otilka: «Otilka, you would make me so happy if, the next time I have a concert in the Czech lands, you played it [Mendelssohn's *Scherzo Capriccioso*] with me — or the *Dumky*» «Otilko, jakou bys mi udělala radost, až bych tak dával někde v Čechách koncert a Ty to hrála se mnou — aneb *Dumky*». KUNA 1989, p. 375.

so characteristic of Dvořák's personality [...] [written] at a time when he was most prone to give way in his work to the momentary moods and emotional dispositions of his own *inner-being*[23].

Based on this excerpt, Šourek seems to view this emotional volatility as more than just an artistic persona; he sees it as a genuine expression of Dvořák's state of mind. He also addresses the vagueness of the dumka's definition — something that Dvořák himself acknowledged; even after having written several pieces that bore this designation, the composer had famously quipped «What is a Dumka?»[24]. Given the term's unclear meaning, Šourek ultimately describes Op. 90 as Dvořák's *personal* take on the genre.

Overall, the emphasis on intimacy is noteworthy in the *Dumky* Trio discourses, and it is in this respect that the discussion differs most drastically from press debates having to do with Dvořák's works in the more public spheres of opera and symphonic composition. Indeed, sincerity was a common thread in music criticism more broadly throughout the nineteenth century. It was often taken for granted in the press that a composer was in earnest and that an abundance of 'feeling', whether personal or national, could never be feigned or fabricated within a composition. Contemporary critical discussions of Giacomo Puccini's operas, for instance, often revolve around perceived notions of 'sincerity' and 'authenticity', as Alexandra Wilson has shown[25]. Richard Taruskin has also made note of the swiftness with which the autobiographical lens tends to be applied by critics of the nineteenth century, the lingering effects of which continue to be felt in music scholarship, and he dissuades the reader from necessarily taking such assessments at face value, using Tchaikovsky's *Pathétique* Symphony, Op. 74 as a case study. «Art is... well artful», writes Taruskin, «and of no art is that truer than the romantic art of confession, of which Tchaikovsky's *Pathétique* is an outstanding example». Taruskin then draws the following conclusion:

> "Always be sincere", the comedy team of Flanders and Swann used to say, "whether you mean it or not". That might have been Tchaikovsky's motto. His matchless ability to live up to it, to "do" sincerity with utter conviction, brought the romantic tradition in music — a thing of artifice, illusion, and manipulated codes — to its very climax[26].

From a certain angle, sincerity was central to the romantic aesthetic, and as demonstrated by the case of Puccini, it continued to be upheld as an important ideal for certain repertories

---

23. Šourek 1930, p. 11: «Jeho dumky nejsou než velmi spontánním výrazem oné rozmarné těkavosti a vznětlivosti nitra, jež byla pro Dvořákovu povahu tak příznačná... v době, kdy nejplněji se ve svém díle poddával okamžitým náladám a citovým disposicím vlastního nitra [...]».

24. Beveridge 1993.

25. Wilson 2007, pp. 216-220; Wilson 2005.

26. Taruskin 2020, p. 801.

well into the twentieth century. Thus, statements claiming that a given piece reflects the composer's «inner being», common though they were, might be taken with a grain of salt when they appear in the Dvořák literature. Nevertheless, it is still worth observing that such statements are far more prevalent in discussions of Dvořák's chamber works than in reviews of his operas and symphonies. Dvořák was never accused of *lacking* sincerity. In fact, his «fervour» was highlighted in some of his earliest Prague reviews; after his official debut concert, featuring the choral piece *Hymnus: Heirs of the White Mountain* [*Hymnus: Dědicové bílé hory*] in 1873[27], one critic had stated that Dvořák wrote the work with the «blood of his heart»[28]. But rarely do reviewers of Dvořák's larger-scale compositions insist on the personal and intimate nature of his music in the way that these writers do. This discrepancy could also be a matter of historical era; initial reviews of the *Dumky* Trio published at the time of its premiere were rather brief, and the more in-depth analyses of Dvořák's chamber works making reference to this aspect of intimacy were written some twenty to thirty years after the *Dumky* Trio's premiere.

The language used to describe Dvořák's different repertories could likewise have been driven by venue, as already noted above. While performances of Dvořák's chamber pieces were typically witnessed by smaller audiences in Prague, the circumstances were rather different for the *Dumky* Trio. The piece was performed repeatedly from January to May 1892 at various venues across the Czech lands (as shown in Table 2, planned by music publisher Velebín Urbánek)[29], and when the tour did make its way to Prague at its midway point in late March, the space in which the program was given was the city's largest concert venue: Rudolfínum. The map shows all of the places that were part of this 'farewell tour' (see Ill. 1). Even though some larger cities like Brno and Olomouc were included on the itinerary, the vast majority of the stops were in small towns, giving the Czech people the rare opportunity to hear Dvořák's music live, with the composer at the piano. Owing to the small performing forces[30] required, the *Dumky* Trio shows that Dvořák's chamber music was uniquely exportable, both on a national and international[31] level, which was certainly helpful in securing its broader acceptance.

---

[27]. For a detailed discussion of the *Hymnus* premiere, see Branda 2021.

[28]. x 1873, p. 88: «není to věru pouhá fráze, pakliže vyslovím, že Dvořák psal skladbu tu "krví srdce svého"».

[29]. Clapham 1979, pp. 112-113.

[30]. Dvořák was not keen on arranging the *Dumky* Trio for piano duet and reluctantly complied when publisher Fritz Simrock urged him repeatedly to do so. See *Dvořák: Letters and Correspondences*. Kuna 1989.

[31]. Clapham 1966, p. 207: «Because of the composer's quarrel with Simrock, the trio was not published until 1894, and consequently it was not heard abroad until more than three years after it had been composed» (performed at St. James's Hall on 13 June 1894).

Table 2: Cities and Dates for Dvořák's 'Farewell Tour'
(as indicated in the 1891 and 1892 volumes of *Dalibor*)

Place	Date
Prague (Měšťanská beseda)	11 April 1891
Pardubice	15 January 1892
Mělník	23 January 1892
Roudnice n. L.	24 January 1892
Nymburk	31 January 1892
Český Brod	1 February 1892
Kolín	2 February 1892
Louny	6 February 1892
Slaný	7 February 1892
Třeboň	13 February 1892
České Budějovice	14 February 1892
Tábor	Date not given
Hořovice	20 February 1892
Velvary	21 February 1892
Litomyšl	27 February 1892
Polička	28 February 1892
Jihlava	5 March 1892
Čáslav	6 March 1892
Mladá Boleslav	19 March 1892
Turnov	20 March 1892
Hořice	24 March 1892
Náchod	25 March 1892
Vysoké Mýto	26 March 1892
Žižkov	28 March 1892
Prague (Rudolfínum/Academic Readers' Society)	31 March 1892
Klatovy	9 April 1892
Rokycany	10 April 1892
Brno	18 April 1892
Boskovice	19 April 1892
Olomouc	1 May 1892
Jičín	4 May 1892
České Budějovice	8 May 1892
Německý Brod	14 May 1892
Rychnov nad Kněžnou	15 May 1892
Jaroměř	16 May 1892
Strakonice	27 May 1892
Písek	28 May 1892

Ill. 1: Map showing the places included on the itinerary of Dvořák's tour.

Dvořák as «Czech cultural export»: Examining the Tour's Press

Finally, much can be extrapolated about Dvořák's chamber music reception from the epithets, headlines, and stylistic discussions that emerged from the tour and the *Dumky* Trio performance in particular. A sample tour programme shows that the concert experience was an interesting mix between formal and casual (see Ill. 2); the note explicitly requests formal attire, but also invites attendees to mingle freely with the musicians after the performance. The programme also makes it clear — right at the top — that all compositions are exclusively by Dvořák, and the *Dumky* Trio is given special prominence, as the last chamber item in the concert, with a note indicating that it is to be preceded by a longer intermission and thereby offset from the other works[32]. The three featured performers are afforded special respect; they are explicitly identified on the programme as «the famous Maestro Dr. A. Dvořák», assisted by «the Czech virtuosos Profs. F. Lachner and H. Wihan»[33]. As might be expected, reviews that were published in the immediate aftermath focus on the 'farewell' aspect of the tour; in a

---

[32]. Firkušný 1993, p. 242.

[33]. *Ibidem*, p. 241. Dalibor, the performing group for the opening and closing numbers, was an amateur orchestra, established in Hořice in 1881. Other performers included Ratibor (an all-male glee club, founded in

PROGRAM

exclusively of Dr. Ant. Dvořák's compositions:

1. Slavonic Dances, Op. 46, no. 1, for large orchestra: Dalibor
2. Trio in F minor, Op. 65, for piano, violin, and cello: Dr. A. Dvořák, Prof. F. Lachner, and Prof. H. Wihan
3. Rondo capriccioso, for violin and piano: Prof. F. Lachner and Dr. A. Dvořák
4. "The Evening Forest Set the Bells Ringing" and "A White Birch Tree Has Run Out," from Op. 63
   Mixed choirs: Vesna and Ratibor
5. a) Peace ("Silent Woods"), from the cycle *From the Sumava*
   b) Rondo, Op. 94, for cello and piano: Prof. H. Wihan and Dr. Ant. Dvořák
6. *Dumky*, Op. 90, for piano, violin, and cello: Dr. A. Dvořák, Prof. F. Lachner, and Prof. H. Wihan
7. Festive March, Op. 54, for large orchestra: Dalibor

The piano was kindly lent by Mr. Robert Rabas, the master brewer.

Beginning at 8:00 P.M.

FORMAL ATTIRE

Longer intermissions following no. 2 and no. 5
Latecomers may enter only after completion of a work
Evening box office from 7:00 P.M. at the staircase

Following the concert, a free gathering in honor
of the guests in the downstairs rooms

ILL. 2: Programme for one of the tour performances. Source: *Dvořák and His World*, edited by Michael Beckerman, Princeton, Princeton University Press, 1993, p. 242.

very real sense, given his pending tenure at the New York Conservatory, Dvořák himself was about to become a «Czech cultural export», and the critics write with this in mind. As a result, reactions in the press to these tour concerts are positively euphoric, stemming from feelings of immense national pride. Several of the reviews were printed together with poetic tributes to Dvořák, most of which underscore the composer's persistent loyalty to his Czech homeland, in spite of his international accolades. The final two stanzas of Josef Pazourek's poem on Dvořák, published in the journal *Lýra*, are illustrative of this type of writing:

Indeed, your compositions are heard with amazement everywhere,
The whole world greets them with jubilation [...]
Yet only a Czech can truly understand the feeling at the bottom of their fiery bosom
Where everything pulsates with life.

1862) and Vesna (a female choir, founded in 1870), featured in the mixed choral number (the fourth item on the concert programme).

He recognizes the Czech kernel, the bond of his own blood
In each and every one of his shining garments;
He knows that it was a Czech soul that polished all the facets
When weaving the motifs into the brocade of the work.

And though the whole world is offering you its gifts and its praise
Even beyond the expands of the seas,
Look — our nation is partaking in one great festivity,
It will devote all its love to you.
And when tempting invitations from abroad come to you,
All of us, though weeping, are bravely calling out:
"Onward for the glory of the motherland!
But leave us your Czech heart here at home"[34].

Others write in a similar vein[35]. In a parallel to the press coverage of Bedřich Smetana after his death in 1884[36], the tone becomes increasingly hagiographic in Dvořák's farewell tour reviews, as critics stood to lose Dvořák to American audiences. The music seems to get lost

---

[34]. Pazourek 1892, p. 1. Firkušný 1993, pp. 240-241.

[35]. Here is another sample of a poetic tribute to Dvořák: «O, prince of music, your alluring, brilliant star is calling you over the far sea; may a new aurora of fame rise there for you; your motherland is happy that the whole world knows you. Your imagination is as vast as the sea you will soon be sailing across into the distance; may the Slavic melodies resound ever there; even there the Czechs will enjoy fame in music. O, do not forget your dear motherland as your fame will be rising to the sky; always remember: "Each to his own", that in the Czech lands this is heard the strongest! O, may the Lord's angel accompany you everywhere, protect you on your artistic pilgrimage, as the wreaths will adorn your features — say: "In the Czech motherland is my cradle". [...] But when one day your heart fills again with longing and your feet stir in the direction of return, and following the inner voice of the heart by which everyone is bound in his heart to his own country: O, know then that all the Czech hearts will go to meet you, will even come flying to meet you; that the arms of all, be they from cities or villages, will lovingly open — to embrace you»; «Ó kníže hudby, tam za širé moře tě volá vábná, zářná hvězda Tvá; nechť vzejde tam Ti nová slávy záře, vlasť raduje se, že celý svět Tě zná. Jak moře veliká Tvá fantasie, po němž tam v dálku brzy budeš plouť; ať zní i tam ty slávské melodie, i tam Čech slavným v hudbě bude slouť. Ó nezapomeň milé vlasti svojí, kdy k nebi sláva Tvá se ponese; vždy vzpomeň: "ku svému jíť mají svoji" — že v Čechách nejvíc zvuk ten ozve se! O provázej Tě všude anděl Páně, chraň na umělé Tebe pouti Tvé, kdy věnce zdobiť budou Tvoje skráně — rci: "v české vlasti kolébka má je". [...] Až jednou však zatouží srdce zase a k návratu se zšine noha Tvá, a kráčejíc po vnitřním srdce hlase, jejž ke svojině každý v srdci má: ó věziž pak, že všecka srdce česká Ti půjdou vstříc, ba vstříc ti poletí; že náruč každá, z města buď neb vesská, se v lásce rozstře — k Tvému objetí». Hakl 1892, p. 1; Firkušný 1993, pp. 236-238.

[36]. St Pierre 2017, pp. 82-85. St. Pierre writes: «Smetana's death in 1884 initiated a change in the type of coverage he received in [...] *Dalibor* and scholarly publications more broadly». She ultimately describes an increasing tendency to portray Smetana as a «proven genius» and unequivocally Czech. As she puts it, this was «a move away from emphasizing Smetana's cosmopolitanism in order to frame him and his works as modern, and toward situating the composer as a symbol of a reimagined, autonomously Czech tradition».

amid the encomiums, and comments on the actual pieces are presented as something of an afterthought, suggesting that critics in the press were reacting less to the music than to the fact that this was meant to be Dvořák's Czech farewell.

Predictably, the reviews draw attention to the Czechness of Dvořák's music, which too can be tied to the nostalgic nature of the tour. Dvořák's upcoming trip abroad made it more crucial than ever to present him to the public as indisputably Czech. More recent scholarship on Dvořák has attempted to clarify the distinctions between the composer's Czech and Slavic styles; this is, for example, the main thrust of Michael Beckerman's piece on Dvořák's *Moravian Duets*[37] as well as David Beveridge's work on the 'dumka', in relation to Dvořák's Piano Quintet, Op. 81[38]. Even though Beveridge has shown that it is erroneous to conceptualise the 'dumka' as a reflection of Dvořák's Czech nationalism, contemporary critics received it as such and were quick to give the work a 'Czech' label. For instance, the reviewer for *Dalibor* opens his discussion of the *Dumky* Trio by noting that the piece, «breathes with proper Czech life» and has successfully made its rounds across the Czech lands; the critic also describes the work as accessible and «easily understandable» on first hearing, in contrast with other, more difficult works that require repeated exposure for full comprehension[39]. Indeed, in spite of current attempts to be more precise in the application of this terminology, Czech critics of the nineteenth century routinely conflated 'Czech' and 'Slav', using the two terms, more or less, interchangeably. Even several decades after the tour, Šourek views the *Dumky* Trio, first and foremost, as «Dvořákian» and as basically Czech, singling out only one theme as having a foreign — specifically Russian — flavour (see Ex. 1)[40].

Ex. 1: Opening cello theme of the fourth movement, *Andante moderato (quasi tempo di marcia)*. Source: Antonín Dvořák, *Trio in E minor, Op. 90*, New York, International Music Company, 1959, p. 6.

In addition to labelling Dvořák's Op. 90 as Czech, several critics use the epithet 'modern' in reference to the work, without elaborating or clarifying their exact meaning. The writer for *Lýra* in Hořice, for example, describes the *Dumky* Trio as «*modern* yet genuinely *Czech* [in] character»[41]. In this context, 'modern' could be understood simply to mean 'recently composed'

---

37. BECKERMAN 1993, pp. 134-156.
38. BEVERIDGE 1993, *passim*.
39. UNSIGNED 1892, p. 153: «pravým českým životem dýšíci».
40. ŠOUREK 1930, p. 14: «Thema, které má ruský lidový nádech».
41. FIRKUŠNÝ 1993, pp. 245-246.

without carrying any deeper connotations. However, it might be useful to reflect on this term in light of Nejedlý's negative review of *Rusalka* from 1901, cited at the beginning of this paper. Nejedlý's main issue with *Rusalka* had to do with the work's supposed lack of modernity and Dvořák's allegedly 'old-fashioned' approach to opera. His criticism of Dvořák in this regard would continue far beyond the *Rusalka* review. In his book *Czech Modern Opera after Smetana* [*Česká Moderní Zpěvohra po Smetanovi*] — written a decade later, in 1911 — Nejedlý devotes only one page to Dvořák, and the brevity of the section alone shows that Nejedlý ultimately sees Dvořák's contributions as irrelevant to discussions of 'modern opera'. In the conclusion of this section, Nejedlý says so explicitly: «it will suffice to draw attention to Dvořák's *musical* influence [on subsequent generations of composers], but his actual operatic works can be cast aside as peripheral to the development of modern Czech opera — as strange anomalies having more to do with Dvořák's personality than the ideological growth of the Czech music drama»[42]. Nejedlý makes it clear that his point of contention lies not with the 'musical' side of Dvořák's art, but with the 'dramatic'[43]. The over-arching agenda of the book is to promote the works of Zdeněk Fibich, to whom Nejedlý gives a full four chapters, while confining Dvořák to the margins of Czech operatic history. The book came in the midst of the 'Dvořák battles', also spearheaded by Nejedlý — a series of attacks on Dvořák's music in the Prague press during the first decade of the twentieth century, prompting equally charged responses from Dvořák's supporters[44].

Nejedlý's arguments in most of his writings are predicated on the notion that Dvořák's operas move in a direction that is opposite to Bedřich Smetana, whose works, in turn, are upheld as the gold standard for Czech opera composition. He categorically dismisses Dvořák's operas mainly because of their variety and their resistance to neat classification. Nejedlý has trouble placing Dvořák's oeuvre within his own teleological conception of opera composition in the Czech lands, and he ultimately classifies Dvořák as a 'regressive' composer. Undoubtedly, much of Nejedlý's criticism of Dvořák was driven by his own distinct biases and agendas, particularly his desire to elevate Smetana's status and posthumously rebrand him as «saviour of the nation»[45], which — apparently, in his view — necessitated a concomitant denigration of Dvořák, who had eclipsed Smetana in international stature and fame. Nejedlý's precise

---

[42]. NEJEDLÝ, 1901, p. 162: «nám zde však stačí vytknouti tento Dvořákův vliv hudební, kdežto jeho vlastní díla operní možno při výkladu o rozvoji moderní české opery ponechati stranou jako thema zvláštní, vztahující se více k umělecké osobnosti Dvořákově než k ideovém vzrůstu českého hudebního dramatu». (The emphasis is mine.)

[43]. John Tyrrell shows that the snub was not directed at Dvořák alone, but that Janáček too was marginalized in Nejedlý's study on Czech opera; TYRRELL, 2010, pp. 103-121.

[44]. For a detailed discussion of the 'Dvořák battles' (or 'Dvořák affair'), see OTTLOVÁ 1996 and LOCKE 2006, pp. 54-58.

[45]. ST PIERRE 2017, p. 94.

motivations are unclear, but his writings would become increasingly political as the twentieth century progressed, and decades later, he would take up a prominent position in the Communist party of Czechoslovakia, as Minister of Culture and Education, affording him an uncommonly large degree of sway over public opinion.

Yet, for all of the criticism levelled against the composer — repeatedly and in the *Rusalka* review, with which the critic struck the first blow — Nejedlý raised no objections to Dvořák's cultivation of chamber music. This perhaps is a function of the uniqueness of the chamber medium. Any assessment of Dvořák's modernity — or lack thereof — is interconnected with issues of genre, and Nejedlý appears to have thought of most genres in terms of 'progressive' and 'regressive' binaries. Unlike the symphonic poem and music drama, which were seen, by Nejedlý and others of his ilk, as appropriate substitutes for their 'out-dated' counterparts — namely, the symphony and conventional opera, chamber music really had no 'updated' equivalent. This eliminated such considerations from the discussion, perhaps safeguarding Dvořák against some of the negative press that he was likely to get for his theatre and orchestral works.

Conclusion

In conclusion, the Czech reception of Dvořák's chamber compositions was remarkably smooth. The area had been identified in the press as a strength for Dvořák when he was just establishing himself on the Prague music scene in the early 1870s, and he seemed to garner praise from all quarters, even from those that were typically hostile towards him. The *Dumky* Trio is a case in point, as it was greeted with wild enthusiasm in the Czech lands. Central to Dvořák's 'last hurrah' in his homeland before heading off to America, it gave rise to the usual ruminations about Dvořák's 'Czechness' in the press. And even later more sober assessments from the early decades of the twentieth century are overwhelmingly positive, drawing attention to the *Dumky* Trio's 'programmatic' and 'operatic' qualities as well as the work's deeply personal and intimate nature. Many elements contributed to Dvořák's relatively uncontroversial chamber music reception, not the least of which is the sheer beauty of the music itself. The positive press had to do with several key factors: the sense that Dvořák was conforming to critical expectations; performances of these works in front of audiences that were perhaps more discerning than average as well as the exportability of the genre; and the fact that chamber music simply seemed to carry less baggage than the more public works of the day, which were the subjects of ongoing aesthetic debates. From a certain angle, it would seem that Nejedlý conceded Dvořák's skill in chamber genres mainly because he had 'bigger fish to fry'. This is ironic, since some of the leading experiments in modernism that were to come from the Second Viennese School in the early years of the twentieth century — shortly after Dvořák's death — would be precisely in the chamber realm[46]. As frustrating as this pigeon-holing was for Dvořák when it came to other domains, the marking out of chamber music as his 'niche' insulated him from criticism, helping to secure, in this area at least, his wider success among the Czechs.

BIBLIOGRAPHY

BECKERMAN 1993
BECKERMAN, Michael. 'The Master's Little Joke: Antonín Dvořák and the Mask of Nation', in: *Dvořák and His World*, edited by Michael Beckerman, Princeton, Princeton University Press, 1993, pp. 134-156.

BEVERIDGE 1993
BEVERIDGE, David. 'Dvořák's «Dumka» and the Concept of Nationalism in Music Historiography', in: *Journal of Musicological Research*, XII/4 (1993), pp. 303-325.

BEVERIDGE 2009
ID. 'A Rare Meeting of Mind's in Kvapil's and Dvořák's *Rusalka*', programme note, in: *Antonín Dvořák: Rusalka*, Prague, Národní Divadlo, 2009.

BOLEŠKA 1912
BOLEŠKA, Josef. 'Dvořákova Komorní Hudba', in: *Antonín Dvořák: Sborník statí o jeho díle a životě*, edited by Boleslav Kalenský, Prague, Umělecká Beseda, 1912, pp. 170-194.

BRANDA 2017
BRANDA, Eva. 'Speaking German, Hearing Czech, Claiming Dvořák', in: *Journal of the Royal Musical Association*, CXLII/1 (2017), pp. 109-136.

BRANDA 2021
EAD. 'Capturing the Zeitgeist: Dvořák's Prague Debut and the Politics of Patriotism', in: *Music & Letters*, CII/2 (2021), pp. 719-757.

BURGHAUSER 1991
BURGHAUSER, Jarmil. 'Dvořákova a Janáčkova Dumka', in: *Hudební Rozhledy*, XLIV/2 (1991), pp. 86-89.

CLAPHAM 1966
CLAPHAM, John. *Antonín Dvořák: Musician and Craftsman*, London, Faber and Faber, 1966.

CLAPHAM 1979
ID. *Dvořák*, New York, Norton, 1979.

---

[46]. The String Quartet No. 2, Op. 10 (from 1908) is generally acknowledged as Arnold Schoenberg's first atonal work.

Db 1882
Db. 'Naše hudební ústavy', in: *Dalibor*, 2nd s., IV/8 and 10 (10 March and 1 April 1882), pp. 57-59, 74-75.

Firkušný 1993
Firkušný, Tatiana. 'Dvořák in the Czech Press: Unpublished Reviews and Criticism', in: *Dvořák and His World, op. cit.*, pp. 230-261.

Hakl 1892
Hakl, Boh. 'Králi Hudby: Dru. Antonínu Dvořákovi', in: *Našinec*, XXVIII/5/51 (1 May 1892), p. 1.

Hoffmeister 1928
Hoffmeister, Karel. *Antonín Dvořák*, English translation by Rosa Newmarch, Westport, Greenwood Press, 1928.

[Hostinský] 1879
[Hostinský, Otakar.] O. H. 'Feuilleton: Koncerty u nás a jinde', in: *Dalibor*, 2nd s., I/13 (1 May 1879), pp. 101-102.

Kuna 1989
Kuna, Milan *et al. Antonín Dvořák: Korespondence a Dokumenty. 3*, Prague, Editio Supraphon, 1989.

Locke 2006
Locke, Brian. *Opera and Ideology in Prague: Polemics and Practice at the National Theatre, 1900-1938*, Rochester-Woodbridge, University of Rochester Press-Boydell & Brewer, 2006 (Eastman Studies in Music, 39).

Nejedlý 1901
Nejedlý, Zdeněk. 'Dvořákova *Rusalka*', in: *Rozhledy*, XI/8 (25 May 1901), pp. 205-209.

[Novotný] 1873
[Novotný, Václav Juda.] x. 'Zprávy z Prahy a z venkova: Druhý koncert filharmonického spolku', in: *Dalibor*, 1st s., I/14 (4 April 1873), pp. 112-116.

Ottlová 1996
Ottlová, Marta. 'The «Dvořák Battles» in Bohemia: Czech Criticism of Antonín Dvořák, 1911-1915', in: *Rethinking Dvořák: Views from Five Countries*, edited by David R. Beveridge, Oxford, Clarendon Press, 1996, pp. 96-110.

Pazourek 1892
Pazourek, Jos. 'Dru. Antonínu Dvořákovi', in: *Lýra: organ hudebního spolku «Dalibor» v Hořicích*, IX/3 (15 March 1892), p. 1.

[Procházka] 1873
[Procházka, Ludevít] P. 'Literatura a umění', in: *Národní listy*, XIII/98 (10 April 1873), p. 2.

Šourek 1930
Šourek, Otakar. *Život a Dílo Ant. Dvořáka. 3*, Prague, Hudební Matice Umělecké Besedy, 1930.

St Pierre 2017
St Pierre, Kelly. *Bedřich Smetana: Myth, Music, and Propaganda*, Rochester-Woodbridge, University of Rochester Press-Boydell & Brewer, 2017 (Eastman Studies in Music, 139).

Šupka 2020
Šupka, Ondřej. *Než nás rozdělí oceán*, Prague, Akademie klasické hudby, 2020.

Taruskin 2020
Taruskin, Richard. *The Oxford History of Western Music. 3: Music in the Nineteenth Century*, Oxford, Oxford University Press, 2010.

Tyrrell 2001
Tyrrell, John. 'Dumka', in: *Grove Music Online*, 2001, <https://www.oxfordmusiconline.com/ grovemusic >, accessed December 2023.

Tyrrell 2010
Id. 'Janáček, Nejedlý, and the Future of Czech National Opera', in: *Art and Ideology in European Opera: Essays in Honour of Julian Rushton*, edited by Rachel Cowgill, David Cooper and Clive Brown, Woodbridge, Boydell Press, 2010, pp. 103-121.

Unsigned 1892
Unsigned. 'Z koncertní síně', in: *Dalibor*, 2nd s., XIII/20 (9 April 1892), pp. 153-154.

Wilson 2005
Wilson, Alexandra. 'Modernism and the Machine Woman in Puccini's *Turandot*', in: *Music & Letters*, LXXXVI/3 (2005), pp. 432-451.

Wilson 2007
Ead. *The Puccini Problem*, Cambridge, Cambridge University Press, 2007 (Cambridge Studies in Opera).

x 1873
x. 'Zprávy z Prahy a z venkova', in: *Dalibor*, 1st s., I/11 (14 March 1873), pp. 87-89.

Czech Song, Jan Ludevít Procházka, and the Salonesque *Musical Entertainments* in 1870s Prague

Anja Bunzel
(Institute of Art History, Czech Academy of Sciences)

On 15 November 1871, the music journal *Hudební listy* (Musical Leaves) announced the *First Private Singing Entertainment* (První soukromá zábava pěvecká), scheduled to take place on 27 November 1871 at the salon of piano manufacturers Joseph Heitzmann and Ferdinand Schloegl in Prague. The founder and editor of *Hudební listy*, Jan Ludevít Procházka (1837-1888), informed the readers that the purpose of these events would be to enable the Czech audience to experience live performances of domestic (i.e., Czech) and Slavic music more generally. The series was meant to introduce audiences to novelties that were cropping up on the Czech music scene, with a view either to new compositions and/or arrangements by Czech composers, or to new publications produced by Czech-based music publishers. The second concert of the series featured Antonín Dvořák's song 'Vzpomínání' (Remembrance), which marked the first time that a work by Dvořák was performed in public, as well as the first time one of Dvořák's compositions was reviewed by renowned music critics. Adding to the field of Czech music studies generally and, in particular, to Jana Vojtěšková's and Jiří Kopecký's work on Jan Ludevít Procházka and Czech music criticism, this essay focuses on the musical events organised by Procházka within the wider framework of Czech national music[1].

I will approach these events chronologically by discussing the repertoire performed from the first concert of the series, on 27 November 1871, to the last, realised on 9 February 1873. In so doing, I will show that the repertoire changed quickly over time, and that Procházka's *Entertainments* did not live on for very long — at least not in an obvious way, as not all composers

---

[1].   On Procházka and his private networks, see Vojtěšková 2011 and Vojtěšková 2013. On Procházka's musical oeuvre, see Venglař 2021. On *Hudební listy*, see Kopecký 2017.

(or performers) programmed in the series were Czech (or, indeed, Slavic), and not all pieces were vocal works. Nevertheless, the examination of Procházka's *Entertainments* offers insights into the quite complex web of cultural agency in 1870s Prague from a number of perspectives: that of the composer, that of the performer, that of the music critic and editor, and that of the concert organiser.

I will argue that within the wider context of Czech musical culture the most important outcomes of these *Entertainments* were not primarily the promotion of individual composers such as Dvořák, or, indeed, the popularisation of new Czech works. Rather, these events offered a platform to explore openly whether and how pan-Slavism might have a place in music and also how it might lead to a more effective formation of national identity in Czech musical culture. Moreover, the events helped to bring together performers, publishers, composers, and audiences in a semi-public or at least 'smaller-than-usual' and seemingly more intimate public setting. Though still effective, the *Entertainments*' contribution to the formation of a Czech national culture was thus more subtle than in other genres (for instance, opera).

***

In the first announcement of the concerts, Procházka explains that the event's special focus on Czech and Slavic song is rooted in «its [i.e. song's] nature and significance, because we see in it the only true and healthy basis of a future Slavic direction in our music»[2]. He adds that the initiative also aims to obtain critical judgement from the public, and create good relationships between composers and publishers as well as composers and performers. The announcement closes with a request directed at poets to offer more texts suitable for musical settings, and at composers to produce songs and duets[3].

TABLE 1 shows the pieces included in the programme for the first concert. All items in the programme originate from Slavic composers (or oral tradition), with the exception of the German composer Robert Franz, whose song 'Die Verlassene' (Ach ihr Wälder, dunkle Wälder) is labelled as 'Bohemian Folk Song' (Böhmisches Volkslied) in the printed score (see Ex. 1)[4].

The words of 'Die Verlassene' originate in the *Rukopis královédvorský* ('Königinhofer Handschrift'), which was a popular source of inspiration during the nineteenth century[5]. It is

---

[2]. See *Hudební* 1871A. «Že klademe zejména váhu na píseň českou a slovanskou vůbec, vychází z povahy a významu této samé, neboť spatřujeme v ní jediný pravý a zdravý základ budoucího směru slovanského v naší hudbě».

[3]. It is also made clear that only songs with both an artistic musical character and a poetic significance will be accepted, while pieces in the Slavonic tone will be granted priority.

[4]. See Franz n.d.

[5]. The Czech poet Václav Hanka claimed to have found this seemingly medieval manuscript in 1817; however, it has been proven that the manuscript was fake. Nevertheless the text and its genesis and reception were influential in the nineteenth century. See Enders 1993.

Ex. 1: Robert Franz, 'Die Verlassene', Op. 40, No. 5, original print (public domain).

perhaps worth noting that Procházka engaged his wife, Marta Procházková, as one of the main singers, in this concert[6]. Furthermore, Procházka made sure to mention that some of the pieces included in the concert had not been published and were played from the manuscript, thus increasing the readership's (and possible audience's) curiosity.

Table 1: Concert programme for the *First Private Singing Entertainment*
Monday, 27 November 1871, 12 noon, Heitzmann and Schloegl[7]

Piece	Composer	Poet	Performer	Publication Status
'Půda vlastenecká'	Karel Bendl		Karel Čech	Manuscript
'Skřivánek'	Mikhail Glinka		Miss Paroubková*	Published in Petersburg
'Jeseň a máj'	Pavel Křížkovský	P. J. Soukop	P. V. Šebesta	Manuscript
'Píseň zlaté rybičky'	Mily Balakirev	Mikhail Lermontov	Miss Kupková	Published in Petersburg
'Na nebi měsíc s hvězdami'	K. Bendl	Vítězslav Hálek (from *Večerní písně*)	Marta Procházková, Miss Paroubková	Published by Starý and Co. in Prague
'Ach vy lesi, tmaví lesi' (Op. 40, No. 5)	Robert Franz	Song from the *Královédvorský rukopis* (Königinhofer Handschrift)	Miss Ambrosová	
'Marie Stuartské nářek z vězení'	Václav Jan Tomášek	From the estate of poets bequeathed by this queen, translation Václav Hanka	M. Procházková	Published by K. V. Enders in Prague
'Ach bolesti, ach žalosti'	Karel Holan (1693)			
Folk song	Josef Leopold Zvonař** (arranger)	From the eighteenth century	V. Šebesta	Published by I. L. Kober in Prague (*Hudební památky*)
Lusatian Folk Songs	-	?	Betty Hanušová	
Trio *Bukovín*	Zdeněk Fibich	From the Singspiel *Bukovín*	Miss Kupková, B. Hanušová, K. Čech	Manuscript

*. Names are given inconsistently in all reports; where possible, I added first names, although I was not able to track them in all cases. With the exception of foreign names, I unified the endings of Czech female surnames as -ová (although sometimes they were given as -ova in the announcements and reviews).

**. On Zvonař, see Berdychová 2007.

In his report of the first concert, Procházka noted that:

---

6. Betty Hanušová married Zdeněk Fibich in 1875.
7. See *Hudební* 1871a and *Hudební* 1871b.

It evoked in us some serious thoughts. The idea of "nationality" is certainly in the foreground during these times; who would not think of national art within this context, and therefore also of national music. We have long been influenced by all things German so that our search for national music might appear like a real "reaction" to many (who are perhaps enthusiastic about artistic "cosmopolitism" (?)); but let us not forget that this is only the beginning of "Slavism" and that it will find for itself a completely new future, and let us remember the results (religious, patriotic, or different in nature) achieved by all those "reactionaries" who acted decisively?! However, as we are "young", we have not yet reached a very clear awareness of what our "Slavic music" is; thus, so far we only recognise by "feeling" when music talks to us in our "mother tongue"[8].

Procházka continued on to discuss the individual pieces performed during the first concert. He singled out the Lusatian folk songs, Karel Holan's arrangement of the late-seventeenth-century song 'Ach bolesti, ach žalosti' (O Pain, o Sorrow), and the eighteenth-century folk song as the ones closest to Czech and Slavic national song, although, in terms of language, they were not fully comprehensible. This remark seems interesting for a number of reasons: first, I personally think that Lusatian Sorbian and Czech are linguistically very close to each other, and possibly closer than Polish and Czech, or Russian and Czech, respectively. Second, Procházka here — perhaps subconsciously — seemed to imply that language does not matter as much as musical features when identifying national traits in music. On the other hand, he foregrounded language by advocating for more national poetry and song as a genre more generally.

Among the art songs featured in the first concert, Procházka's favourite was Pavel Křížkovský's 'Jeseň a máj' (Autumn and May). In his capacity as editor of the music journal *Dalibor*, Procházka published the piece as the journal's twelfth musical supplement in 1874. Procházka further praised the song's strong emotional qualities and simple, truly national singing style. He also valued Franz's 'Die Verlassene', which was performed in Czech. According to Procházka, it had a clear Slavic character, although the uniform rhythm did not correspond to the Slavic spirit. Here, of course, one might bear in mind that Franz was a German composer and the original words to his setting were German. The author continues to offer short descriptions and critiques of the other pieces featured on the concert programme, with Zdeněk Fibich's trio

---

8. See *HUDEBNÍ* 1871b: «Vyvolala v nás vážné myšlénky. Myšlénka "národnosti" zajisté stojí v naší době velice v popředí; kdož by tu nepomýšlel také na národní umění a tedy i na národní hudbu. Jsme ode dávna tak příliš ve všem německému vlivu podrobeni, že mnohým snad (uměleckým "kosmopolitismem" (?) nadšeným) připadá naše snažení po národní hudbě jako pravá "reakce"; považme však, jak je "Slovanstvo" posud mladé a že mu tedy náleží zcela nová budoucnost a považme k jakým výsledkům dospěli všichni ti "reakcionáři", kteří proudem své doby (buď náboženským, vlasteneckým neb jiným) dali se unést k činům rozhodným?! Že však jsme "mladí", proto také nedospěli jsme ještě k úplně jasnému vědomí, jaká jest ta naše "hudba slovanská", nýbrž dosud více pouze "citem" poznáváme, pak-li k nám "mateřským jazykem" promluví».

from *Bukovín* being characterised as a «truly artistic effort of the young composer»[9]. Here, Procházka drew a clear distinction between 'artistic' and 'folk' song, a categorisation which surfaces also in other places.

The comprehensive report concludes with a long quote from a statement related to the same concert, published in the paper *Národní listy* (National Leaves). It does not offer much originality, as it primarily quotes Procházka's announcement and praises the initiative as presaging a «happy, promising future»[10]. Procházka's decision to include this long quotation in his own journal may thus be interpreted as a strategic move rather than an attempt at broadening public discourse.

Much like the first concert, the second focused on vocal repertoire and included works by both local and international composers; this time around, all composers were Slavic in origin (see TABLE 2).

TABLE 2: CONCERT PROGRAMME FOR THE *SECOND FREE MUSICAL ENTERTAINMENT*
SUNDAY, 10 DECEMBER 1871, 4PM, HEITZMANN AND SCHLOEGL[11]

PIECE	COMPOSER	POET	PERFORMER	PUBLICATION STATUS
Love Song ('Vzkázání')	Karel Bendl	Eliška Krásnohorská	Vávra	Manuscript
Aria 'Váňy', from the Singspiel *Žizň za carja*	Mikhail Glinka	Nestor Kukelnik	Klementa Kalašová	
'Bůh kázal slunci pláti' (No. 12), from the *Persian Songs*	Anton Rubinstein	Friedrich Bodenstedt	Miloslava Havelková	
Aria from *Rusalka*	Alexander Dargomyzhsky	From the Singspiel *Rusalka*	K. Čech	
'Přilítlo jaro z daleka', Op. 5	Zdeněk Fibich	Vítězslav Hálek (from *Večerní písně*)	Emilie Bubeníčková	Published by Em. Wetzler in Prague
'Vzpomínání'	Antonín Dvořák	E. Krásnohorská	E. Bubeníčková	Manuscript
'Už noč ložitsja na polja'	D. Alexandrova*	?	Klementa Kalašová	
'Přádelnice'	Stanisław Moniuszko	Jan Czeczot	K. Kalašová	
Ballad from the Singspiel *Rogněda*	Alexander Sěrov	Dmitry Averkiev	M. Havelková	
Trio from the Singspiel *Rusalka*	A. Dargomyzhsky	Alexander Pushkin	E. Bubeníčková, Vávra, K. Čech	

*. Most likely Alexandra Dormidontovna Alexandrova-Kochetova.

---

9. *Ibidem*: «Právě uměleckou snahu mladého skladatele».
10. Review *Národní listy*, printed in HUDEBNÍ 1871B: «Šťastná, mnohoslibná budoucnost».
11. See HUDEBNÍ 1871B; review HUDEBNÍ 1871C.

This second concert was no longer called a 'Singing Entertainment' ('zábava pěvecká'), but rather a 'Free Musical Entertainment' ('volná zábava hudební'), pointing to the extension of options with respect to programmable genres. The word 'free' most likely refers to the relatively loose structure of the events and open-minded programming policy of the organisers; the concerts were not free of charge, however, and neither were audience members nor performers encouraged to freely and/or spontaneously contribute to or change the music programme. Immediately following the second event, a very short report appeared in *Hudební listy*, stating that all four singers, Emilie Bubeníčková (1844-1920), Klementa Kalašová (1850-1889), Karel Čech (1844-1913), and a singer called Vávra (probably Antonín Vávra) were applauded enthusiastically by the audience[12]. The songs by Karel Bendl, Fibich, Dvořák, and, of the Russian pieces, the Moscow singer D. Alexandrova's (probably Alexandra Dormidontovna Alexandrova-Kochetova) composition were all warmly received. Finally, the reviewer noted that the small excerpt from Alexander Dargomyzhsky's opera *Rusalka* «evoked the vivid desire to soon hear this piece in its entirety on our stage»[13]. One observation might be worth mentioning here: for the first concert, Procházka stated that the Franz song lacked Czech musical sentiment and that the Lusatian folk songs were close to the Czech style but were not fully understandable linguistically by the audience. This then opens up the question of how Stanisław Moniuszko's 'Přádelnice' (The Spinning Woman) was performed (and understood)[14].

The famous Russian pianist Věra Timanova's visit to Prague heavily impacted programming for the third concert. This event consisted primarily of piano works by Fryderyk Chopin, Anton Rubinstein, Fibich, and Vilém A. Mayer, alongside a vocal work by Alexander Sěrov, and two songs to words by Eliška Krásnohorská, composed by Jindřich Pech and Bendl (see Table 3). Procházka features here as both organiser and pianist, while Fibich takes on the dual role of composer and pianist. Both share a certain degree of agency through their capacities as performers and creative forces behind the scenes. Likewise, Timanova acts as an agent not only through her performances, but also by adding a piece to the programme that had not been announced (Chopin's Mazurka in A Minor). It is not clear from either the announcements or the reviews whether she played that piece as an encore, or whether the concert concluded with the four-hand piano performance by Fibich and Procházka, with Timanova adding the mazurka somewhere in between (see Table 3).

---

[12]. Not all these performers are known today. On Emilie Bubeníčková and Karel Čech, see Ludvová 2022; on Klementa Kalašová, see Milotová 2015, pp. 134-153.

[13]. See *Hudební* 1871c: «vzbudily živé přání, uslyšeti brzo celé dílo na našem jevišti».

[14]. It seems that it was performed in Czech, as the Polish original would have been 'Prząśniczka'. However, Procházka did not comment on this aspect at all and only gave the Czech translation of the title in his review.

Table 3: Concert programme for the *Third Free Musical Entertainment*
Thursday, 21 December 1871, 7pm, Heitzmann and Schloegl[15]

Piece	Composer	Poet	Performer	Publication Status
Overture from *Sardanapal*, piano reduction for four hands	Vilém A. Mayer	Byron (tragedy)	Ludevít Procházka, Zdeněk Fibich	
'Opuštěna'	Jindřich Pech	Eliška Krásnohorská	Miloslava Havelková	Appeared with Em. Starý and Co.
'Noc'	Karel Bendl	E. Krásnohorská	M. Havelková	
Scherzo in E Major, Op. 54	Fryderyk Chopin	–	Věra Timanova	
'Bůh kázal slunci pláti', Op. 34, No. 12, from the *Persian Songs*	Anton Rubinstein	Friedrich Bodenstedt	M. Havelková	
Ballad from the Singspiel *Rogněda*	Alexander Sěrov	Dmitry Averkiev	M. Havelková	
Etude in E major, Op. 72, No. 3	F. Chopin	–	V. Timanova	
'Trepak'	A. Rubinstein	–	V. Timanova	
Mazurka in A minor*	F. Chopin	–	V. Timanova	
Overture from *Pražský žid*, piano reduction for four hands	Zd. Fibich	Kolárov (tragedy)	Procházka, Zd. Fibich	

*. This piece is not included in the programme announcement; however, the review reveals that the pianist added this piece to the concert.

The third concert received a long review, possibly because it also provided a forum to extoll the precocious talent of the sixteen-year old pianist Timanova. It seems that this visit also enabled, or perhaps demanded, a change in focus regarding the programme, which was given over mainly to piano pieces. The reviewer used this occasion to address more general aspects regarding Mayer and Fibich, both of whom had already been heard in public (Mayer with a symphonic performance of his *Helena*, and Fibich with various performances). The reviewer concludes that an orchestral performance of Fibich's composition *Pražský žid* (The Jew of Prague), given this time in a version for piano four hands, would be a great experience. In so doing, he effectively steers the discourse towards large-scale works and performances, and away from the *Musical Entertainments* originally planned as intimate performances in a smaller setting[16]. In this regard, Heitzman and Schloegl's *Entertainments* served as a space where new works could be tested out on a smaller scale and with less effort.

While the first three concerts of the series took place within a month, a slightly longer break followed the third concert. The next one was not realised until February 1872. The general

---

[15]. See *Hudební* 1871 d.

[16]. See *Ibidem*.

concept of the event remained similar to the initial events. Again, the programme featured a combination of published and unpublished vocal and piano works by local and international composers, given by well-known local performers (see TABLE 4). Aside from some composers already known from previous performances (for example, Václav Jan Tomášek, Mikhail Glinka), some new names entered the scene — Václav Hořejšek, František Pivoda, and Jan Hugo Voříšek, for instance. This seems to have been a general principle that guided programming for these concerts, which enabled lesser-known composers to be heard alongside well-known names. According to the review, two of the performers, Otilie Langerová and M. Kučerová, were students of Pivoda's. The mention of this constellation enabled the readership to contextualise the performance, but it also helps us as historians to place the events within their own context, as they appear to have enabled young local students to perform for distinguished audiences[17].

TABLE 4: CONCERT PROGRAMME FOR THE *FOURTH FREE MUSICAL ENTERTAINMENT*
SATURDAY, 3 FEBRUARY 1872, 6 PM, SCHLOEGL[18]

PIECE	COMPOSER	POET	PERFORMER	PUBLICATION STATUS
Symfonická věta	Vilém A. Mayer	–		
Duettino	Mikhail Glinka	?	Otilie Langerová, M. Kučerová	
Písně vesnické 'Ta má malá chaloupka' 'Za našimi humny květe mák'	František Pivoda	?	Fr. Prošek	Manuscript
Eclogues No. 20 and 21	Václav Jan Tomášek	–	Karel Slavkovský	
'Ten tam můj klid'	M. Glinka	Goethe, from *Faust*	M. Kučerová	
'Večernice'	Václav Hořejšek		Fr. Prošek	Manuscript
'Kogda bezzadotno'	Mily Balakirev		O. Langerová	
Rhapsody for Piano, No. 3 and 4	Jan Hugo Voříšek	–	K. Slavkovský	

Following another two-month break, the *Musical Entertainments* moved to a new venue, with a fifth concert announced as taking place at home of the Švertásek brothers[19], although the reason for the change in venue may not be ascertained from announcements in the press. The programme reveals a small extension in repertoire with performances by the Hřímalý brothers

---

[17]. See *HUDEBNÍ* 1872E.

[18]. This event was announced several times; it was popularised through the performers rather than through the programme. *HUDEBNÍ* 1872B; *HUDEBNÍ* 1872C; *HUDEBNÍ* 1872D.

[19]. The form that is used in the paper is 'Švertásků'. It is the genetive of the name Švertásek; I am using the nominative in all places.

238

on the violin and cello[20]. One of the brothers, Vojtěch, was also featured as a composer (see Table 5). Furthermore, the programme included a song by *Hudební listy*'s co-editor, Josef Richard Rozkošný, thus extending his impact on this music-cultural practice into two different activities (although Procházka remained the main editor).

Table 5: Concert programme for the *Fifth Free Musical Entertainment* Wednesday, 10 April 1872, Švertásek brothers[21]

Piece	Composer	Poet	Performer	Publication Status
Trio for piano, violin, cello	František Zdeněk Skuherský	–	Slavkovský, Hřímalý brothers	
Slovak Folk Songs 'Pod Krivaňom' 'Navštivenie falešnej'			Betty Hanušová	
'Starý dub'	Josef Richard Rozkošný	Vojtěch Šmilovský	Karel Čech	
Song	Kochanovský	?	K. Čech	
'Proto'	Antonín Dvořák	Eliška Krásnohorská	Miss Kupková	
'Sirotkovo lůžko'	A. Dvořák	E. Krásnohorská	Miss Kupková	
'Mladý cikán'	Josef Leopold Zvonař	Jaromír Picek	K. Čech	
Romance	Alexander Dargomyzhsky	?	K. Čech	
Duet: 'Rybičky'	Vojtěch Hřímalý*	A. Hejduk	Miss Kupková, B. Hanušová	
Duet: 'Výstraha'	V. Hřímalý	Ladislav Staněk	Miss Kupková, B. Hanušová	
Duet: 'Jaro'	V. Hřímalý	Boleslav Jablonský	Miss Kupková, B. Hanušová	

*. This is Vojtěch Hřímalý junior; his father, who was called Vojtěch, too, was also a composer. However, the duets can be found in the Czech national library and thus authorship may be verified as belonging to the same Vojtěch Hřímalý who also performed as a violinist in this concert. For the score, see Hřímalý n.d.

Entirely devoted to chamber music, the programme for the final concert included string music by Slavic and non-Slavic composers ranging from Joseph Haydn to Dvořák, which redirected attention to the Hřímalý brothers' musical skills and away from the potentially significant role that vocal music might play in the formation of Czech national

[20]. The Hřímalý brothers were well known as a string quartet in the following cast: Jan (first violin), Vojtěch (second violin), Bohuslav (viola), Jaromír (cello).

[21]. See *Hudební* 1872f.

music (see Table 6). Indeed, in the space of a single season, the *Musical Entertainments* had moved from purely vocal affairs to chamber music events, with their concomitant emphasis on performance. Thus, 'Czech local colour' was highlighted in this season not primarily through musical composition, but also through the performers hired, the venues used, the organisers who undertook the ventures, and the audiences who attended.

Table 6: Concert programme for the *Sixth Free Musical Entertainment*
Friday, 5 July 1872, 7pm, Švertásek brothers[22]

Piece	Composer	Poet	Performer	Publication Status
String quartet Op. 17, No. 5 in G major	Joseph Haydn	–		
Polonaise for Violin and Piano Accompaniment	Ferdinand Laub	–	Jan Hřímalý	
Adagio from Trio Op. 13	Antonín Dvořák	–		
'Studien für den Pedalflügel', Op. 56, No. 2.4	Robert Schumann, arranged for two violins and piano by Vojtěch Hřímalý	–		
'Noční zpěv' (string quartet)	Jean Vogt	–		
Quartet in E-flat Major, Op. 74	Ludwig van Beethoven	–		

The announcement for the second series in November 1872 continued to highlight programming local composers in public concerts, and mixing this repertoire with new foreign (especially Slavic) repertoire was emphasized as the purpose of the series[23]. It began with a concert featuring a rich programme of string, piano, and vocal music (see Table 7). Besides such well-known Czech composers as Dvořák and Fibich, a further opening towards German composers is noticeable, especially through the programming of a song by Richard Wagner to words by Mathilde Wesendonck. This was the only female poet featured in the *Entertainments* besides Eliška Krásnohorská, settings of whose texts were apparently regular occurrences within the context of the *Musical Entertainments*. The inclusion of Wagner in November 1872 seems most notable considering the divided reception of Wagner in 1870s Prague[24]. Another change was the geographical move of the event to the Konviktsaal, which was an established concert venue at the time. It may be safe to assume that the performances had advanced from the small, intimate, salon-style gatherings given at the piano manufacturers Heitzmann and Schloegel to more sophisticated concerts.

---

22. See *Hudební* 1872g. In the announcement the concert's focus on the string quartet surrounding the Hřímalý brothers was emphasised.

23. See *Hudební* 1872h.

24. Procházka, a student of Smetana's, and, from 1874, his successor as editor of *Hudební listy*, František Pivoda, were key figures within this context. See Kopecký 2017.

Table 7: Concert programme for the *First Free Musical Entertainment*, Second Season Friday, 22 November 1872, 12 noon, Konviktsaal

Piece	Composer	Poet	Performer	Publication Status
Quintet for string quartet and piano	Antonín Dvořák	–	Karel Slavkovský, Vojtěch Hřímalý, Lederer, Krehan, Neruda	
Song by Eichendorff	Zdeněk Fibich	Joseph von Eichendorff	Betty Hanušová	
'Útěcha pěvcova'	Z. Fibich	Justin A. Ch. Kerner	B. Hanušová	
'Houslař'*	Z. Fibich	Anderson**	B. Hanušová	Premiere
Gavotta for piano	J. P. Gotthard***	–	Lilli Striková	
Cavatina Op. 91, No. 3	Joachim Raff	–	L. Striková	
'Zwei welke Rosen', Op. 13, No. 1	Robert Franz	Georg von Hauenschild	Karel Čech	
'Stille Sicherheit', Op. 10, No. 3	R. Franz	Nikolaus Lenau	K. Čech	
'Träume'	Richard Wagner	Mathilde Wesendonck	K. Čech	
Canon for piano	Ladislav Zelenský	–	K. Slavkovský	
Promenade	L. Zelenský	–	K. Slavkovský	
Valse impromptu	V. J. Hlaváč	–	K. Slavkovský	

*. In the review, the song is referred to as 'Hudec'.

**. According to the thematic catalogue, Fibich did not set any poem by Anderson; it is possible that this is a mistake. The catalogue lists a piece titled 'Der Spielmann' for 22 September 1872, to words by Adalbert von Chamisso. Hudec 2001, p. 229.

***. In the review, the piece is credited to «J. P. Gotthard, actually Pazdírek» («J. P. Gottharda, vlastně Pazdírka»).

The review for this concert is quite comprehensive, but not very telling with respect to the role of these events in the advancement of Czech music. Rather, it provides a detailed technical analysis of each individual performance. It concludes with the modest request to have printed programme booklets including the lyrics of the songs, or to improve the singers' pronunciation so that such booklets would be unnecessary[25]. This statement reveals some hidden criticism; it also bears witness to the challenges faced by singers of multilingual musical programmes.

The second concert of the second season was announced for Sunday, 22 December 1872, again in the Konviktsaal. While a programme was not published, the concert was advertised on account of its performers: Helena Röslerová, Marta Procházková, Kar. Paroubková, and Vojtěch Hřímalý[26]. The third and final concert of the second (and last) series was enriched by the violinist Václav Kopta, who had arrived in Prague from North America. Kopta's presence

[25]. See *Hudební* 1872i.

[26]. See *Hudební* 1872j.

ensured that the programme would include a number of violin pieces; the vocal works were merely announced as 'songs' without further specification (see TABLE 8).

TABLE 8: CONCERT PROGRAMME FOR THE *THIRD FREE MUSICAL ENTERTAINMENT*, SECOND SEASON, SUNDAY, 9 FEBRUARY 1873, 12 NOON, KONVIKTSAAL[27]

PIECE	COMPOSER	POET	PERFORMER	PUBLICATION STATUS
Sonata in D Minor	Friedrich Wilhelm Rust (arranged by Ferdinand David)	–	Václav Kopta	
Song	Josef Rheinberger	?	Eleonora Korteová	
Song	Robert Franz	?	E. Korteová	
Song	Vilém A. Mayer	?	Karel Čech	
Song	Zdeněk Fibich	?	K. Čech	
Gavotte for piano	Ladislav Želenský	–	Žofie Ditrichová	
Intermezzo	Johannes Brahms	–	Ž. Ditrichová	
Giga noc variazioni	Joachim Raff	–	Ž. Ditrichová	
Songs Op. 1 and Op. 4	Bohdan Kirchner	?	E. Korteová	
Song	Mily Balakirev	?	K. Čech	
Song	Fryderyk Chopin	?	K. Čech	
Ballad and Polonaise	Henri Vieuxtemps	–	V. Kopta	

***

In this chapter, I have brought together and contextualised the musical works programmed as part of the *Musical Entertainments* organised by Jan Ludevít Procházka in early-1870s Prague. Aside from the window this may provide on lesser-known nineteenth-century repertoire performed in Prague during the Czech national revival, a number of music-cultural observations emerge from this examination. The *Musical Entertainments* form part of our received musicological knowledge, especially on account of Dvořák's debut, but they have

---

[27]. See *HUDEBNÍ* 1872K. The concert was first announced for Sunday, 5 January 1873. The announcement included only the names of the performers (but not the programme): Žofie Ditrichová, Eleonora Korteová, Karel Čech, Neruda. The concert was postponed until 9 February 1873, and a string quartet was added to the performers, without mentioning concrete names (*HUDEBNÍ* 1872A). Three days before the concert, on 6 February 1873, another announcement followed, stating that this would be the third and last performance of the cycle, and that the performers would be joined by the Prague violinist Václav Kopta, who had just arrived from America (*HUDEBNÍ* 1873A; review *HUDEBNÍ* 1873B). The review is a summary of repertoire and performers rather than a detailed account of content and/or audience reactions. The concert was also announced in *DALIBOR* 1873A, and again, with emphasis on Kopta from America, in *DALIBOR* 1873B.

never been scrutinised holistically through the lens of Czech musical practice of the time. Yet, as this chapter has shown, the *Musical Entertainments* were perhaps not primarily intended to showcase individual composers or works, and if so, this showcasing was certainly not limited to Antonín Dvořák, but was equally geared towards the creative work of Zdeněk Fibich, or Karel Bendl, for instance, both of whom were also programmed quite often. Furthermore, the *Entertainments* reveal Eliška Krásnohorská, primarily known today as Smetana's librettist, as an inspiration for many more composers. Besides Dvořák, composers such as Jindřich Pech and Karel Bendl set her texts. The singing entertainments were a platform for public engagement with Czech national identity in music — outside the world of opera and large-scale works, as these genres had not been explored altogether too productively by Czech composers at the beginning of the 1870s.

Furthermore, it is important to consider Procházka's equal acknowledgement of the role of the performer in defining musical culture, an aspect often neglected in today's music-historical considerations. Some of the concerts were announced and/or reviewed primarily for the sake of their performers rather than their programmes. Sometimes famous foreign performers were invited to perform as part of the series; sometimes young performers — for instance, students residing in Prague — could showcase their skills and gather experience. Some of the performers were also close to the organiser (for instance, Marta Procházková as Jan Ludevít Procházka's wife), and quite often major players took on more than one role (for example, when Procházka performed piano works together with Fibich, or when Vojěch Hřímalý composed and arranged works performed in concerts that featured him as a violinist).

Perhaps it was this spirit of mutual inspiration and close proximity between composing, learning, performing, listening, and reviewing which lay at the heart of Procházka's initial idea, and thus at the heart of his calling the concerts '*Free*' *Entertainments* and adding an intimate and spontaneous element to them. As ephemeral events, these concerts were important in enabling exchange and discourse, but they also had an influence on the publishing business, and possibly on the private careers and revenues of Procházka (and also his singer wife), Heitzman and Schloegl, and the Švertásek brothers, especially at the beginning. Later, once the concerts had moved to the Konviktsaal, intimacy appears to have given way to greater sophistication.

Possibly more importantly, contemporary journalistic practice gave Procházka the opportunity to reflect on the issue of a distinct Czech and/or Slavic musical identity at a broader public and less ephemeral level[28]. To a certain extent, Czech song became 'publicly intimate'

---

[28]. The significance of this aspect may be surmised from various other contemporary publications on song as a potential ideal 'Czech national genre', for instance Václav Juda Novotný's (1849-1922) piece *On the Development of National Songs and Its Significance* (O vývinu písně národní a jejím významu), which was published across the first seven numbers of *Dalibor* in 1874 (Novotný 1874).

through these *Entertainments*[29]. However, as promising as song was as a genre suited to making the Czech identity public, Procházka's *Entertainments* also served their traditional functions as salons, namely, as spaces of innovation, experimentation, and inspiration, where composers could introduce and test out their new — possibly large-scale — works with keen performers and smaller audiences. They provided a more 'intimate' and low-cost setting than larger venues (see, for instance, the piano performance of excerpts from Fibich's *Pražský žid*).

In the end, one must ask if Procházka succeeded in bringing together local and international composers and audiences to explore pan-Slavic potentials for the formation of Czech national song (and Czech national culture). The *Musical Entertainments* survived only a little over two years — two seasons: one including six concerts, and a second comprising three events. They never had a set day of the week (or month), or, indeed, a set time of the day. Venues changed, too. Sometimes concerts had to be postponed. These circumstances suggest that Procházka's *Musical Entertainments* never gained an established foothold in Prague's musical life — one that audiences would anticipate as part of their everyday musical life. Only the first concert was labelled 'Singing Entertainment'; other — often purely instrumental — genres were quickly added to the programmes. In light of this, perhaps Procházka's aim was a little too ambitious in a Prague characterised by a fast-moving musical culture. Not only did his own activity as editor of *Hudební listy* cease in 1873 (he moved to *Dalibor*), but other musical initiatives mushroomed during the 1870s. For instance, there were the *Chamber Music Entertainments* (Zábava komorní hudby); furthermore, musical associations were founded, and other concert series and/or stand-alone concerts outside of series took place with increasing frequency. Despite its move from the private and semi-public domain into the open public, musical culture remained ephemeral and highly mutable. Furthermore, Czech opera endured as the main focus of public attention, and was discussed intensely during that time; there was simply less room in the print media for small-scale genres.

Nevertheless, it is initiatives like Procházka's *Singing* (or later, *Musical*) *Entertainments* that enabled encounters, inspiration, revenue, and discourse. The works programmed in these concerts, and the overarching idea of pan-Slavism as a unifying element in music-cultural practice may be overshadowed by the large-scale works and greater discussions about individual protagonists at the time. However, their effect on contemporary music-cultural practice may have been larger than has been assumed to date. It is my hope that this small glimpse into Procházka's *Entertainments* may ignite further research on aspects of cultural agency and the formation of greater institutional structures that consider chamber music repertoire through the lens of themes, social circles, and cross-regional cultural exchange, to enable a more diverse picture of nineteenth-century (Czech) music and musical culture.

---

[29]. On the idea of 'public intimacy' and song, see ROECK 2009.

Bibliography

BERDYCHOVÁ 2007
BERDYCHOVÁ, Tereza. *Josef Leopold Zvonař, hudební teoretik a významný zjev hudby*, unpublished Bachelor's Degree Thesis, Brno, Masaryk University, 2007.

DALIBOR 1873A
Dalibor, I/5 (31 January 1873), p. 38.

DALIBOR 1873B
Dalibor, I/6 (7 February 1873), p. 48.

ENDERS 1993
ENDERS, Julius. *Rukopis zelenohorský a královédvorský: vznik, styl a básnická hodnota staročeské orální poesie*, Prague, Neklan, 1993.

FRANZ n.d.
FRANZ, Robert. *Sechs Gesänge für eine Singstimme mit Begleitung des Pianoforte*, Leipzig, Kistner, n.d.

HŘIMALÝ n.d.
HŘIMALÝ, Vojtěch. *Čtyři dvojzpěvy pro ženské hlasy s průvodem piana*, Prague, Em. Starý, n.d.

HUDEBNÍ 1871A
Hudební listy, II/38 (15 November 1871), p. 321.

HUDEBNÍ 1871B
Hudební listy, II/41 (6 December 1871), pp. 347-348.

HUDEBNÍ 1871C
Hudební listy, II/42 (13 December 1871), p. 356.

HUDEBNÍ 1871D
Hudební listy, II/43 (20 December 1871), p. 302.

HUDEBNÍ 1872A
Hudební listy, IV/2 (10 January 1872), p. 15.

HUDEBNÍ 1872B
Hudební listy, III/3 (18 January 1872), p. 23.

HUDEBNÍ 1872C
Hudební listy, III/4 (25 January 1872), p. 31.

Hudební 1872d
Hudební listy, III/5 (1 February 1872), p. 41.

Hudební 1872e
Hudební listy, III/6 (8 February 1872), p. 47.

Hudební 1872f
Hudební listy, III/14 (4 April 1872), p. 116.

Hudební 1872g
Hudební listy, III/27 (4 July 1872), p. 226.

Hudební 1872h
Hudební listy, III/46 (14 November 1872), p. 379.

Hudební 1872i
Hudební listy, III/48 (28 November 1872), p. 395.

Hudební 1872j
Hudební listy, III/50 (12 December 1872), p. 410.

Hudební 1872k
Hudební listy, III/52 (28 December 1872), p. 426.

Hudební 1873a
Hudební listy, IV/6 (6 February 1873), p. 46.

Hudební 1873b
Hudební listy, IV/8 (20 February 1873), p. 63.

Hudec 2001
Hudec, Vladimír. *Zdeněk Fibich: tematický katalog*, Prague, Bärenreiter, 2001.

Kopecký 2017
Kopecký, Jiří. 'Introduction', in: *Retrospective Index to Music Periodicals*, 2017 <https://www.ripm.org/?page=JournalInfo&ABB=HUL>, accessed December 2023.

Ludvová 2022
Ludvová, Jitka. 'Čech, Karel', and 'Bubeníčková, Emilie', in: *Historický ústav AV ČR, Biografický slovník*, 2022 <http://biography.hiu.cas.cz/Personal/index.php/BUBEN%C3%8D%C4%8CKOV%C3%81_Emilie_1.12.1844-10.12.1920>, accessed December 2023.

MILOTOVÁ 2015

MILOTOVÁ, Nina. *Kulturní dějiny Podřipska 1860-1914 v kontextu českého národního hnutí*, unpublished Ph.D. Diss., Olomouc, Palacký University Olomouc, 2015.

NOVOTNÝ 1874

NOVOTNÝ, Václav Juda. 'O vývinu písně národní a jejím významu', in: *Dalibor* II/1 (3 January 1874), pp. 1-2; II/2 (9 January 1874), pp. 9-10; II/3 (16 January 1874), pp. 17-20; II/4 (23 January 1874), pp. 25-27; II/5 (30 January 1874), pp. 33-34; II/6 (6 February 1874), pp. 41-43; II/7 (13 February 1874), pp. 49-51.

ROECK 2009

ROECK, Bernd. 'Von intimer Öffentlichkeit zu öffentlicher Intimität: Über ein Paradigma der Moderne', in: *Öffentliche Einsamkeit: Das deutschsprachige Lied und seine Komponisten im frühen 20. Jahrhundert*, edited by Michael Heinemann, Hans-Joachim Hinrichsen and Carmen Ottner, Cologne, Dohr, 2009, pp. 7-25.

VENGLAŘ 2021

VENGLAŘ, Petr. *Hudební tvorba Ludevíta Procházky*, unpublished Diploma Thesis, Olomouc, Palacký University Olomouc, 2021.

VOJTĚŠKOVÁ 2011

VOJTĚŠKOVÁ, Jana. 'Umělecké kontakty Jana Ludevíta Procházky', in: *Musicalia*, III/1-2 (2011), pp. 85-124.

VOJTĚŠKOVÁ 2013

Album Jana Ludevíta Procházky z let 1860-1888 / The Procházka Album (1860-1888), edited by Jana Vojtěšková, Prague, Koniasch Latin Press, 2013.

«Die edelste und künstlerischeste aller Kunstformen»: The Committee for the Promotion of Chamber Music — A *fin-de-siècle* Initiative in Zagreb[1]

Vjera Katalinić
(Croatian Academy of Sciences and Arts, Zagreb)

Introduction

At the beginning of the nineteenth century, the lack of representative orchestral ensembles in the towns and courts of continental Croatia (i.e., Civil Croatia) was compensated for by the presence of chamber ensembles, usually trios or string quartets. They were first active at aristocratic courts (including the residence of Maksimilijan Vrhovec, the Bishop of Zagreb[2]), performing on special occasions. Some noble families had a small group of permanently employed musicians (such as the Erdődy family at their estates in Burgenland and Hrvatsko Zagorje[3]), or hired and gathered them together occasionally (such as counts Prandau and Pejačević at their estates in Slavonia). The need for more professional musicians, especially singers and string players, was prompted by a desire for regular theatrical events. Thus, it was a group of musicians, first united in a chamber ensemble, who initiated the institutionalization of professional music making, and consequently, appropriate musical education.

---

1. The material for this paper was elaborated within the NetMus19 project (IP 06-2016-4476; 2017-2021), and additionally researched and prepared for print within the MusInst19 project (IP 02-2020-4277; 2021-2025), both financed by the Croatian Science Foundation.

2. In his memoirs (*Diarium*), Bishop Maksimilian Vrhovac wrote that on 22 November 1819, a string quartet comprising the general Greth, the deputy Sivini, lawyer and musician Wisner von Morgenstern, and a certain Laforest performed at his palace. See Goglia 1930, p. 8.

3. Hrvatsko Zagorje is the north-western region of Civil Croatia. The Erdődy family owned estates there in Novi Marof and Varaždin. Among the musicians employed by the family were Ignaz Pleyel and Jan Křtitel Vaňhal. For more on the musical aspect of the family in the late eighteenth and early nineteenth centuries see Seifert 1995, and on migration of musicians in the region see Katalinić 2014.

Vjera Katalinić

Chamber Music and National Identity

When the Societas filharmonica Zagrabiensis (or, colloquially, Musikverein) was founded in 1827 in Varaždin and Zagreb, as well as in some other towns (Križevci, Karlovac, Osijek), it was the first step towards the organisation of Varaždin and Zagreb schools, in 1828 and 1829 respectively. At the concert on 18 April 1827 that marked the beginning of the Zagreb Musikverein, the joint forces of professionals and amateurs performed Ludwig van Beethoven's Septet, Op. 20[4], thereby pointing to future pedagogic directions and efforts. Both musicians and audiences in Zagreb were very pleased that a society orchestra was soon formed to perform at various occasions. Some of this society orchestra's members also participated in the opera orchestra. The foundation of the National Theatre in Zagreb (1861) prompted the formation of the theatre's own orchestra for stage music performances; this orchestra soon began to participate in staging operetta repertoire, and with the founding of the National Opera Department (1870), the large orchestra also executed symphonic repertoire at special academies (the so-called *quodlibet* concerts[5]). However, the national issue was present and foregrounded in vocal and stage works because language — according to Herder's ideas — was the main means of representing a nation without a national state. This foregrounding of language also occurred in other Slavic nations within the Habsburg Empire and, since the 1867 and 1868 Compromises[6], in the Austro-Hungarian Monarchy. Thus, rousing songs and a national opera[7] came into being during the first wave of the National Revival movement in the 1830s and 1840s (peaking during the 1848 Revolution), as well as during the second wave, in the 1860s and 1870s, after the abolishment of neo-absolutism in 1861. The high point occurred in 1861, with the foundation of the Croatian National Theatre and ten years

---

[4]. Besides Beethoven's chamber piece, on the programme were Mozart's overture to *Don Giovanni*, a vocal quartet by an unknown composer, a *Concert polonaise* by Mayseder (performed by Laveczari), the overture to Rossini's *L'Italiana in Algeri*, variations for clarinet by Louis Spohr (performed by Korneg), the Andante from Haydn's Symphony No. 94 ('Surprise'), and finally, a choral piece with soloists by Wisner V. Morgenstern called *Hymne an die Musik*.

[5]. These concerts, insofar as they were first continuous orchestral music making in Zagreb, actually prepared the path for the establishment of an independent symphonic orchestra, specialised for an adequate repertoire. Thus, the Zagreb Philharmonic Orchestra was officially founded only in 1921.

[6]. Following the Austro-Hungarian Compromise in 1867, the 1868 Croatian-Hungarian Compromise regulated the relationships between these two monarchical entities within the parliamentary system. The following period, especially from the 1870s and 1880s until the beginning of the Great War, is marked by important juridical and educational reforms (for example, the foundation of the modern university in Zagreb) that influenced a rather stable cultural environment, despite the constant misbalances within the Dual Monarchy.

[7]. The premiere of the 'first national opera' *Ljubav i zloba* [Love and Malice] by Vatroslav Lisinski (1819-1854) was announced in 1846 in some major European newspapers in Milan, Paris, and Vienna. On Lisinski and his output there exist many publications; one of the most recent ones is the volume Tuksar et al. 2021.

later, with the organization of the National Theatre's opera department. Composer Ivan Zajc was hired to take over the directorship of the opera, establish an appropriate ensemble, and compose national operas; he successfully drew on his experiences in Milan and Vienna and led the ensemble until 1889, building up a standard operatic repertoire. His own operas represented a change in national attitudes: his three eminent national-historical operas *Mislav* (1871), *Ban Leget* (1873), and *Nikola Šubić Zrinjski* (1876) were followed by operas rooted in traditional Slavic texts and ended with operas that tried to follow Wagnerian structural processes and contemporary topics.

On the other hand, chamber music reflected international tendencies and only occasionally resulted in instrumental variations and fantasies on national or folk themes, or pieces composed 'in the spirit of folk music', created by Croatian composers. During the first half of the century, such pieces may be found in the oeuvre of the blind guitar virtuoso Ivan Padovec (who wrote for piano as well as for guitar)[8]. Other pieces of this nature were composed by Vatroslav Lisinski (mostly for piano) as well as Antun Kirschhofer[9], a violin teacher and composer, among others. On the other hand, in the later period, similar chamber works were composed by the musicologist, ethnomusicologist, and composer Franjo Ksaver Kuhač. Furthermore, Antun Schwarz, a violinist, violin teacher, and conductor, composed some chamber music for his students with 'national' titles such as *Mladi Hrvat* [A Young Croat] for two violins; meanwhile, cello teacher Ivan Oertl penned *Slavjanin* [A Slav] for cello solo. Both these pieces were performed as part of a student concert in 1868[10]. On the same occasion, a Concertino for six violins, cello, and piano by Schwarz was also presented, suggesting that chamber music by local composers furnished both fields: the nationalistic and the generally stylistic. This was the case for the chamber output of the national opera composer Ivan Zajc, who nevertheless predominantly promoted an international style. However, some of these pieces may be considered *Salonmusik*, especially those by Padovec and Kuhač, and some were meant to be performed in the ballroom (dance music by Lisinski) or in the concert hall (Lisinski, Zajc). The newly established Musikverein (1827) and its school (1829), thus declared their national and international attitudes through the repertoire of their concerts: they successfully balanced the standard repertoire with pieces by domestic composers of various stylistic orientations.

---

[8]. Padovec mostly composed fantasies and variations on popular operatic themes, but exceptionally also composed some national pieces for piano (dedicated to Ljudevit Gaj, the leader of the Croatian National Movement) and for guitar. See Katalinić – Majer-Bobetko 2006.

[9]. Kirschhofer's *Variations on the Patriotic Theme* were performed at a concert of the choral society of clerics in 1841, organised in honour of the Zagreb Bishop Juraj Haulik. See Goglia 1930, p. 127.

[10]. It was performed by the two violin students Kornelia Kerin and Arnold Janda, and the other piece by G. Felbinger, on 25 July 1868, along with other chamber pieces by Charles August de Bériot (a violin solo), variations for cello solo by Mercadante, and arrangements of excerpts from operas by Meyerbeer and Donizetti. See Miklaušić-Ćeran 2001, p. 118, illustration no. 6.

Accordingly, arias, overtures, and chamber pieces by Seyfried, Paer, Mayseder, Rossini or Boieldieu may be found on programmes side by side with pieces by Padovec, Lisinski or Georg Carl Wisner von Morgenstern (one of the founders of the Musikverein, a teacher at the school and composer). However, analysis of the Musikverein's public concert programmes, and to some extent of its school, point to the dominance of orchestral pieces (both vocal-instrumental and instrumental), probably with the intention of demonstrating increasing capacity for larger performances. There are a few exceptions: small groups of professionals and students sometimes performed as members of chamber ensembles, mostly in the second half of the century. Furthermore, chamber pieces were mostly performed either on recitals given by domestic and guest performers, or in private music gatherings in salons. Musikverein teachers participated in chamber ensembles, sometimes even together with amateurs, both in private and in public. For example, in 1871, a Musikverein concert opened with Beethoven's Trio in C Minor, performed by teachers Ivan Zajc, Ivan Oertl, and Josip Eisenhuth[11].

Owing to the organization of music schools and ensembles, various vocal and instrumental soloists visited Zagreb, participating in performances of the standard operatic repertoire as well as national operas, to the approval of local audiences. Throughout the period, good soloists were gladly accepted and greeted by these audiences, such as the pianist Johann Nepomuk Hummel in 1815, violinist Treichlinger from Vienna in 1832, pianist Franz Krommer in 1838, and violinist Leopold Jansa, as well as the soprano Frisch from Odessa in 1839, Franz Liszt, violinist Albert Küstner from Berlin in 1846, and many others, who came to Zagreb much more frequently during the second half of the century. Organizers in Zagreb constantly endeavoured to attract and retain quality and educated musicians[12]. They also made efforts to bring back local musicians who had studied or worked abroad, such as the pianist Alois Pusch and the violinst Antun Schwarz (who returned to Zagreb after studying in Vienna), but even more, although with less success, the Croatian female singers who developed their careers in European and American theatres, such as Ilma de Murska, Matilda Marlow, Irma Terputec Terée, and Milka Ternina. Only Ternina (who was probably the most famous among them) returned to Zagreb definitively on the eve of the Great War after many successful appearances elsewhere, especially as a Wagnerian singer in Bayreuth and New York. She ended her career in Zagreb as a singing teacher at the Conservatory (later the Music academy)[13].

---

[11].   *Ibidem*, p. 118, illustration no. 7.

[12].   One of them was the violinist Antun Kirschhofer, who came from Budapest as a trained musician, embraced his new environment, and stayed in Zagreb as a music teacher and conductor of the Musikverein orchestra; he also conducted the theatre orchestra and performed as a soloist or in chamber ensembles.

[13].   For more on their activities and destinies, see Katalinić 2015.

CHAMBER MUSIC INITIATIVES IN ZAGREB:
EDUCATING PERFORMERS AND AUDIENCES

Throughout the nineteenth century, there was nonetheless a demand by more educated music lovers for performances of quality chamber music, hitherto mostly left to individual initiatives. On several occasions during the century, local professionals and amateurs, as well as music students, organized chamber performances in order to promote this sublime art. In 1845, a piano trio with pianist Josip Poličanski, violinist Silvio Medunić, the cellist Johann Köck performed a trio by Karl Reissiger[14]. In 1865 and 1866, a string quartet with Antun Schwarz (a Musikverein violin teacher), Adolf Felbinger (a builder), Emanuel Simm (also a Musikverein teacher and choralist in the Cathedral), and Ivan Oertl (a Musikverein cello teacher) performed a few times, but the audience was not large enough to satisfy the organizers[15]. Ludmilla (Ljudmila) Weiser, a female virtuoso and professional violinist from Zagreb, gave a few concerts in the Zagreb theatre and various concert halls in 1864, then together with the singer Matilda Mallinger in 1865, and accompanied by the pianist Anna Krupka of the Vienna Conservatory in 1866, before touring in European cities[16]. The Musikverein teachers also organized student chamber ensembles who later participated in school concerts. Some of the teachers were also skilful composers, so the standard chamber repertoire was expanded with pieces composed to suit the specific performance level of the students involved. However, chamber music was introduced into the school curriculum only in 1894 when Franjo (Fantišek) Jilek (the student of Zdeněk Fibich) was appointed the first chamber music teacher. This overlapped with the growing interest in professional chamber music.

Chamber performances with local music teachers took place on various occasions, already from the 1840s and 1850s on, increasing in later decades. Furthermore, in 1882 and 1883 some amateur musicians organized a series of private chamber concerts with invited guests[17], but such actions were mostly short-lived[18]. In 1884, the «First Croatian Amateur Quartet» (as it was referred to in the local press) was active in Zagreb, composed of musicians Aurel Waisz, later a music teacher in London; Oto Žert, later a member of the Vienna opera and philharmonic orchestras; Mirko Waisz, later a cello teacher in Boston; and medical doctor Aleksandar Kuhar. Yet, despite good reviews, its members later spread professionally all around the world. In 1890, Musikverein professor Đuro Eisenhuth founded a string quartet and a family piano trio with his brother Josip (cello) and his

---

[14]. GOGLIA 1930, p. 10 and p. 38.

[15]. Occasionally, depending on the repertoire performed, the quartet was joined by the pianist Vlaho Budmani (later a piano teacher in London) and cellist Antun Goglia, a music historian in Zagreb. See *ibidem*, pp. 10 and 38.

[16]. JEIĆ 2018.

[17]. These private concerts were organized in a residence at Duga ulica no. 22. See GOGLIA 1930, p. 39.

[18]. *Ibidem*.

daughter Luisa (piano) who performed not only in their family salon but also in public, mostly in the Musikverein hall[19].

The Expansion of Chamber Music: Guest Performances and Consequences

As noted earlier, some individual guest virtuosi gave concerts in Zagreb as soon as the city became safe and far away enough from the Turkish border. The first music visitors were touring theatre companies, and during the nineteenth century, Zagreb had already built up a substantial audience for various music events. At first, the appearances of these companies were organised in the theatre[20] and in the *Narodni dom* [People's House] hall. Later, after 1876, guest musicians often performed in the newly erected concert hall of the Musikverein. Concerts with chamber pieces were performed by Julius Epstein (a Zagreb-born pianist who had settled in Vienna), the cellist Heinrich Röver (in 1854)[21], and a Swedish female vocal quartet (in 1869). Guest performers may have visited Zagreb upon invitation from the Musikverein Board[22], such as the singer Carlotta Patti (in 1875), or a trio which included Teodor Ritter, Gustav Holländer, and Sigmund Bürger[23]. One representative guest ensemble was a Florentine string quartet (Jean Becker, Enrico Masi, L. Chiostri, F. Hilfert) who visited Zagreb in the 1870s[24]. The cellist David Popper appeared at the theatre on several occasions: with Sophie Menter in 1875 and in April 1886 with Alfred Reisenauer (a court pianist from Weimar) at the Musikverein, where his farewell concert was given for the benefit of the Musikverien's pension funds[25]. In 1876, guest performers included harpist Therese Zamara, and in 1877, violinist Pablo de Sarasate. In 1890, the Hellmesberger quartet started a series featuring guest performances by esteemed chamber ensembles. The increased arrival of chamber musicians in Zagreb was most certainly encouraged by the opening of a new concert hall, but also by the audience's interest in quality performers.

---

[19]. *Ibidem*, p. 11.

[20]. Concerts at the Zagreb National Theatre have been documented by posters and leaflets, kept in the Archives of the theatre (Department for History of Croatian Theatre, Croatian Academy of Sciences and Arts in Zagreb). Most of them have been digitized and are accessible at <https://dizbi.hazu.hr/a/?pr=l&msq=kazali%C5%A1ne+cedulje&ps=10>, accessed december 2023.

[21]. Röver had been performing as a cellist in the Hellmesberger Quartet since 1859.

[22]. The Musikverein has been out of service since March 2020, when a disastrous earthquake in Zagreb forced its Board to displace the documentation during the work in progress on the extensive renovation of the building. Due to this temporary unavailability, researchers can rely only on published literature and rare digitized sources.

[23]. Goglia 1930, p. 10.

[24]. *Ibidem*, p. 9.

[25]. Miklaušić-Ćeran 2001, p. 118, illustration no. 13.

As a result, this encouraged the opening of chamber music courses at the Musikverein school, and in turn more regular chamber performances.

This fascination with chamber music and the need to cultivate this kind of sublime art was explicitly expressed in 1896 by both musicians and audiences. In a review in the *Agramer Zeitung*, probably by Ernst Schulz, it is claimed:

> In no type of music is there such a sensitive void in our art life as in the care of chamber music. We have recently received inquiries from many sides, would it not be possible to establish an association that would enable this noblest and most artistic of all art types which simultaneously forms heart and soul and which values the most outstanding works by Mozart, Beethoven, Schubert, Schumann, as well as more recent pieces by Tchaikovsky, Dvořak, Smetana, Goldmark, that other cultural towns have cultivated already for some time. Now, as we have heard, this idea has taken a more solid form and a number of art-loving musicians have already found themselves determined to carry out their plan as soon as possible. In the next few days we will be able to announce the programmes of the chamber music performances to be organized[26].

During the 1890s, the enthusiasm of Zagreb music lovers for chamber music was triggered by the guest performance of the aforementioned Hellmesberger string quartet from Vienna[27]. In January 1894, a critic enthusiastically announced the performance of the new Bohemian String Quartet in the Musikverein Hall: «The excellent reputation that precedes this quartet, which a Viennese music critic calls the first of the existing associations for chamber music, will undoubtedly contribute to the complete success of the quartet»[28]. A few days later, a review by Ernst Schulz confirmed this praise:

---

[26]. [SCHULZ] 1896A: «In keinem Zweige der Musik besteht in unserem Kunstleben eine so empfindliche Lücke, wie bei der Pflege der Kammermusik. Von vielen Seiten empfingen wir in letzterer Zeit Anfragen, ob es nicht möglich wäre, eine Vereinigung zu constituiren, die es ermöglichen würde, diese edelste und küstlerischeste aller Kunstformen, die Herz und Gemüth zugleich bildet und die Werthschätzung für die hervorragendsten Werke Mozarts, Beethovens, Schuberts, Schumanns, dann der neueren Componisten Čajkovski's, Dvořaks, Smetanas, Goldmarks bei uns in der Weise zu cultiviren, wie das in anderen Kunststädten längst eine eingebürgte Institution ist. Nun hat diese Idee, wie wir vernehmen, festere Formen gefaßt, und es hat sich bereits eine Anzahl kunstbegeisterter Musiker gefunden, die fest entschlossen sind, ihren Plan der baldigsten Verwirklichung zuzuführen. In den nächsten Tagen schon werden wir in der Lage sein, die Programme der zu veranstaltenden Kammermusik-Aufführungen bekannt zu geben».

[27]. GOGLIA 1930, p. 11.

[28]. See *AGRAMER* 1894: «Der ausgezeichnete Ruf, welcher diesem Quartette, das ein Wiener Musikkritiker das erste der bestehenden Vereinigungen für Kammermusik nennt, vorangeht, wird ohne Zweifel beitragen, einen vollständigen Erfolg des Quartetts zu erzielen».

> Seldom, very seldom, has our city experienced such a full musical enjoyment as last night, when the Bohemian string quartet in the Musikverein Hall made us forget for a while that we live in Zagreb, where chamber music is one of the utmost rarities. Three young Czech artists, the gentlemen Hoffmann, Suk and Nedbal, aged between 20 and 22, and Prof. Vihan, who stepped in instead of the fourth youth who had fallen ill, had taken on the thankless task for Zagreb to produce here a pure classical music and to show what may be achieved by developed ability, fiery love for art and deep understanding of music. Our time is poor in famous quartets; the Hellmesberger and Rosé quartets have achieved world recognition, but yesterday we heard a four-leaf clover which, if it holds out in its current course, will become a first-ranked star on the musical horizon[29].

This quote reveals several issues for the critic that should be pointed out: firstly, the assessment that chamber music is real classical music and that good chamber music in Zagreb at that time was rare. This refers primarily to the occasional crisis of musical theatre, which, due to the need to raise the necessary funds, reached for 'banal' forms of entertainment such as operettas or guest appearances by obscure magicians or acrobats[30]. Certainly, the term 'classical music' does not refer to the period of classicism, but to the canonical musical works of previous periods; this is evident from the repertoire.

Another important point emerges from the evaluation of the Bohemian String Quartet's performance: that the quality they achieve results from knowledge and professionalism (i.e., good schooling), love of art, and understanding of music. Both views refer to the restricted opportunities for music education offered in Zagreb at that time. The Musikverein school, following its establishment in early 1829, gradually developed and expanded, but during the first

---

[29]. [SCHULZ] 1894: «Selten, sehr selten hat unsere Stadt einen derart vollen musikalischen Genuß gehabt, als gestern Abend, da das böhmische Streichquartett im Musikvereinssaale uns eine Zeit lang vergessen ließ, daß wir in Agram leben, wo die Kammermusik zu den größten Raritäten gehört. Drei junge čechische Künstler, die Herren Hoffmann, Suk und Nedbal, im alter von 20 bis 22 Jahren, und Prof. Vihan, der an Stelle des erkrankten vierten Jünglings eingesprungen war, hatten die für Agram leider sehr undankbare Aufgabe übernommen, hier reine classische Musik zu produciren und zu zeigen, was ausgebildetes Können, feurige Liebe zur Kunst und tiefes Verständniß der Musik zu leisten im Stande sind. An berühmten Quartetten ist unsere Zeit arm, die Quartette Hellmesberger, Rosé haben Weltruf erlangt, aber gestern hörten wir ein vierblättriges Kleeblatt, das, wenn es in seinem begonnenen Laufe aushält, ein Stern erster Größe auf dem musikalischen Horizonte werden wird». Also see GOGLIA 1930, p. 12.

[30]. August Šenoa, a prolific writer and theatre critic, was an ardent enemy of the operetta and various other 'light' pieces for the musical stage, especially the cheap Viennese farces and burlesques that «deserve to sleep in the archives». However, he had to admit that they attracted audiences to the theatre and thus brought in necessary income (ŠENOA 1934, p. 29). Stjepan Miletić, the first professional intendant and highly deserving person of the Zagreb National Theatre at the end of the nineteenth century, was like-minded. His repertoire makes it obvious, but he could not have kept his standards for more than four years (1894-1898).

half of the century it still owed its existence to the private initiative of an association financed by membership and tuition fees. In 1861, it became a provincial institute (Landesinstitut) and began receiving the first subsidies for its educational activities. The period from 1890 on was important in this development, when the school actually gained the structure of a conservatory (1891) with 17 highly qualified teachers and 220 students[31]. But delays in the formal and legal implementation of conservatory-level status — probably primarily due to financial and partly to political reasons — delayed the establishment of the conservatory until 1916. As a result, the school's more gifted students continued to go abroad for additional education and often stayed there if they achieved international success.

The Committee for the Promotion of Chamber Music

Sporadic guest performances of eminent ensembles seemed insufficient for the continuous promotion of this sublime type of music. A series of actions followed: three weeks after the 1896 appeal in the press, again in the *Agramer Zeitung*, one can read about the first chamber concert of the Musikverein performances that featured local musicians and Musikverein members. The critic Ernst Schulz pleaded the cause in this introductory text:

> The maintenance of classical chamber music should be the ideal goal of every association that is called to be the guardian of the people to be educated musically; because apart from the fact that these works by the classical masters reveal the purest art form, they are the most eminent instructive material, which can only have a stimulating and fruitful effect on a possible future musical genius. Where is such a talent supposed to get to know the wonders of polyphony in our country[32]?

It was precisely Ernst Schulz, a music critic of the Zagreb daily *Agramer Zeitung*, who advocated and promoted chamber music in his role as a member of the newly established Committee for the Promotion of Chamber Music, founded in late 1896. Along with him, the society founders included the builder and architect Herman Bollé (1845-1926), senior clerk and politician Carl von Mihalovich (1830-1918), lawyer, legal councillor, amateur cellist, and

---

[31]. Šaban 1977, pp. 101-113 and pp. 232-233: Šaban rightly names this period (1890-1920) after the vice-president of the Musikverein, the historian Vjekoslav Klaić. During his era, there was a significant increase in the number of the staff as well as the number of students so that their number in 1920 has almost doubled (see p. 103).

[32]. Schulz 1896b, p. 4: «Die Pflege der classischen Kammermusik sollte das idealste Ziel jeder Vereinigung sein, die berufen ist, die Hüterin im Reiche des musikalisch zu erziehenden Volkes zu sein, denn abgesehen davon, daß diese Werke der classischen Meister die reinste, geläuterste Kunstform zutage treten lassen, sind sie ja das eminenteste instructive Material, welches nur fördernd und befruchtend auf ein eventuelles zukünftiges Musikergenie wirken kann. Wo soll denn ein solches bei uns die Wunder der Polyphonie kennen lernen?».

Ill. 1: Announcement of a series of three concerts in the 1899/1900 season, *Agramer Zeitung*, 17 November 1899, p. 8. Photo by V. Katalinić.

prolific music writer Antun Goglia (1867-1958), director of the Zagreb Opera Franjo Rump(e)l, and engineer Robert Weiss[33]. Their task was publicly stated in Schulz's text from December 1896, when the name of the Committee appeared for the first time: *Comité zur Pflege der Kammermusik in Agram*. Their idea was to organize a local chamber ensemble, a quartet, to give regular (several times a year) chamber music concerts. The intendant of the National Theatre, Stjepan Miletić, found suitable musicians in the theatre orchestra (concertmaster Adolfo Pick, Josip Čermak, and Adolf Lutz), and they were joined by Professor Hinko Geiger, a cellist from the Musikverein School. Although the first two concerts on 5 February (the beginning of the Committee's activity) and 27 March 1897 were well received[34], it seems that the members, due to their other obligations, failed to maintain the planned pace of performance. Further, it is possible that an event profile featuring local performers failed to attract sufficient audiences. Thus, the Committee was encouraged to try to revive the audience's interest in this elite field

---

[33]. GOGLIA 1907, p. 3. Jelena Vuković mentions the Committee in her diploma theses (VUKOVIĆ 1998, pp. 26-32), mostly based on Goglia's writings.

[34]. Audience interest at the beginning of the Committee's activity was very modest, so that the small Musikverein hall was sufficient. However, in the second season, when well-known international ensembles were invited, interest increased to such an extent that the large hall had to be used. See GOGLIA 1907, pp. 3-4.

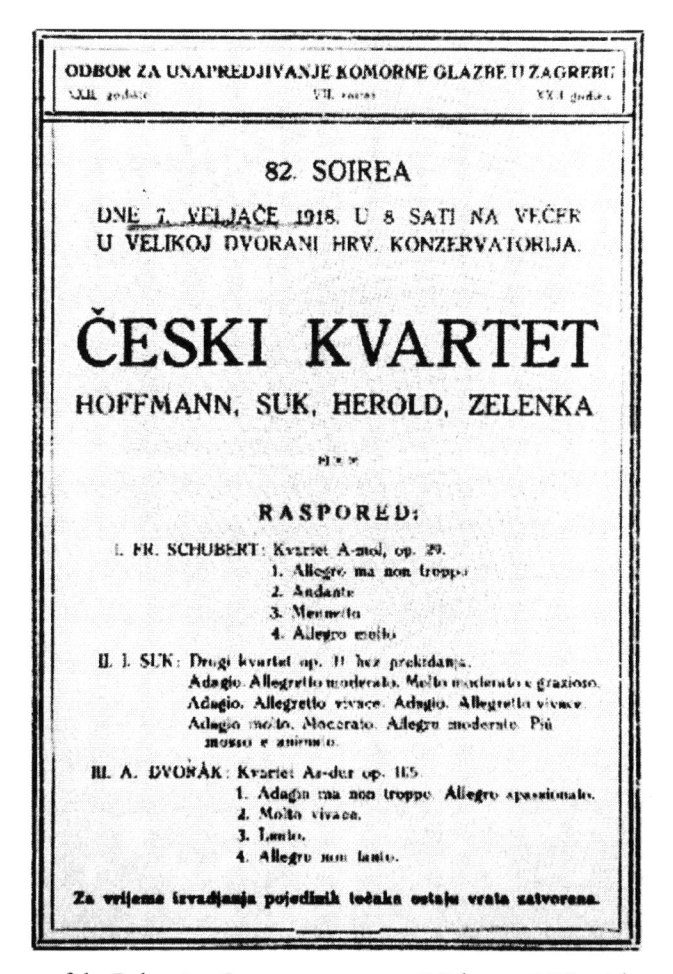

ILL. 2: Programme of the Bohemian Quartet, concert on 7 February 1918, with quartets by Schubert, Suk and Dvořák. Digitized material from the Archives of the Croatian Music Institute, <https://hgz.eindigo.net/?pr =iiif.v.a&id=11773&tify={%22pages%22:[17],%22view%22:%22info%22}>, accessed December 2023.

of music by inviting excellent foreign ensembles. For the next 21 years (until the end of 1918), the Committee sought to organize up to three chamber concerts a year on a regular basis during the first six seasons, four concerts during the next four seasons, and later usually three annually, with some reductions during the Great War. Some ensembles performed several times, almost regularly, and some of them returned in reconfigured ensembles. Among them, the Bohemian Quartet stands out, especially its first guest appearance, with the prominent young violinist Josef Suk and violist Oskar Nedbal (both in their 20s), so that the ensemble received excellent reviews and was invited to Zagreb for a total of nine performances (in 1917, in Zagreb, their performance also marked the 10th anniversary of the quartet's existence). A 'ladies' string quartet' also attracted attention, with violinists Marie Soldat-Roeger and Elsa V. Plank, Natalie Bauer-Lechner (viola), and Lucy Herbert-Campbell (cello), performing quartets by Luigi Cherubini,

Joseph Haydn, and Ludwig van Beethoven in 1899. In addition, solo pieces were performed by Marie Soldat-Roeger (Introduction and Rondo from the violin concerto by Henri Vieuxtemps) and Lucy Herbert-Campbell (Air by J. S. Bach and Nocturne by F. Chopin). These two female musicians would later return to Zagreb, in 1901, with Ilona Eibenschütz as a piano trio.

The repertoire of these guest chamber ensembles (from duos to sextets) was mostly standards, with compositions by Haydn, Mozart, Beethoven, Schubert, Schumann, Chopin, Brahms, Smetana, Dvořák, Grieg, Franck, Cherubini, Bach, Mendelssohn, Spohr, and some Russian composers (Tchaikovsky, Rimsky-Korsakov, Borodin, Glazunov). To some extent it was the Quartetto Triestino that brought a different repertoire with Claude Debussy, as well as the highly awaited Bachmann Trio from Dresden in 1910, that performed a Piano Trio by the then-contemporary Croatian female composer Countess Dora Pejačević. During the Committee's twentieth and final season, on 4 April 1918, a string quartet formed specifically for that occasion by distinguished musicians residing in Zagreb — the virtuoso Zdravko Baloković (violin I), his teacher Václav Huml (viola), Miroslav Schlick (violin II), Juro Tkalčić (cello), and Milan Stančić (piano) — performed Pejačević's String Quartet Op. 31 and Piano Quintet Op. 40, both to excellent reviews[35].

Research to date reveals that the Committee organised a total of 42 performances by 18 chamber ensembles in its 21 years of existence (its activities ended roughly with the end of the Austro-Hungarian Empire). In addition, it organized 28 recitals by prominent soloists (e.g., pianists Ernst von Dohnányi and Wilhelm Backhaus, violinist Bronislav Huberman, and cellist Pablo Casals) and seven guest appearances by orchestral ensembles, including the Wiener Tonkünstler Orchestra with Oskar Nedbal. The Committee also tried to hold concerts during wartime: in 1914 not a single chamber ensemble came, but this was somewhat compensated by solo performances.

The Board acted as a separate company; tickets were purchased only for members of the Committee (either as subscriptions for the season, or individually). Tickets for guests were offered only exceptionally, so that the membership would be promoted and enlarged. Goglia described the interest for the new society:

> Immediately in the second season, the interest in these performances grew so much that not all members could fit in the small hall of the music institute, so the soirées had to be held in the big hall. In the same year, Their Imperial and Royal Highnesses Archduke Leopold Salvator and Archduchess Blanca joined our community, who showed the keenest interest in the committee's efforts during their entire stay in Zagreb[36].

---

[35]. The reviewer Kazimir Krenedić praised her distinguished and serious style, her energetic instrumentation and especially the beauty of some Slavic motives in the third movement of the quartet; cited in GOGLIA 1930, p. 44.

[36]. GOGLIA 1907, p. 4.

The reviewer (probably Erich Schulz, although the reports were not signed) always pointed out the presence of the highest nobility and outstanding citizens, underscoring their interest in the activity of the Committee. He also announced the guests, and sometimes gave additional information, mostly gleaned from the foreign press, such as Waldemar Meyer's Stradivari violin (Quartet Waldemar Meyer, 21 November 1899).

The Committee tried to present the best artists available, not only chamber ensembles, but later, in the sixth season, the Czech philharmonic ensemble. They also attempted to introduce some exquisite local performers (singers, pianists, etc.) who joined chamber ensembles as guests. This gave them the opportunity to enter performers' networks, and provided a means of presenting them to the local audiences as musicians of highest quality. The founders of the Committee worked closely with the Musikverein, of which they were all members. Their repertoire was somewhat compatible with the Musikverein's guests, and often the same performers gave concerts for both organisers, which are sometimes difficult to separate[37]. The Musikverein also provided its facilities to the Committee, offering first the small hall, and later, when interest in the Committee's programmes increased, a large one. Even after the Committee's abolishment, the Musikverein apparently maintained good relationships with some of the guests, so they continued to collaborate in the new state — the Kingdom of Serbs, Croats and Slovenes, later named the Kingdom of Yugoslavia.

Conclusion

The research presented here provides the basis for further research within the project on private musical initiatives and music institutionalization in nineteenth-century Croatia. One fruitful avenue for further exploration is a survey of newspaper articles to reconcile data that do not match the preserved documentation. However, based on the material presented here, it is nonetheless possible to draw some conclusions. First, encouragements to organise more systematic performances of chamber music overlap with periods of diminished need to confirm national identity (which was more associated with opera and vocal music), and these encouragements grew stronger throughout the nineteenth century. Second, the interest in chamber music, considered 'pure classical' and sublime music, increased in relation to less elite forms of musical entertainment, primarily operettas and various acrobatic performances.

---

[37]. It is still unknown whether the documentation of the Committee has been preserved or not. Many programme leaflets have been kept in the archives of the *Musikverein* but it will not be possible to do further investigations until the end of the renovation of its building, hopefully from 2026 on. Thus, this investigation and reconstruction of its repertoire was mainly done according to the writings of Antun Goglia (Goglia 1907; Goglia 1930) and press reports.

The objectives of such initiatives, especially of the Committee for the Promotion of Chamber Music, was to develop the taste and interest of the audiences, educate them, and encourage local musicians to make quality chamber music themselves. Third, the Committee's elitist tendencies are also evident in special socially organized concerts for distinguished and non-standard audiences, and the reviews emphasised the presence of the political elite on such occasions (such as Count Károly Khuen-Héderváry and his wife, the highest administration, and some representatives of the House of Habsburg, some of them even being members of the Committee). Thus, through the organisation of chamber concerts, the elitism of the music salon was fully achieved on a larger scale. Fourth, with the development of the Musikverein school, especially after 1890, when its structure showed all the features of a conservatory, the Committee's incentives began to yield more and more results, especially owing to the model of high-quality and attractive invited ensembles and demanding repertoire. This resulted in the greater engagement of chamber music teachers at the Musikverein's school, and thus more frequent student performances in chamber ensembles. At the same time, music-school teachers were increasingly organized into more or less long-lived ensembles, without isolating their performances (only) to the level of salon music, i.e., private musical entertainment. An almost symbolic turning point, after the dissolution of the Committee for the Promotion of Chamber Music at the end of 1918, was the founding of the Zagreb Quartet in 1919, with excellent domestic musicians, whose activity was not interrupted even in turbulent times. These same musicians influenced the foundation of a series of other chamber ensembles of various specialized types (including the Zagreb Soloists with Antonio Janigro, in 1953), which is still active today.

BIBLIOGRAPHY

AGRAMER 1894
'Concerte', in: *Agramer Zeitung*, 15 January 1894, p. 5.

GOGLIA 1907
[GOGLIA, Antun]. *Deset godišta komorne glazbe 1897-1906*, Zagreb, Odbor za unapredjivanje komorne glazbe u Zagrebu, [1907].

GOGLIA 1930
ID. *Komorna muzika u Zagrebu*, Zagreb, Tisak nadbiskupske tiskare, offprint from the journal *Sv. Cecilija*, 1930.

JEIĆ 2018
JEIĆ, Jadran. 'Ludmilla Weiser – prva profesionalna hrvatska violinistica i violinska virtuoskinja. Bio-bibliografska studija prigodom 170 godina od njezina rodenja', in: *Arti musices*, XLIX/1 (2018), pp. 69-108.

Katalinić 2014
Katalinić, Vjera. 'Glazbene migracije i kulturni transfer: Vaňhal i neki suvremenici', in: *Radovi Zavoda za znanstveni rad Varaždin*, xxv (2014) pp. 219-228.

Katalinić 2015
Ead. '«Verstummt der süssen Stimme Schall»: The Destiny of Four Croatian Singers in the 'Long 19th Century", in: *Diasporas*, no. 26 (2015), pp. 153-169.

Katalinić – Majer-Bobetko 2006
Ivan Padovec (1800-1873) and His Time, edited by Vjera Katalinić and Sanja Majer-Bobetko, Zagreb, Croatian Musicological Society, 2006.

Miklaušić-Ćeran 2001
Miklaušić-Ćeran, Snježana. *Glazbeni život Zagreba u xix. stoljeću*, Zagreb, Croatian Musicological Society, 2001.

[Schulz] 1894
[Schulz, Ernst]. 'Das Concert des Böhmischen Streichquartetts', in: *Agramer Zeitung*, 20 January 1894, p. 2.

[Schulz] 1896a
[Id]. 'Kammermusik in Agram', in: *Agramer Zeitung*, 10 November 1896, p. 4.

Schulz 1896b
Id. 'Concert des Landes-Musikinstitutes', in: *Agramer Zeitung*, 1 December 1896, pp. 4-5.

Šaban 1977
Šaban, Ladislav. *150 godina Hrvatskog glazbenog zavoda*, Zagreb, Hrvatski glazbeni zavod, 1977.

Seifert 1995
Seifert, Herbert. 'Musik und Musiker der Grafen Erdödy in Kroatien im 18. Jahrhundert', in: *Studien zur Musikwissenschaft*, xliv (1995), pp. 191-208.

Šenoa 1934
Šenoa, August. *Kazališna izvješća. 1*, Zagreb, Binoza, 1934 (Sabrana djela, 15).

Tuksar et al. 2021
Music, Arts and Politics: Revolutions and Restorations in Europe and Croatia, 1815-1860, on the Occasion of 200th Anniversary of Vatroslav Lisinski and 160th Anniversary of the Death of Ban Josip Jelačić, edited by Stanislav Tuksar, Vjera Katalinić, Petra Babić and Sara Ries, Zagreb, Croatian Musicological Society, 2021.

Vuković 1998
Vuković, Jelena. *Glazbeni život Zagreba od 1890. do 1920. u orisu glazbene kritike na njemačkom jeziku*, unpublished Master's Thesis, Zagreb, University of Zagreb, Academy of Music, 1998.

Chamber Music 1850-1918: Violin and Chamber Music in Lisbon in the Early Days of the Republic

Hélder Sá
(INET-md, Universidade de Aveiro)

Introduction

THE FIRST PORTUGUESE REPUBLIC held political power from October 1910 to May 1926. This regime followed the assassination of King Carlos and his son Prince Luís Filipe in 1908, which precipitated the fall of the monarchy two years later[1]. In 1910, Lisbon was the political and musical centre of the country; it housed Portugal's only opera house, the Teatro de São Carlos (S. Carlos Theatre – TSC)[2], and the only state music school, the Royal Conservatoire[3]. The new regime significantly impacted Lisbon's musical milieu because new elites associated opera with the monarchy, which resulted in dwindling support for this genre of musical entertainment[4]. Indeed, one of the immediate consequences of the Republic was the suspension of the 1910-1911 opera season at São Carlos[5]. With opera performances cancelled, symphonic music flourished, and two new orchestras carried out regular seasons, which was unprecedented[6]. More subtle, but nonetheless evident, political change also affected chamber music performances. This chapter offers an overview of concerts that showcased the violin in chamber music performances within Lisbon, identifying key artists, repertoires, and

---

[1]. SERRÃO 2001.

[2]. In 1908, a fire destroyed S. João Theatre, in Oporto.

[3]. In 1910, the new Republican authorities renamed the Royal Lisbon Conservatoire as Lisbon Conservatoire (ROSA 2010).

[4]. CARVALHO 2011, p. 183.

[5]. MOREAU 1999, p. 161.

[6]. NERY 2015, pp. 38-41; SÁ 2022, pp. 33-126.

performance contexts during the First Portuguese Republic. The research elaborates upon the work of Teresa Cascudo and Maria José Artiaga, which focuses on the increase of instrumental performances after 1870 and examines its relevance during the Republic[7].

Cascudo provides a concise overview of Portugal's classical music scene between 1870 and 1918, delving into the key figures of this era and their activities. Particularly emphasised are the varied facets of Michel'angelo Lambertini, who played a pivotal role during this period as an entrepreneur, musicologist, music promoter, pianist, conductor, editor, musical critic, and collector of musical instruments. The publication highlights the noticeable absence of thorough studies on many prominent themes, such as the internationalisation of Portuguese musicians, opera's role as an international spectacle, the increasing prominence of instrumental music, and nationalist and modernist trends of this period. The journey of several Portuguese musicians — pianists Artur Napoleão, Óscar da Silva, Raimundo de Macedo, Alexandre Rey Colaço, and José Viana da Mota, violinists Nicolau Ribas, Bernardo Moreira de Sá, Alexandre Bettencourt, and cellists Guilhermina Suggia and David de Sousa — to prominent conservatories of the time (Leipzig, Berlin, Weimar, Frankfurt, Paris, and Brussels) contributed to bridging the Portuguese music scene with the practices of those musical hubs. This led to a particularly notable growth in chamber music concerts in Portugal.

Artiaga's study explores the transformations in concert repertoire spanning 1870 to 1900 across Portugal's major cities, Lisbon and Oporto. The findings challenge prevailing assumptions about Portuguese musical culture, particularly the perceived dominance of opera and Italian music. They unveil a multifaceted musical panorama shaped by the influence of French culture. Lyrical genres such as opera, operetta, and zarzuela were prominent, accompanied by the emergence of various chamber music ensembles and recitals. Furthermore, the study underscores the pivotal role of Austro-German repertoire, which gained increasing significance, particularly from 1879 onwards, within the realm of instrumental music. This shift marks a distinct departure from previous assumptions and aligns Portuguese musical practices more closely with the Austro-German tradition during this period.

My survey in this chapter addresses two main categories of events: those featuring foreign touring violinists, and still others showcasing musicians living in Portugal. I begin with recitals given by the Sociedade de Concertos de Lisboa (Lisbon Concert Society – SCL), an association that hired only foreign violinists during the period my study concerns. In the second part of the chapter, I discuss the activity of resident violinists, with a focus on several specific case studies.

---

[7].   CASCUDO 2002; ARTIAGA 2007.

FOREIGN VIOLINISTS

Michel'angelo Lambertini, José Viana da Mota, Luís de Freitas Branco, Alberto Pedroso, Alberto Joyce, Cecil Mackee and Pedro Joyce Dinis created the Sociedade de Concertos de Lisboa (Lisbon Concert Society – SCL) in 1917[8]. During the First Republic, this society hosted recitals by internationally acclaimed violinists. The society's work might be considered the extension of a similar initiative carried out earlier by the Sociedade de Música de Câmara (Chamber Music Society – SMC). Although the society folded in 1911, its activities significantly impacted the Lisbon music scene during the first decade of the 1900s[9]. The programming of these societies aligns with a movement towards the assimilation of Portuguese musical practices with European conventions. Dating back to the mid-nineteenth century, this movement is characterised by a proliferation of associations dedicated to the promotion and performance of instrumental music. According to Cascudo, this intensification became feasible as a result of a growing appreciation for instrumental works by prominent composers of the Baroque and Classical periods. This was coupled with advancements in the German music printing industry, which allowed for the complete printing of compositions by J. S. Bach, Ludwig van Beethoven, Felix Mendelssohn, W. A. Mozart, and Robert Schumann[10].

Over ten seasons between 1900 and 1911, the Chamber Music Society organized 76 concerts. It also promoted a short-lived music school dedicated to this repertoire. Early concerts were spearheaded by a resident string quartet, whose members included Francisco Benetó (violin), Cecil Mackee (violin), António Lamas (viola), and Luís da Cunha Menezes (cello). Subsequently, more Portuguese musicians became involved in the initiative, with the majority of the programming being ensured by national instrumentalists. The SMC also hired well-known foreign performers such as violinists Mathieu Crickboom, Jacques Thibaud, and Eugène Ysaÿe. A further remarkable initiative of the SMC was a composition competition for violin and piano sonatas and string quartets, held in 1908-1909[11]. At the beginning of the Republic, during the SMC's last regular season (1910-1911)[12], the society's five recitals included sonatas for violin and piano by Edvard Grieg, Guillaume Lekeu, and Luís de Freitas Branco, with trios and quartets by Beethoven, Grieg, Joseph Haydn, Mendelssohn, Carl Reinecke, and Schumann, as well as August Klughardt's Piano Quintet, and Johan Svendsen's Octet (see TABLE 1, p. 268).

---

[8]. BASTOS 2010, p. 1229; TAVARES 2015.

[9]. MACHADO 2002, pp. 77-82.

[10]. CASCUDO 2002, pp. 61, 65.

[11]. *Ibidem*, p. 81. The winners were Luís de Freitas Branco with his Violin Sonata No. 1 and Júlio Neuparth with the String Quartet Op. 28.

[12]. In 1914, SMC tried to resume its activity with two concerts (*ibidem*, p. 82).

TABLE 1: 1910-1911 SEASON, SMC[13]

28 December 1910: George F. Handel – Sonata for two violins; **Joseph Haydn** – Trio (not specified); **Ludwig Van Beethoven** – Quartet (not specified) by Francisco Benetó, Cecil Mackee (violins), António Lamas (viola) Luís da Cunha Menezes (cello), Isaura Lambertini (piano) (*E.M.*, 8 Jan. 1911, 7; *A.M.*, 15 Dec. 1910, 240; 31 Dec. 1910, 246).

30 January 1911: Carl Reinecke – Piano Trio Op. 38; Edvard Grieg – String Quartet Op. 27 by Francisco Benetó, Cecil Mackee (violins), António Lamas (viola), Luís da Cunha Menezes (cello), Ofélia Freire (piano) (*E.M.*, 5 Feb. 1911, 6; *A.M.*, 15 Jan. 1915, 7; 31 Jan. 1911, 14).

22 February 1911: Antonín Dvořák – String Quartet Op. 96; **Edvard Grieg** – Violin Sonata Op. 13; **August Klughardt** – Piano Quintet Op. 43 by Francisco Benetó, Cecil Mackee (violins), António Lamas (viola), Luís da Cunha Menezes (cello), Luísa Campos (violin), Ester Campos (piano) (*A. M.*, 28 Feb. 1911, 31).

6 April 1911: Ludwig Van Beethoven – Piano Trio (not specified) by Isaura Lambertini (piano), Cecil Mackee (violin), Camila Avila (cello); **Luís de Freitas Branco** – Violin Sonata no. 1 by Francisco Benetó (violin), Carlos Andrade (piano); **Robert Schumann** – String Quartet (not specified) by Francisco Benetó, Estela d'Ávila (violins), António Lamas (viola), Camila d'Avila (cello) (*A. M.*, 15 Apr. 1911, 57).

14 June 1911: Felix Mendelssohn – Piano Quartet by Michel'angelo Lambertini (piano), Francisco Benetó (violin), Cecil Mackee (viola), Luís da Cunha Menezes (cello); **Guillaume Lekeu** – Violin Sonata by Michel'angelo Lambertini (piano), Francisco Benetó (violin); **Johan Svendsen** – String Octet by Luísa Campos, Estela d'Ávila, Branca Ochoa, Francisco Benetó (violins), Pedro de Freitas Branco, Cecil Mackee (violas), Somers Cocks, Luís da Cunha Menezes (cellos) (*A. M.*, 15 Jun. 1911, 95).

After this season came to an end, a critique, likely written by Michel'angelo Lambertini (one of the promoters of both societies and editor of the magazine *A Arte Musical*), highlighted the challenges of gaining acceptance from the Lisbon audience[14]. It was considered unsustainable to maintain the same programming approach, based on performing significant chamber music compositions, in the future. Thus, the SMC promoters sought a different model, founded on virtuosity, and still seen as the ideal approach in «musically semi-barbaric» countries like Portugal. To achieve this, the society was willing to increase the engagement of renowned performers for recitals featuring instrumental and vocal duos, with the intention of avoiding virtuosity that lacked musical depth, which the critic referred to as «impure virtuosity». This endeavour was not successful, as the society concluded its activities shortly thereafter. Only later, with the Lisbon Concert Society, would this concept be developed, as we will see.

---

[13]. *Eco Musical* (*E. M.*) and *A Arte Musical* (*A. M.*).
[14]. *ARTE* 1911, p. 175.

Between 1918 and 1925, the Lisbon Concert Society held its recitals at the Teatro República (Republic Theatre)[15] and the S. Carlos Theatre. In this period, SCL showcased nine violinists in performances of duos with piano, two trios, and six quartets, over a total of 38 recitals (see Tables 2 and 3)[16].

Table 2: Violin and Piano Recitals, SCL

Dates	Musicians	Place
19 and 21 March 1918	Francisco Costa (vn), Tomás Teran (pf)	TSL
11 and 12 June 1918	Juan Maném (vn), José Viana da Mota (pf)*	TSL
13 and 14 April 1919	Jules Boucherit (vn), Magdalena Tagliaferro (pf)	TSL
16 and 17 March 1920	Mathieu Crickboom (vn), Marthe Dron (pf)	TSC
8 and 9 November 1920	Lydie Demergian (vn), Andre Solomon (pf)	TSC
27 and 29 November 1920	Henry Wagemans (vn), Lazare Levy (pf)	TSC
28 and 30 April 1923	Paul Kochanski (vn), Tomás Teran (pf)	TSC
3 and 4 June 1924	Manuel Quiroga (vn), José Castro (pf)	TSC
12 and 13 November 1925	René Benedetti (vn), André Lermythe (pf)	TSC

*. The cellist Pablo Casals also played at this concert.

Table 3: Trios and Quartets, SCL

Dates	Musicians	Place
28 and 30 January 1918	**Paris Trio***: Yvonne Astruc (vn), Sra Marguerite Caponsachi (vc), Lucie Caffaret (pf)	TSL
7 January 1920	**Ricardo Viñes Trio**: Joseph Bilewski (vn), André Levy (vc), Ricardo Viñes (pf)	TSC
18, 19, and 20 April 1920	**Rosé Quartet**: Arnold Rosé (vn), Paul Fischer (vn), Anton Ruziska (va), Friedrich Buxbaum (vc)	TSC
29 and 30 March 1921	**Rosé Quartet**: Arnold Rosé (vn), Paul Fischer (vn), Anton Ruziska (va), Friedrich Buxbaum (vc)	TSC
21 and 22 April 1921	**Poulet Quartet**: Gaston Poulet (vn) Henri Giraud (vn), Émile Macon (va), Louis Ruyssen (vc)	TSC
22 and 23 May 1923	**Hague Quartet**: Sam Swaap (vn), Adolf Poth (vn), Jean Devert (va), Charles van Isterdael (vc)	TSC

[15]. This theatre was inaugurated in 1894 with the designation Teatro Dona Amélia, in honour of the queen of Portugal at that time. It was later renamed as Teatro S. Luís, a name it still carries today, in memory of one of its main advocates, Luís de Braga Júnior, the Viscount of São Luiz de Braga. Between 1910 and 1928, it was known as Teatro República.

[16]. Moreau 1999; Tavares 2015.

7 and 8 May 1924	**Léner Quartet**: Jeno Léner (vn), Josef Smilovits (vn), Sandor Roth (va), Imre Hartmann (vc)	TSC
11 and 12 December 1924	**Zimmer Quartet**: Albert Zimmer (vn), Frédéric Ghigo (vn), Louis Baroen (va), Jacques Gaillard (vc)	TSC
25 and 26 May 1925	**Paris Trio**: Yvonne Astruc (vn), Marguerite Caponsacchi (vc), Maledeine de Valmalète (pf)	TSC
29 and 30 December 1925	**Pró-Arte Quartet**: Alphonse Onnou (vn), Laurent Halleux (vn), Germain Prévost (va), Robert Maas (vc)	TSC

*. The pianist M. Jeiseler also played in this concert.

As evidenced by the preceding data, all violinists who performed at the SCL during this timeframe were of foreign origin. This trait is reminiscent of another institution, the Orpheon Portuense, located in Oporto[17]. A comparative analysis of the performances offered by these two societies reveals instances where certain ensembles played in both cities within a few days of each other, implying potential collaboration between the promoters to engage performers and likely sharing some of the associated costs[18].

The duo repertoire for the Lisbon Concert Society was varied, featuring 37 composers from the Baroque to the early twentieth century (GRAPH 1)[19]. Fritz Kreisler emerges as the composer most represented in these events, with 16 presentations (half of the recitals had one or two pieces), followed by Beethoven (13), Camille Saint-Säens (10), J. S. Bach (8), Giuseppe Tartini (7), and Franz Schubert (5).

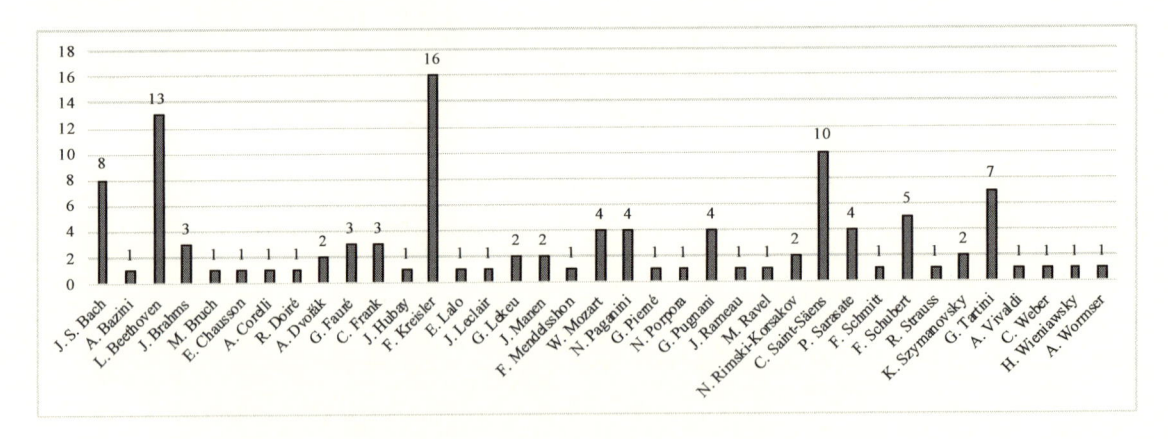

GRAPH 1: VIOLIN AND PIANO REPERTOIRE BY COMPOSER, SCL, 1917-1926

---

[17]. ARAÚJO 2014.

[18]. Concerts with the same groups at Orpheon Portuense (HORA 2014): Paris Trio — 3 and 5 January 1920; Rosé Quartet — 12 and 14 April 1920; Rosé Quartet — 31 March and 1 April 1921; Zimmer Quartet — 13 and 19 December 1924.

[19]. MOREAU 1999; TAVARES 2015.

Among the features less frequently observed in SCL programmes was the incorporation of new compositions. Even so, national premieres like Kreisler's miniatures, Karol Szymanowski's *Nocturne and Tarantella* Op. 28, *Mithes* Op. 30, and Maurice Ravel's *Tzigane* (given in Lisbon just one year after its London premiere) were included[20]. With respect to Kreisler's compositions, six out of the eight violinists in duos performed them, showcasing a genuine trend among virtuosos of that era. Conversely, Szymanowski's works were featured by just two violinists — Paul Kochansky and René Benedetti — with the former closely collaborating and premiering several of the composer's pieces.

These premieres resonated in the Lisbon press. In the case of the performances of *Mithes* and *Tzigane*, by René Benedetti and pianist André Lermythe, in November 1925, Luís de Freitas Branco, one of the most notable Portuguese composers of this period, hastened to analyse the musicians' performance. He characterized Benedetti as a competent violinist, endowed with good technique, albeit with a weak sound and «lacking an excess of personality». He described Lermythe as a «too discreet accompanist» before delving into considerations about Szymanowski and Ravel and their compositions. Regarding *Tzigane*, the critic emphasised Ravel's irony and genius:

> As he had already done in the ingenious ballet *La Valse*, based on Viennese dance patterns, he resorted to technical steps, types of rhythm, special cadences and other characteristic elements of Bohemian arias by geniuses such as Tivadar Nachez or [Pablo de] Sarasate, and created a masterpiece, evoking the old pieces of virtuosity from the good Romantic times of Wieniawski or Vieuxtemps. A very modern paradox! The genre that overshadows cultured and serious musicians: the virtuosity piece, adopted by one of our most cultured and refined composers[21]!

Trios and quartets with violin by Beethoven loomed large in 16 of 20 recitals, with quartets representing a full 75 percent of the repertoire featured at these events. Audiences were treated to works by Mozart (7), and Johannes Brahms (6). Haydn, Schubert, and Schumann also figured prominently (5 each) (see Graph 2, p. 272)[22].

---

[20]. See Schwarz 1995. Some of Kreisler's compositions were attributed to other composers. Later, Kreisler admitted authorship.

[21]. Freitas Branco 1925, p. 2: «Como já tinha feito no genial bailado "A Valsa", para as formulas da dansa [*sic*] vienense, recorreu aos passos de técnica, aos tipos de ritmo, ás cadencias especiais e mais elementos característicos das arias boémias do genero Tivadar Nachez ou Sarasate, e criou uma obra-prima, evocação das velhas peças de virtuosidade dos bons tempos românticos de Wieniawsky ou Vieuxtemps. Paradoxo bem moderno! O género que dantes mais fazia velar a face aos músicos cultos e sérios: a peça de virtuosidade, adoptado por um dos compositores mais cultos e requintados da época actual!».

[22]. Moreau 1999; Tavares 2015.

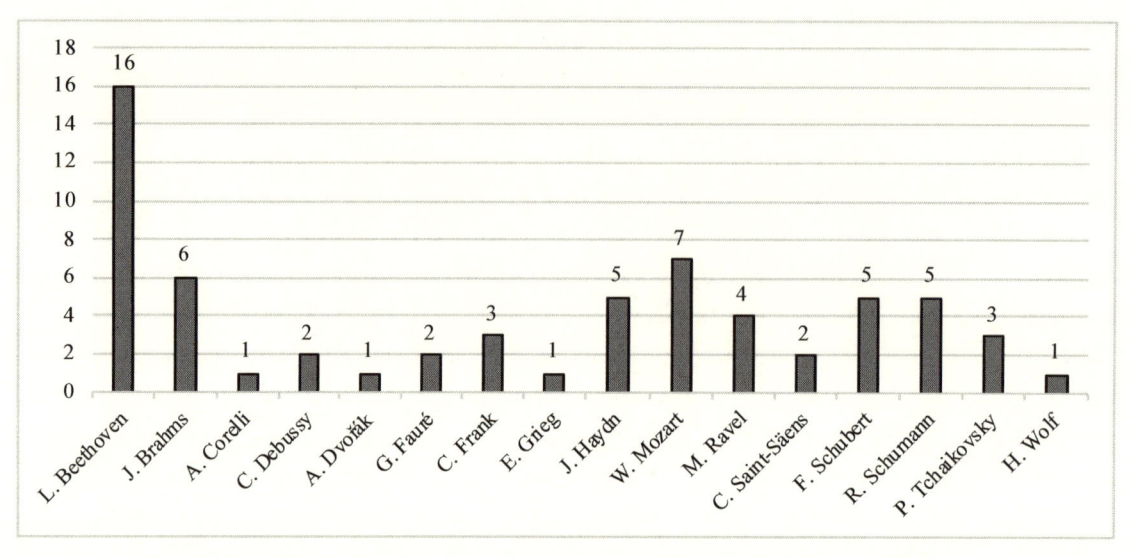

GRAPH 2: TRIOS AND QUARTETS WITH VIOLIN BY COMPOSER, SCL, 1917-1926

The number of composers represented in performances by these ensembles is much smaller than those given by duos (16 *versus* 37 composers). The latter's repertoire was steeped in the Classic and Early Romantic canon — Haydn, Mozart, Beethoven, and Schubert — and their followers. But these musicians also included works by living or recently deceased composers such as Hugo Wolf, Antonín Dvořák, Claude Debussy, Camille Saint-Saëns, Gabriel Fauré, and Maurice Ravel. In sum, they hail mainly from Central Europe, especially France, Austria, and Germany.

Taking a broader view, it should be noted that Beethoven's absolute prominence in these recitals is identical to repertoires that had been played at quartet societies all over Europe since the nineteenth century[23]. Indeed, with regard to the Portuguese context, Artiaga has shown the predominance of compositions by Beethoven, Mendelssohn, and Haydn in chamber music events presented in Lisbon between 1874 and 1876. She further observed that the music of Beethoven, Mendelssohn, and Strauss dominated concert programs during the last three decades of the nineteenth century.

Without the performances of the duos, the events promoted by SCL could hardly be viewed as a 'new' form of musical entertainment for the recently established Republic. Indeed, these duets seem to align with the new programming model that Lambertini advocated for the Chamber Music Society in 1911, emphasising virtuosity to meet the expectations of Lisbon audiences. This approach was only successfully implemented in the SCL.

---

[23].   See MAHAIM – LEVIN 1996; WEBER 2008; CASCUDO 2021.

Resident Violinists

Many of the concerts in which resident violinists took part could be described as benefit concerts, following the prevalent model in Europe during the 1800s. Francisco Benetó (1875-1945) was probably the most sought-after violinist for these concerts and was described as «artist» or «teacher», a move that distinguished him from amateur musicians who also participated in these events. On 27 June 1912, the pianist Alfredo Napoleão (1842-1917) promoted a concert at the hall of the *Illustração Portugueza*, a Lisbon magazine. He collaborated with three musicians, including Benetó and amateurs Leonor de Magalhães Correia (singer) and Esther Bensaúde (pianist)[24]. The programme included eight moments that alternated music for solo piano, violin and piano, and voice and piano. It featured late Classical and Romantic repertoire from Beethoven, Fryderyk Chopin, Robert Schumann, Mendelssohn, Schubert, Richard Wagner, Anton Rubinstein, and Alfredo Napoleão himself. According to the critic for *Illustração Portuguesa*, Benetó played Beethoven's Sonata Op. 24 and Napoleão's *Allegro de Concert* Op. 49[25] «brilliantly»[26].

Apart from playing in events organized by other musicians and institutions, Benetó, as a few other violinists, also promoted his own recitals, known as «Benetó Concerts». For these events, Benetó played virtuosic pieces, sonatas and concertos, frequently accompanied by piano or small orchestras that included his students and friends. On 8 April 1915, Benetó performed, for the first time in Portugal, *La Chasse* by Kreisler/Cartier, *Symphonie espagnole* (Spanish Symphony) by Édouard Lalo, *Pierrot (Serenade)* by Alberto Randegger and *Scherzo Tarantellá* by Henryk Wieniawski[27] (see Ill. 1, p. 274). The critic Luís Cunha praised Benetó's mastery and virtuosity, also highlighting his merit as a teacher for having managed to «establish a notable bow school»[28]. The event also featured vocal and piano performances by amateurs Maria Ferraz Bravo and Irene Gomes Teixeira, respectively, similar to Napoleão's concert.

The presence of these amateur performers was also notable in a unique concert series, which was uncommon in the Lisbon music scene: the complete presentation of Beethoven's violin sonatas by pianist Alexandre Rey Colaço (1854-1928) and violinist Júlio Cardona (1879-

---

[24]. Esther Bensaúde probably joined Leonor Correia at the piano.

[25]. Napoleão composed this seldomly-played piece in the 1890s while living between Rio de Janeiro and Buenos Aires. In this concert, he also played *Fantasia e 2ª Polonaise*, Op. 59 for piano solo. To consult his catalogue, see Pinto 1913, pp. 60-61.

[26]. Michel'angelo Lambertini's Music Programme Collection (1909-1916), Biblioteca Nacional de Portugal, BNP (Portuguese National Library), Shelfmark: M 5 R, 2116. See also *A Arte Musical*, 30 June 1912, p. 112; *Illustração Portuguesa*, 8 July 1912, p. 55.

[27]. BNP, Shelfmark: M 5 R, 2217.

[28]. Cunha 1915, p. 61.

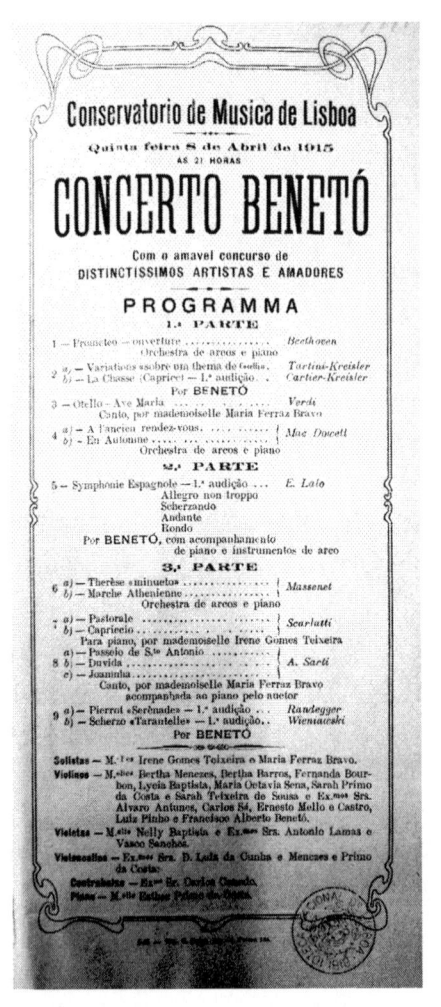

ILL. 1: Francisco Benetó's concert, 8 April 1915, Lisbon Conservatoire, BNP.

1950)[29]. Thematic orchestral concerts dedicated to German or French music, or specifically to Wagner or Beethoven, were quite frequent. However, events focusing on a single composer or featuring a whole set of compositions were unusual in Lisbon. Colaço and Cardona, both teachers at the Lisbon Conservatoire, accomplished the cycle through five recitals held between January and March of 1915. These performances took place at the *Grémio Literário*, a society founded in 1846 by renowned Portuguese figures like historian Alexandre Herculano and poet Almeida Garrett with the aim of fostering social interaction and intellectual activity among its members.

---

[29]. SÁ 2019; SÁ 2022, pp. 168-175. Later, Cardona and Colaço intended to play the Piano Trios by Beethoven with the cellist João Passos. The first concert was on November 18, 1915, but, due to several problems, they cancelled the project (see *A Arte Musical*, 15 November 1915, p. 191; 30 November 1915, p. 198; *A Capital*, 17 November 1915, p. 2).

ILL. 2: First recital of the Beethoven Violin Sonatas by Colaço and Cardona, 28 January 1915, Grémio Literário, EJC.

As mentioned earlier, the performances also featured participation by amateur singers and Colaço's piano students, who also played music by Beethoven. These recitals garnered media coverage, which emphasised Beethoven's genius as well as the high standing and competence of the performers. The reviewer for *Eco Musical* unequivocally underscored the value of these events, writing:

> Colaço proposed to play these ten colossal portions of Beethoven's heritage chronologically. Even if they aren't the most valuable part of that heritage, their complete knowledge and comparative study is quite interesting. [...] Colaço partnered for this project with Júlio Cardona, a violinist with an accomplished reputation and an easy and remarkable technique[30].

---

[30]. *Eco* 1915: «Colaço propôs-se apresentar pela ordem cronológica essas dez parcelas da colossal herança que Beethoven deixou à posteridade, e conquanto elas não sejam, em geral, o mais valioso quinhão dessa herança, o seu conhecimento integral dando ocasião ao estudo comparativo, não deixa de ser sumamente interessante. [...] Colaço, neste seu novo empreendimento é coadjuvado por Júlio Cardona, um violinista cuja reputação está feita e

In the first recital (on 28 January 1915), Colaço and Cardona played the two Sonatas Op. 12, Nos. 1 and 2 and *Romance* Op. 40[31] (see ILL. 2, p. 275). *Ecco Artístico* published a favourable review: «The performance was clean, with refined attention to the score. Júlio Cardona's tuning was precise, and the performance was wise enough regarding what the master wrote and with no other effects»[32]. If we consider accounts of these performances in the press, the following recitals demonstrated Colaço's and Cardona's artistic expertise and prestige in Lisbon. However, the scope of these presentations was significantly limited to audiences in Lisbon, as they were exclusively intended for the members of *Grémio Literário*.

The lack of audience attendance is indeed a prevalent characteristic in numerous other chamber music concerts from this period in Lisbon, which did not attain the same level of popularity as symphonic concerts. In the events organized by Benetó, as well as the series by Colaço and Cardona, efforts were made to overcome this limitation through the joint participation of students and teachers, thereby maximizing the number of attendees at these performances.

The Academia de Amadores de Música (Academy of Music Amateurs – AAM) and the Sociedade Nacional de Música de Câmara (National Society of Chamber Music – SNMC) also played significant roles, providing platforms for resident violinists in Lisbon during the First Republic. The former was established in 1884 and encompassed musical education and the promotion of both orchestral and chamber concerts[33]. The AAM had a significant musical impact from its inception and continued to operate during the First Republic, although its activity diminished during this period, with efforts focused on chamber music concerts at the expense of orchestral concerts. In contrast, the SNMC, was solely dedicated to concert promotion and remained active from 1919 to 1974[34]. This institution was established through

---

que tanto se distingue por uma facilidade técnica admirável». (The copy consulted for this chapter may be found in Espólio Júlio Cardona, EJC, Museu Nacional da Música, Shelfmark: 3337.)

[31].   EJC, Shelfmark: 2717. There were also two voice pieces and a piano Sonata in the programme: *In questa tomba oscura* (In this Dark Tomb) WoO 133 and *Die Ehre Gottes aus der Natur* (The Glory of God in Nature) Op. 48 No. 4 by Angelo da Mota Marques (voice) and Francesco Codivilla (piano) and *Andante Favori* WoO 57 played by Ema Campos.

[32].   EJC, Shelfmark: 3337: «A execução foi bastante cuidada sendo de notar o escrupulo que houve em observar a partitura na sua integralidade. Júlio Cardona esteve preciso na afinação e consciencioso na execução não se preocupando com efeitos para se sentir estritamente ao que o mestre escreveu».

[33].   Apart from the S. Carlos Theatre Orchestra, mainly dedicated to opera, the AAM orchestra, which was composed of a mix of students, professional and amateur musicians — a unique feature in the Portuguese musical context — was the only regular orchestra in Lisbon from the 1890s to the 1910s. This institution, along with its violin teachers like Victor Hussla and Andrés Goñi, played a key role in mentoring female violinists, especially considering that during the nineteenth century, playing the violin in Portugal was largely limited to men (ROSA 2009, pp. 170-217; CASCUDO 2010, pp. 8-9; SÁ 2022, pp. 274-288).

[34].   BASTOS 2010, p. 1230.

the initiative of the violinist António Fernando Cabral, alongside João Carlos Valente and João Gomes da Silva, musicians in the early stages of their respective careers. To advance their undertaking, these musicians sought out the collaboration of three experienced educators from the Lisbon Conservatory: the pianist José Viana da Mota, then serving as the Conservatory's headmaster; Júlio Cardona, appointed as the artistic director and conductor of the Society's orchestra; and the composer Luís de Freitas Branco, who assumed the role of conductor for the Orpheon[35].

Another common characteristic of events promoted by these institutions is the significant inclusion of Portuguese composers, mostly contemporaries and part of the Lisbon musical circle, alongside canonical repertoire. On 16 May 1916, pianist and composer António Fragoso (1897-1918) premiered his Trio Op. 2 for violin, cello, and piano in a recital exclusively devoted to his compositions[36]. Flaviano Rodrigues (violin), João Passos (cello) and Fragoso played this trio, dedicated to Tomás Borba, Fragoso's teacher at the Conservatoire and head of the AAM. The following year, on 2 June 1917, Fragoso promoted another recital at the Academy, presenting *Suite Romantique* (Romantic Suite) for violin and piano with Fernando Cabral (1900-1976). This violinist, who premiered several compositions by António Fragoso and Frederico de Freitas (1902-1980), also performed Beethoven's Violin Sonata Op. 30 No. 2, Fauré's *Berceuse* and Philipp Scharwenka's *Alla Polacca* Op. 104 No. 4.

The violinist and composer Flaviano Rodrigues (1891-1970) was another regular presence at the AAM. Some of his compositions for violin and piano — *Um Fado*, *Poemeto*, and *Romanza* — were performed by Flaviano himself during the final years of the Republic, between 1922 and 1925, alongside other pieces such as *Fantasie* and *Le Cigne* (The Swan) by Saint-Saëns, *Legende* by Henryk Wieniawski, and *Danses Tziganes* (Gipsy Dances) by Tivadar Nachéz[37] (see ILL. 3, p. 278).

In the early seasons of the Sociedade Nacional de Música de Câmara, the most prominent violinists were Fernando Cabral, one of the promoters and his former teacher, Júlio Cardona. The inaugural concert of this society, held on 11 April 1920, was attended by high-ranking political figures, including the President of the Republic and the Minister of Education, and took place in the hall of the Lisbon Conservatory[38]. The event began with Cardona and José Viana da Mota playing Fauré's Violin Sonata Op. 13. The remaining works included songs by Giacomo Carissimi, Fauré and Pierre-Alexandre Monsigny, two choral works by J. S. Bach, and a *Concerto Grosso* by Handel, played by a 28-piece orchestra[39].

---

[35]. *Revista do Conservatório Nacional de Música*, 1 May 1920, pp. 4-5.

[36]. AAM Archive (AAAM), *Programas 1909-1927*.

[37]. *Ibidem*, 14 May 1922.

[38]. *Revista do Conservatório Nacional*, 1 May 1920, p. 6.

[39]. Arquivo Histórico do Conservatório Nacional (*National Conservatory Historical Archive* – AHCN), Shelfmark Box 702. Bundle. 1811. *Aluguer do Salão, Documentos referentes a 1915-1921*.

ILL. 3: Academia of Music Amateurs' concert, 14 May 1922, AAAM.

During the first season, Fernando Cabral's performances included Guillaume Lekeu's Violin Sonata, Luís de Freitas Branco's String Quartet, Mozart's Piano Quartet K. 478, António Tomás de Lima's Trio, Fragoso's *Suite Romantique* and Beethoven's *Romance* Op. 40 and Sonata Op. 96. The focus on programming Portuguese composers was widely recognized by critics from the outset. In the second concert, the SNMC presented Freitas Branco's String Quartet in full premiere, prompting a comment from Adriano Mereia, in *Diário de Notícias*:

> In yesterday's concert, the spotlight fell on Freitas Branco's "String Quartet",
> and it's worth mentioning that the new musical ensemble played a role in the
> selection process. The piece, now introduced by four accomplished performers[40], is

---

40.   Fernando Cabral and Armando Gomes (violins), Asdrubal Godinho (viola) and Júlio Almada (cello).

deserving of recognition and applause. Having rested in a drawer for an extended period, waiting for compassionate hands to bring it to the forefront, it has finally emerged as a testament to rectify an injustice. Especially noteworthy is that the "Quartet", composed, to the best of our knowledge, a decade ago, bears the hallmark of its era in terms of both its essence and artistry. It exhibits a considerable touch of impressionism, within a form that transcends traditional moulds, and through the deliberate use of harmony as a potent vehicle for expression, there is also an undeniable technical skill[41].

In subsequent seasons, this society introduced thematic concerts focused on a single composer, such as Beethoven and J. S. Bach, as well as featuring Portuguese music. The most prominent distinction between the National Society of Chamber Music and the Lisbon Concert Society lies in the nationality of their performers. The former predominantly engaged national instrumentalists, whereas the events of the latter were consistently presented by international soloists, who came to Lisbon expressly for this purpose. Another distinction between this society and the Lisbon Concert Society lies in the number of performers featured in each event. In the gatherings organized by the SNMC, as well as in those by the AAM, the programs were distributed among multiple performers, rather than being entrusted to a single chamber music group as was the case in SCL's events.

Alongside the gamut of activities discussed so far, resident violinists also took part in chamber music ensembles contracted by numerous theatres within the city[42]. These ensembles were primarily sextets, comprising two violins, a viola, a cello, a double bass, and a piano, and they played a significant role in enhancing the local music scene with a diverse repertoire that encompassed salon and art music. Sometimes their performances were combined with other types of entertainment such as moving pictures.

On 18 February 1913, for instance, at the Trindade Hall, a *Soirèe Concerto* was, in fact, a three-part event[43]. It included the screening of films in the first and third parts. Performed by the resident sextet, the purely musical second part of the event featured music by Saint-Saëns and Ernest Guiraud. Violinist António Tomás de Lima (1887-1950) also played Hubert

---

[41]. Mereia 1920, p. 2: «No concerto de ontem coube a vez ao "Quarteto de Cordas" de Freitas Branco, e dever é dizer-se que a nova agremiação musical teve dedo na escolha, porque a obra agora tornada conhecida por quatro executantes de mérito, é das dignas de se considerarem e aplaudirem. Deixada por mais tempo amarelecer numa gaveta à espera que mãos piedosas a trouxessem à luz, surgia simplesmente uma iniquidade. Tanto mais que o "Quarteto" tendo, pelo que sabemos, quase um decénio de escrita, tem também estampada, pelo espírito e pela factura, a época a que pertence. Há nele uma boa dose de impressionismo na forma menos cingida aos antigos moldes e no emprego da harmonia como meio expressivo muito determinante, e há, ao mesmo tempo, indiscutível habilidade técnica».

[42]. *Boletim da Associação de Classe dos Músicos Portugueses* (1911-1913), BNP, Shelfmark: P.P. 16961 V.

[43]. BNP, Shelfmark: M 5 R, 2146.

ILL. 4: Olympia and Trindade Theatre's advertisement, BNP.

Léonard's *Souvenir de Haydn* Op. 2 and Charles Oberthur's *Berceuse* Op. 299 arranged for violin, harp, and cello. The impresario who ran this theatre also managed the Olympia Hall and promoted concerts joining the two sextets. In its advertisements, the company highlighted musicians' names as an assurance of quality (see ILL. 4). In these advertisements, the violinists Francisco Benetó, Laureano Forsini, Flaviano Rodrigues, Carlos Sá, César Leiria, Francisco Remartinez, João Pires, Frederico Fonseca, and Victor Bregante are prominently featured, as they were among the most sought-after performers in Lisbon's musical circles.

The following season, between 15 November 1914, and 3 January 1915, the Olympia Theatre held eight chamber music sessions. Dedicated to the 'Classical repertoire', they took place on Saturdays, at four o'clock in the afternoon. A third of the programme included Beethoven's music. Mozart, Schubert, Grieg, César Franck, Alexandre Moskowsky, Saint-Saëns and Júlio Neuparth's Quartet were part of the selection. According to Ernesto Vieira, a well-known teacher, musicologist and critic of that period, this concert cycle had small audiences because the concerts were scheduled at inconvenient times, which led to economic losses for the promoter[44]. Once again, the same pattern previously identified by Artiaga before the Republic emerges: Austro-German and francophone composers, with Beethoven standing out, are among the most frequently presented in Lisbon theatres in terms of the classical repertoire. There is often a concern to include national composers in the programming.

CONCLUSION

The programmes and performers I have enumerated thus far suggest meaningful nuances with respect to the involvement of violinists performing chamber music in Lisbon during the First Republic. What must also be taken into account is the position and influence of foreign soloists compared to resident musicians. The involvement of foreign virtuosos in the programming of the Lisbon Concert Society represented a significant contrast compared to other concert-promoting organisations such as the Chamber Music Society, the Academy of Music Amateurs, and the National Society of Chamber Music. In the pre-Republican era, the Chamber Music Society had predominantly relied on national or locally-based instrumentalists, occasionally engaging a few international soloists. However, with the advent of the Lisbon Concert Society, there was a notable shift. Specifically concerning violinists, the programming now became the exclusive domain of foreign musicians, who were contracted to perform in two or three concerts. During the early 1920s, these violinists included Mathieu Crickboom, Paul Kochanski, and Manuel Quiroga for duo performances and Yvonne Astruc, Joseph Bilewski, Arnold Rosé, and Gaston Poulet, who participated in trios or quartets. Considering Lambertini's public statement in 1911, when the activities of the Chamber Music Society came to an end and the idea of returning to programming models based on virtuosity emerged, it is reasonable to infer that this shift aimed to reverse the limited engagement of the Lisbon audience with chamber concerts.

These violinists, a minority compared to the local instrumentalists, normally performed almost equally in piano duos and quartets, although evidence exists for three events with foreign violists playing in trios. This balance between duos, often emphasising virtuosic music, and ensembles composed of three or four members, appears to once again align with Lambertini's vision, seeking to satisfy both the interests of the Lisbon audience and society's sustainability, and echoing the goals pursued in the Chamber Music Society.

---

[44].   *Eco Musical*, 1 February 1914, pp. 33-34.

The repertoire performed in duos encompasses a diverse geographical and chronological range, totalling 37 composers. Among these, the most prominent were Kreisler, Beethoven, Saint-Saëns, Bach, Tartini, and Schubert. The presence of Kreisler's compositions, consistently featured in these recitals, along with the introduction of debut performances by contemporary composers, contributes a touch of modernity to a model historically associated with the nineteenth century. Less innovative was the repertoire presented by trios and quartets. In these events, canonical composers such as Beethoven, Mozart, Brahms, Schubert, Haydn, Schubert, and Schumann prevailed, generally adhering to the pattern previously verified by Artiaga in the last three decades of the nineteenth century.

With respect to resident violinists, what emerges through a study of concert programmes is their adaptability. This may be explained as an adjustment to a small musical environment, which required the ability to adapt to various settings, including orchestral and chamber music. The data suggests that local violinists mainly took part in chamber music events promoted by other musicians, schools, and musical societies. Recitals promoted by violinists were not widespread, although players such as Francisco Benetó proved notable exceptions to this tendency. Besides his participation in concerts organized by other musicians and the Chamber Music Society, where he played a pivotal role, Benetó organized annual concerts featuring his students and close friends, presenting virtuoso repertoire.

Similar to the SCL's programming, Beethoven's influence was prominent in the different highlighted contexts where resident violinists performed. The cycle presented by Cardona and Colaço, dedicated to the complete performance of Beethoven's violin sonatas, stands out as the most significant instances, even though it represents a unique occurrence within Lisbon's musical landscape. Another clear indicator of Beethoven's importance was the 'Classical Concerts' series hosted by the Olympia Theatre.

This chapter has also revealed another significant aspect related to repertoire: the presentation of music involving the violin composed by contemporary Portuguese composers, often presented as premieres. This practice was particularly highlighted in the programming of the Academy of Music Amateurs and the National Society of Chamber Music, thanks to the contributions of violinists Fernando Cabral, Júlio Cardona, and Flaviano Rodrigues.

In sum, this investigation of chamber music during the First Republic period in Lisbon underscores the absence of a substantial connection between the choice of repertoire and the performance venues. These concerts took place in a variety of locations, including auditoriums, foyers, and multipurpose halls, with no apparent consistent correlation between specific musical content and venue type or organizer. This observation underscores the dynamic nature of Lisbon's musical landscape during this time, where diverse chamber ensembles frequented a range of spaces, contributing to the city's cultural milieu.

Bibliography

Araújo 2014
Sociedade Orpheon Portuense (1881-2008): Tradição e Inovação, edited by Henrique Gomes de Araújo, Porto, Universidade Católica Editora, 2014.

Arte 1911
[Lambertini, Michel'angelo]. Untitled review, in: *A Arte Musical*, 15 November 1911.

Artiaga 2007
Artiaga, Maria José. *Continuity and Change in Three Decades of Portuguese Musical Life 1870-1900*, unpublished Ph.D. Diss., London, University of London, 2007.

Bastos 2010
Bastos, Patrícia. 'Sociedade Nacional de Música de Câmara (SNMC)', in: *EMPxx* 2010, vol. IV, p. 1230.

Carvalho 2011
Carvalho, Mário Vieira de. 'A República e as Mudanças na Cultura Musical e Músico-Teatral', in: *A Vida Cultural na Lisboa da I República (1910-1926)*, edited by Álvaro Costa Matos and João Carlos Oliveira, Lisboa, Câmara Municipal de Lisboa, 2011, pp. 165-184.

Cascudo 2002
Cascudo, Teresa. 'A Música em Portugal entre 1870 e 1918', in: *Michel'angelo Lambertini: 1862-1920*, edited by Maria Helena Trindade, Ana Paula Tudela and Carla Capelo Machado, Lisbon, Instituto Português de Museus-Museu da Música, 2002, pp. 61-71.

Cascudo 2010
Ead. 'Academia de Amadores de Música (AAM)', in: *EMPxx* 2010, vol. I, pp. 8-9.

Cascudo 2021
Un Beethoven Ibérico: Dos Siglos de Transferencia Cultural, edited by Teresa Cascudo, Granada, Comares, 2021.

Cunha 1915
Cunha, Luís. Untitled review, in: *A Arte Musical*, 15 April 1915.

Eco 1915
Untitled review, in: *Eco Musical*, 23 February 1915.

EMPxx 2010
Enciclopédia da Música em Portugal no século xx, edited by Salwa Castelo-Branco, 4 vols., Lisboa, Temas e Debates-Círculo de Leitores, 2010.

FREITAS BRANCO 1925
FREITAS BRANCO, Luís de. Untitled review, in: *Diário de Lisboa*, 18 November 1925.

HORA 2014
HORA, Tiago Manuel da. 'Orpheon Portuense (1881-2008): Actividade Artística', in: *A Sociedade Orpheon Portuense (1881-2008): Tradição e Inovação*, CD, edited by Henrique Luís Gomes de Araújo, Porto, Universidade Católica Editora, 2014.

MACHADO 2002
MACHADO, Carla Capelo. 'A Actividade Musical de Michel'angelo Lambertini', in: *Michel'angelo Lambertini 1862-1920, op. cit.*, pp. 73-91.

MAHAIM – LEVIN 1996
MAHAIM, Ivan. 'The First Complete Beethoven Quartet Cycles, 1845-1851: Historical Notes on the London Quartett Society', translated and edited by Evi Levin, in: *The Musical Quarterly*, LXXX /3 (1996), pp. 500-524.

MEREIA 1920
MEREIA, Adriano. Untitled review, in: *Diário de Notícias*, 26 April 1920.

MOREAU 1999
MOREAU, Mário. *O Teatro de S. Carlos: Dois Séculos de História. 1*, Lisbon, Hugin Editores, 1999.

NERY 2015
NERY, Rui Vieira. *Os Sons da República*, Lisbon, Imprensa Nacional Casa da Moeda, 2015.

PINTO 1913
PINTO (Sacavém), Alfredo. *Horas d'Arte (Palestras Sobre Música)*, Lisbon, Ferin, 1913.

ROSA 2009
ROSA, Joaquim Carmelo. *Struggling at the Margins: Musical Education in Lisbon (1860-1910)*, unpublished Ph.D. Diss., London, University of London, 2009.

ROSA 2010
ID. 'Escola de Música do Conservatório Nacional (CN)', in: *EMPxx* 2010, vol. II, p. 415.

SÁ 2019
SÁ, Hélder. 'As Sonatas de Ludwig van Beethoven para Piano e Violino por Alexandre Rey Colaço e Júlio Cardona: Uma Revisitação dos Concertos de 1915 através da Imprensa da Época', in: *Post-ip: Revista do Fórum Internacional de Estudos em Música e Dança*, IV (2019), pp. 106-115.

SÁ 2022
ID. *O Violino em Portugal na Primeira República: Contextos, Protagonistas e Repertórios*, unpublished Ph.D. Diss., Aveiro, Universidade de Aveiro, 2022.

SCHWARZ 2001

SCHWARZ, Boris. 'Kreisler, Fritz', in: *Grove Music Online*, <www.oxfordmusiconline.com>, accessed February 2024.

SERRÃO 2001

SERRÃO, Joaquim Veríssimo. *História de Portugal (1910-1926): História Diplomática, Social, Económica e Cultural. 12*, Lisbon, Verbo, 2001.

TAVARES 2015

TAVARES, Elsa. *A Sociedade de Concertos de Lisboa Durante e Depois da Presidência de Viana da Mota – Continuidade ou Ruptura? (1917-1960)*, unpublished Master's Diss., Lisbon, Universidade Nova de Lisboa, 2015.

WEBER 2008

WEBER, William. *The Great Transformation of Musical Taste: Concert Programming from Haydn to Brahms*, Cambridge-New York, Cambridge University Press, 2008.

NATIONAL IDENTITIES AND CULTURAL TRANSFER

Modern French Chamber Music in Britain and César Franck

David Reißfelder
(Cologne, Germany)

The decades around 1900 in musical Europe were characterised by an increasing sense of nationalism on the one hand and by intensifying international relations on the other. Musical life in late Victorian and Edwardian Britain typically demonstrates this dualism: concerts flourished, especially but not only in London, and offered the public the opportunity to become acquainted with a wide and cosmopolitan repertoire. Both prominent and less prominent composers and artists from the Continent visited the British Isles to present their works. Authoritative circles of British academics, critics, and musicians fostered this transfer while simultaneously decrying the marginalisation of homegrown music, which they emphatically promoted.

One of the most rapid transformations occurred in the Anglo-French musical liaison[1]. The introduction and dissemination of progressive French repertoire within Britain began before the turn of the century; at first, these activities were mostly received with reluctance. From around 1907, however, this cultural transfer started to gain momentum, with several French composers repeatedly presenting their works in person. Avant-garde French music was championed foremost by a small group of amateur enthusiasts: French engineer Tony Guéritte, *homme de lettres* G. Jean-Aubry, and English financial journalist and music critic Edwin Evans conceived a systematic campaign to bring French chamber music to England. Their Société des Concerts Français (1909-1915) administered a concert series in London and recitals across Britain under the auspices of local societies. In lectures and articles, critics described a lively French musical scene involving different factions that were united by their aim to present a genuine expression of a French 'national spirit'. Jean-Aubry and Evans proposed the widely held notion of a French renaissance as a pattern for how British composers could achieve the expression of their own national musical voice. The highly loaded debate surrounding a

---

[1]. This paper draws on the Ph.D. dissertation published as Reißfelder 2022.

British national music fiercely pitted Francophiles against more conservative critics such as Ernest Newman.

The music of César Franck was belatedly introduced to Britain. Practically unknown at the time of his death in 1890, Franck came into vogue shortly thereafter, with his popularity reaching its peak by 1920. His small corpus of chamber music, especially the Violin Sonata, was valued as a body of 'modern classics'. Alongside the fervent promotion of the music of his pupils and younger compatriots, Franck emerged posthumously as a key figure of the so-called modern French school. The popular success (after an initial period of irritation and resistance) of the 'school's' eventual figureheads, Claude Debussy and Maurice Ravel, was not an isolated phenomenon but followed a process of rapprochement similar to the one that characterised the reception of Franck and other precursors[2]. By the First World War, French music — to a great extent, modern chamber music — would become an integral part of British repertoire. An examination of its presence and influence in Britain adds layers to our understanding of the multi-faceted phenomenon of musical modernism. It also challenges a now superseded but still prevalent view of British musical culture as insular, reactionary, and overly Germanophile.

SAINT-SAËNS AND OTHER EARLY CONTACTS WITH FRENCH CHAMBER MUSIC

Particularly in the domain of chamber music, German repertoire had indeed dominated nineteenth-century Britain. The two most renowned series — the Musical Union (1845-1881), by violinist-impresario John Ella, and the Popular Concerts, affectionately called 'Pops' (1859-1904) — established a canon focused on 'classics' and later embraced the works of Franz Schubert, Robert Schumann, and contemporaries like Johannes Brahms and Antonín Dvořák[3]. Austro-German artists such as Joseph Joachim personified an aesthetic of musical idealism that was also taken up by composers and teachers like Hubert Parry and Charles Villiers Stanford in their endeavour to create an indigenous tradition of British instrumental music[4]. At this time, French music played little to no part in the chamber music canon. On the contrary, critics frequently associated it with long-standing stereotypes representing the very opposite of the ideals of serious instrumental music: lightness, elegance, charm, and superficiality[5].

The only French composer who managed to gain a solid position in British concert life before 1900 was Camille Saint-Saëns. He sought refuge in England from the Paris upheavals

---

[2]. For the reception of Debussy and Ravel's orchestral music in Britain, see KELLY 2020.

[3]. See BASHFORD 2007 for a detailed study of the Musical Union.

[4]. For concert programming, see WEBER 2008; for the term 'idealism', see most recently WEBER 2020. For Parry and Stanford, see DIBBLE 1992; DIBBLE 2002.

[5]. See the account of the presence of French music and a history of cultural Anglo-French relations in RODMELL 2021.

in 1871 and made his London pianistic debut that year. Hans von Bülow and Alfredo Piatti introduced his Cello Sonata Op. 32 in 1873 at the Pops. More ensemble works followed in the 1870s and were repeatedly taken up after their first performances. The Suite for Cello and Piano Op. 16 and Piano Trio Op. 18 were both played for the first time by the Dutch London-based pianist Willem Coenen as part of his series dedicated to modern chamber music. Saint-Saëns appeared as pianist for a performance of his Piano Quartet Op. 41 with Leopold Auer, Benno Holländer, and Jules Lasserre in 1876, and he turned pages for von Bülow for the Cello Sonata two years later. By 1880, pianists Edward Dannreuther, Karl Heinrich Barth, Mary Krebs, and Agnes Zimmermann, along with violinists Joachim, Wilhelm Wiener, Henry Holmes, Wilma Norman-Neruda, and Ludwig Straus, had also all performed Saint-Saëns's music in London.

Initially, Saint-Saëns enjoyed the ambiguous reputation of a Wagnerian, but English critics found in his chamber music «nothing but what is thoroughly orthodox, recalling fairy-like and fanciful themes of the Weberian school»[6]. Nevertheless, in his trifold capacity as composer, pianist (or organist), and conductor, Saint-Saëns made a name for himself in Britain and secured prestigious commissions, including one from the Philharmonic Society for the *Symphonie avec orgue* Op. 78 (1886). Like Edvard Grieg, a favourite among the English, Saint-Saëns was awarded an honorary doctorate from the Universities of both Cambridge (1893) and Oxford (1907). In the year before the orchestral commission, Saint-Saëns wrote his Violin Sonata Op. 75 for a tour in Yorkshire, premiering it with Otto Peiniger in Huddersfield in November 1885[7]. His later chamber music (including the String Quartet Op. 112, premiered by the Ysaÿe Quartet during its Popular Concerts season in 1901, see below) was acknowledged as a sound addition to the repertoire but failed to make a deeper impression on British critics. It was, as a whole, characterised as «more scholastic than inspired»[8]. References to Saint-Saëns's nationality were conspicuously absent from most press reviews. The composer owed his wide popularity to his conventional Classic-Romantic style rather than to his Frenchness.

As for Saint-Saëns's compatriots, their works were for a long time limited to scattered or solitary performances in Britain. Gabriel Fauré's Violin Sonata Op. 13 was presented in 1877 (the year of its first Paris performance) at London's Musical Union, where Édouard Lalo's Piano Trio in B minor had been played once in 1861. Charles Hallé introduced the Piano Trio Op. 32 by Benjamin Godard in 1886. It was the Dutch violinist Johannes Wolff, a favourite of Queen Victoria, who would muster the courage for a broader, systematic support of French music[9]. He announced a revival of the Musical Union in 1894 with the express purpose of

---

[6]. *The Athenaeum*, 2 June 1877, p. 713 (about the Piano Trio Op. 18).

[7]. RATNER 2002, pp. 180ff. (with later date of first performance).

[8]. *The Musical Standard*, 19 January 1901, p. 45 (about String Quartet Op. 112).

[9]. For Wolff's biography, see STRAETEN 1933, p. 373.

presenting unfamiliar chamber works, especially of French origin. In the first Wolff Musical Union concert, Cécile Chaminade and Charles-Marie Widor appeared side by side performing their own works. Later guests of honour included Saint-Saëns, Louis Diémer and the wind players Paul Taffanel and Charles Turban (in a Quintet for Piano and Winds by Anton Rubinstein), as well as Fauré alongside Francis Thomé. Most observers generally noted that French chamber music had an affinity with German models and measured it accordingly, with a slightly patronising attitude. Only a few began to discern new and original traits in the music from across the Channel:

> [...] perhaps English amateurs do not yet understand the French school, and are only in love with the stodgy, pseudo-classical style of composition affected by second-rate German composers. These defects do not belong to Mdlle. Chaminade's compositions. [...] M. Widor's compositions are exceedingly graceful and very French in tone, but they have not the fire of Mdme. Chaminade's[10].

> M. Fauré's work [Piano Quartet Op. 45] [...] is so new in style and original in conception that it demands more attention than can be expected so late in the evening. The restlessness of its tonality and the originality which marks every moment make it at first somewhat hard to follow; but it is full of good and often beautiful ideas, and it breathes throughout a spirit of earnestness which should commend it to musicians. The composer is hardly at all known in this country [...]. It is to be hoped that he [Arthur Chappell, the manager of the Popular Concerts] will continue his researches in the same direction, and enable English amateurs to hear some of the chamber music of M. César Franck, a composer whose influence on French music has had a marked and lasting effect[11].

The Establishment of Franck's Chamber Music in Britain

This mention of Franck's name in the context of Eugène Ysaÿe's first appearance at the Pops, where he introduced Fauré's Piano Quartet Op. 45 in 1891, is conspicuous. One year after Franck's death, his music was still almost unknown in Britain. From his small corpus of chamber music, only the early Piano Trio in F-sharp minor Op. 1, No. 1 had been introduced to Britain, in 1861. Pianist Karl Klindworth, a friend of Franz Liszt and Richard Wagner, violinist Henry Blagrove, and cellist Hugo Daubert had included it in their series of progressive chamber concerts alongside works by Schumann, Fryderyk Chopin, Franz Berwald, and George

---

10. *The Musical Standard*, 26 May 1894, p. 441. The main works at the Wolff Musical Union concert were Chaminade's Piano Trio in A minor and Widor's Piano Quartet in A minor.

11. *The Saturday Review*, 14 November 1891, p. 558.

Macfarren[12]. It was positively received in the press — much better than Schumann's Piano Trio in F Major, in fact — but very seldom repeated[13]. One performance was undertaken by another champion of Liszt's, pianist Walter Bache, in 1867[14]. Despite limited knowledge of Franck's music in 1890, some obituaries alluded reverently to the composer's considerable influence and projected a rising reputation, though perhaps not great popularity among the British public:

> By the death of M. César Franck [...] France loses one of her most accomplished and most esteemed musicians. Popular indeed, in the ordinary sense, his works never were and perhaps never will be, for popularity for its own sake was the last thing the amiable composer sought to win. But though somewhat *caviare* [*sic*] to the general public, almost all his works are highly esteemed by musicians, and it is quite probable that the reputation of some of them will increase rather than diminish as they get to be better known. Little of his music has been performed in this country [...][15].

Franck's late chamber works were among the first to be introduced to British audiences. Their premieres were systematically undertaken by English pianist Fanny Frickenhaus and French-born, London-based violinist René Ortmans (1863-1949); together with Ortmans' quartet, they premiered the Violin Sonata (1893), Piano Quintet (1896), and String Quartet (1897). Frickenhaus (*née* Evans, 1849-1913) had studied in Brussels and had already performed French music in London in the early 1880s; later, she would play Debussy[16]. Ortmans appeared regularly in London from 1885 onward, subsequently also teaching and conducting. An overstrained arm prohibited him from continuing to play modern chamber music with his quartet[17]. Other first performances of Franck included piano works (*Prélude, choral et fugue*, Théophile Ysaÿe, 1896), organ pieces, and orchestral music (parts of *Psyché* and *Rédemption* and the Symphony in D minor, Charles Lamoureux and Édouard Colonne, 1896). After 1900, major provincial choral festivals took up the performance of oratorios (for example, *Les Béatitudes* in English translation, Glasgow, 1900)[18].

---

[12]. ALLIS 2012, pp. 146ff.

[13]. «The trio performed on Tuesday night, unequal as it is, displays such extraordinary power and imagination, that it is incomprehensible how a man of such manifest genius as the author should have been content with the obscurity into which he has retired». *The Musical World*, 16 March 1861, p. 171.

[14]. Andrew de Ternant identified Bache's performance as the first. In a kind of musicological deception, he described a meeting of Franck and Bache in Paris and a visit of Franck to London in 1877. In fact, Franck never visited Britain. TERNANT 1925; see also STOVE 2012, pp. 184-187.

[15]. *The Musical World*, 15 November 1890, p. 906.

[16]. See also WENZEL 2018.

[17]. STRAETEN 1933, pp. 190ff.

[18]. See the overview in STOVE 2011. For the context of the orchestral performances, see LANGLEY 2012.

Perhaps surprisingly, given the previous reception of French music, some of Franck's works quickly became established. The Violin Sonata in particular emerged as a well-liked 'modern classic'. From the beginning, critics portrayed it as an earnest composition differing from «ordinary French music» and rather being influenced by the «modern German school»[19]. Noted were its «[...] undoubted originality, [...] severe style and extremely modern harmonic design»; the opening movement was often linked to Grieg[20]. In contrast to chamber music by Franck's compatriots Godard, Fauré, Widor, and Chaminade, the Sonata was soon taken up by English musicians and played as early as 1894 by Maud Branwell and Marie Motto at a Royal College of Music student concert.

The Piano Quintet and String Quartet received more ambiguous reviews from the press and musicians alike. Their extraordinary ambitiousness was appreciated but at first perceived as appealing only to a limited circle of music lovers. Both works were repeated for the first time in 1901 (apart from a private performance of the Quintet in 1898 with Fauré as pianist at the home of Frank Schuster, who was also to become an illustrious friend and supporter of Elgar's[21]). Substituting for the almost seventy-year-old Joachim, Eugène Ysaÿe and his quartet became guests for the Pops season and gave the British premieres of Saint-Saëns's String Quartet Op. 112 and Vincent d'Indy's Piano Quartet Op. 7. With his Franco-Russian sympathies — balanced by respect for the German classics — Ysaÿe was proclaimed «man of the moment» and seen as Joachim's successor[22]. Just as Joachim had persistently advocated for Schumann and Brahms despite much British prejudice, Ysaÿe now championed the newest chamber music in London. While in 1901 it was still doubtful whether Franck would ever equal Schumann and Brahms in rank[23], a decade later, the significance of his works — the more austere Quintet and Quartet included — was beyond question:

> César Franck's pianoforte quintet has received quite a lot of attention lately
> [...]. This noble quintet was until recently much neglected; indeed the same may
> still be said of César Franck's other works proportionally to their merit. This is
> difficult to understand considering the immense effect he has had upon modern
> musical thought, French musical thought in particular. Apart from his remarkable
> innovations in harmony, his form is quite individual, and worthy of careful study by
> the musician. Certain it is that his influence is far-reaching, and powerful, although
> far too little acknowledged[24].

19. *The Athenaeum*, 22 April 1893, p. 515; *The Musical Times*, 1 May 1893, pp. 278ff.
20. *The Times*, 21 April 1893, p. 4.
21. Fauré related this performance late at night in a letter to his wife. FAURÉ 1951, pp. 27ff.
22. *The Musical Standard*, 6 April 1901, p. 207.
23. *The Athenaeum*, 6 April 1901, p. 441.
24. *The Violin and String World, Supplement to The Musical Standard*, 25 February 1911, p. 12.

Franck's chamber music, by the beginning of the First World War, was regularly performed by British musicians. Twenty years after his death, he was unreservedly perceived as 'modern' and appeared in concert series focused on contemporary (and often British) repertoire, such as the Concerts of Modern Chamber Music, organised by composer-pianist Joseph Holbrooke, and recital series of newly formed ensembles like the London String Quartet, the English String Quartet, and the Philharmonic String Quartet[25]. Still, the public seemed to withhold its ultimate affection from Franck, except for the Violin Sonata. In 1915, the young composer and critic Philip Heseltine noted two popular misconceptions of Franck — that he was a formalist and that he was «dear old gentleman» (known as «père Franck») — in his analytical notes for a Quintet performance by the Philharmonic String Quartet (see ILL. 1, pp. 296-298). That same year, *Times* critic H. C. Colles, criticising the British echoing of the French eulogy, described a problematic relationship between meaning and form in Franck's music, which he contended became especially obvious in sonata form — the Violin Sonata, once again, excepted. Colles saw this as a reason for the partly passive British reception of Franck:

> The Violin sonata has been played perhaps too often, the String quartet not quite often enough, but no one can say that any one of his later and more characteristic works for instruments has been neglected in this country. At the same time our acceptance of Franck has been rather passive; he has been praised by the precious; the keepers of "the classical tradition" have opened their door by one chink to admit him into the circle of the elect, while at the same time the assailants of "the classical tradition" and of all tradition have not despised him. English musical journalists emulate the paeans of such accomplished French critics as M. D'Indy and M. Rolland, who find Franck to be the saviour of music, the restorer of the symphony, and who attribute to his beneficent influence nearly every species of musical development since 1870. [...] For in spite of all the enthusiasm, real and affected, Franck's music has not gripped the heartstrings of a people (at any rate of this people) in a decisive way. It has remained the property of musicians, and been taken on trust by the public which cares most about it when it gets the added interest of interpretation by a great artist[26].

Nonetheless, in a 1917 lecture series on the foundations of twentieth-century music, Edwin Evans portrayed Franck as Beethoven's first successor in the symphonic field, implicitly strengthening a connection that Franck's pupil d'Indy had already established. Evans coined

---

[25]. The London String Quartet was established in 1908 by founding members Albert Sammons, Thomas W. Petre, Harry Waldo Warner, and Charles Warwick-Evans. The English String Quartet was founded in 1902 by Thomas Morris, Herbert Kinze, Frank Bridge, and Ivor James. The Philharmonic String Quartet was established in 1915 by Arthur Beckwith, Eugene Goossens, Raymond Jeremy, and Cedric Sharpe. For an overview of ensembles, see MEADMORE 1929.

[26]. COLLES 1915, p. 206.

7

CÉSAR FRANCK (1822-1890) Quintet in F minor, for
Piano and Strings

(Composed in 1879. Produced in January, 1880, by the Société
Nationale, Paris, Saint-Saëns, to whom the work is dedicated,
playing the piano part).

I. Molto moderato quasi lento.
Allegro.
Piu Presto—Tempo I. Allegro.
II. Lento, con molto sentimento.
III. Allegro non troppo ma con fuoco.

PIANO—WILLIAM MURDOCH.

The popularity of César Franck's music in this country has been—at any rate for the large body of concert-goers who receive music emotionally rather than intellectually—somewhat hindered by the excessive zeal of hierophantic persons who would fain interpret it to the multitude. The popular mind, forgetting a little and perhaps exaggerating a little of what it has been told, too frequently carries away two outstanding impressions which serve to make up a very inadequate and wholly fallacious connotation of César Franck and his work. The first fallacy is that of Franck the formalist. Franck, most conscientious of artists, always took the most meticulous care to cast his subject-matter in a form exactly suited to its precise expression, but, emphatically, form and structure were with him, as with all other great composers, merely means by which the music might be rendered more lucid, more readily intelligible. The music must, and indeed can very well speak for itself, and the layman need not be in the least debarred from apprehending its import by the fact that he has but little technical knowledge of musical forms and their evolution. The other fallacy concerns the essence rather than the externalities of Franck's music. It has given rise to the conception of Franck as a shadowy, saint-like creature, remote, rather unreal, moving in a sphere where the throbbing heart of humanity is scarcely perceptible : outwardly, a simple-minded, benevolent person, leading an uneventful life—almost a " dear old gentleman."

ILL. 1: Programme notes (excerpt) by Philip Heseltine for the concert of the Philharmonic String Quartet, 26 October 1915. Published with the permission of the Royal College of Music, London.

8

Nothing could be farther from the truth, nor could any un-biassed listener attribute the authorship of this intensely vital and human Quintet to so vague and emasculated a person as this figment of misguided minds.

The most salient characteristic of all Franck's music is a passionate reaching-upwards to the plane of ecstasy and spiritual exaltation, which is the quintessence of all sincere religion, theistic or otherwise. In Franck's life externals counted for little. "He lived" (as has been said of Wordsworth) "a life of excitement and passion, and he preached a doctrine of magnificence and glory."

The Quintet is distinguished, as regards workmanship, by close adherence to its thematic texts, the clearest logic in development, and a certain rhythmic interrelation of the themes, which, throughout the work, seem to grow quite naturally one out of another.

The opening phrase is announced by the strings *dramatico*—

The piano replies with a gentle, caressing phrase that seems to plead against the hard ferocity of the preceding subject. The whole introduction is a kind of dialogue based upon these two phrases.

The first subject of the *Allegro* is commenced by the strings in octaves, and continued by strings and piano in alternation, each enlarging upon the other's point. It is in three sections—

and after three bars more of B—

9

a flowing passage for the first violin leads to a new melody in the viola—

which is taken up by the other strings, worked to a rapid *crescendo*, and finally merged in an important theme, evolved rhythmically from the third section of the first subject—a typical expression, with its insinuating, persisting rise and fall, of that quality of aspiration mentioned above as being characteristic of all Franck's work—

It is first stated by the piano, and at its climax the first violin enters with a passionate outburst—

This practically completes the actual material of the first movement, but its melodic developments are endless and resourceful in the extreme.

The final climax, built up on the opening rhythm of the introduction, the first section of the principal subject and a transformation of the pleading phrase, now allotted to the strings, is terrific ; but exhaustion seems to follow, and the movement dies softly away.

The second movement has all the eerie tranquillity of the lull that succeeds a violent storm. The greater part of it is pervaded by a grey, half-light atmosphere, and there is no climax of more than three or four bars' duration. The opening theme is announced by the first violin in short, almost gasping phrases, with a soft accompaniment of iterated chords on the piano. A short, sighing phrase for the piano leads to its repetition, an octave higher, the piano part being this time in arpeggio form, the term 'progressive academicism' to describe the specific relationship between tradition and innovation in recent French music and to sum up what he saw as the motto of the Franckist tradition: «loyalty to principle [in the formal construction] combined with the utmost liberality in detail»[27]. Franck's music arguably presented a stronger link to the German tradition than Fauré's: original elements like cyclic design and chromatic harmony could be seen as the continuation of Beethoven, Liszt, and Wagner. Franck's music also had less affinity to salon style than that of Fauré, whose music, with its greater emphasis on instrumentation and colour, was often and stereotypically regarded as 'frivolous'. It was described as such by John F. Runciman, critic for the *Saturday Review*, who also repeatedly expressed a strong personal dislike for Franck[28]. This was, however, no longer the mainstream view of French music in Britain.

TABLE 1: SELECTED BRITISH FIRST PERFORMANCES OF FRENCH CHAMBER MUSIC

DATE	WORK	PERFORMERS (SERIES; PLACE, IF NOT LONDON)
5 March 1861	Franck: Piano Trio Op. 1, No. 1	Karl Klindworth, Henry Blagrove, Hugo Daubert
6 December 1873	Saint-Saëns: Cello Sonata Op. 32	Hans von Bülow, Alfredo Piatti (Popular Concerts)
19 June 1877	Fauré: Violin Sonata Op. 13	Alfred Jaëll, Leopold Auer (Musical Union)
9 November 1891	Fauré: Piano Quartet Op. 45	Benno Schönberger, Eugène Ysaÿe, Ludwig Straus, William Whitehouse (Popular Concerts)
19 April 1893	Franck: Violin Sonata	Fanny Frickenhaus, René Ortmans
22 November 1894	Fauré: Piano Quartet Op. 15	Fauré, Johannes Wolff, Louis van Waefelghem, Leo Stern (Wolff Musical Union)
28 March 1896	Franck: Piano Quintet	Frickenhaus, Ortmans, Alfred Mistowski, L. Szczepanowski, B. Albert
27 March 1897	Franck: String Quartet	Ortmans, Szczepanowski, Alfred Hobday, Albert
12 January 1901	Saint-Saëns: String Quartet Op. 112	Ysaÿe Quartet (Popular Concerts)
19 October 1904	Debussy: String Quartet	Vera Warwick-Evans, Herbert Kinze, Frank Bridge, Ivor James (Royal College of Music)
3 December 1907	Chausson: Piano Quartet Op. 30	Ricardo Viñes, Parisian Quartet (Newcastle)
5 December 1907	Ravel: String Quartet	Parisian Quartet (Sheffield)
11 June 1915	Ravel: Piano Trio	Alfredo Casella, Yvonne Astruc, Jean Charron (Société des Concerts Français)
26 June 1917	Debussy: Violin Sonata	Joseph Jongen, Désiré Defauw (War Emergency Entertainments)
20 December 1917	Fauré: Violin Sonata Op. 108	Harold Samuel, Defauw (War Emergency Entertainments)

[27]. EVANS 1917, p. 349.

[28]. RUNCIMAN 1914, p. 75: «The best that can be said of such music [Fauré's] is that it is charming»; RUNCIMAN 1902, p. 767: «But Franck! — laborious, conscientious, working always as one explaining the mysteries of form and development to a school-class — [...]. His is modern kapellmeister music».

DAVID REIßFELDER

THE SOCIÉTÉ DES CONCERTS FRANÇAIS AND THE
SYSTEMATIC PROMOTION OF MODERN FRENCH CHAMBER MUSIC

The recognition of Franck was related to a broader contemporaneous trend: the establishment of the most recent French music in Britain. This development — difficult to imagine only a few years earlier — was largely facilitated by a systematic campaign led by a small Anglo-French clique. The first such venture was undertaken by Paris-born singer and pianist Lucie Barbier (*née* Hirsch, 1875-1963), who had come to Manchester with her husband, a professor of French. With a broad range of professional contacts in both France and England, she organised two series of eight 'French Concerts' from 1907 to 1909, which brought César Géloso, Henry Février, Paul Bazelaire, Reynaldo Hahn, Saint-Saëns, Victor Gallois (who had scandalously won the 1905 Prix de Rome over Ravel), Fauré, and d'Indy to Manchester. Debussy had to cancel his appearance at short notice[29].

The day after the first 'French Concert' in Manchester, another group of French musicians began a small tour from Newcastle over to Leeds and Sheffield, and eventually to London. At five concerts, the Quatuor Willaume (advertised as the Parisian Quartet[30]), pianist Ricardo Viñes, and singer Hélène M. Luquiens performed Ernest Chausson's Piano Quartet Op. 30, Ravel's String Quartet (both for the first time), Debussy's String Quartet, and Fauré's Piano Quartet Op. 15 along with piano pieces and songs (see ILL. 2, pp. 301-302, for the programme and TABLE 1, p. 299, for other selected first performances). The tour's main initiators were French engineer and music enthusiast Tony J. Guéritte (1875-1964), who had moved to Newcastle in 1899 and settled in Surbiton (Surrey, now Greater London) in 1907, and the critic and writer G. Jean-Aubry (1882-1950)[31], who later also became Guéritte's brother-in-law. Jean-Aubry, well-connected in musical circles, had in 1906 co-founded the Cercle de l'Art moderne in his hometown of Le Havre, where the Quatuor Willaume, Viñes, Luquiens, and composers such as Ravel, Florent Schmitt, Albert Roussel, and Déodat de Séverac presented French avant-garde music.

Surprisingly, the French musicians' tour met with a mostly warm response. An elaborate and reverent review emphasising the performers' crucial role in conveying the radically new idiom was written by Arthur Symons, a poet and essayist influenced by the French symbolists:

---

[29].   See the dissertation by Barbier's granddaughter based on her papers and letters (at the National Library of Wales, Aberystwyth): STONEQUIST 1972. For a focus on the later London concerts, see the master's thesis PIATIGORSKY 2018. A summary is also given by RODMELL 2021, pp. 174-176.

[30].   The Quatuor Willaume (Gabriel Willaume, Georges Morel, Émile Macon, and Louis Feuillard) was the regular quartet at concerts of the Société des Concerts Français and performed in Britain until 1914.

[31].   Born Jean-Frédéric-Émile Aubry, he chose the pen name G. Jean-Aubry. For his broad activities, see RODRIGUEZ 2004.

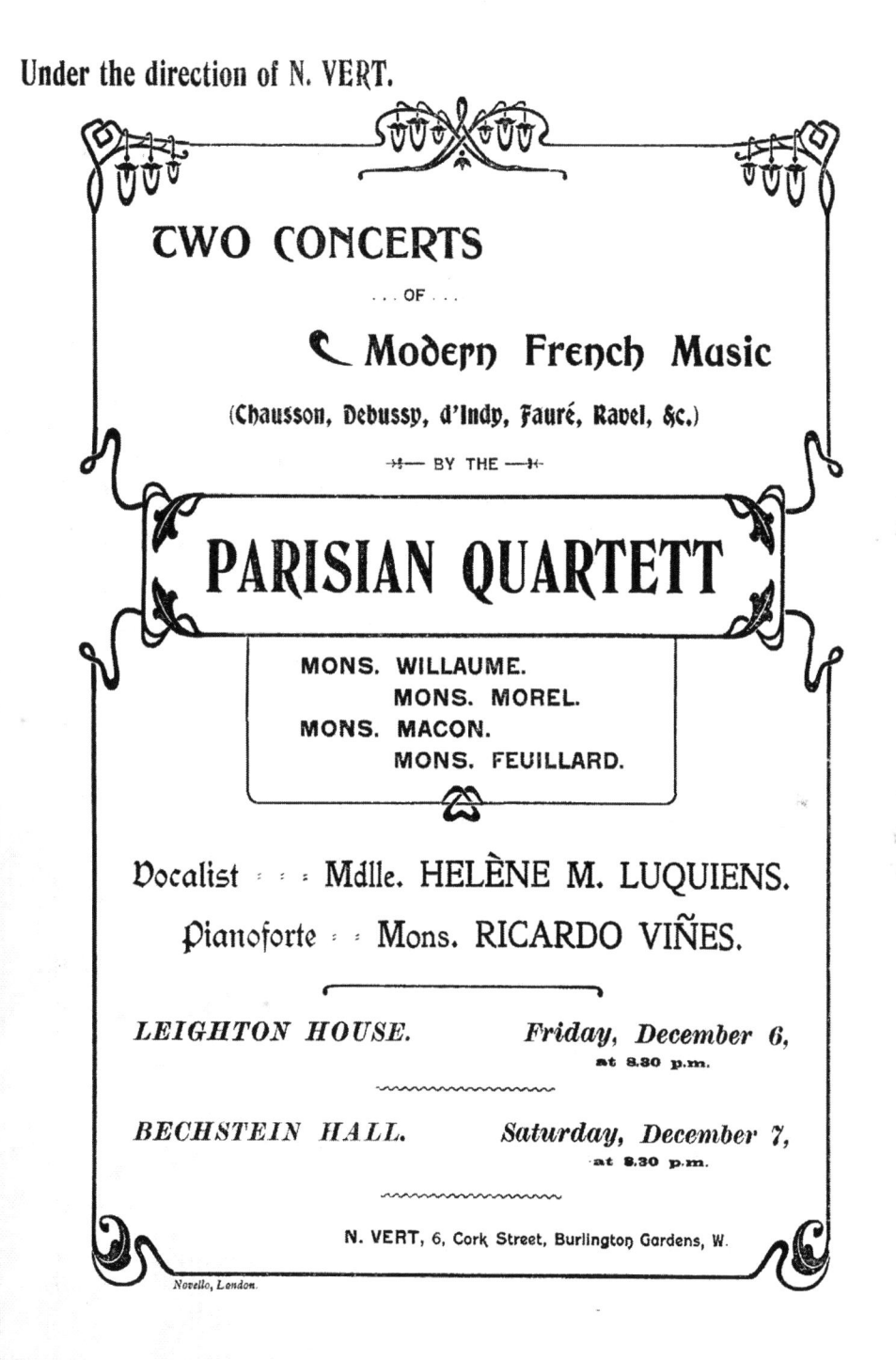

ILL. 2: Programme sheet for the London concerts of Guéritte's tour, December 1907. Published with the permission of the Wigmore Hall Archive.

THE PARISIAN QUARTETT.

Programme for

BECHSTEIN HALL,

Saturday, December 7, at 8.30.

QUARTET in C for Piano, Violin, Viola and Violoncello - - - *Gabriel Fauré.*
MM. RICARDO VIÑES, WILLAUME, MACON, FEUILLARD.

SONGS	(a) "Lied Maritime"	- - - *Vincent d'Indy.*
	(b) "Apaisement"	- - - *Ernest Chausson.*
	(c) "La Chanson Perpétuelle"	- *Ernest Chausson.*

(With string quartet accompaniment.)
Mlle. HÉLÈNE M. LUQUIENS.

PIANO SOLO	(a) "Danse au bord de l'eau"	- - *Albert Roussel.*
	(b) "Toccata"	- - - *Ernest Chausson.*
	(c) "Paysage"	- - - *Claude Debussy.*

Mons. RICARDO VINES.

INTERVAL.

SONGS	(a) "L'Invitation au Voyage"	- - *Henri Duparc.*
	(b) "Clair de Lune"	- - - *Gabriel Fauré.*
	(c) "La Fée aux Chansons"	- - *Gabriel Fauré.*

Mlle. HÉLÈNE M. LUQUIENS.

PIANO SOLO	(a) "3rd Impromptu"	- - *Gabriel Fauré.*
	(b) "Le lac vert"	- - - *Vincent d'Indy.*
	(c) "Alborada del Gracioso"	- - *Maurice Ravel.*

Mons. RICARDO VINES.

1ST QUARTET for two Violins, Viola and Violoncello - - *Claude Debussy.*
MM. WILLAUME, MOREL, MACON, FEUILLARD.

BECHSTEIN GRAND PIANOFORTE.

Miniature Score of Debussy's Quartet on Sale at the Hall.

The adventure of the Parisian Quartet in England was a hazardous one, and it is pleasant to know that is has succeeded. Two Frenchmen, one a man of letters, M. Jean Aubry, living in France, the other, M. Guéritte, living in the North of England, both enthusiastic admirers of the "new" music in their country, planned, with rash confidence, a series of five concerts, beginning in Newcastle and ending in London. Nothing but the very latest French music was given [...]. An organisation more perfectly arranged it would be difficult to imagine. Each separately is a fine player, and they move together like one man. Music, whose secret had seemed closed, opened at their touch; good or bad, whatever it had to give, they gave; they almost deceived one, at times, into thinking that the trivial was charming, or the meaningless significant, so much skill and sympathy did they put into their generous playing. Exactly the same must be said of the accomplished singer, Mlle Luquiens, and of the brilliant pianist, M. Viñes. The songs, all their bright and dim monotonies, all that was diaphanous in them, and their occasional touches of feeling, this singer gave us with a perfect fidelity to the sense of what she had apprehended in its full meaning, the music and the words. The voice and the method were exactly suited to the particular quality of most of these songs that hummed or soared in the air. The songs, and most of the piano music, was a kind of music of insects, and the Catalan pianist, nervous and deliberate, made over again on the piano, with his bird-like pounces upon the notes, which responded eagerly to his fierce caresses, a new music which is "cruelle et câline", a thing made to astonish, intoxicate, or subdue. He puts no passion into music that is without it, but he draws from it all its essence, makes it ring like bells and veils it in bright mist, follows it in all its excessive speeds, and lingers with it in its gardens under the rain; he is a kind of malign attendant spirit, letting it loose and accompanying it on its freakish errands. Of the nine composers whose music was thus faithfully interpreted to us, two stood out from the others with a definite superiority. These were Ernest Chausson, who seems to close the past, and Claude Debussy, who seems to open the future[32].

Encouraged by the positive reception of their enterprises, the executive committee of the Manchester 'French Concerts' and Guéritte briefly joined forces. But that same year, in 1909, Barbier moved to Aberystwyth (Wales) with her husband, and ceased arranging concerts at the same level as before, although she continued to give lectures and be active in the University Musical Club. The merged organisation, now based in London and adopting the name Société des Concerts Français, hosted twenty-eight concerts in the capital between 1909 and 1915 (see ILL. 3, p. 304)[33]. It also collaborated with local societies to disseminate modern French chamber and vocal music throughout Britain. Alongside the Frenchmen Guéritte and Jean-Aubry, another crucial figure for this undertaking was English music aficionado Edwin Evans. He had discovered Debussy already in the 1890s and, as a critic,

---

[32].   Symons 1907, p. 723.

[33].   For a list of the concerts and reproductions of programme books, see Reißfelder 2022, pp. 118-135.

ILL. 3: Cover of the programme book of the 5th Concert of the Société des Concerts Français in London, 1909. Published with the permission of the Wigmore Hall Archive.

relentlessly promoted modern French, Russian, and British music[34]. Guéritte later credited Evans with first conceiving of the Société[35].

The Société's London programmes — in contrast to the Manchester concerts — mostly featured young, avant-garde French composers. In its first year, 1909, Debussy, Roussel, Ravel, Schmitt, and Hahn all appeared in person. Later guests included the lesser-known Amédée Reuchsel, Maurice Reuchsel, Louis Dumas, Léon Moreau, and Ernest Moret, as well as composers «who belong to the French school, although not of French nationality»[36]. Most composers played or accompanied their own works. Older music was presented as well, for example by Saint-Saëns, Lalo, Emmanuel Chabrier, and Paul Dukas. However, popular opera or orchestral composers like Hector Berlioz, Charles Gounod, Georges Bizet, and Jules Massenet were strikingly absent. Using the 1907 tour engineered by Guéritte and Jean-Aubry as a model, small groups of French artists would give a few concerts in various cities with a similar programme under the aegis of the Société. Such a journey — from Helensburgh over to Edinburgh and Southport down to London — was made in 1913, for example, by the Parisian Quartet, pianist Mme Feuillard, and violinist André-Louis Mangeot. Chausson's Concert Op. 21 was the main work and enthusiastically received[37]. Increasingly, French repertoire of the seventeenth and eighteenth centuries was included and mixed with the modern. In 1912, the specialists of the Société des concerts d'autrefois gave a whole concert of early music[38].

The 1907 tour concerts included no works by Franck, but his Violin Sonata was played by composer César Géloso and violinist Marcel Chailley at Barbier's first concert in Manchester. Franck's *Prélude, choral et fugue* (performed by Blanche Selva) and two songs were presented

---

[34]. Previous research has largely overlooked Evans, but see SCAIFE 1994, pp. 174-188. Evans' own account of the discovery and exploration of modern French music can be found in the translator's preface to JEAN-AUBRY 1919A.

[35]. GUÉRITTE 1945: «On his advice the Société des Concerts Français was founded in 1907, and during its 10 years of existence he was one of its most active committee members. The chamber music programmes of the Société were heard in some 130 concerts throughout Great Britain, and contained the names of 75 composers, of whom 15, including Debussy, d'Indy, Ravel, Roussel.&c., were present; 407 works were performed, 240 being thus heard for the first time here».

[36]. With these words, the programme book of 29 March 1912 announced a concert with guests George Enescu and Frédéric d'Erlanger. On later occasions, Alfredo Casella and (Mme) Poldowski (*alias* Régine Wieniawski, *alias* Lady Dean Paul) attended in person.

[37]. *The Times*, 15 February 1913, p. 10. Concert sheets are held in the André-Louis Mangeot Collection, Royal College of Music, London. The given name of the pianist, wife of the Quartet's cellist Louis Feuillard, could not be found.

[38]. *The Daily Telegraph*, 18 January 1912, p. 11. This society was founded by flautist and regular visitor to England Louis Fleury. He had already played at a Société concert in London in 1910 as a member of the Société moderne d'instruments à vent.

at Barbier's last event, for which d'Indy was the guest of honour[39]. In London, all three late chamber works were given by the Société. Critics who preferred the introduction of more recent music sometimes expressed scepticism over the Société's inclusion of older and better-known works, such as ones by Saint-Saëns[40]. In 1911, however, a commentator opined that the «sheer beauty» of Franck's Piano Quintet «quickly obliterated all other impressions received during the concert» played by the Parisian Quartet, which had included the String Quartet Op. 12 by deputising cellist Louis Dumas and piano pieces by Gabriel Dupont[41].

The Société's programmes reflected the aesthetic divide in French musical life: some were dedicated to Scholists (*scholistes*) such as d'Indy, Roussel, Déodat de Séverac, and Albéric Magnard, others to so-called Impressionists such as Ravel, Schmitt, Hahn, André Caplet, and Désiré-Émile Inghelbrecht. Whereas the latter group was often found guilty of striving solely for effects and occasionally accused of being Debussy imitators, composers with a connection to Franck and his circle were mostly positively received. Chausson's style especially seemed to merge the more solid and logical (German) elements of his teacher with the adventurous harmonic turns of Fauré and the original ventures into instrumental colour and texture that more sympathetic concertgoers began to embrace in Debussy and Ravel's music[42]. One review summed up the first performance of Chausson's Piano Quartet during the 1907 tour by Viñes and the Parisian Quartet thus: «in addition to being intellectual, the music was strongly emotional; moreover, from a harmonic point of view it seemed more spontaneous than that of Ravel»[43]. This dichotomy mirrored the difference between «musique cérébrale» and «musique sensorielle» used by Edwin Evans (following Michel-Dimitri Calvocoressi) to characterise the opposing factions in the French musical milieu[44].

After the outbreak of the First World War, the Société presented only three more concerts in London in 1915. The Belgian composers Joseph Jongen, Guy Weitz, and Victor Vreuls were the main guests, and Ravel's Piano Trio had its British first performances. Jongen and Weitz had fled to England and attended in person. All three were associated with

---

[39]. *The Musical Times*, 1 January 1908, p. 46; *The Musical Standard*, 20 March 1909, p. 181.

[40]. CLUTSAM 1911: «At his best, Saint-Saëns could never plead guilty to having inspired a single bar of the latest development of French art».

[41]. *The Musical Times*, 1 February 1911, p. 116.

[42]. See, for example, *The Manchester Guardian*, 12 January 1914, p. 8.

[43]. *The Athenaeum*, 14 December 1907, p. 777. The review also included a short introduction: «In France César Franck opened up new paths and Vincent d'Indy, Debussy, and other composers look on him as the head of the modern French school. In this country Franck, for a long time ignored, is now recognized as a notable composer of the second half of the nineteenth century; and his D minor Symphony and various chamber works are already familiar. Vincent d'Indy and Ernest Chausson both studied with him; and Debussy and Ravel, to name two other prominent composers, if not so directly connected with Franck, have undoubtedly been influenced by his works».

[44]. EVANS 1909, p. 394. See SCAIFE 1994, p. 180.

Franck, and not just because of their native country[45]. Jongen quickly plunged into London musical life: the Belgian Quartet with Jongen as pianist, his compatriots Désiré Defauw and Emile Doehaerd, and English violist Lionel Tertis regularly combined modern French, Belgian, and British works[46]. A related ensemble, the Allied (String) Quartet — with Defauw as first violinist, cellist Doehaerd, and changing combinations for the inner voices — continued to present first performances of French and English works until the 1920s, among them chamber music by Arnold Bax (Piano Quintet, 1917), Fauré (Piano Quintet in C minor, 1921), and E. J. Moeran (String Quartet in A minor, 1923). The Allied Quartet also played with composers Frank Bridge (String Sextet, 1919), Schmitt (Piano Quintet, 1919), and Ravel (*Introduction et allegro*, 1922)[47].

These Belgian artists were regularly involved in another concert series solely dedicated to French music: after the sudden demise of the Société des Concerts Français (despite the announcement of further seasons in its last programme book[48]), singer and composer Isidore de Lara started up a similar venture. In 1914, he had initiated the War Emergency Entertainments to provide work for British musicians during the war, and soon added a series of 'All British Concerts'[49]. In the summer of 1916, de Lara complemented these with an inaugural French recital:

> In the course of a brief address, Mr. de Lara said that he hoped, with the sympathy and patronage of the French Ministry of Fine Arts, to embark in the autumn on a campaign on behalf of French music. There was no time to listen to the music of Germany, but it undoubtedly was a time to listen to that of a nation we love, respect, and revere. Up to the present there had been no unity between French and English musicians, and this, surely, was the season to bring it about. He hoped that the same thing would be done in Paris for English music as the Société

---

[45]. The publication of Jongen's second Violin Sonata had been commented upon before: «We do not know whether M. Joseph Jongen is or is not an avowed follower of César Franck. [...] one catches a faint but unmistakable echo of the work of the older composer. [...] By this M. Jongen identifies himself with the modern French classical movement, which owes its very existence to the stimulating vitality of Franck's art». BONAVIA 1910.

[46]. The ensemble's first concert included Jongen's own Piano Quartet, Frank Bridge's Phantasy Quartet, Mozart's Piano Quartet in G minor, and songs by Debussy, Defauw, and Pierre de Bréville. *The Observer*, 13 June 1915, p. 14.

[47]. For more concerts of the ensemble, see WHITE 2006, pp. 30 and 54-63.

[48]. The programme book of the twenty-eighth concert in the seventh season on 25 June 1915 is held in the Fonds Joseph Jongen, Conservatoire royal de Bruxelles.

[49]. The War Emergency Entertainments ultimately encompassed 1259 concerts, including 171 British concerts with 266 new works. *The Times*, 1 July 1919, p. 14. Nevertheless, even promoters of British music like Evans viewed de Lara's concerts sceptically, and they never received as much attention as similar enterprises. See also ANGELL 2014, pp. 192-197.

des Concerts Français had done in the past, and he hoped to do in the immediate future for the art of our Allies[50].

The twenty concerts between 1916 and 1918 primarily served as vehicles for known works, some of which already had become 'modern classics', like Fauré and Franck's Violin Sonatas, Debussy and Chausson's Quartets, and Ravel's *Introduction et allegro*. But they also facilitated first performances, including Debussy and Fauré's new Violin Sonatas in 1917, as well as lesser-known repertoire by Magnard (Quintet for Piano and Winds), Erik Satie (*Sonatine bureaucratique*), and Alexis de Castillon (Piano Quintet). As usual at the War Emergency Entertainments, the concerts were accompanied by short introductory talks by organiser de Lara, Harry Levy-Lawson[51], conductor Thomas Beecham[52], and critics Jean-Aubry and Evans.

THE DEBATE OVER NATIONAL CHARACTER AND FRENCH MUSIC AS A MODEL

From the beginning of the promotion of modern French repertoire around 1907, concerts were complemented by independently held lectures and articles in the press, for both academic and broader audiences. The French-born Michel-Dimitri Calvocoressi was one of the first to portray and analyse piano music by Debussy, Ravel, Déodat de Séverac, and others. He wrote for the *Musical Times* on various aspects of modern music, and in 1913 gave four lectures on French music at Oxford[53]. Calvocoressi and his fellow critic Edwin Evans both emphasised the different groups and aesthetics in French musical life but also what they saw as a common ground: the original and individual expression of national character as it had been

---

[50]. *The Daily Telegraph*, 20 July 1916, p. 10. For a list of de Lara's French concerts and the ultimately fruitless attempts to establish British concerts in Paris, see REISSFELDER 2022, pp. 176ff. and pp. 191-197. Some programme books are held in the Fonds Joseph Jongen, Conservatoire royal de Bruxelles.

[51]. Levy-Lawson (Lord Burnham) was proprietor and director of the Daily Telegraph and president of the Anglo-French Society, which co-organised the French concert series with de Lara from 1917.

[52]. Beecham «spoke on behalf of that "youngest of the arts", French music, defending it against misunderstanding, and implying that something more is needed than the quiet appreciation it has received in this country. [...] the clear and concise treatment of instrumental music, in which, without vaguely seeking inspiration in the heavens but "keeping their feet on the earth", their composers have exhibited a sense of proportion, economy, and style worthy of imitation». *The Times*, 1 May 1918, p. 8.

[53]. For his first English article, see CALVOCORESSI 1906. For a short biography and a summary of the Oxford lectures, see *The Musical Times*, 1 September 1913, pp. 573-575. In 1914, Calvocoressi moved to England and remained there. For recollections and observations, see CALVOCORESSI 1933, pp. 279-313.

embodied in French music of the seventeenth and eighteenth centuries[54]. Franck was almost unanimously portrayed as the catalytic figure behind this reawakened French musical movement, although Calvocoressi also hinted at the «dangers of Franckism» — namely, formalism and intellectualism[55]. Even more conservative academics and critics who held little regard for most French music, such as Alexander Mackenzie and Ernest Newman, acknowledged Franck's far-reaching influence[56]. This one-sided narrative was deplored, however, by Herman Klein, a friend and early British promoter of Saint-Saëns — who before 1900 had been considered the foremost French composer of instrumental music[57].

The expression of national character in music lay at the core of the debate about a genuinely British school of composers[58]. Jean-Aubry was most vocal in depicting the French movement as leading musical Europe. It was his deep belief that it provided an ideal model for other European countries (as Spain had shown) — not as a compositional pattern to imitate but as a model for finding the way (back) to self-expression, liberated from so-called alien influences. Jean-Aubry and Evans both lamented the overwhelming authority of German instrumental music in the nineteenth century, as it had led to musical uniformity across Europe: an imperial musical state in contrast to the federal republic that Evans welcomed after 1920[59]. In their eyes, British music especially suffered under this hegemony (a view shared by many British observers) and consequently stood to profit greatly from its close partner under the *entente cordiale*:

> Britain has known, musically speaking, a glorious past. This for two centuries had no continuation, having too readily given place to foreign influence; but to-day British music is striving to free itself, to reconquer an independence of spirit, which will assure it henceforth a grandeur like that which it has too easily forgotten. France for about fifty years has been confronted with the same problem; she also had known a wonderful musical epoch which, little by little, had dropped out of mind; musical art had disappeared; people were actually accepting the idea that France was not a

---

[54]. For example, Evans 1909; Evans 1910a; Evans 1910b. A comment from an anonymous (sceptical) listener on Evans' 1910 lecture was published in *The Musical Herald*, 1 February 1910, p. 55.

[55]. Calvocoressi 1912. The article was part of a chronological course on French music for the members of the Home Music Study Union.

[56]. See the reports on their lectures in Mackenzie 1907 and Newman 1909.

[57]. «Let it not be forgotten that there was a time when Saint-Saëns was regarded as the leader of advanced French musical thought. [...] he was one of those who prepared the way for that movement [of the younger musicians like Debussy and Ravel]. His sin in other eyes was that he did not go hand in hand with César Franck». Klein's reply was directed at and appeared directly after Jean-Aubry's attack on Saint-Saëns. See Jean-Aubry 1917b, p. 16.

[58]. See Ball 1993 for an overview of the debate.

[59]. Evans framed it thus in a speech at a dinner given in his honour with many prominent composers present. *The Musical Times*, 1 February 1923, p. 127.

country capable of serious music-making. Suddenly, however, French musical art came to life again, and the history of French music of to-day is that of a resurrection. At a time when Britain is thinking, and rightly so, of "nationalising" her musical creativeness, it cannot be useless to see how her great nation-friend compassed this[60].

Arguing against this reasoning, Newman was one of the Francophiles' most persistent antagonists. Even though he acknowledged Debussy's groundbreaking novelties (some of which he regarded as mannerisms), he was critical of what he saw as the French's increasing obsession with national character[61]. Such dissent originated in the critics' varying understandings of nationalism: what Jean-Aubry and Evans valued as a healthy reaction against uniformity and as crucial for originality, Newman saw as a danger, namely «selecting a few mental traits and elevating them to the dignity of national characteristics». Newman rather looked forward to that French composer who would «roar out from a great chest a great song that will shatter some of these facile theories about French elegance»[62]. Consequently, he also objected to English nationalists who urged the pursuit of folksong and Tudor music[63]. Against an essentialist concept of nationalism, Newman contended that a *British* music was needed, not a *national* music — and French music could be of no use towards that end. He considered it foolish to substitute one model for the other and attributed large parts of the French achievements to local conditions and mindsets. For Newman, Elgar's music was English; for Francophiles and the French, it was only a (pale) imitation of German music[64]. Accordingly, the debate about an appropriate model was inseparable from the aesthetic debate between (German) expression and sentiment and (French) cerebral objectivity and cleverness — between 'modern' and 'modernist'[65].

Rising to prominence during the First World War, Eugene Goossens was a close friend of Evans, and in Evans' eyes he was one of the most promising, authentically English composers. Newman, by contrast, denounced some of Goossens' works (such as the piano cycle *Kaleidoscope*

---

[60]. JEAN-AUBRY 1917A, pp. 14ff. Jean-Aubry wrote this short introductory book especially for British readers. Two years later, Evans' translation of Jean-Aubry's collected volume *La musique française d'aujourd'hui* was published; see JEAN-AUBRY 1919A.

[61]. NEWMAN 1910A; NEWMAN 1910B.

[62]. In a review of Jean-Aubry's *La musique française d'aujourd'hui*. NEWMAN 1917, p. 441.

[63]. NEWMAN 1912.

[64]. «And while a certain school of critics, by reason of some strange blindness, regard this Anglo-French or Anglo-Russian music at one remove as the music out of which an English renaissance is to come, music like Elgar's is considered by them to be German». NEWMAN 1918, p. 472. Jean-Aubry likened Elgar's role to Saint-Saëns's insofar as both had adapted German forms to national requirements. JEAN-AUBRY 1919B, p. 198. For the controversies between Evans and Newman, see SCAIFE 1994, pp. 159-162.

[65]. For the two terms relating to Elgar, see McGUIRE 2008.

Op. 18) as mere French imitations[66]. In a lecture for the newly established Arts League of Service in London in November 1919, Goossens counter-intuitively took up Newman's concerns but regarded them as overcome:

> All new movements in art produce a crop of imitators, and it is only to be expected that with such a drastic revolution of musical speech, such as France gave birth to at the beginning of this century, many would succumb entirely to the new influence rather than profit by its teaching, and in no other country was this so apparent as in our own, where, for a short time, in our endeavours to rid ourselves of the ponderous German influences to which we were enslaved, we seemed likely to revert to the other extreme and become entirely Gallic, both in speech and manner. This fortunately did not entirely happen, and the development in power and significance of the music of Vaughan Williams is only to quote one example of how, under foreign influence, the level-headed musician can assimilate and expand, without sacrificing either the personal or the national characteristic to be found in the work of all real artists[67].

British composers such as Goossens, Frank Bridge, John Ireland, Rebecca Clarke, Ralph Vaughan Williams[68], and Cyril Scott indeed responded eagerly to the new French sounds. The latter two excepted, they also played French music in concert[69]. It provided a different kind of model as a welcome alternative — or rather complement — to the familiar German examples. Chamber music held a special significance in this development: many French composers had been first introduced to Britain through, and remained especially associated with, chamber music. At the same time, homegrown chamber music gained momentum in Britain. It was more broadly and consistently cultivated by composers and more regularly presented in concerts, and ever more frequently by newly founded ensembles such as the London String Quartet and the Philharmonic String Quartet (see above). Recent French and British works were often presented side by side. Whether progressive Francophone elements were signs of imitation or emancipation remained open to debate: in the words of one author, Goossens' Rhapsody for Violoncello and Piano Op. 13 would «be regarded as "French" by many English, and "English" by many French»[70].

---

[66]. Evans' article series *Modern British Composers'* was programmatic. See EVANS 1919; NEWMAN 1918, p. 472.

[67]. GOOSSENS 1919, pp. 9ff.

[68]. During the winter of 1907/1908, Vaughan Williams took composition lessons with Ravel in Paris. Ravel was Calvocoressi's suggestion, whereas Evans had first recommended d'Indy. ADAMS 2013.

[69]. Bridge participated in the British premiere of Debussy's String Quartet and played Fauré's Piano Quartet Op. 15 with the composer in 1914. For more discussion of the composers' involvement with French music and its impact on their own works, see REIßFELDER 2022.

[70]. *The Daily Telegraph*, 8 January 1917, p. 6.

Bibliography

ADAMS 2013
ADAMS, Byron. 'Vaughan Williams's Musical Apprenticeship', in: *The Cambridge Companion to Vaughan Williams*, edited by Alain Frogley and Aidan J. Thomson, Cambridge, Cambridge University Press, 2013 (Cambridge Companions to Music), pp. 29-55.

ALLIS 2012
ALLIS, Michael. 'Performance in Private: «The Working Men's Society» and the Promotion of Progressive Repertoire in Nineteenth-Century Britain', in: *Music and Performance Culture in Nineteenth-Century Britain: Essays in Honour of Nicholas Temperley*, edited by Bennett Zon, Farnham, Ashgate, 2012, pp. 139-171.

ANGELL 2014
ANGELL, Jane. 'Music and Charity on the British Home Front during the First World War', in: *Journal of Musicological Research*, XXXIII/1-3 (2014), pp. 184-205.

BALL 1993
BALL, William Scott. *Reclaiming a Music for England: Nationalist Concept and Controversy in English Musical Thought and Criticism, 1880-1920*, Ph.D. Diss., Columbus (OH), Ohio State University, 1993; Ann Arbor (MI), UMI Research Press, 1993.

BASHFORD 2007
BASHFORD, Christina. *The Pursuit of High Culture: John Ella and Chamber Music in Victorian London*, Woodbridge, Boydell Press, 2007 (Music in Britain, 1600-1900, 3).

BONAVIA 1910
F. B. [BONAVIA, Ferruccio]. 'New French Music', in: *The Manchester Guardian*, 29 December 1910.

CALVOCORESSI 1906
CALVOCORESSI, Michel-Dimitri. 'A Few Remarks on Modern French Pianoforte Music', in: *The Monthly Musical Record*, XXXVI/426 (1906), pp. 123-124.

CALCOVORESSI 1912
ID. 'Franckism and Impressionism. A Study of Extremes', (Home Music Study Union, Course on French Music, Sixth Paper), in: *The Music Student*, IV/7 (1912), pp. 285-287.

CALVOCORESSI 1933
ID. *Musicians Gallery: Music and Ballet in Paris and London: Recollections*, London, Faber & Faber, 1933.

CLUTSAM 1911
G. H. C. [CLUTSAM, George H.] 'Music. Yesterday's Concerts', in: *The Observer*, 26 February 1911.

COLLES 1915
COLLES, H. C. 'César Franck and the Sonata', in: *The Musical Times*, LVI/866 (1915), pp. 206-209.

DIBBLE 1992
DIBBLE, Jeremy. *C. Hubert H. Parry: His Life and Music*, Oxford, Clarendon Press, 1992.

DIBBLE 2002
ID. *Charles Villiers Stanford: Man and Musician*, Oxford, Oxford University Press, 2002.

EVANS 1909
[EVANS, Edwin.] 'Musical Party Strife in France', in: *The Academy*, 7 August 1909.

EVANS 1910A
ID. 'French Music of To-day', in: *Proceedings of the Musical Association*, XXXVI (1909-1910), pp. 47-74.

EVANS 1910B
ID. 'The Significance of Contemporary French Music', (Report on Lecture at the Incorporated Society of Musicians), in: *The Musical Times*, LI/804 (1910), p. 107.

EVANS 1917
ID. 'The Foundations of Twentieth Century Music', in: *The Musical Times*, LVIII/894 (1917), pp. 347-351.

EVANS 1919
ID. 'Modern British Composers. IV. Eugène Goossens', two parts, in: *The Musical Times*, LX/916-917 (1919), pp. 265-268, 329-334.

FAURÉ 1951
FAURÉ, Gabriel. *Lettres intimes*, edited by Philippe Fauré-Fremiet, Paris, La Colombe, 1951.

GOOSSENS 1919
GOOSSENS, Eugène. *Modern Tendencies in Music*, (Lecture for the Arts League of Service, 27.11.1919), London, [1919].

GUÉRITTE 1945
GUÉRITTE, T. J. 'Mr. Edwin Evans', in: *The Times*, 16 March 1945.

JEAN-AUBRY 1917A
JEAN-AUBRY, G. *An Introduction to French Music*, English translation by Percy A. Scholes, London, Cecil Palmer & Hayward, 1917.

JEAN-AUBRY 1917B
ID. 'Camille Saint-Saëns: Wagner and French Music', in: *The Musical Times*, LVIII/887 (1917), pp. 13-16.

JEAN-AUBRY 1919A
ID. *La musique française d'aujourd'hui*, Paris, Perrin, 1916; English translation by Edwin Evans, *French Music of To-day*, London, Kegan Paul, Trench, Trubner, 1919.

JEAN-AUBRY 1919B
ID. 'British Music Through French Eyes', in: *The Musical Quarterly*, V/2 (1919), pp. 192-212.

KELLY 2020
KELLY, Barbara L. 'French Connections: Debussy and Ravel's Orchestral Music in Britain from *Prélude à l'après-midi d'un faune* to *Boléro*', in: *The Symphonic Poem in Britain, 1850-1950*, edited by Michael Allis and Paul Watt, Woodbridge, Boydell Press, 2020 (Music in Britain, 1600-1900, 26), pp. 115-146.

LANGLEY 2012
LANGLEY, Leanne. 'Joining Up the Dots: Cross-Channel Models in the Shaping of London Orchestral Culture, 1895-1914', in: *Music and Performance Culture in Nineteenth-Century Britain: Essays in Honour of Nicholas Temperley*, *op. cit.*, pp. 37-58.

MACKENZIE 1907
MACKENZIE, Alexander. 'Phases of Modern French Music', (Report on Lecture at the Royal Institution), in: *The Musical Herald*, 1 March 1907.

McGUIRE 2008
McGUIRE, Charles Edward. 'Edward Elgar: «Modern» or «Modernist»? Construction of an Aesthetic Identity in the British Music Press, 1895-1934', in: *The Musical Quarterly*, XCI/1-2 (2008), pp. 8-38.

MEADMORE 1929
MEADMORE, W. S. 'British Performing Organizations. (2) Present-Day Organizations', in: *Cobbett's Cyclopedic Survey of Chamber Music. 1*, edited by Walter Willson Cobbett, London, Oxford University Press, 1929, pp. 203-212.

NEWMAN 1909
NEWMAN, Ernest. 'César Franck and the Modern French School of Composers', (Report on Lecture in Liverpool), in: *The Manchester Guardian*, 23 January 1909.

NEWMAN 1910A
ID. 'A Note on Debussy', in: *The Musical Times*, LI/807 (1910), pp. 293-296.

NEWMAN 1910B
ID. 'Debussy on Nationality in Music', in: *The Musical Times*, LI/813 (1910), pp. 700-702.

NEWMAN 1912
ID. 'The Folk-Song Fallacy', in: *The English Review*, XI/10 (1912), pp. 255-268.

NEWMAN 1917
ID. 'The New French Recipe', (Reprint from the *Birmingham Post*, 20 August 1917), in: *The Musical Times*, LVIII/896 (1917), p. 441.

Newman 1918
Id. 'Mr. Ernest Newman on French and English Music', in: *The Musical Times*, LIX/908 (1918), pp. 471-472.

Piatigorsky 2018
Piatigorsky, Anna. *The Campaign for French Music: The Société des Concerts Français and the Critical Reception of French Music in Britain 1907-1915*, unpublished M.Mus. Thesis, Melbourne (VIC), University of Melbourne, 2018.

Ratner 2002
Ratner, Sabina Teller. *Camille Saint-Saëns, 1835-1921: A Thematic Catalogue of His Complete Works. 1: The Instrumental Works*, Oxford, Oxford University Press, 2002.

Reißfelder 2022
Reißfelder, David. *Paris in London. Kammermusikalische Begegnungen um 1900*, Hildesheim, Georg Olms Verlag, 2022.

Rodmell 2021
Rodmell, Paul. *French Music in Britain 1830-1914*, Abingdon-New York, Routledge, 2021 (Music in Nineteenth-Century Britain).

Rodriguez 2004
Rodriguez, Philippe. 'Georges Jean-Aubry: infatigable passeur des arts', in: *Cahiers Maurice Ravel*, VIII (2004), pp. 199-135.

Runciman 1902
Runciman, John F. 'Busoni, Ysaÿe and Others', in: *The Saturday Review*, 20 December 1902.

Runciman 1914
Id. '«Frivolous» Music', in: *The Saturday Review*, 18 July 1914.

Scaife 1994
Scaife, Nigel Clifford. *British Music Criticism in a New Era: Studies in Critical Thought 1894-1945*, unpublished Ph.D. Diss., Oxford, University of Oxford, 1994.

Stonequist 1972
Stonequist, Martha Elisabeth. *The Musical Entente Cordiale, 1905-1916*, unpublished Ph.D. Diss., Boulder (CO), University of Colorado at Boulder, 1972; Ann Arbor (MI), UMI Research Press, 1972.

Stove 2011
Stove, R. J. 'Franck after Franck: The Composer's Posthumous Fortunes', in: *The Musical Times*, CLII/1914 (2011), pp. 44-60.

Stove 2012
Id. *César Franck: His Life and Times*, Lanham (MD), Scarecrow Press, 2012.

STRAETEN 1933
STRAETEN, Edmund van der. *The History of the Violin: Its Ancestors and Collateral Instruments from Earliest Times to the Present Day. 2*, London, Cassell, 1933.

SYMONS 1907
SYMONS, Arthur. 'French Music in London', in: *The Saturday Review*, 14 December 1907.

TERNANT 1925
TERNANT, Andrew de. 'César Franck and His Opus 1 in England', in: *The Musical Times*, LXVI/989 (1925), pp. 609-610.

WEBER 2008
WEBER, William. *The Great Transformation of Musical Taste: Concert Programming from Haydn to Brahms*, Cambridge, Cambridge University Press, 2008.

WEBER 2020
ID. 'Musical Canons', in: *The Oxford Handbook of Music and Intellectual Culture in the Nineteenth Century*, edited by Paul Watt, Sarah Collins and Michael Allis, New York, Oxford University Press, 2020, pp. 319-341.

WENZEL 2018
WENZEL, Silke. 'Fanny Frickenhaus', in: *MUGI. Musikvermittlung und Genderforschung: Lexikon und multimediale Präsentationen*, edited by Beatrix Borchard and Nina Noeske, 2018, <https://mugi.hfmt-hamburg.de/artikel/Fanny_Frickenhaus.html>, accessed December 2023.

WHITE 2006
WHITE, John. *Lionel Tertis: The First Great Virtuoso of the Viola*, Woodbridge, Boydell Press, 2006.

Chamber Concerts for Champagne Socialists: Quartets and Contradictions at Manchester's Ancoats Brotherhood at the End of the Long Nineteenth Century

Geoff Thomason
(Royal Northern College of Music, Manchester)

For those who know Manchester, Ancoats is an area to the east of the city centre, in the hinterland behind Victoria Railway Station, roughly enclosed by the angle of the railway line and Great Ancoats Street and intersected by two main thoroughfares, the Oldham and Rochdale Roads. Today it has become quite gentrified, with the former mills and warehouses which once operated as powerhouses of Britain's Industrial Revolution now converted into desirable apartments, but during the nineteenth century it was one of the poorest of the city's inner suburbs.

In 1844, Friedrich Engels described Ancoats thus in *The Condition of the Working Class in England*:

> In the [...] broad district included under the name Ancoats, stand the largest mills in Manchester lining the canals, colossal six and seven-storied buildings towering with their chimneys far above the low cottages of the workers. The population of the district consists, therefore, chiefly of mill hands and, in the worst streets, of hand weavers. The streets nearest the heart of the town are the oldest, and consequently the worst. Farther to the north-east lie many newly built-up streets, here the cottages look neat and cleanly [...] the vacant building lots between them larger and more numerous. But this can be said of a minority of the houses only, while cellar dwellings are to be found under almost every cottage; many streets are unpaved and without sewers, and worst of all, this neat appearance is all pretence [...]. For the construction of the cottages individually is no less to be condemned than the plan of the streets. All such cottages look neat and substantial at first, their massive

ILL. 1: Ancoats in 1895 — Manchester Libraries, Information and Archives.

brick construction deceives the eye, and, on passing through a newly-built working-men's street, one is inclined to agree with the assertion of the Liberal manufacturers that the working population is nowhere so well housed as in England. But on closer examination it becomes evident that the walls of these cottages are as thin as it is possible to make them[1].

In the course of the nineteenth century the native population of Ancoats was swelled by numbers of Italian immigrants, earning it the nickname of Manchester's 'Little Italy'. It was also home to many Irish immigrants escaping the potato famine of the late 1840s[2]. This accounted for the high percentage of Roman Catholics and Roman Catholic churches in the area. While standards of living remained poor, commercially it was one of the city's most successful areas: the mills in which most of its residents were employed benefitted from the convenience of transport offered by its proximity to the railway and to the Rochdale and Ashton Canals and the River Medlock. The wealth it generated, however, together with the cultural capital it supported, was concentrated in Manchester's southern suburbs such as Didsbury or Withington, or further south in the expanding commuter towns of North Cheshire. Several of these, such as Bramhall, Bowdon or Alderley Edge, owed their creation in the nineteenth century to the coming of the railway.

Drawing attention to the parallels between the development of Manchester's cultural life in the nineteenth century and its industrial and commercial expansion, several writers have questioned the notion that both followed different trajectories. John Seed has discussed the role of the city's emergent, culturally literate middle classes as patrons of the visual arts[3], while Wilfred Allis, in his discussion of the city's Gentlemen's Concerts, has argued in favour

---

1. ENGELS 1892, pp. 56-57.
2. REA – RICHARDSON 1988.
3. SEED 1988.

ILL. 2: Charles Rowley by Ford Madox Brown, 1885 – © Manchester Art Gallery / Bridgeman Images.

of seeing the concerts' conscious social exclusivity as their principal attraction[4]. Elsewhere, Richard Roberts and John K. Walton have examined the role of middle-class patronage exercised through local government[5]. The latter's analysis is relevant here, as it was through his involvement in local government that one individual was to exercise his concern for the cultural life of Ancoats' residents.

Charles Rowley (1839-1933) was born in Ancoats, into a family of thirteen children[6]. He served his time in its workshops and helped run soup kitchens during the Cotton Famine of the 1860s. Politically a Fabian socialist, he was elected as a council member for Ancoats in 1875, serving, among other things, on the Sanitation Committee, through which he established public baths and wash-houses. He was also a firm believer in bringing the arts to the people. He organised band concerts and was instrumental in setting up the Manchester Art Museum in Ancoats. He was also the founder of 'Recreation in Ancoats'. As he noted in his autobiographical *Fifty Years of Work without Wages*:

> In the autumn of 1881 we started a Sunday afternoon meeting in the New Islington Hall. Sir Henry Roscoe F.R.S. gave the first lecture, the subject being

---

[4]. ALLIS 1995.
[5]. ROBERTS 1983; WALTON 1983.
[6]. ROWLEY 1900.

"John Dalton". We had some music each day and met from three to five. These afternoons were a great success from the first. We got together from five to nine hundred people, mostly men. Not going for the rhetorical or popular in any way, we have avoided the dry, the pompous and the patronising [...][7].

In 1889 the programme was expanded to include extra-mural activities and became the Ancoats Brotherhood, but the pattern of Sunday meetings was retained. Guest speakers, many known to Rowley personally, delivered their lecture between two recitals of music. Surviving programmes reveal these lectures as bearing out Rowley's claim to have avoided the «rhetorical or popular», preferring instead themes of a political, philosophical, ethical or moral nature. Speakers from the 1890s include Henry Simon on 'Cremation' (one of the few papers to have survived through publication), Richard Pankhurst, (husband of the women's suffrage campaigner Emmeline Pankhurst) on 'Federation, Citizenship, Ethics', and the *Manchester Guardian*'s music critic Arthur Johnstone on 'Beethoven'[8]. There are early signs too, in lectures on Nelson, General Gordon and 'True Patriotism', of an emphasis on national identity which was to grow over the coming years. Rowley included in his book what he maintained were genuine testimonials from those who attended, such as this from Fred Walker, described as a wire drawer in an Ancoats workshop: «To say what the Ancoats Recreation movement has been to me would be to give an account of the social and educational sides of my life for the past twenty-one years, so strongly has the Ancoats Recreation movement influenced me»[9]. Or, R. Cross, a commercial traveller: «I often am amazed when I think how much I owe to those meetings in Ancoats. Unlike most other organisations, "Ancoats" touches life at every point. I was like thousands of other young men who are without any definite plan, and are aimlessly drifting along. It is just at that stage where the movement you founded becomes of such value»[10]. Given the language in which they are couched, it is tempting here to speculate as to whether these really are the verbatim comments of poorly-educated Ancoats workers or paraphrases by Rowley himself.

Jonathan Rose, in *The Intellectual Life of the British Working Classes* has warned against popular assumptions that educational movements such as that at Ancoats were wholly motivated by a patronising, middle class, 'we know what's good for you' attitude[11]. Rowley himself countered any suggestion that the lectures and recitals were either poorly attended or over the heads of those who heard them. Reviewing the meeting which relaunched the project as the Ancoats Brotherhood in March 1889, the *Manchester Guardian* recorded further testimony

---

[7]. *Ibidem*, p. 199.
[8]. SIMON 1892.
[9]. ROWLEY 1900, pp. 217-218.
[10]. *Ibidem*, pp. 218-219.
[11]. ROSE 2001.

from Rowley as to the success of his venture. More significantly it reported his defence of the Brotherhood's activities having their own pro-nationalist, patriotic agenda. His argument suggests that he, at least, had clear ideas as to the values his patrons should be encouraged to aspire to:

> [...] audiences ranged from a thousand to four hundred, and many of these were regular members [...]. Why should they not meet and talk about subjects upon which they wanted to form just and workable opinions? [...] All social subjects which interested them as neighbours and citizens might be faced. Had they any local patriotism, or even truly national patriotism[12]?

The theme of 'national patriotism' was taken up elsewhere. A lecture entitled simply 'Patriotism', given by the barrister A. Woodroofe Fletcher shortly after the relief of Kimberley and Ladysmith in the Second Boer War, distinguished «the patriotism of the last few weeks [which] was based on a very lofty principle of morality or conduct» with «what they heard now [which] was not so much national patriotism as Imperial patriotism in very large letters»[13]. Imperial patriotism he defined as, «the increasing of the Empire's borders and the swallowing-up of small nations which followed as a consequence, [and] was not a policy consistent with the brotherhood of the human race»[14]. Five years later an address by Manchester University's Professor Sadler deplored the failure to instil patriotic values in the nation's schools, not merely because young children possessed impressionable minds, but because «[...] in those schools where we were dealing with newly-arrived immigrants it was desirable to do more than we were doing to let them know what the conditions were in the country into which [...] they had come»[15].

By the beginning of the twentieth century, Manchester's already substantial immigrant population had been swelled by large numbers of Polish and Russian Jewish refugees, many of whom, according to surviving alien registration records, settled in areas to the north and north west of Manchester city centre, or over the municipal border in the neighbouring town of Salford. Census returns for 1901 record 8,094 Russians, including Polish nationals, living in Manchester, as opposed to 2,935 German, Austrian or Swiss. Yet, unlike their Teutophone counterparts, the Russian/Polish community was largely working class and therefore took little or no part in the city's concert life. There is also no evidence that they came within the orbit of the activities of the Ancoats' Brotherhood.

---

[12]. *Manchester* 1889, p. 12.

[13]. *Manchester and Lancashire* 1900, p. 10. The relief of Kimberley had taken place on 15 February, that of Ladysmith on 28 February.

[14]. *Ibidem.*

[15]. *Manchester and Lancashire* 1905, p. 8.

Music at Ancoats

Rowley notes that the musicians who performed at the Ancoats meetings often gave their services free[16]. Both men and women took part, although the latter initially appeared only as singers or pianists. One name that appears consistently in these early concerts is that of the cellist Carl Fuchs.

Ill. 3: Carl Fuchs – RNCM Archives.

Fuchs (1865-1951) was a German-born cellist who later adopted British citizenship. A student of Bernard Cossmann at the Hoch Conservatoire in Frankfurt, his playing had sufficiently impressed Clara Schumann that she provided a letter of introduction to Charles Hallé in Manchester[17]. One of several foreign musicians active in the city, not least in the Hallé Orchestra (of which he became principal cellist), he is of particular importance in that he became a member of the string quartet which Adolph Brodsky founded shortly after his arrival

---

16. Rowley 1900, pp. 199ff.: «Quite as fortunate have we been in our music […]. Here the list of kind and voluntary helpers is endless».

17. Dated 20 January 1887. Copy at RNCM CF/1/33.

ILL. 4: Adolph Brodsky – RNCM Archives.

in Manchester in 1895, and which in turn emerged as the mostly frequently heard chamber ensemble at the Ancoats Brotherhood. Although the lack of any direct correspondence leaves a question mark over the extent of Fuchs' influence on the planning of the early Ancoats recitals, the numerous instances in which they became a vehicle for his own performances might, however, offer a clue.

Prior to Brodsky's arrival, the earlier Ancoats programmes consisted primarily of several short pieces or movements from longer works, with an emphasis on the Austro-German canon. Composers represented prior to the first appearances of the Brodsky Quartet at Ancoats include J. S. Bach, Ferdinand David, Karl Anton Eckert, W. A. Mozart, Felix Mendelssohn, Ludwig van Beethoven, Franz Schubert, George Frideric Handel, Robert Schumann, David Popper, Joseph Haydn, Max Bruch and Johannes Brahms. These account for over half the known works performed, with Beethoven the most performed within this group. Several of the remaining pieces are moreover by composers on the fringes of the Austro-German tradition, such as Josef Rheinberger, Franz Liszt, and Niels W. Gade.

The Russian violinist Adolph Brodsky (1851-1929) was a native of the port city of Taganrog. He had studied in Vienna with Joseph Hellmesberger and consolidated his reputation by giving the first public performance of Pyotr Il'yich Tchaikovsky's Violin concerto with Hans Richter and the Vienna Philharmonic in December 1881. For most of the 1880s he taught at the Leipzig Conservatoire while remaining active as a performer. It was there that he formed his first string quartet. Brodsky left Germany in 1891 to become leader of the New York Symphony, resigning two years later after a union dispute with conductor Walter Damrosch. By the end of 1894 he was in Berlin when Charles Hallé invited him to Manchester to replace Willy Hess as leader of his orchestra and Professor of Violin at his recently opened Royal Manchester College of Music. On 25 October 1895, Hallé died, and Brodsky was appointed to succeed him as the College's Principal, a post he held until his own death in January 1929.

Brodsky had given regular chamber concerts throughout his tenure in Leipzig. There he came into contact with, among others, Brahms, Edvard Grieg, and Ferruccio Busoni, as well as Ethel Smyth, whose violin sonata he premiered. His Leipzig programmes bear out the Conservatoire's reputation for conservatism, straying but little from a largely nineteenth-century Austro-German repertoire and with all but one of the forty-odd programmes containing music by Beethoven.

In Manchester Brodsky lost little time in forming a new quartet, with second violinist Christopher Rawdon Briggs and Hallé violist Simon Speelman as well as Fuchs. Their own series of Brodsky Quartet Concerts was established in 1896, and as early as November 1895 they had made their debut at Manchester's Schiller-Anstalt. Founded in 1859 in commemoration of the centenary of the birth of Friedrich Schiller, the Schiller-Anstalt, situated in Nelson Street south of the city centre, functioned as a social meeting place for Manchester's German community[18]. Much of this social activity centred around concerts, for the organisation of which Carl Fuchs was also responsible, and which frequently invited major German musicians to perform. The clarinettist Richard Mühlfeld, for example, appeared there in 1900, playing the Brahms clarinet quintet with the Brodsky Quartet. Richard Strauss was a guest artist in 1904.

The audience profile of the Schiller-Anstalt — German, middle class, affluent (as early as the 1890s patrons could book tickets by telephone) — was a gift to Brodsky's own grounding in, and preference for, the Austro-German chamber music canon. The repertoire overlaps considerably with that of the Brodsky Quartet Concerts, which at this stage enjoyed a regular venue at the city's Gentlemen's Concert Hall[19]. Indeed, some years later,

[18]. Nelson Street was also home to the Pankhurst family. The Schiller-Anstalt building was demolished in 1930.

[19]. Demolished in 1903 and replaced by the Midland Hotel, where the Brodsky Quartet Concerts initially moved.

ILL. 5: The Brodsky Quartet c.1900 – RNCM Archives.

an anonymous correspondent to the *Manchester Guardian* commented that «the support for music in Manchester is mainly from the large colony of Germans residing there»[20]. It is no surprise, then, that the quartet's first appearance at an Ancoats concert, on 15 November 1896, consisted of movements from Schubert's *Death and the Maiden* quartet and the first of Beethoven's *Rasumovsky* quartets. At their next recital, in February 1898, Arthur Johnstone, music critic for the *Manchester Guardian*, lectured on Beethoven, with musical examples played by the Brodsky Quartet and pianist Sydney Vantyn of the Liège Conservatoire. Such a fusion of the spoken and performed sections of the afternoon's proceedings proved an innovation. The precedent was followed in February 1908 when Carl Fuchs lectured on 'Beethoven and the Violoncello'. Not only did Brodsky's concentration on the predominantly canonic Austro-German repertoire demonstrate his own preferences, it appears to have found an echo in those of the Brotherhood's founder.

Rowley's testimony to the success of the Brotherhood, quoted above, singles out Beethoven in the context of 'the best of the fine arts'. Beethoven is also the only composer to have been accorded the honour of forming the subject of an Ancoats lecture. In addition to those already mentioned, a lecture on Beethoven was given by a Mr. T. W. Surette on 31 October 1911, on which occasion the programme carried a quote from Spitta: «A perfectly lucid musical vitality, sufficient always unto itself, is to be found only in Mozart: Haydn and

---

[20].   *MANCHESTER* 1913, p. 13.

Beethoven are more open to poetic influences, Beethoven very much more than Haydn». And from Tchaikovsky: «Mozart reaches neither the depths nor the heights of Beethoven. And since in life too, he remained a careless child, his music has not that subjective tragic quality which is so powerfully expressed in that of Beethoven»[21].

T. Whitney Surette was a staff lecturer on music for the American Society for the Extension of University Teaching. He had previously given a series of lectures on the Beethoven symphonies in conjunction with a Beethoven cycle given by Hans Richter with the Hallé Orchestra in 1907, on which occasion he was introduced by Rowley[22]. In the 1880s Rowley presented to Manchester University a series of twelve panels by Ford Madox Brown — a personal acquaintance — depicting leaders in the arts and sciences. Many are from antiquity, the Middle Ages, or the Renaissance: Homer, Cicero, Aristotle, Bacon, Michelangelo and Shakespeare. The only 'modern', representing music, is Beethoven.

By the turn of the century the Brodsky Quartet had become regular performers at the Ancoats Brotherhood, giving at least one annual concert. Although they played complete works rather than excerpts, their repertoire remained notably small. Known to Fuchs and violist Simon Speelman from Henry Rensburg's concerts in Liverpool, cellist Henry Smith joined them in February 1900 for the Schubert string quintet, heard with Beethoven's Quartet Op. 18, No. 6. The following year brought *Death and the Maiden* again, with Beethoven's Op. 29 String Quintet, a favourite work of Brodsky's which he performed several times in Leipzig but where its status as a rarity in Manchester concerts was commented on in local press reviews. In the twenty two Ancoats concerts given by the Quartet between 1900 and early 1914, only fifteen composers are represented, of which Beethoven, with twenty five performances, is far and away the most common[23]. Schubert comes second with nine (still mostly the string quintet or *Death and the Maiden*), with six pieces each by Mozart and Haydn, five by Mendelssohn, two each by Brahms and Bach, and one by Schumann. Less familiar works include those by composers whom Brodsky had championed in Leipzig; Robert Volkmann — another personal favourite — Tchaikovsky and Grieg. Visiting artists included Julius Klengel, Brodsky's cellist in Leipzig.

This emphasis on the Austro-German canon is understandable in a city whose musical profile, as evidenced by other major institutions such as the Hallé Orchestra and the Gentlemen's Concerts, mirrored a German émigré population which had been growing in size and influence since the 1840s. Not all were active musicians; some, like Gustav Behrens, first Secretary to the Council of the Royal Manchester College of Music, chose to use industrial wealth to promote music in the city. A major coup had been the appointment of Hans Richter as successor to Hallé as conductor of the Hallé Orchestra and Gentlemen's Concerts, in the latter capacity

---

21. Ancoats Brotherhood programmes are held in Manchester Central Library.
22. *Manchester* 1907, p. 7.
23. This includes the cycle of six concerts that the Brodsky Quartet gave in January and February 1914.

ousting the short tenure of Frederic Cowen and thereby provoking the accusation from W. H. Cummings, Principal of London's Guildhall School of Music, that this was «the result of the Teutonic influence in Manchester»[24].

Rowley remained firm in his claim that his organisation existed for the benefit of the people of Ancoats. In reality, by the turn of the century, the situation was otherwise. The Brotherhood already hosted such activities as a cycling club and regular trips to the continent that would have been well beyond the financial means of the average mill worker. In November 1906, the *Manchester Courier* published a lengthy but anonymous attack on Rowley and the Brotherhood, citing it as a venture which had long since left its original aims behind. The writer targeted the Brotherhood's concerts in particular:

> The civilisation of Ancoats has now been going on apace for so long that it is time a protest were raised against the idea that Ancoats now requires it. The well-dressed people who make incursions thither [...] where they sit and flatter themselves that they are doing a good work, but their self-sacrifice in appreciating the fine music [...] is fully rewarded by their receiving an entertainment free that would mean cabs, evening dress and gold in Peter Street[25].

Peter Street was the site of the Free Trade Hall, Manchester's principal concert hall and home to the Hallé Orchestra. The writer continues:

> The mental pabulum [...] is too strong for the palate of the men and women who left school in the Fourth and Fifth Standards, ten, fifteen, twenty years ago. Therefore objection is taken to this patting of Ancoats on the back [...] this swooping down of silks and satins on a maligned district [...] the committee is now more or less a medium for the provision of splendid concerts [...]. But they are all now pretty well to do, the poorest not very poor, and the man who does not go out of Ancoats is not one of them [...]. The Sunday afternooners are chiefly those who may have had — "A dinner not severely plain, a pint or two of really good champagne"[26].

The above implies that this new breed of audience did not merely sit alongside the attentive mill workers of Ancoats, but effectively replaced them. This tension between the kind of working class audience envisaged by Rowley and the affluent middle class audience

---

[24]. ALLIS 1995, p. 116: «Cowen's contract was terminated, and the treatment brought an angry letter from the Principal of the Guildhall School of Music [...] who thought the treatment of Cowen to be shameful and probably the result of the Teutonic influence in Manchester». Adolph Brodsky refers to Cowen's replacement by Richter in a letter to Ferruccio Busoni of 3 November 1898. Berlin: Staatsbibliothek Preußischer Kulturbesitz, Mus NL F Busoni B II 1062.

[25]. *MANCHESTER AND LANCASHIRE* 1906, p. 10.

[26]. The quotation is from *After Horace* by A. D. Godley, first published in his *Lyra Frivola* of 1899.

which the Brotherhood's concerts came to attract created one of a number of moral dilemmas which presented themselves during the history of the organisation. This audience will also have included members of Manchester's German community which patronised the Brodsky Quartet Concerts and those at the Schiller-Anstalt. It was presumably to them that Captain Schlagintweit, the German Consul in Manchester, addressed his own view of patriotism in January 1913, appealing to «Germans who became naturalised Englishmen not to forget or to deny the land of their birth» and urging the individual «never to forget the race from which he springs [...]» and to, «devote all his spare energies to acting as mediator, conciliator and interpreter between his old and his adopted country»[27].

Amid such a wealth of German music, where, then, were the complementary lectures on other aspects of German culture? Throughout the Edwardian years one looks in vain among the lectures which were regularly given on other foreign cultures, such as Hilaire Belloc on 'Modern France', Councillor Butterworth on 'The Canadian Outlook', or the Rev. Hudson Shaw on 'Ravenna'[28]. Plenty of lectures also contributed to the Brotherhood's implicit promulgation of a more nationalist outlook: the Dean of Ely on 'An Ideal Church, from the Church of England Point of View' a series of six lectures on 'The Works of Chaucer', Philip Carr on 'The National Theatre Movement', or Belloc again on 'The Battle of Crecy: Its Importance in Military History'[29]. Yet, in Rowley's agenda of inculcating national pride which such lectures were intended to support, there was little celebration of British music beyond a handful of songs and slighter piano pieces by composers such as Ralph Vaughan Williams, Granville Bantock, Landon Ronald and Cyril Scott, all of them largely the preserve of female performers. However, any suggestion that the Brotherhood was intrinsically anti-German at this period is countered by the fact that since before the turn of the century the trips to the continent organised for members — or at least the affluent patrons who could afford them — included several to Germany. In 1913 the *Manchester Courier* was able to report that: «Thirty-seven members of the Ancoats Brotherhood left London Road Station yesterday afternoon en route for a week's visit to North Germany. It was the fifteenth party of its kind organised by the Brotherhood [...]»[30]. Then, on 23 February 1913, in the programme for the Manchester Trio (Edward Isaacs, Arthur Catterall and Carl Fuchs) playing Brahms, Schumann and Beethoven, there appeared a cartoon with the caption *Teutonic satire*. The scene is a society salon where an eminent German singer is performing:

---

[27]. *MANCHESTER AND LANCASHIRE* 1913A, p. 13. The address to the Brotherhood on 5 January was entitled 'Leaves from a Consul's Notebook' and his wife Therese sang in the concert which followed.

[28]. 17 January 1904; 21 January 1906; 13 January 1909. Belloc was MP for the local constituency of Salford South 1906-1910.

[29]. 18 January 1903; 23 January 1910; 22 January 1911.

[30]. *MANCHESTER AND LANCASHIRE* 1913B, p. 4.

CHAMBER CONCERTS FOR CHAMPAGNE SOCIALISTS

HOSTESS: *Oh, pray don't leave off Mr. Rosencranz... That was a lovely song you just began!*

EMINENT BARITONE: *Yes matame... Bot it tit not harmonise viz de cheneral gonverzation. It is in B vlat, and you and your vrends are talking in G! I haf a song in F, and a song in A sharp... bot I haf no song in G!*

ACCOMPANIST: *Ach – berhaps to obliche matame, I could transpose de aggompaniments – ja!*

So — Germans give us great music, but it's okay to make fun of them. More seriously, by 1913 lectures were already beginning to reflect the growing tension between Britain and Germany, adopting an overtly political tone and giving more prominence to nationalist topics. In December 1913, when Dr. David Starr Jordan spoke on 'War and Manhood', the programme reproduced an (uncredited) article 'The Case of Herr Brandt and the Octopus of Appeasement', highlighting Karl Liebknecht's role in blowing the whistle on false statistics used to stimulate the German arms trade[31]. The following month the Dean of Manchester spoke on 'Democracy, Its Merits and Its Dangers'[32]. At the same time the Brodsky Quartet began a series of six recitals consisting almost entirely of music by Haydn, Schubert, Beethoven, Mozart, Schumann, Brahms, Mendelssohn, and Bach.

There were signs, too, that Manchester's interest in chamber music was diminishing. In addition to the letter cited earlier commenting on a substantial support for concerts from the city's German community, a further letter from William Eller to the *Manchester Guardian* in October 1913[33] criticised «the steady falling off in subscriptions to the Hallé concerts» and «the still more marked falling off in support for the Brodsky Quartet Concerts»[34]. Comments were also made about the indifference of Manchester audiences to other than visiting foreign artists. After the outbreak of war, the music critic Samuel Langford noted in the *Manchester Guardian* that:

> The war seems so violently to have affected the liking for music that not only is the supply of chamber music cut off but appreciation has been strangely lacking for the few chamber concerts we have had [...]. The sense that in quartet-writing music is near to becoming an artifice, appealing chiefly to the initiated and the "Fancier", steals over the most musical occasionally[35].

After war was declared in August 1914, the Brotherhood swung into anti-German mode with a vengeance. On 25 October it reproduced 'The Divine Mission of the Kaiser.

---

[31]. 7 December 1913.
[32]. 11 January 1913.
[33]. ELLER 1913.
[34]. *MANCHESTER* 1913, p. 13.
[35]. LANGFORD 1915, p. 3.

Proclamation to his Eastern Army. The Devil is His God': «Remember you are the elect people. The spirit of the Lord has descended upon me because I am the Emperor of the Germans. I am the Instrument of the Almighty [...]. Destruction and death to all who resist my will [...]. May all the enemies of the German people perish [...]. God, who speaks through me, commands you to execute his will»[36]. The Ancoats Brotherhood was well aware of the scale of what was to come: the lecture for that day was 'Armageddon and After' by Mr. B. N. Langton-Davies. A month later an (uncredited) article was reproduced attacking German housing policy as vastly inferior to that in Britain, including the footnote, «Let us hear no more of German "Kultur", or progress in education»[37].

In January 1915, MP George Roberts spoke on 'Labour and International Peace'. The programme reproduced a letter by Sir T[homas] Jackson: «[...] The letters in your columns have exposed [...] the shallowness of German pretentions to discovery in many fields of science and literature. No-one will dispute their supremacy in music, but their claim to distinction in the other arts is [...] simply amazing»[38]. His diatribe even went so far as to deride the nineteenth century completion of Cologne cathedral as an example of megalomania and bad taste. Jackson's comment may well articulate the cultural dilemma in which the Ancoats Brotherhood found itself. While speakers waged a national opposition to German culture, German music somehow required defence from criticism.

The Brodsky Quartet was, initially, not in a position to contribute to the implied debate. At the outbreak of war, Brodsky, on holiday in Marienbad, was interned in Austria and Fuchs, visiting his family, in Germany. The musical contributions to the Ancoats meetings experienced an understandable reduction in the number of male performers and a glut of vocal recitals by largely female singers. Some of these saw it as their patriotic duty to abandon the Austro-German repertoire completely, even, in one instance to include military songs, as Amy Brooke did in January 1915 when she sang her own compositions *Gallant Belgium* and *When Lancashire Leads the Way*. Others continued to draw, at least in part, on the Lieder tradition — admittedly usually singing in English — among a growing number of songs by French and English composers. The appearance of names like Claude Debussy, Cécile Chaminade, Vaughan Williams or Sir Granville Bantock suggests, not just an eschewing of the German school, but also a growing turn, especially by female singers, from the canonic to the contemporary.

The lack of male performers also created an opening for women beyond their traditional roles as singers or pianists. As early as October 1914, the anti-Kaiser diatribe quoted above appeared in a concert that featured an all-female string quartet. True, they played Haydn; but more significantly they played Frank Bridge — completely uncharted territory for the

---

36. This had appeared in the *Manchester Guardian*, 12 October 1914, p. 10.
37. 15 November 1914.
38. 3 January 1915.

Brodsky Quartet. The year 1914 also witnessed the first of several recitals by the all-female Edith Robinson Quartet, featuring Brodsky's pupils. Other Brodsky pupils who appeared included the violinist Ethel Richmond and Arthur Catterall, whose own quartet (Catterall, John Bridge, Frank Park and Johan Hock) gave several recitals. Another featured quartet was led by Catterall's second violinist, John Bridge. Its novel programme on 24 October 1915 complemented Schubert's A minor quartet with music by Frank Bridge and Percy Grainger. As Bella Baillie, the Manchester soprano Isobel Baillie made her Ancoats debut during the war, as did a young Eric Fogg, whose mother was Baillie's teacher, while his father conducted Crumpsall Male Voice Choir, who also featured in the Ancoats programmes at this time. Baillie and Fogg appeared together in November 1917, in a programme of English and French songs and piano music by Debussy and Cyril Scott[39].

Adolph Brodsky's return to the UK in 1915 marked a resumption of his quartet's Ancoats appearances, with Walter Hatton replacing the still-interned Carl Fuchs[40]. There is little evidence of Brodsky's own preferences having been nuanced by European politics. While the Brotherhood heard such lectures as Shakespeare and patriotism, 'The True Meaning of the British Empire', or 'The Fascination of Belgium before the Savages Came', Brodsky was still flying the cultural flag for Mozart, Schubert, Mendelssohn and above all Beethoven in a concert given on 13 January 1918[41].

In short, Brodsky introduced no changes to the repertoire he had offered before the war. Neither did his Ancoats concerts offer any striking differences from those the Quartet gave elsewhere in Manchester and the North West. It is telling, for example, to see that the Brodsky Quartet concert mentioned above was followed by one a fortnight later in which the Catterall Quartet offered quartets by Ernő Dohnányi, Anton Arensky and Aleksandr Borodin. Brodsky's wife Anna contributed her own anti-German polemic when she spoke on *Kerensky and the Revolution in Russia* in October 1917, praising the Revolution but roundly blaming the Germans for supporting the Bolshevik threat to democracy.

> There is certainly no doubt that the weakening of Russia was always a part
> of the policy of the Hohenzollerns. There is also no doubt that it is the German

---

[39].   11 November 1917. They also appeared together on 2 December 1917, on which occasion Fogg played some of his own compositions.

[40].   Fuchs' membership of the quartet was effectively brought to an end by the war. Even after his release, Hatton was more often than not Brodsky's regular cellist. Fuchs did, however, continue to appear independently. The composition of the Brodsky Quartet after the war was fluid, particularly after the death of Simon Speelman in 1921. The roles of second violin and viola were frequently taken by John Bridge and Frank Park in the post-war years. Fuchs did not rejoin the quartet on a more permanent basis until 1926.

[41].   Sir Sidney Lee, 17 January 1915; Sir Francis Younghusband, 12 November 1916; Edna Walter, 6 February 1918.

government which was and is one of the chief agents of Russia's present collapse and disaster. When the Revolution came so suddenly and passed so swiftly, so bloodlessly, with such a wonderful absence of revengeful deeds, and brought so much joy and happiness to the whole population of Russia, our enemies were taken by surprise, and during the first weeks following the great event they could not do anything to harm the great event, but later Germany did her utmost to prevent the organisation of Russia under her new-found freedom. Russia swarmed with German spies, who worked in the front and in the rear, spreading their wicked propaganda, against the Provisional Government, against our allies, against the war, and for a separate peace[42].

Given later the same day, Brodsky's recital with the pianist John Wills was at least tactful enough to stick to music by Tchaikovsky, Sergey Rachmaninov, and Grieg. Otherwise not a word is heard against the continued presence of German music in the markedly anti-German environment which the Ancoats Brotherhood had become.

By 1918 the Brodsky Quartet were giving noticeably fewer Ancoats concerts, reinforcing their tendency to look somewhat predictable alongside the more varied fare which was now increasingly on offer. Younger performers were introducing more contemporary repertoire. Singers were looking more consistently beyond the German Lieder tradition. Women were taking their place alongside their male counterparts as string players and or even as composers. In addition to concerts by the all-female Edith Robinson Quartet there were, for example, appearances by the violinists Gertrude Barker and Joanna (Jo) Lamb and another unnamed, but all-female string quartet[43]. To the socialist minds of the Ancoats Brotherhood, the political import of the war which had contributed to these changes was never in doubt, but this was a war which threw down a challenge to German cultural values. In terms of music, the challenge it posed could only be met by recourse to a fair amount of compromise. Unable to apply its anti-German polemic to German music, the Ancoats Brotherhood communicated the message that music was a special case, above and immune from political differences. In this it unwittingly found a staunch ally in the Brodsky Quartet.

Several lectures deal with the war's aftermath in terms of problems or questions. J. R. Clynes spoke of 'Our Present and Future Food Problems'[44] while Councillor Mellor asked 'Do We Want More and Better Houses for Manchester?'[45]. Meanwhile the programme for 1918-1919 contained a diatribe from one Dr. Muhler, a former director of Krupps, reminding patrons that: «The Prussia of today can only inspire the nations of Europe with a deeper

---

[42]. Brodsky 1918.
[43]. 25 October 1914.
[44]. 29 December 1918.
[45]. 23 February 1919 (replacing the advertised lecture: Prof. Ramsay Muir on 'A New Europe').

hatred [...]. She will force every foreign people to subordinate their civilisation to her own barbarism [...]»[46].

The inclusion by the Brodsky Quartet that season of the 'barbarism' of Beethoven and Mendelssohn might suggest that Muhler was ironically correct in one aspect of German civilisation. Europe was now a palpably changed landscape, but the problems and questions posed by the Ancoats speakers shied away from addressing its own cultural dilemma. As for Charles Rowley, he placed himself and the Brotherhood in a position which obviated any need to seek a resolution. Although he lived well into his nineties, dying in 1933, lectures were abandoned by 1924. Shortly thereafter, Rowley, reluctant to cede control of his brainchild to a successor, simply called a halt to the Brotherhood *per se*[47].

As a case study, the involvement of the Brodsky Quartet in the Ancoats Brotherhood's activities symbolises this cultural dilemma. It also demonstrates the extent to which Brodsky's own largely inflexible musical preferences risked becoming increasingly out of step with the changing attitudes of his adopted city towards those cultural traditions which had shaped it. Undoubtedly such changing attitudes were profoundly influenced by the First World War, but it would be naïve to see this and the political tensions leading up to it as the sole cause of the change, especially in a city with so large and culturally literate a German population as Manchester. The discourse of chamber music in Manchester both during and after the war reveals that the war itself acted more as catalyst than as cause. The Ancoats Brotherhood played its own part in enabling more women to take centre stage as chamber musicians and provided a forum for younger musicians. Both were able to contribute to a growing presence for contemporary music that challenged the reliance on a largely canonic repertoire that had been the mainstay of the Brotherhood's recitals in its earlier days. Just what role that repertoire played in its own activities during the war years remained ambiguous. Clearly, one could be beastly to the Bosch, but not to Beethoven.

BIBLIOGRAPHY

ALLIS 1995
ALLIS, Wilfred. *The Gentlemen's Concerts: Manchester 1777-1920*, unpublished M.Ph. Thesis, Manchester, University of Manchester, 1995.

BRODSKY 1918
BRODSKY, Anna. *The Birth of Free Russia*, Manchester, Sherratt & Hughes, 1918.

---

[46]. Winter programme 1918-1919.
[47]. *MANCHESTER* 1924A, p. 10. See also *MANCHESTER* 1924B, p. 11.

ELLER 1913
ELLER, William. 'Letter', in: *Manchester Guardian*, 7 October 1913.

ENGELS 1892
ENGELS, Friedrich. *The Condition of the Working Class in England in 1844*, translation by Florence K. Wischnewetzky, s.l., Allen and Unwin, 1892.

LANGFORD 1915
LANGFORD, Samuel. 'The Edith Robinson Quartet Concert', in: *Manchester Guardian*, 15 March 1915.

MANCHESTER 1889
Untitled review, in: *Manchester Guardian*, 5 March 1889.

MANCHESTER 1907
'Beethoven's Symphonies. Mr. Surette's Explanatory Lecture', in: *Manchester Guardian*, 30 September 1907.

MANCHESTER 1913
'An English Lover of Music (letter)', in: *Manchester Guardian*, 7 October 1913.

MANCHESTER 1924A
'The Ancoats Sunday Lectures to be Discontinued', in: *Manchester Guardian*, 9 October 1924.

MANCHESTER 1924B
'End of the Sunday Lectures: Tribute to Mr. Rowley's Work. Movement that Influenced Many Others', in: *Manchester Guardian*, 13 October 1924.

MANCHESTER AND LANCASHIRE 1900
'Ancoats Brotherhood and Patriotism', in: *Manchester Courier and Lancashire General Advertiser*, 12 March 1900.

MANCHESTER AND LANCASHIRE 1905
'Teaching of Patriotism. Address by Professor Sadler', in: *Manchester Courier and Lancashire General Advertiser*, 6 March 1905.

MANCHESTER AND LANCASHIRE 1906
'What's in a Name?', in: *Manchester Courier and Lancashire General Advertiser*, 17 November 1906.

MANCHESTER AND LANCASHIRE 1913A
'Unpatriotic Germans: Consul's Appeal to his Fellow Countrymen', in: *Manchester Courier and Lancashire General Advertiser*, 10 January 1913.

MANCHESTER AND LANCASHIRE 1913B
'Manchester Day by Day', in: *Manchester Courier and Lancashire General Advertiser*, 12 May 1913.

REA – RICHARDSON 1988
REA, Anthony – RICHARDSON, Neil. *Manchester's Little Italy: Memories of the Italian Colony of Ancoats*, Manchester, Neil Richardson, 1988.

ROBERTS 1983
ROBERTS, Richard. 'The Corporation as Impresario: The Municipal Provision of Entertainment in Victorian and Edwardian Bournemouth', in: *Leisure in Britain 1780-1939*, edited by John K. Walton and James Walvin, Manchester, Manchester University Press, 1983, pp. 137-158.

ROSE 2001
ROSE, Jonathan. *The Intellectual Life of the British Working Classes*, New Haven (CT), Yale University Press, 2001.

ROWLEY 1900
ROWLEY, Charles. *Fifty Years of Work Without Wages: (laborare est orare)*, London, Hodder and Stoughton, 1900.

SEED 1988
SEED, John. 'Commerce and the Liberal Arts: The Political Economy of Art in Manchester, 1775-1860', in: *The Capital of Culture: Art, Power and the Nineteenth-Century Middle Class*, edited by Janet Wolff and John Seed, Manchester, Manchester University Press, 1988, pp. 45-82.

SIMON 1892
SIMON, Henry. *Cremation: A Lecture Written for the Ancoats Brotherhood, Manchester*, Edinburgh, R & R Clark, 1892.

WALTON 1983
WALTON, John K. 'Municipal Government and the Holiday Industry in Blackpool, 1876-1914', in: *Leisure in Britain 1780-1939, op. cit.*, pp. 159-186.

Abstracts and Biographies

CHRISTOPHER CAMPO-BOWEN, *Antonín Dvořák's String Quartets Opp. 105 and 106 and the Question of Late Style*

The last two string quartets composed by Antonín Dvořák — the String Quartet in G Major, Op. 106, and the String Quartet in A-flat Major, Op. 105 — have long occupied a curious place in accounts of the composer's life and works. Given their genre and their chronological position within the composer's life, these quartets have been frequently apostrophised as the last pieces of 'absolute music' that Dvořák ever wrote. In this chapter, I re-evaluate the historical position of the Opp. 105 and 106 quartets in Dvořák's life with an eye toward a vexed question in music history: that of 'late style'. I suggest that the example of Dvořák's last works exposes the contingency and exclusionary nature of the label 'late', and his willingness to shift genres, audiences, and aesthetic principles in the last years of his life places him outside conventional biographical and musical models. Dvořák's last string quartets present an opportunity to rethink how we construct narratives of the careers of composers, and how we unwittingly perpetuate exclusionary models that privilege certain identities, certain world views, and certain kinds of music.

CHRISTOPHER CAMPO-BOWEN is Assistant Professor of Musicology in the School of Performing Arts at Virginia Tech. He completed his Ph.D. in musicology at the University of North Carolina at Chapel Hill. He holds a B.A. in Music from Stanford University and an M.M. in Orchestral Conducting from The Catholic University of America in Washington D.C. Christopher's research focuses on music in the Habsburg Monarchy in the nineteenth and twentieth centuries, especially on the relationships between music, ethnicity, gender, and empire, and he is particularly interested in how conceptions of ruralness in Czech operas structured notions of subjectivity and identity. His book projects include his monograph *Visions of the Village: Ruralness, Identity, and Czech Opera* (under contract with Oxford University Press) and, with Anja Bunzel, the collected edition *Women in Nineteenth-Century Czech Musical Culture: «Apostles of a Brighter Future»* (Routledge, 2024). His work has previously appeared in *Nineteenth-Century Music*, *Cambridge Opera Journal*, and *The Musical Quarterly* and at various national and international conferences.

***

ANDREW DERUCHIE, *Saint-Saëns's Second String Quartet and the Art of Composing 'Oldly'*

According to the received music-historical narratives, after 1900 the long-lived Camille Saint-Saëns (1835-1922) faltered creatively, entrenched his art in the past, faded into irrelevance, and became a curmudgeonly opponent of the modernists. This reception owes to assumptions of twentieth-century historiography, but insights from the emerging interdisciplinary field of age studies reveal that it also problematically reflects culturally-ingrained stigmas surrounding aging and old age. Taking as a touchstone the Second String Quartet (1918), which Saint-Saëns linked to experiences of aging, this essay proposes a more sympathetic view of his old-age career. The composer's writings evince an outlook theorists call generativity, whereby the elderly, engaged and productive, view themselves as teachers of young. In this light, the Quartet evinces neither creative decline nor intransigence. Close analysis of form, pitch organization, and musical narrative reveal the composer's engagement with modernist innovations and his ongoing exploration of new possibilities. Through these means he demonstrated, as a lesson to posterity, how music could evolve according to the classicising values in which he foresaw the aesthetic cornerstones of the art form's future.

A historical musicologist, ANDREW DERUCHIE specialises in orchestral and chamber music of the nineteenth and twentieth centuries, with a special emphasis on French topics. Areas of interest included intersections between compositional practice and cultural history, aesthetics, and musical form. He is the author of *The French Symphony at the Fin de Siècle: Style, Culture, and the Symphonic Tradition* (University of Rochester Press, 2013) and publications on Saint-Saëns, d'Indy, Mahler, and Debussy. Currently an Assistant Professor of musicology at the University of Manitoba, he has also held posts at the University of Otago and the University of Ottawa.

***

CHRISTIANE STRUCKEN-PALAND, *César Franck: The String Quartet at the Nexus of Tradition and Innovation*

César Franck's *String Quartet* in D minor (1889) — his only contribution to the genre — is characterised by an experimental overall design which nonetheless ties in with genre traditions of absolute music that arose in the wake of Beethoven. Characterised by symphonic monumentality, it is especially marked by the conspicuous use of cyclically recurring elements; the central theme in particular, whose careful process of creation may be traced through the study of sketches and which recurs in many ways — as adaptation, transformation or reminiscence — in the other movements, and which plays a special role as guarantor of the work's unity. Especially in the outer movements, Franck breaks from their traditional function as the setting up of a dramatic conflict or its apotheotic resolution and instead develops new formal dramaturgies. The first movement is distinguished by the radical formal independence of the introduction: Franck designs it as a self-contained formal section and at the same time integrates it into the movement by treating it as the exposition of a second, broken, sonata form, its components scattered as interpolations throughout the movement. In this alternating the interweaving of two formal processes Franck's individual concept of form stands at odds with the traditionally dramatic, forward-thrusting momentum of traditional sonata movements. This concept continues in the final movement, itself increasingly dominated by retrospective moments and regressions, through which the musical process is interrupted and then suspended. Characteristic of this are the reminiscences of previously heard movements at the beginning of the final movement and in the coda. These thematic recapitulations, their relationship, and how they function in the course of the movement are examined more closely. The finale no longer functions as the final point of a teleological development that spans the whole movement, but becomes a reflection of the beginning. The thematic recapitulations are oriented towards psychological mechanisms of experience, such as associations and memories, and in so doing make the temporal distance perceptible to the same degree as they attempt to bridge it, seemingly paradoxically, at the same time.

CHRISTIANE STRUCKEN-PALAND studied organ at the Musikhochschule in Cologne, as well as Romance languages and classical philology at the city's University. In 2006 she was awarded a doctorate for her thesis on Cyclic Principles in the instrumental works of César Franck. She is currently a collaborator in education at the Ministry of Education. In 2003 she was awarded a grant from the German Academic Exchange Service (DAAD) for research in Paris, and in 2006-2007 a grant for study at the Paul Sacher Foundation in Basel. In 2006 she founded the International César Franck Association and has continued to serve as its president. Her numerous publications have centered on the works of the nineteenth and twentieth centuries, in particular on Franck, Saint-Saëns, Fauré, and Honegger, as well as teaching materials on music and Latin. She is the editor of a complete critical edition of Franck's organ and harmonium works (Bärenreiter-Verlag, Kassel), has held posts as organist, and has an active career as a performer on the organ.

***

FRANÇOIS DE MÉDICIS, *The Franck Quintet: Dramatic Character, Style, and Relationship to the Beethoven Instrumental Tradition*

This chapter provides an examination of the links between César Franck's Quintet and the nineteenth-century Beethovenian instrumental traditions. To this end, various significant musical characteristics are analysed: cyclic form, tension curves (shaped for the effects of climax and apotheosis), topoi, development of contrasting ideas, and the narrative trajectory that spans the entirety of the work (*Per aspera ad astra*; the ride to the abyss). Some of these characteristics find comparison in three works from the Beethovenian tradition, which also share the general key of F minor with Franck's work: Beethoven's *Appassionata* Sonata, Op. 57; Liszt's *Funérailles*; and Brahms's Piano Quintet, Op. 34. A historiographical examination of Vincent d'Indy's commentary on the relationships between Franck's works and the Beethovenian tradition follows. The analysis of the Quintet reveals the need for greater nuance within some of d'Indy's ideas, and throws some of his other assumptions into question, suggesting Franck's work more nearly approaches the style of Beethoven's second period, rather than his third.

FRANÇOIS DE MÉDICIS is Professor of Musicology at the Université de Montréal. Author of *La maturation artistique de Debussy dans son contexte historique (1884-1902)* (Brepols, 2020), he co-edited *Debussy's Resonance* (2018) with Steven Huebner, and *Musique et modernité en France, 1900-1945* (2006) with Sylvain Caron and Michel Duchesneau. With Fabien Guilloux, he also co-edited a critical edition of Saint-Saëns's Violin Sonatas (Bärenreiter, 2021). His many articles on French and Russian music from 1880 to 1945 focus on composers such as Bonis, Debussy, Koechlin, Milhaud, Scriabin, and Stravinsky.

***

NANCY NOVEMBER, *Challenging Tradition: All-Female String Quartets of the Late Nineteenth and Early Twentieth Centuries*

The string quartet was traditionally firmly located in the male domain. A 'strong genre', associated with technical mastery and the highest compositional achievements in the eighteenth and early nineteenth centuries, it was composed by men (including, notably, the main exponents of the Viennese Classical canon), performed by men (in both public and private settings), and written about by men. Women were largely excluded from its sphere, except as audience members at concerts, which started to flourish in the early and mid-nineteenth centuries. But starting around the 1870s, the social taboo against women learning string instruments was eased, and women started to participate not only in private string quartets but also in public. This was partly a function of changing access to conservatoire training for women, and notable female performers, including the Czech violinist Lady Halle (Wilma Norman-Neruda) and the Canadian violinist Nora Clench. Both of these women had access to the Austro-German tradition through teachers and repertoire, which helped them to establish their reputations and their string quartet leadership, in a still almost exclusively male arena. How were female quartet players, and all-female string quartets received, and how did this change? In reviews of the time we find references to purity, uniformity, and invisibility of female performers, which seem to be an effort to contain the covert voyeurism evident elsewhere — for example in iconography (including photographs). What persists and changes today in the ways we currently understand all-female string quartets of our time? I consider aspects of voyeurism and technical excellence.

NANCY NOVEMBER is a Professor of Musicology in the University of Auckland's School of Music. Combining interdisciplinarity and cultural history, her research centers on chamber music of the late eighteenth and nineteenth centuries, probing questions of historiography, canonisation, and genre. She is the recipient of a Humboldt Fellowship (2010-2012) and three Marsden Grants from the New Zealand Royal Society. She recently publish the monographs *Opera in the Viennese Home from Mozart to Rossini* (CUP, 2024), *The Age of Musical Arrangements in Europe, 1780-1830* (CUP, 2023), *Beethoven's Symphonies Arranged for the Chamber: Sociability, Reception, and Canon Formation* (CUP, 2021), edited a book on Beethoven's *Eroica* Symphony (CUP, 2020), and has published books and editions on a broad range of chamber music from the nineteenth century.

***

SYLVIA KAHAN, *Reportage of Chamber Music in the Paris Daily Papers, 1860-1914*
Between 1860 and 1914, the Paris daily newspapers regularly covered the musical activities of opera divas, international conductors, violin and piano virtuosos, and composers, and occasionally featured articles about operas, ballets, and symphonies. But, curiously, the coverage of chamber music and chamber musicians was a mixed bag — this, despite the fact that chamber-music societies, especially string-quartet societies, were multiplying and prospering, occupying an increasingly large place in concerts and soirees. This study provides an overview of the coverage of chamber music and critical responses to its Paris performances between 1860 and 1914 by three major daily newspapers, *Le Figaro*, *Le Gaulois*, and *Le Temps*. These topics were discussed routinely in professional music journals, but unevenly in the non-specialist press: in *Le Figaro* and *Le Gaulois*, both of which catered to an aristocratic and upper-bourgeois readership, the genre was rarely deemed worthy of coverage, while the music journalists of the more liberal *Le Temps* were indefatigable champions of both the genre and the instrumentalists who devoted themselves to the repertoire. Press coverage of three of the most popular chamber-music ensembles, the Société philharmonique, the Société de musique de chambre pour instruments à vent, and the Quatuor Capet serve as case studies. The disparity in press coverage and its implications are considered at the conclusion.

SYLVIA KAHAN is Professor of Music at the Graduate Center and the College of Staten Island, City University of New York, where she teaches both Musicology and Piano. She has performed as concerto soloist, recitalist, and collaborative pianist in venues throughout the United States and Europe. As a musicologist, she specializes in French music of the *Belle Époque* and the early twentieth century, with an emphasis on music salon culture and the role of women in music patronage. Her book, *In Search of New Scales: Prince Edmond de Polignac, Octatonic Explorer* (University of Rochester Press, 2009), broke new ground in the history of octatonicism, and her two award-winning biographies of Winnaretta Singer-Polignac, *Music's Modern Muse* (University of Rochester Press, 2003) and *Winnaretta Singer Polignac: Princesse, mécène et musicienne* (Les presses du réel, 2018), have inspired concert programmes at Lincoln Center and at international music festivals as well as several television documentaries produced in the United States and France. A new book on Marie-Blanche de Polignac is forthcoming.

***

ABSTRACTS AND BIOGRAPHIES

ISABELLE PERREAULT, *Constructing and Re-Mediating the Ethos of a Music Lover: The Case of Marguerite de Saint-Marceaux*

This chapter charts Marguerite de Saint-Marceaux's (1850-1930) influence on the creation and circulation of French chamber music at the turn of the twentieth century. A key figure of Parisian high society under the Third Republic, Mme de Saint-Marceaux acted as a veritable epicentre for the networks of musicians, artists, and critics that fashioned musical modernity. The diary she kept between 1894 and 1927 is an exceptional archive that highlights private activities, kindred encounters between creators, and the formation of intimate circles, all of which inflect the course of the music scene even as they remain peripheral to it. Here I explore the *salonnière*'s tactical engagement with the musical world of her time, her ostensible interest in contemporary music, and her sustained efforts to provide visibility for chamber music by means of her receptions — an engagement that must be understood as part of the process whereby she constructed her ethos as a lover of music. More specifically, I look at discursive framings pertaining to music and the scenography of the 'enlightened amateur'. I further aim to measure the extent to which the *salonnière* was implicated in the development of her milieu's sensibilities and listening habits, and, in so doing, to identify the sociological mechanisms whereby musical tastes are consolidated through social dynamics grounded in distinction (BOURDIEU 1979).

ISABELLE PERREAULT holds a Ph.D. in French Literature and is a research fellow at the Observatoire interdisciplinaire de création et de recherche en musique (OICRM, Université de Montréal). Her research interests include the relationships between music and literature in nineteenth and twentieth-century France, as well as the experience of the senses acting as a signifying power in twentieth-century texts. Following a postdoctoral fellowship funded by the Social Sciences and Humanities Research Council of Canada (SSHRC, 2020-2021) and devoted to research focused on the 'memory of modernity' through musical reference in contemporary French narrative, Perreault's more recent works focus on listening as a model, a motif, and a sensitive disposition in literary reading and criticism since 1950.

***

KATHRYN M. FENTON, *The Musical Art Quartet, Alice Warder Garrett, and American Musical Diplomacy in the Early Twentieth Century*

The world wars sparked a surge in patriotism and nationalism, both in Europe and abroad. In the United States, a surge of '100% Americanism' dominated the political and cultural conversation (Higham). In the arts, and especially so in music, Americans demonstrated a keen interest in how to promote American-born musicians and music, particularly in the face of what they viewed as European chauvinism in the musical world (Crawford, Horowitz, Levy). Alice Warder Garrett, a well-known American art patron during the first half of the twentieth century, sponsored several musicians as well and corresponded with leading composers and performers of the day. In the years between the wars, she sponsored a newly formed string quartet, The Musical Art String Quartet, led by Sascha Jacobsen. She frequently invited them to her home in Baltimore to perform both the standard works of the quartet literature and new works by American composers. When her husband accepted an appointment as American Ambassador to Italy the early 1930s, Garrett invited the ensemble to accompany them abroad. There the quartet played for guests at the couple's temporary home in Capri and embarked on a tour of Italy, as documented in a scrapbook from Garrett's time in Italy. The scrapbook, correspondence, and other materials from the Garret papers as well as American newspaper coverage of the quartet, suggest that Garret's interest in the ensemble went beyond a solely aesthetic one. An examination of these materials in the light of the '100% Americanism', the rising interest of the United States' government in diplomacy, and recent scholarship on musical diplomacy (Ansari, Fosler-Lussier, Geinow-Hecht, Statler) reveals that Garrett seems to have used her position as the wife of an Ambassador to promote the artistic achievements of American musicians in Italy, thereby attempting to demonstrate newfound American-European cultural equivalence — something American musicians had been fighting to promote since the early nineteenth century. The tour can thus be seen as one example of the continued efforts to secure the United States' new footing as a power on the world stage.

KATHRYN M. FENTON is an Assistant Professor at Stephen F. Austin State University in Texas. She received her Ph.D. from the University of Western Ontario in 2012, and her research examines issues of American musical identity formation during the Gilded Age and Progressive Era. Her first book, *Puccini's «La fanciulla del West» and American Musical Identity* (Routledge, 2020), explored the tensions surrounding the world premiere of Puccini's opera. Her current book project examines the musical patronage of one Puccini's American contacts and her efforts to improve the prestige of American music and musicians in Italy.

***

EVA BRANDA, *Evaluating Dvořák's 'Niche': The 1892 Farewell Tour, the Dumky Piano Trio Op. 90, and Perceptions of Dvořák as Chamber Music Composer*

In his scathing review of Dvořák's *Rusalka*, critic Zdeněk Nejedlý writes: «In the name of Dvořák's true followers, we have to ask the master most earnestly not to be taken off course by flattery, which leads him to [fateful] paths [...] and to return to the domain where he reigns supreme in the world: chamber music» (NEJEDLÝ 1901). Known for his rather severe criticism of Dvořák's operas, Nejedlý was nevertheless willing to acknowledge Dvořák's skill in the realm of chamber music. Indeed, this was the one area in which Dvořák's Czech critics seemed in agreement, as confirmed by another contemporary critic Josef Boleška, who claimed that enthusiasm in Prague for Dvořák's chamber works had reached cultish levels (BOLEŠKA 1912). This chapter explores Dvořák's Czech reception as a chamber music composer — an area that was identified early on as his niche. Specifically, it examines Dvořák's tour of the Czech lands in 1892, ahead of his American sojourn. The centrepiece of the tour programme was the *Dumky* Piano Trio, Op. 90 (1891). Much like the *Slavonic Dances* that had kickstarted Dvořák's career — and with the added nostalgia that comes from being pitched as a 'farewell' to Czech audiences — the piece proved to be an ideal vehicle for affirmations of Dvořák's 'Czechness' and his chamber music prowess. Using the *Dumky* Trio as a case study, this chapter seeks to tease out broader chamber music discourses and to understand why, relative to other genres, Dvořák's reception in this area was comparatively uncontroversial.

EVA BRANDA holds a Ph.D. in musicology from the University of Toronto and teaches at Wilfrid Laurier University. With special attention to Dvořák, her research focuses primarily on reception issues in the late nineteenth century. Dr. Branda's work has appeared in the *Journal of the Royal Musical Association, Music & Letters, Nineteenth-Century Music Review*, and *Cambridge Opera Journal*. She will also be contributing a chapter on the Czech symphonic tradition to the book *A History of Music in the Czech Lands*, to be published by Cambridge University Press in 2024.

***

ANJA BUNZEL, *Czech Song, Jan Ludevít Procházka, and the Salonesque «Musical Entertainments» in 1870s Prague*

On 15 November 1871, the music journal *Hudební listy* (Musical Leaves) announced the *First Private Singing Entertainment* (První soukromá zábava pěvecká), scheduled to take place on 27 November 1871 in the salon of the piano manufacturers Joseph Heitzmann and Ferdinand Schloegl in Prague. The founder and editor of *Hudební listy*, Jan Ludevít Procházka (1837-1888), informed the readers that the purpose of these events would be to enable the Czech audience to experience live performances of domestic (i.e., Czech) and Slavic music more generally. The series was meant to introduce audiences to novelties that were cropping up on the Czech music scene, with a view either to new compositions and/or arrangements by Czech composers or to new publications produced by Czech-based music publishers. The second concert of the series featured Antonín Dvořák's song 'Vzpomínání' (Remembrance), which marked the first time that a work by Dvořák was performed in public, as well as the first time one of Dvořák's compositions was reviewed by renowned music critics. Adding to the field of Czech music studies generally and, in particular, to Jana Vojtěškové's and Jiří Kopecký's work on Ludevít Procházka and Czech music criticism, this essay focuses on the musical events organised by Procházka within the wider framework of Czech national music. Approaching these events chronologically, this chapter shows that the repertoire changed quickly over the course of time, and that Procházka's *Entertainments* did not live on for very long. Arguably, within the wider context of Czech musical culture, the most important outcomes of these *Entertainments* were not primarily the promotion of individual composers such as Dvořák, or, indeed, the popularisation of new Czech works. Rather, these events offered a platform to explore openly whether and how pan-Slavism might have a place in music and might lead to a more effective formation of national identity in Czech musical culture. Moreover, the events helped to bring together performers, publishers, composers, and audiences in a semi-public or at least 'smaller-than-usual' or seemingly more intimate public setting.

ANJA BUNZEL holds a research position at the Musicology Department of the Institute of Art History, Czech Academy of Sciences. She gained her B.A. and M.A. from Freie Universität Berlin, Germany, and her Ph.D. from Maynooth University, Ireland. Her research interests include private music-making in Central Europe during the nineteenth century, nineteenth-century song, and music and gender. She is co-editor of *Musical Salon Culture in the Long Nineteenth Century* (Boydell, 2019), sole author of *The Songs of Johanna Kinkel: Genesis, Reception, Context* (Boydell, 2020), and has contributed to *Clara Schumann Studies*, edited by Joe Davies (CUP, 2021). She is a member of the editorial boards of *Studia Musicologica* (AK Journals) and *Global Nineteenth-Century Studies* (Liverpool University Press) as well as of the advisory board of *Irish Musical Studies* (Boydell Press).

***

VJERA KATALINIĆ, *«Die edelste und küstlerischeste aller Kunstformen»: The Committee for the Promotion of Chamber Music — A «fin-de-siècle» Initiative in Zagreb*

In late nineteenth-century Zagreb, various musical events took place quite regularly: the National Theatre performed operas from the standard repertoire as well as national pieces; its orchestra gave concerts of symphonic music; and the school of the National Music Institute organised regular concerts of their students and professors. An additional and complementary organiser of chamber concerts, founded in late 1896, was the so-called Committee for the Promotion of Chamber Music, with its task proclaimed in its title. A small intellectual circle among members of the Musikverein of various professions (an architect, two musicians, a politician, a music critic, and an engineer) answered the demands of audiences to invite the best international chamber ensembles, thus giving them the opportunity to hear and to cultivate «the most outstanding compositions by Mozart, Beethoven,

Schubert, Schumann, as well as more recent pieces by Tchaikovsky, Dvořák, Smetana, and Goldmark, that other cultural towns have cultivated already for some time». From the beginning of 1897 until the end of World War I, they organised almost one hundred concerts of famous contemporary ensembles: soloists with accompaniment (such as Pablo Casals, Fritz Kreisler, etc.), trios (such as the Russian piano trio), quartets (such as Quartetto Triestino, Quartett Rosé), and even chamber orchestras (such as Wiener Tonkünstler Orchester with Oskar Nedbal) were invited and sharpened the taste and demands of the Zagreb audiences. This chapter analyses the list of invited guests, their repertoire, the reception of the audiences as well as their impact on musical life in Zagreb during a turbulent period that ended with the disintegration of the Habsburg Empire.

VJERA KATALINIĆ serves as scientific advisor and director for the Institute for the History of Croatian Literature, Theatre, and Music at Croatian Academy of Sciences and Arts in Zagreb. She is also a full professor at the University of Zagreb, Music Academy, and president of the Croatian Musicological Society. Her fields of interest include musical culture in the eighteenth and nineteenth centuries, the mobility of music and musicians and their networks, and the music archives in Croatia. A leader of various national and EU projects, Katalinić is currently researching the institutionalisation of modern bourgeois musical culture in nineteenth-century Croatia.

***

HÉLDER SÁ, *Chamber Music 1850-1918: Violin and Chamber Music in Lisbon in the Early Days of the Republic*

From 1910 to 1926, Portugal lived under a democratic regime that replaced the previous monarchy. These political changes affected Lisbon's musical sphere, particularly opera and symphonic concerts. The impact on chamber music practices was more subtle. This investigation explores the role of the violin during the early years of the Republic, identifying key players, chamber music repertoire, and performative surroundings. Furthermore, it verifies whether the conclusions of ARTIAGA 2000 and CASCUDO 2002 regarding repertoire changes from 1870 onwards apply to chamber practices involving the violin. The data proceed from primary sources and period press articles, namely the specialised magazines *A Arte Musical* and *Eco Musical*. During this period, the Sociedade de Concertos de Lisboa (Lisbon Concert Society – SCL) hosted touring violinists such as Mathieu Crickboom, Paul Kochansky, Manuel Quiroga and René Benedetti, performing duos with piano. The SCL also promoted recitals with trios and quartets featuring the violin. Yet, in Lisbon, most of the events involved Portuguese or foreign violinists living in the city, namely Júlio Cardona, Pedro Blanch, Francisco Benetó, Fernando Cabral, António Tomás de Lima and Flaviano Rodrigues. The repertoire played in the SCL duo recitals covered a wide chronological span from Baroque to the early twentieth century. The trio and quartet repertoire included the Classic and Early Romantic canon and their followers. This information corroborates previous research, widening its spectrum to chamber repertoire with violin and shows continuity with late nineteenth-century practices. Research identified the same violinists in different contexts, although the boundaries between the repertoires can hardly be associated with performance venues. This analysis leads us to believe that these categorisations may not have been assumed by these musicians and are thus mere musicological frameworks that can scarcely explain the complexity of their performing experiences.

HÉLDER SÁ studied violin at the Porto Music Conservatoire, ESMAE (Escola Superior de Música e Artes do Espectáculo), and University of Aveiro. He completed his master's degrees in violin and music education, as well as a Ph.D. in Music with a research project entitled *O Violino em Portugal na Primeira República: Contextos, Protagonistas e Repertórios*. He teaches violin and is a member of INET-md. He published his studies in AVA

Musical Editions, UA Editora, and Comares. His investigations deal with the historical musicology and the performance of Portuguese repertoire from the late nineteenth century and the first half of the twentieth century.

***

DAVID REIßFELDER, *Modern French Chamber Music in Britain and César Franck*

In the nineteenth century French chamber music only slowly gained a foothold in British concert life. By 1920, however, it had not only secured its place in the repertoire, it constituted a focal point in the debate about British music. Camille Saint-Saëns was the first Frenchman who succeeded with his ensemble works, beginning from the 1870s. In connoisseur circles, Gabriel Fauré was much esteemed two decades later, but failed to achieve unreserved success. It was César Franck who emerged posthumously as a key figure of the so-called 'modern French school' and whose chamber works (notably the Violin Sonata) became established as 'modern classics'. The popular success of the movement's eventual figureheads, Claude Debussy and Maurice Ravel, followed a similar process of *rapprochement* after an initial period of irritation and resistance. The amateur-led Société des Concerts Français (1909-1915) was largely responsible for familiarising the British public with the French avant-garde and its different aesthetic factions. After the beginning of World War I, singer and concert entrepreneur Isidore de Lara continued dedicated modern French recitals until 1918. Concurrently, critics such as Edwin Evans, G. Jean-Aubry, and Michel-Dimitri Calvocoressi emphasised the importance of the French movement in lectures and articles. Indeed, the French people's focus on national character was highly significant at a time when the British were ardently debating their own national music. Authors with more Germanophile leanings, such as Ernest Newman, remained more sceptical and disputed the assertion that the French movement provided an ideal model. As homegrown chamber music gained momentum in Britain, many young composers responded eagerly to the new sounds from the Continent.

DAVID REIßFELDER was research associate and Ph.D. candidate at the University of Zurich from 2018 to 2021. He holds a B.A. and M.A. in musicology and history from Heidelberg University. He also studied at King's College London and spent a research stay at King's College, Cambridge, where he worked on Charles Villiers Stanford and the Cambridge University Musical Society. His publications include articles for *Musik-Konzepte* (on Klaus Ospald), *Göttinger Händel-Beiträge* (Arthur Balfour), and *MGG Online* (Edwin Evans and Benjamin Dale). He currently works for the German Science and Humanities Council.

***

GEOFF THOMASON, *Chamber Concerts for Champagne Socialists: Quartets and Contradictions at Manchester's Ancoats Brotherhood at the End of the Long Nineteenth Century*

Founded in 1881 as Recreation in Ancoats by the Manchester councillor Charles Rowley, the Ancoats Brotherhood, as it was renamed in 1889, sought to bring cultural education to one of the most deprived areas of Manchester. It offered a series of lectures from leading figures alongside concerts of chamber music given by local musicians, not the least being the quartet founded by Adolph Brodsky after his appointment as Principal of the Royal Manchester College of Music in 1895. Its intended audience of mill workers marks it out in contrast to other musical societies in Manchester, such as the Schiller-Anstalt, aimed at the city's large, middle-class and culturally literate German community. Contemporary concert programmes, letters and newspaper reports, as well as Rowley's own writings, reveal two principal themes in the developing career of the Brotherhood. One is the parallel between the gradual shift in its chamber repertoire towards that also heard at the Schiller-Anstalt or the Brodsky Quartet concerts, and the metamorphosis of its audience into one of bourgeois liberals who shared Rowley's political sympathies. The other is the tension between the Brotherhood's allegiance to a predominantly Austro-German musical canon in the years leading into and during the First World War. In particular, the Brodsky Quartet's long-standing concert series at the Brotherhood reveals an increasing desire to maintain the primacy of this Austro-German canon in the face of growing anti-German and British nationalist sentiment, articulated by its respected and influential speakers. It also sheds light on the role of the First World War in facilitating the appearance of women as chamber musicians, bringing with them a different and often more contemporary repertoire, which itself offered a substantial challenge to the Austro-German hegemony.

GEOFF THOMASON recently retired from his position as Deputy Librarian (Research) at the Royal Northern College of Music in Manchester. After reading music at the University of Manchester, he gained his Ph.D. with a thesis on the Manchester career of the violinist Adolph Brodsky. His research focuses on music in Manchester in the late nineteenth and early twentieth centuries, particularly the impact of the First World War on the city's musical life. As a music librarian, he has held several posts at the national and international level for the International Association of Music Libraries. A keen practical musician, he is active as a composer and arranger as well as an orchestral and chamber player. Thomason is a Liveryman of the Worshipful Company of Musicians and was recently named Honorary Fellow of the UK and Ireland branch of the International Association of Music Libraries.

INDEX OF NAMES

INDEX OF NAMES